CANADA
UNDER
MULRONEY

D1527625

CANADA UNDER MULRONEY

AN END-OF-TERM REPORT

ANDREW B. GOLLNER & DANIEL SALÉE

EDITORS

Véhicule Press

MONTRÉAL

Dépôt légal, Bibliothèque nationale du Québec and the National Library of Canada, 4th trimester 1988

CANADIAN CATALOGUING IN PUBLICATION DATA

Main entry under title:
Canada under Mulroney

ISBN 0-919890-88-1

1. Canada — Politics and government — 1984–
I. Gollner, Andrew B. II. Salée, Daniel

FC630.C36 1988   971.064'7   C88-090375-9
F1034.2.C36 1988

Cover illustration by AISLIN
Special appreciation to Paul Davies
Design and imaging by ECW Production Services, Sydenham, Ontario
Printed and bound by Les Editions Marquis Ltée
Published by Véhicule Press, P.O.B. 125, Place du Parc Station, Montreal, Quebec H2W 2M9

Canadian distribution

University of Toronto Press
5201 Dufferin Street
Downsview, Ontario M3H 5T8

U.S. distribution

University of Toronto Press
340 Nagel Drive
Buffalo, New York 14225-4731

Printed in Canada

CONTENTS

SOCIAL JUSTICE

STREAMLINING THE ADMINISTRATIVE MACHINERY

ACKNOWLEDGEMENTS

This volume is based on a set of papers presented at a conference in May 1988, assessing the Mulroney government's term in office. The conference was sponsored by Concordia University's Political Science Department, and was made possible by the generous support of the Social Sciences and Humanities Research Council, the Jean H. Picard Foundation, the office of the Rector and of the Dean of Arts and Sciences at Concordia University. We are grateful for their assistance which made the conference and this book possible. In the preparation of the manuscript for publication, we also wish to acknowledge the invaluable assistance of Bell Canada's Governmental and Social Affairs Department.

INTRODUCTION:

A Turn to the Right? Canada in the Post-Trudeau Era

ANDREW B. GOLLNER and DANIEL SALÉE

The chapters in this book were written near the end of the Mulroney government's first term in office, in mid-1988. They offer up-to-date, comprehensive and penetrating analyses of the past four years of Conservative rule and of the government's record of delivering on its 1984 electoral promises of "economic renewal, social justice and national reconciliation."

Canadian voters are being called to the polls in 1988 to choose a new federal government. The exercise of free choice between competing political alternatives, the right of citizens to keep their representatives accountable and the constitutional safeguards that have been put in place to uphold the above, are generally considered as the three pillars of a democratic society.

As we have painfully learned over the past few decades, these preconditions of democratic rule have been frequently unable to guarantee stability for democratic systems, legitimacy for political rulers and satisfaction for those who have elected people to high office.

As editors of this volume, we did not set out to bring forth the latest news on the "crisis of democracy." The event itself is, after all, old news — and citizens, as well as scholars, are destined to be scratching their heads about the subject for a long time to come.

We also did not set out to provide a convenient hit list of government shortcomings, simply as a means of increasing the ammunition of opposition parties during the 1988 electoral campaign.

We aimed, rather, to fill a void that tends to loom particularly large during electoral campaigns. Namely, the absence of comprehensive, meaningful and preferably objective assessment of a ruling party's record in office, and of its faithfulness (if we can use such a word in an era of widespread voter cynicism) to the mandate on which it was elected.

Election campaigns tend oftentimes to be dominated by the rhetoric of new things to come, new styles to follow. In the heat of the campaign, the record of the past is heavily muddied, and citizens have only a faint recollection of the promises made to them four or five years earlier by competing political parties. Even more curious, voters are often ignorant of their government's record of delivery on the many promises it undertook to get elected in the first place.

In the land of hockey, as in most parliamentary democracies, voter attention during election times is frequently diverted from the scoreboard. The spotlight is on the new line-up of players and on promises of new plays to come. The emphasis is on change rather than reflection, on style rather than issues, on process rather than substance. It is usually after the noise of the campaign has subsided that citizens turn back to look at the scoreboard, only to find that they are still not winning. The above largely explains the incredible volatility of public opinion between elections and the low level of public satisfaction with politicians and public officials. It is increasingly commonplace to consider that the holding of elected officials to their electoral promises is unrealistic, archaic and naïve. One of our modest objectives with this book is to help move people and politicians away from this mentality.

In spite of our earlier promises not to dissect yet again the infected body of contemporary democratic praxis, we do wish to make an important observation, and one that is central to our thinking. We do not link the supposed "ungovernability" of our society with the supposedly excessive demands of citizens (demand-overload) — or with what Daniel Bell and neo-conservatives so colourfully labelled as the 'Revolution of Rising Entitlements' (1975). We suggest that many of our recent problems of governance stem largely from the public's growing ignorance of the vital policy choices it faces, and from the frequent propensity of office seekers in all segments of the ideological divide to treat their electorate as suckers.

Of course, we also tried to be realistic. We sought clarity and objectivity from each of the authors presented in this text. But we also know that in spite of academia's claim to have achieved comparative advantage over everyone else in society in the provision of these commodities, clarity and objectivity rarely flow freely from scholarly pens. Academics, just like their political colleagues, are quite good at hauling in the gullible. And so we thought it better to dispense with exaggerated claims of objectivity. In our haste to purge ourselves and our contributors of subjectivism and of partisan political postures, we had to remind ourselves of Gunnar Myrdal's eloquent observation: " . . . there can be no view except from a viewpoint" (1978).

Thus the chapters that make up this book do not add up to a value-free menu. The best that we could offer was an unloaded dice. The reader will find here both pro and anti-government declarations. Some authors speak for clearly vested interest, while others subscribe to ideological stances that are noticeably non-centrist. Disneyland may insist on covering up Mickey Mouse's private parts; we are however much more open minded, and to academic purists, no doubt much more messy. We did not select our writers according to their ideological or political preferences. The selection is bound to irritate the Left, the Right, as well as the Centre, and we are naturally delighted with that prospect.

In short, this book does not provide a one sided, or ideologically consistent report card, but a lively cross-section of perceptions, and a vivid illumination, from different angles, of the Mulroney government's post-1984 performance. As such, the book will not only clarify the strategic policy issues facing the voting public, and thereby broaden public awareness of our policy choices, but will also be of significant use to students and scholars wishing to have a better understanding of political management and public policy-making in the Mulroney years.

Some readers will probably find that our selection of policy areas suffers from omissions. No text is to be found on agricultural policy, on environmental policy or on immigration policy for example. We did not seek to be specific. Annual reviews of specific policies perform this task very well.[1] Such yearly publications meet the current need for policy evaluation on the short term. By focusing on the key areas which the government seems to have

11

given priority, the texts gathered in this book offer a more global picture of the performance of the Mulroney government, and provide a clearer picture of the policy choices that confront Canadians entering the 1990s.

A TURN TO THE RIGHT?

Western democratic societies have evolved between the late 1940s and the mid-1970s within the ideological context of a "social democratic" consensus. This is not to say that we have witnessed the political dominance of social-democratic or socialist parties, but rather the virtually unqualified acceptance, throughout the political spectrum, of the Keynesian idea that the market economy is not self-regulating and periodically generates turmoil. This was a problem thought not likely to disappear spontaneously but through a more active role of the state in the regulation of demand and in the organization of the market at the macro level. In light of the social welfare problems created by the consequences of unemployment and other inadequacies of the market economy, it was assumed as one analyst points out

> ... that the state was superior to the private insurance market in fulfilling the role of protecting individuals against the vicissitudes of economic life. It was assumed that without the state people would be helpless victims of the 'blind' and unpredictable market. Furthermore, it seemed 'natural' that the state's welfare role should be extended into education and health. The rationale for this was not merely the relief of suffering but the creation of more equal opportunities. 'Social justice' where this term refers to the correction of a pure market determination of income so as to produce some desired social 'outcome,' became perhaps the most predominant feature on the masthead of the new consensus (Barry, 1987: 2).

Despite recent studies and analyses questioning whether a Keynesian "revolution" ever took place in Canada (Noël, 1987; Campbell, 1987) it can be safely said that Canada has adopted the fundamental tenets of the social democratic consensus, and generally — if loosely — complied with a Keynes-inspired model of policy-making and state intervention. Though more reactive than acting out of an actual commitment for Keynesianism, Canadian governments since World War II have implemented through the years a series of socioeconomic policies which, characteristically, have led to a spectacular growth in social expenditures (Moscovitch and Albert, 1987) and consequently to an appreciable increase of the state's overall societal reach.

Around the end of the 1960s, a new economic phenomenon began to slow down the process of hitherto unbridled state growth. Stagflation, the combined effect of concurrent high levels of unemployment and inflation, was increasingly challenging the appropriateness of Keynesian policies as tools of economic rectification and democratic political economy. By the mid-1970s, stagflation and the attendant economic decline had become an unequivocal reality for policy-makers to contend with. Traditionally, when unemployment rose, demand fell and so did prices. And vice versa. The Keynesian strategy had tended to encourage demand in time of high unemployment, and conversely, to discourage it in inflationary periods so as to maintain a relative degree of stability. Stagflation however necessitated action on both fronts simultaneously. An unlikely accomplishment. As one student of the Keynesian experiment in Canada recently observed, Canadian policy-makers thus faced a confusing and unsettled economy. The phenomenon of stagflation made the Keynesian tools seem to be inappropriate. It appeared that the best that could be done in this regard was to choose to deal with either inflation or unemployment. Choosing between the greater of two evils put the government in a politically awkward situation. The government's policy focus swung back and forth between the two, depending which was causing more political controversy at any particular moment (Campbell, 1987: 167).

This pattern was broken finally in 1975 when, in a dramatic about face, the Trudeau government opted in favour of the fight against inflation with its prices and wages controls initiative. Paradoxically, if this policy "involved the reconstruction of the power and authority of the Canadian state in the market economy" (Campbell, 1987: 189), it also meant the breakdown of the fragile post World War II social consensus. The vehemence with which the price and wage controls were received and criticized indicated the emergence of an impasse as to what the global priorities and orientation of social management should be. To a large extent, the politics of the 1980s bear the imprint of that impasse.

Contrary to the normal cyclical crises which regularly affect capitalist economies, the economic decline of the late 1970s and early 1980s has led to a structural reconsideration of the traditional bases of socioeconomic life since World War II. The hard, all too painful new economic reality faced by Canadians (recession, de-investment, flight of foreign capital, the new international division of labour, pressures for higher wages in the late 1970s, decline in productivity gains, etc.) really underlies a crisis in the process of capital accumulation, "one in which the whole dynamics of accumulation linked to the process of valorization and to the temporary resolution of the contradictions between the relations of production and relations of exchange are put in question" (Houle, 1983: 133). Like most of the other Western capitalist societies, Canada was facing on the eve of the 1984 election an organic crisis that hit at the very core of its societal foundations: enter the Progressive Conservative government of Brian Mulroney.

Political scientists and other analysts have tended to situate the Mulroney government on the right of the Canadian political spectrum. In recent years, the ruling federal party has been frequently lumped together with the 'new right,' the neo-conservative/neo-liberal tide that appears to have washed over a number of other countries. Canada, it seems, has entered what has been dubbed elsewhere as the era of "neo-politics" (Medcalf and Dolbeare, 1985). The Canadian Tories have indeed been swept up by the wave of fundamental socioeconomic and political challenges currently eroding the foundations of the post-war societal orthodoxy in the Western world. They entered the 1984 election with the mission of reshaping and reformulating the social contract by which Canadians have lived over the past three or four decades. The Tories have never hidden their intentions to restructure the state and to privatize social and economic life in Canada. Consider for example these comments by Brian Mulroney prior to the 1984 election:

> The tragic process of swedenizing of Canada must come to a halt (. . .). I am a Canadian and I want to be free, to the extent reasonably possible, of government intrusion and direction and regimentation and bureaucratic overkill (. . .).
>
> As we contemplate the sad state of this splendid nation, we search for reasons why things are as they are. One major reason is that we have a federal government committed to a social democratic collectivist philosophy. There is no room in

its vocabulary for words like risk, sacrifice, reward, initiative, enterprise and profit.

It is absolutely clear that the private sector is and must continue to be the driving force in the economy (. . .). The role and purpose of government policy will relate primarily to how we can nurture and stimulate the Canadian private sector. A Progressive Conservative government will create an overall economic environment which provides exactly this kind of support. (1983: *Passim*)

On the surface, Mr. Mulroney's comments bear striking resemblance to the ideologically-inclined pronouncements of Ronald Reagan and Margaret Thatcher. The natural proclivity of political scientists is to search for labels to qualify the policy stance of the Mulroney government, and not infrequently the term' neo-conservative' and/or 'neo-liberal' are the ones that are applied to it. This classification is particularly convenient because it has been used so often and so convincingly in reference to the political praxis in the U.S.A. and the U.K., to which Mulroney appears to have been aspiring.

In our view the above attempts to ideologically pigeonhole Canada's Tories as neo-conservatives/neo-liberals are rather misplaced. For one, the terms neo-conservative and neo-liberal are fraught with imprecision and in most cases are used in a rather cavalier and inappropriate manner. These notions in short are often muddled and at best they convey varied or complementary meanings.

Some like to establish a clear distinction between the two. To quintessential neo-conservative Irving Kristol, neo-conservatism is inclined to the belief that a predominantly market economy is a necessary if not sufficient precondition for a liberal society; sees economic growth as indispensable for social and political stability; believes in a "social insurance state" i.e. a state that takes a degree of responsibility for helping to shape preferences that the people exercise in a free market — to elevate them; and looks upon family and religion as indispensable pillars of a decent society (1983: 76–77). Neo-liberalism on the other hand is a "process of disengagement from social democratic liberalism (. . .). It is also a disengagement from the upper middle class, Bohemian point of view which has been so popular in these last ten years and found many recruits within the liberal social democratic movements. It represents a disengagement from the limits to growth perspective that was so popular among the liberals in the last 15 years" (Kristol in Peters & Keisling, 1985: 181).

Charles Peters, the editor of *The Washington Monthly* and self-styled neo-liberal views the difference more summarily: "if neo-conservatives are liberals who took a critical look at liberalism and decided to become conservatives, we (neo-liberals) are liberals who took the same look and decided to retain our goals but to abandon some of our prejudices. We believe in liberty and justice and a fair chance for all, in mercy for the afflicted and help for the down and out. But we no longer automatically favour unions and big government or oppose the military and big business" (1985).

Finally, others claim that the distinction between the two strands is a blurred and invalid one. They believe "liberal-conservative" would be a more appropriate term to qualify the ideological reorientation of the 1980s since neo-liberal components seem to determine neo-conservatism in important ways (Mouffe, 1986: 35).

Between neo-conservatism and neo-liberalism, there is hardly more than a variation in degree and nuance as to how to achieve the reforms and changes that the proponents of each strand think are needed to face up to what they see as the abuses of the Welfare state and Keynesian economics. While neo-conservatives will tend to insist more on traditional moral values and social ethics, and may even consider state intervention to insure that a modicum of conventional morality be imposed on society (e.g. legislation against abortion, compulsory prayer in the schools), they are just as likely as their neo-liberal counterparts to assert the paramountcy of the market and of individualism, though the neo-liberal will tend to favour a more minimalist state (Barry, 1987). The so-called New Right blends these two tendencies into its socioeconomic project.

Admittedly, Mulroney's Conservatives share a number of ideas with their counterparts in the U.S.A. and the U.K. But do these occasional overlaps with British and American neo-conservatism constitute sufficient grounds to label the Mulroney period as a neo-conservative enterprise? Several contributors to this volume might disagree, while others are at ease with the term.

Beyond the labels, beyond the ideological categories and classification, a fact remains: the policy agenda of the 1980s has taken a turn which seems to break away from the public policy logic we have grown accustomed to over the last three or four decades.

Whether this is a neo-conservative or neo-liberal phenomenon may, in the end, be a problem of very little relevance. It is almost commonplace to say that there is today in the dominant political discourse a growing commitment to a greater degree of economic laissez-faire, and to the enhancement of the individualization of the social sphere. A commitment which seems to translate, wherever it has been formulated with more or less success into policies of deregulation, privatization, de-welfarization and tighter management of human resources. This new commitment is really what is at the heart of the current political/ideological reorientation. It must be understood in itself, in its implications, and not with reference to some desire for terminological precision or taxonomic correctness.

The Mulroney government's election to office in 1984 raised and continues to raise on the eve of a new federal election, a number of questions. Is the Tory government ideology driven or is it simply a pragmatic or opportunistic vehicle following the winds of change? Is this a government that has been engaged in a process of redirecting the ingrained public consumptionist tastes of Canadians or is it one that broadly speaking has been responding to newly developing, and more individualistic public demands? The turn to the right that we have spoken about earlier, and which many of the chapters documents — is it largely the product of a Tory agenda and how different would things be under a Liberal or NDP government?

While neo-conservative labels are frequently attached to Mulroney's legislative performance by left leaning academics how is it that Canada under the Tories has clearly not experienced the extremes of Thatcherite or Reaganite state decompression? What is it about the Canadian societal fabric that, in spite of shallower traditions of welfarism than found in Britain, enabled it to withstand efforts to engineer a major tear in its social safety net? Is that tear yet to come? To what extent has the 'New Right' restructuring we have spoken about earlier been realized in Canada under Mulroney, and how much of it is merely political rhetoric that appears to be taken at its word only by classification driven political scientists? And most importantly, how enduring is the shift to the Right likely to be? Have public tastes really shifted, and is the dismantling of the welfare state, the reduction of government intervention, and the rise to prominence of the marketplace in all spheres of life likely to become the wave of the future?

17

The authors of the various chapters of this book have addressed these and other important questions and a number of interesting conclusions have emerged.

One of the conclusions drawn is that the behaviour of the Mulroney government does not lend itself to easy ideological interpretations. The utilization of neo-Marxist, neo-conservative, neo-liberal, corporatist or most other blinkers to explain the behaviour of the Mulroney regime oftentimes neglects to inform us about some glaringly atypical behaviour on the part of the government. The atypical behaviour is of course clearly the product of the fact that the Mulroney regime, in spite of its rhetoric, has turned out to be surprisingly non-doctrinaire. A few years ago, Anthony Westell has observed that in Canada " . . . regional loyalties and interests have always been more important than ideology." (Westell, 1982: 33) Westell correctly prognosticated that the then Conservative Party leader, Mr. Joe Clark was going to be challenged " . . . by members of his party who want to return ideology to politics — who believe they can defeat the Liberals by offering the neo-conservative view to voters" (1982: 33).

Mr. Westell of course was partly right. Joe Clark did end up impaled on his party's ideological bayonet, but that bayonet has proven to be of great use only in leadership contests and in the context of campaign rhetoric. As the Meech Lake accord and a host of other post-1984 Tory initiatives have shown, Canadians still very much prefer to drive into the future with regional rather than ideological mirrors.

In 1984, Canadians voted for a line-change and manifestly not for a neo-conservative menu. This is clear from three years of opinion surveys that show an intensified appetite for goods and services normally found in the stockrooms of the staunchest of Canadian Social Democrats, the NDP.

What The Tories' first term in office has also shown is a sobering responsiveness by the government to the Canadian imperative. As many of the papers in this book demonstrate, particularly those written from the Eastern and Western parts of the country, Mulroney's government has become increasingly adept at surf-boarding over our uniquely Canadian socio-political waves. The likelihood of radical neo-conservative ideological designs being enforced upon Canadians by the Tories or by anyone else, is highly unlikely in the future.

It is also clear that Canada under Mulroney is not such a different place from what it would have been had the Liberals been in power. The NEP, FIRA, the regulatory matrix of the 1960–70 decade have all been on the hit list of Liberal party strategists prior to 1984. Former Liberal transport minister, Lloyd Axworthy is the father of Canadian airline deregulation, and the efforts to come to grips with social expenditures goes well back before 1984. With a few minor exceptions, Meech Lake is acceptable to the vast majority of federal Liberals.

To be sure, the Tories' free-trade deal with the U.S.A. is one policy initiative that John Turner's Liberals have chosen to dramatically distance themselves from, especially during the homestretch leading up to the next election. To what extent this posture by the Liberal leader will resemble the previous Liberal party leader's electoral flip-flop on price and wage control, is left to the future. The ground for such a turn-about is of course well prepared. Federal liberals have historically not been known to be strong anti-continentalist. Their Quebec cousins are pro free-traders and much of the Liberal fury is directed not against the concept of free-trade as such but against Mulroney's variant. Mulroney's free trade deal may be torn up by John Turner if he is elected to office, but that action alone may not stop the Liberals from concocting a free-trade deal of their own with the U.S.A. The king is dead, long live the king! The unbearable lightness of politics has given wings to far less air-worthy projects in the past. In short, the realignment taking place in Canada under Mulroney is a reactive one, that has yet to find its balance, and it is a realignment that most observers feel would have taken place regardless of who controlled the keys to the executive washrooms of the Langevin block.

By the 1980s, Canada's socioeconomic edifice was shaken as its structural weaknesses became more apparent and unavoidable. The profound recession, unprecedently high interest rates and the intensification of the fiscal crisis of the state in the early 1980s indicated without a doubt the magnitude of the problem. Because of its increasingly limited financial latitude, the Canadian state has been forced to consider cutting down on its expenditures, reorient its various interventions and strategies or action, and review the organization and management of its activities. As attested to by a series of governmental commissions of inquiry, reports and task forces, from the 1979 Lambert Commission on financial management and accountability to the 1986 Nielsen Task Force on government programmes, through the 1981 parliamentary Task force on

Federal-provincial relations, the monumental MacDonald Commission on economic union, the Forget Commission on unemployment, and of course with the constitutional revisions of 1981–1982,
the new Charter of rights and Meech lake, the politics of the 1980s
have been the politics of state restructuring. It is impossible to
understand fully recent Canadian politics if one does not grasp this
phenomenon, and the extent to which it has pervaded the political search for solutions to the crisis. The significance of the rise of
the so-called New Right in Canadian politics lies in this very
search. In tune with Mulroney's early calls for the termination of
the "swedenizing of Canada" and for the revival of the individualistic and entrepreneurial spirit, this search has given shape to
a rhetoric and to actual policies wherever feasible aimed at challenging the collectivistic gains made during the unfettered expansion
of welfarist social measures. The policy commitment to the reinforcement of market mechanisms in all aspects of societal life, and
to the reorientation of social welfare programs toward assistance
rather than insurance objectives (toward selectivity rather than
universality) was without a doubt a central dimension of the
search.

What is also clear, however, is that Canada under Mulroney did
not move as sharply to the right as some had expected, and that
the shift to the right is unlikely to be longlasting. Had the pre-1984
public policy fabric of Canada been held together by ideological
stitches, Tory efforts to tear it apart would have had much greater
chances of succeeding. But since the growth of government and
state expansion in the post-World War II era has been a largely
pragmatic response to objective necessities (albeit with a number
of poorly designed and executed responses to those necessities) the
task of neo-conservative reconstruction is far more difficult to sustain in this country. The heavy and criss-crossing regional winds
blowing across our land, unlike in Britain, or elsewhere, will also
surely scatter the neo-conservative clouds that some would like
Canada to be blanketed in from sea to sea. And perhaps, Anthony
Westell's comments are equally apposite: "The trend to the right
may not last more than a few years, because . . . the market
economy will not be able to deliver the stability and security that
people now, quite reasonably demand" (1982: 34).

If we have any advice to offer to Canadians during this election
year, it is one drawn from our national sport — keep your eyes on
the play, don't lose track of the score, and beware of distracting

20

line changes. Whether the 'New Right' perceptions of the role of the state is well founded, whether its perception of the inherent ills of the Welfare state is correct, whether the solutions it has offered to reestablish some kind of socioeconomic stability are desirable is not really the object of this book. Rather it is the performance of one government, the Mulroney administration, that is under scrutiny here. A government which, through its particular discourse and attitudes seems to have entrusted itself with the mission of presiding over the "reconstruction" of Canadian society and politics. How well has the Mulroney government been able to achieve its project is really the central question raised by this book. By extension — though implicitly — the book tries to shed some light on the feasibility of the New Right alternative in the Canadian context.

NOTE

1 See, in particular, the annual publication of the Carleton University School of Public Administration *How Ottawa Spends*.

REFERENCES

Barry, Norman (1987). *The New Right*, (London: Croom Helm).

Bell, Daniel (1975). "The Revolution of Rising Entitlements," *Fortune*.

Campbell, Robert (1987). *Grand Illusions. The Politics of the Keynesian Experience in Canada*, (Peterborough: Broadview Press).

Houle, François (1983). "Economic Strategy and the Restructuring of the Fordist Wage-Labour Relationship in Canada," *Studies in Political Economy*, No. 11.

Houle, François (1987). "Du libéralisme classique au néo-liberalisme: la soumission de L'État aux lois du marché" in Lizette Jalbert and Lucille Beaudry (eds.), *Les métamorphoses de la pensée libérale*, (Montréal: Presses de l'Université du Québec), pp. 29–64.

Kristol, Irving (1983).. *Reflections of a Neo-Conservative*, (New York: Basic Books).

Medcalf, Linda and Dolbeare, Kenneth, M. (1985). *Neopolitics. American Political Ideas in the 1980s*, (Philadelphia: Temple University Press).

Moscovitch, Allan and Albert, Jim (eds.) (1987). *The Benevolent State. The Growth of the Welfare State in Canada*, (Toronto: Garamond Press).

Mouffe, Chantal (1986). "L'offensive du néo-conservatisme contre la démocratie" in Lizette Jalbert and Laurent Lepage (eds.) *Néoconservatism et restructuration de l'État*, (Montréal: Presses de l'Université du Québec).

Mulroney, Brian. (1983). *Where I Stand*, (Toronto: McClelland and Stewart).

Myrdal, Gunnar (1978). "Institutional Economics," *Journal of Economic Issues*, Vol. XIII, No. 4.

Noël, Alain (1987)."L'après-guerre au Canada: politiques keynesiennes ou nouvelles formes de régulation?" In Gérard Boismenu and Gilles Dostaler (eds.) La "théorie générale" et le keynesianisme, (Montréal: ACFAS), pp. 91–107.

Peters, Charles, (1985). "A Neo Liberal Manifesto" in Charles Peters and Philip Keisling (eds.) A New Road for America: The Neo-Liberal Movement (New York: Madison Books).

Peters, Charles and Keisling, Philip (eds.) (1985). A New Road for America (New York: Madison Books).

Westell, Anthony (1982). "Political Trends: Is Canada Turning Right?" The Canadian Business Review, Spring.

NATIONAL RECONCILIATION

... *a priority goal of my Ministers will be to breathe a new spirit into federalism and restore the faith and trust of all Canadians in the effectiveness of their system of government. A constant process of consultation and cooperation must be restored* ....

My government's management of federal-provincial relations will pursue three basic objectives: to harmonize policies of our two orders of government, to ensure respect to their jurisdictions, and to end unnecessary and costly duplication ....

The reality of Canada is one of distinct regional identities, each rooted in many generations of history; of diverse cultures; of regional economic strengths: a country of many parts whose people share a profound attachment to one Canada.

My Ministers are determined to achieve a national consensus which will reflect that reality. A national consensus is also needed to reduce the persistent isolation of Canada's regions, to meet the challenges of economic and social disparity, to revitalize the strengths of our traditional resource industries ....

Ultimately, such a consensus must be reflected in the fundamental law of our land, for it is obvious that the constitutional agreement is incomplete so long as Quebec is not part of an accord. While their principal obligation is to achieve economic renewal, my Ministers will work to create the conditions that will make possible the achievement of this essential accord. In this work the cooperation of all partners of Confederation will be necessary.

— Speech from the throne, November 5, 1984.

National Reconciliation: The Mulroney Government and Federalism

RICHARD SIMEON

INTRODUCTION

A central theme of the Progressive Conservative's 1984 campaign was Brian Mulroney's pledge to foster "National Reconciliation." It was time, he argued, notably in a speech at Sept-Isles, "to breathe a new spirit into federalism," and reverse the "serious deterioration in federal-provincial relations" of the previous decade.

The commitment to reconciliation involved a number of related elements. First, was the acceptance of a more provincialist and communitarian vision of Canada, in contrast to the "liberal nationalism" of Trudeau (Romanow, Whyte and Leeson, 1984). "There is room in Canada for all identities to be affirmed ... for all aspirations to be affected." Second was a commitment to reduce inter-regional conflict. Third, he would work with the "duly elected" government of Quebec to "convince the Quebec National Assembly to give its consent to the new Canadian constitution." Fourth, there would be a renewed commitment to reduce regional disparities. Fifth, there would be an end to federal "intrusions" into areas of provincial jurisdiction. Ottawa would "not duplicate provincial programs or launch programs that are incompatible with provincial programs." It would be guided by the "principle of respect for provincial authority." Finally, there was a commitment to "co-operative federalism" and to a model of policy-making in the federal system which depended on extensive collaboration between the two senior orders of government.

Governing Canada, then, was to be a cooperative, collaborative partnership between two equal orders of government.

It would be hard to imagine a sharper repudiation of the model of federalism which had been pursued by the Trudeau government, especially in the period 1980 to 1984. Trudeau's drive had been to stop, and then reverse, what he considered the drift towards provincialization and decentralization in Canadian federalism. Where Mulroney talked of regional diversity, Trudeau emphasized the primacy of the national, pan-Canadian community. Where Mulroney talked of equal orders of government, Trudeau had asserted the ultimate authority of the central government. Where Mulroney talked of respect for provincial jurisdiction, Trudeau had pushed federal authority to its limits, on the constitution, energy and health care policy. Where Mulroney talked of collaboration among 11 first ministers, Trudeau emphasized federal unilateralism, with Ottawa by-passing the provinces to deliver its own programs and to forge direct links with citizens and interest groups (McRoberts, 1985). Where Mulroney talked of cooperation, Trudeau had derided the assumptions of cooperative federalism, arguing that it placed the interests of governments ahead of citizens, tended inevitably to "lowest common denominator" solutions, and eroded the legitimacy and authority of the federal government while elevating a group of irresponsible provincial politicians to the status of national leaders. Trudeau's model, by contrast asserted the virtues of "competitive federalism" (Milne, 1986).

Mulroney's federalism was a return to an older model of Canadian federal politics, in at least two respects. First, it reasserted the primacy of the traditional Canadian preoccupation with territorial politics, based on region and language. It paid less heed to the growth of alternative conceptions of the bases of political division — gender, multiculturalism, individual rights and the like — which had been fostered especially by the advent of the Charter of Rights. Second, it reasserted the primacy of elite accommodation — leaders dealing with leaders — which had been challenged both by Trudeau's assertion of mobilizing citizens against governments and by the growth of demands for a more participatory style of politics.

Mulroney's emphasis on reconciliation struck a responsive chord. Canada had just passed through an extraordinary period of conflict and turmoil, symbolized by the bitter constitutional debate, the battles over energy, and other issues. A decade of regional and linguistic tensions seemed to have called the very

26

existence of the country into question. There was a profound sense of "institutional failure." The institutions of parliamentary government at the centre seemed incapable of effectively representing all parts of the country or of bridging regional differences.

The mechanisms of intergovernmental relations seemed to have become arenas for intergovernmental posturing and for the articulation of deeply divided visions of federalism. Surveys showed a strong desire to reduce the wrangling and to find more fruitful bases for cooperation. If many thought that Trudeau's pushing of the system to its limits had been a necessary catharsis, many now felt it was time for a renewed search for harmony.

Other factors also suggested that conditions were propitious for the kind of reconciliation Mulroney advocated. With the Referendum and the subsequent disarray of the PQ in Quebec, the drive had gone out of the state-based nationalism which had defined Quebec politics since the 1960s. Now there was a profound disillusionment with political action; if nationalism remained, it was less political nationalism than what Courchene labelled "market nationalism" (Courchene, 1977). With the defeat of the PQ in 1985, there would be a federalist government in Quebec with which the Tories could negotiate. Regional divisions had also become attenuated. Western province-building had been driven by world energy prices; now, the collapse of these prices — and those of related commodities — diminished the regional conflict, and the competition among governments for revenues. For the west, the problem now was less how to gain greater autonomy for themselves, and more how to ensure their ability to exercise influence at the centre.

Political factors also helped to create the conditions for harmony. The massive Tory victory ensured that for the first time in many years, the government in Ottawa had significant support in all parts of the country, presumably enhancing Ottawa's capacity to work out accommodations within its own processes, and reducing the sense of exclusion which had been such a powerful source of provincialist support. Moreover, the Liberals in power had faced a solid bloc of provincial governments of different partisan stripe. While it is clear that federal-provincial conflict is inadequately explained by the partisan composition of the various governments, the fact that Mulroney would be dealing with Premiers of the same party ensured at least a short honeymoon period.

Thus, in 1984 Canadians elected a government committed to

reconciliation, and the underlying conditions provided a solid base on which that aspiration could be realized. Four years later, there is little doubt that tensions within the federal system have been sharply reduced. The sense of federal-provincial warfare has disappeared. Nevertheless, the Mulroney approach raises a number of important questions. Some arise from internal contradictions within the Mulroney approach itself. These turn primarily on the relationship between its aspirations for federalism, and its equally important commitment to a more market-oriented and less interventionist role for government in the economy. Other questions — crystallized especially by the Meech Lake debate — turn on the strength of alternative images of Canada, and especially the perceived conflict between collaborative federalism, on the one hand, and changing conceptions of citizen-state relations and effective government on the other.

We will return to these questions, but will first explore the Mulroney record, with particular reference to his two key initiatives: free trade with the United States and the Meech Lake Accord, both of which nicely illustrate the dilemmas in the Mulroney approach.

THE RECORD

Once in office, the new government moved quickly to demonstrate the new "spirit of cooperation," and to bring the provincial governments "within the circumference of federal policy-making." At the November, 1985, First Ministers' Conference, Mulroney stated that provinces were to be involved in national decision-making as "trusted partners in the business of managing the federation, partners equally dedicated to its unity and prosperity" (Milne, 1986: 221). "I believe," he said, "that in a federalist state you should govern to the extent humanly possible, in harmony with the provinces" (Graham, 1986: 391). The new government would show greater deference to provincial priorities; there would be less emphasis on imposing its will, or on "direct delivery" of federal programs. Such rhetoric, while a sharp contrast from the immediately preceding period, was not new in Canadian federalism: a similar orientation guided the early years of the Pearson Liberals, and indeed the Trudeau years prior to 1980 (Simeon, 1972).

28

The most obvious manifestation of the Mulroney commitment was a veritable explosion in intergovernmental conferencing, beginning with the first FMC on the Economy, in February, 1985, a love-in at which all first ministers lauded the new spirit. They agreed to hold First Ministers conferences on the economy at least annually for the first five years. Between 1980 and 1984, there had been an annual average of five First Ministers' conferences; in the first year of the Mulroney mandate there were 13. There were 353 ministerial meetings, compared to an annual average of 82 in the previous four years. And there were 72 meetings of deputies, compared with an average of 45 in the previous period (Milne, 1986; 223). More meetings were now held outside Ottawa; more were chaired by provincial ministers; and more were focussed on provincial agendas. Thus Mulroney restored intergovernmental discussions — and especially the FMC — as a central arena of national policy-making.

The new government also moved quickly to remove the chief "irritants" in the federal-provincial relationship. The much-hated National Energy Program, already battered by the drop in oil prices, was rapidly dismantled. In a later defence of the free trade agreement, Pat Carney, the federal Trade Minister, claimed that the Tories had moved first to end the NEP — and now, with the agreement, had ensured that no federal government would ever again be able to repeat it. The Western Accord was signed in March, 1985. Prices were to be set by the market; a host of taxes associated with the NEP were to be terminated or phased out; PIP grants and the bias towards exploration on Canada lands would be ended (Hawkes and Pollard, 1987:156). More than any other initiative, Mr. Mulroney claimed, the agreement underscored the "reconciliation among Canadians . . . and progress toward renewed federalism" (First Ministers Conference, 1985).

The Accord was soon followed by an agreement deregulating gas prices. On the East Coast, in the Atlantic Accord, signed with Newfoundland, Ottawa agreed to joint management and pricing of offshore oil and gas resources, and agreed that the provinces would receive all "province-type" revenues as if the resources were located on land. The new model was a jointly shared responsibility.

In other, less salient areas, further progress was made. Ottawa got out of the lottery business. Ottawa collaborated with the provinces in the development of a joint declaration on the goals of regional development policy. The provinces were insulated from the first round of federal deficit-cutting. In regional development, Economic and Regional Development Agreements were signed with a number of provinces which had failed to come to agreement with the previous government; and there was less emphasis on direct delivery of federal programs. Responsibility for much of the IDRP program was transferred to the provinces; and it was henceforth to be targeted more directly to the least developed regions (Savoie, 1986: 91). In 1987, new regional development agencies, emphasizing local decision-making and greater responsiveness, were created in the Atlantic region, and in the West.

The primary tests of the new collaborative model came in the two major policy initiatives undertaken by the first Mulroney government: the negotiation of a Free Trade Agreement with the United States, and the search for a constitutional settlement with Quebec which culminated in the Meech Lake Accord.

The free trade initiative raised immediate questions for federalism for several reasons. First was the "constitutional gap" identified by the Macdonald Commission. Constitutional interpretation seemed to suggest that while the federal government had plenary authority to negotiate and ratify any international treaty, that power did not extend to the power of implementation. For that purpose, the federal-provincial division of powers prevailed: Ottawa could not implement those provisions of treaties which fell into provincial jurisdiction. That would not be a problem so long as a trade treaty dealt only with the federal tariff: it was a problem if it dealt with non-tariff barriers, since many of the subsidies, procurement and other programs were undertaken by provincial governments. That had been underlined by the softwood lumber dispute, in which it was provincial stumpage and management practices which were held to constitute unfair subsidies by United States authorities. Non-tariff barriers were clearly on the Free Trade agenda; and American negotiators made it clear that any agreement must include provincial practices. Federalism was also involved because of the historic regional differences on free trade versus protection, themselves grounded in regional economic differences; and because any agreement was likely to have divergent regional impacts. Finally, provinces themselves had become increasingly involved in international economic relationships, and were unlikely to give the federal government *carte blanche* to negotiate an agreement with so many potential implications for them (Simeon, 1987).

30

Thus the question became: how should provinces be involved in the negotiations? In the initial skirmishing, some provinces took the position that negotiating a trade agreement should be a fully collaborative process. The Canadian trade negotiators should take their instructions from and report to the First Ministers as a group; and it would be they who would approve the deal and agree on its implementation. Such a model was too much even for Mulroney's collaborative federalism: Ottawa was prepared to consult with and inform the provinces, but not to take instruction from them. The critical question of ratification and implementation was left aside.

Eventually a process was agreed: First Ministers would meet to review progress every 90 days; and mirror meetings of ministerial and officials meetings would be held. This was the pattern that prevailed through the negotiations. Three provinces — Ontario, Manitoba and Prince Edward Island — opposed the draft agreement that was reached, and continued to assert that provinces had the right to veto important sections of the agreement which they held to infringe on areas of provincial jurisdiction. Federal negotiators, on the other hand, had worked hard to reach a deal which had as few hostages to provincial powers as possible — indeed, this may be one reason for the limited character of the agreement, which says little about existing subsidies and other non-tariff barriers. Moreover, federal officials argued that Ottawa did in fact have the authority itself to implement the disputed parts of the agreement, perhaps under the Peace, Order clause, but more likely by asserting that all provisions fell within the ambit of the federal trade and commerce power. Indeed, the reach of the trade and commerce remains a grey area, and the issue, may well end up in the courts.

Thus collaborative processes have their limits for the Tories. It does not extend to the requirement for unanimity before any initiative can be taken; nor does it preclude the implicit threat of recourse of the courts if intergovernmental accommodation breaks down. Despite these limits, however, the negotiation of the free trade agreement marks how far along the collaborative path we have travelled. In earlier rounds of Canada–U.S. trade discussions, and even in the negotiation of the 1965 Autopact with such massive consequences for Ontario, provinces had been barely informed as to what was happening, though they had been consulted and informed during the previous round of negotiations under the General Agreement on Tariffs and Trade.

THE MEECH LAKE ACCORD

Meech Lake represents the epitome of the Mulroney approach to federalism, both in its substance, and in the process by which it was achieved. The "spirit of Meech Lake" has become another name for "national reconciliation." Securing Quebec's voluntary acceptance of the constitutional settlement of 1982 was a central goal for Mulroney: it was both to be a great act of strengthening the country, healing the gaping wound left by Quebec's earlier exclusion; and, more prosaically, it was a way of cementing the new-found Conservative strength in Quebec. The crucial political task was to find a way to meet Quebec's minimum demands — a restoration of the Quebec veto on constitutional amendment, some formal recognition of Quebec's status as a distinct society within Canadian federalism, and the like — while simultaneously respecting the equality of all provinces which had been enshrined in the 1982 amending formula, and ensuring that in squaring this circle, federal powers would not be irreparably constrained.

The government began with the assumption that such a delicate balancing act, given the divergent views in the country at large, could only be achieved through the finest arts of federal-provincial diplomacy. There was no natural consensus "out there," no vision of Canada and Quebec to be mobilized through popular appeal. The new 1982 amending formula required the unanimous agreement of 11 governments, and it was these governments which must be brought on side. Thus, following the revelation by the new Quebec government of its basic conditions for agreement, Mulroney appointed Senator Lowell Murray as Minister of State for Federal–Provincial Relations and Norman Spector as Secretary to the Cabinet for Federal–Provincial Relations — two respected negotiators — and charged them with finding the basis for agreement. With virtually no public fanfare, the two shuttled among Quebec and the other provinces, seeking to lay the grounds for consensus. Only when the groundwork was laid was a formal First Ministers conference held.

Following the pattern of elite accommodation, it was held in camera, at the Meech Lake Conference centre. Following the Prime Minister's view that crucial decisions can only be made among top leaders, the only official present was Spector. It was later argued that only the talents of a professional negotiator were able to ensure that at the end of the day, tentative agreement on a new accord was reached.

Only then was the issue thrown open to public discussion. Three weeks later, in an extraordinary bargaining session, lasting all day and through the night, all 11 first ministers signed the final legal text of the Accord. Again, participants are unanimous in testifying, it was only the extraordinary atmosphere of crisis, exhaustion and peer group pressure which kept the consensus intact. And even then, this could be achieved only by writing an Accord with crucial elements left ambiguous or undefined.

Under the 1982 formula, the text then had to be ratified by each legislature, within three years, before becoming part of the constitution. This process too was to be constrained by the requirements of executive federalism. Any alteration, in any legislature, would necessitate reopening the intergovernmental discussion. Hence the government stated that only if "egregious errors" were found in the text could amendments be accepted; otherwise legislatures must pass it unamended. Again, there was a sense that the consensus was so fragile and so finely balanced that any such change could lead to its rapid unravelling, with little chance of putting it back together.

The text of the Accord reinforced the assumptions of national reconciliation and collaborative federalism — in the recognition of Quebec as a "distinct society," and in provincialist changes to the amending formula and senate and judicial appointments. High levels of federal-provincial cooperation were to be required in the future by the extension of the unanimity rule to a further group of amendments, by joint appointment of senators and judges, and by the operation of the new provision with respect to the spending power. The legitimacy of collaborative federalism was recognized by the constitutional provision for annual first ministers' conferences on the economy and on the constitution.

Thus, since 1984, the Mulroney government has done much to advance its strategy of improved interregional and intergovernmental harmony. Two basic questions remain: how successful has it been? And what are the implications of this model for the future of Canadian federalism? How does one judge the Mulroney project for federalism?

QUALIFIED SUCCESS

The most cursory survey of the federal scene today shows that levels of interregional conflict, so deep and apparently irreconcilable in the 1970s, are now much attenuated. Gone is the sense of a national fabric stretched almost to the tearing point. Regional divisions have not disappeared — they are after all a permanent part of the "background noise" of Canadian politics, but, in comparison to the 1970s and early 1980s, they are much muted. Mulroney's style and commitment must be given a large part of the credit for this. The major regional irritants have been removed; federal discretionary spending has been carefully doled out to all regions.

Nevertheless, it would be wrong to give the Conservative government full credit for these changes. The determinants of the intensity of regional differences are more systematic, as Joe Clark, another Prime Minister equally dedicated to regional reconciliation, found when he had tried to bridge the differences between Central Canada and the West over energy in 1979. Thus it was the rise of energy prices which fuelled regional conflicts in the 1970s — and their decline in the 1980s has led to the diminution of regional conflict. Moreover, the fact that the Tories had won large majorities in every province, and were able to deal with a majority of provinces with conservative regimes smoothed the political path.

Mulroney, too, has found it difficult to bridge regional competition for economic development and federal largesse. Indeed, he has found that attempts to shore up and solidify support in one area provokes anger and resentment in others. Federal discretionary spending in procurement and other areas is a potent instrument for this. But this is a double-edged sword, more likely to provoke jealousy than gratitude. Thus the Canadair decision — along with other spending in Quebec — provoked outrage in Manitoba. Quebec and New Brunswick have sparred over frigates, and the list goes on. Moreover the West has been reminded that it is not enough simply to be proportionately represented in the governing party. In a parliamentary system, the weight of numbers still remains with central Canada. Thus, the western sense of being unrepresented in Ottawa has been rekindled. This helps explain some of the erosion of western support for the Tories, and, more important, explains the current search for more institution-alized means of securing the interests of the less populous regions at the centre — notably the call for a "Triple E" Senate.

The longer-run implications of the Mulroney strategy are also deeply ambiguous. This is most evident with the Free Trade initiative. One of its great appeals to Mulroney was that it promised to address historic grievances in the west and east by finally laying to rest the National Policy. (This was also a central justification advanced by the Macdonald Commission.) No longer would resentment be driven by the sense that the peripheries were compelled to buy their goods at higher than world prices from Central Canada, and to sell their resources at less than world value on uncertain world markets. Now every region could buy and sell at world prices. Moreover, the restraints that the international agreement imposed on Ottawa would in the future prevent it undertaking industrial policies which discriminated against peripheral reasons. Pat Carney, for example, told westerners that having already dismantled the NEP, the Tories were now signing an international agreement which ensured that never again could such a program be undertaken.

In the short-run, there is much to this assessment of free trade. The longer-run implications, however, may be rather different. To the extent that free trade ends up conferring its benefits and costs differently on different regions, it could well fuel the politics of regional jealousy. The Free Trade Agreement has protected Canadian regional development policies, but they remain potentially vulnerable to U.S. trade law. Hence, in the long run, the ability of the federal government to act as the "national insurance agent" and the redistributor of resources among regions may well be attenuated. Even more fundamentally, free trade essentially puts an end to the National policy's dream of creating an east–west economy. It continues the postwar trend of de-linking the Canadian regional economies; each now functions independently in the world, their destinies tied not to each other, but to North American and global markets. Free trade is based on the assumption that economic integration compelled by government action is a recipe for conflict; and thus that harmony will be promoted by disengagement. However, one wonders whether it is possible to sustain a commitment to regional redistribution and equalization in the absence of extensive economic ties among regions. Thus, free trade could exacerbate regional differences, while reducing the capacity of the federal government to alleviate them.

Some aspects of Meech Lake may have somewhat the same logic. It too says that future conflict will be avoided by ensuring that the interests of national majorities will not be imposed on regional majorities — through the extension of the unanimity rule, and the extension of the right to opt-out of Constitutional amendments or shared cost programs with fiscal compensation. The thrust is to protect each region from the others, and from the national government. It removes some causes of regional grievance; but does less to create the conditions for developing national consensus which transcends such differences.

Linguistic conflict has also sharply declined. Again, some of the primary reasons are systemic — notably the decline of state-based Quebec nationalism. Nevertheless, here, surely, Mulroney deserves considerable credit. He began with the Tory electoral coalition, in which many previous PQ activists, such as Lucien Bouchard, played a major role in the Tory sweep. While this is reminiscent of Duplessis' cooperation with the Tories in an earlier era, and much opportunism was no doubt at work, the Tories have helped break the sterile pattern of a Quebec politics fundamentally polarized between nationalists centered in Quebec City and anti-nationalists centered in Ottawa.

The central achievement is, of course, the Meech Lake Accord. The political challenge was to square two circles, while not breaking a third. How to reconcile a model of linguistic dualism based on the notion that Quebec is the social and political base for francophone Canadians — the model defended by successive Quebec governments and nationalist movements — and the model of dualism based on the rights of linguistic minorities in all parts of the country — the model so passionately defended by Pierre Trudeau. How to reconcile the notion that the government of Quebec plays a special role as the primary political expression of the distinctive Quebec society — the *sine qua non* of all Quebec governments in modern times — with the idea that all Canadian provinces are juridically equal? And how to reconcile both of these with the maintenance of a strong central government?

To its defenders, Meech Lake does all these things. It defines dualism simultaneously as including the presence of anglophones and francophones in all parts of the country, and as the existence of Quebec as a distinct society. Both dimensions are to be principles

36

of interpretation of the whole constitution. In asserting that all governments have the duty to "preserve" national dualism, it is an advance on the 1982 constitution, which extended only to guarantees of minority language education rights. It gives Quebec the obligation of promoting its distinct society, but carefully avoids defining the distinctiveness, and explicitly denies any associated transfer of jurisdiction. It squares the second circle by giving Quebec a constitutional veto which simultaneously applies to all the other provinces — the same model as the Liberals' opting out legislation of 1965, and as the Victoria Charter of 1971.

This is a creative compromise — bought at the price of clarity and precision. Its great achievement is to have secured the voluntary acceptance by Quebec of the 1982 constitutional settlement. Recent events, however, show that it is no clear guide to the resolution of linguistic conflicts — whether within Quebec or in Saskatchewan and Alberta. Meech Lake, even when enacted, will provide no authoritative resolution to the question. Indeed, it has been pointed out that the lack of content creates the possibility for future conflict and disillusion depending on how the interpretive chips fall.

Finally, the Mulroney government has restored a large measure of intergovernmental harmony. Federal-provincial conferences are no longer the arena for the articulation of mutually exclusive ideologies about federalism. We no longer see the clashes between province and country-building economic strategies. Federal-provincial conferences have proliferated, and have seldom been the scene of aggressive posturing. Once again, there are systematic reasons: the decline of regional conflict, partisan — and perhaps more important, ideological — congruence among most of the governments, the departure from the political scene of most of the central actors of the earlier period, fiscal restraints which have curbed the expansionist drive at both levels, and so on. Numerous communiqués testify to intergovernmental consensus on a host of issues, such as regional development strategy. The government has been able to win majority provincial support for most of its major initiatives. Governments have lined up against each other in court less often. Where there is disagreement, it is more likely to be expressed privately.

Yet it is unrealistic to think that all is intergovernmental harmony. There remain important regional differences in interest — and when Ottawa intervenes on one side or another — as in the

Canadair decision — intergovernmental disagreement erupts. Fiscal restraint has meant that provinces could not continue to be exempt from federal deficit reduction measures, and limits have been placed on intergovernmental transfers. Policy and bureaucratic differences continue to fuel intergovernmental conflict, as in the Ottawa–Ontario disputes over securities regulation. There remain sharp divisions over free trade, with three provinces opposed to it. The federal government has taken the position that it does indeed have the authority to implement all parts of the agreement, and the question may well end up in the courts.

Despite these caveats, Mulroney's record in achieving "national reconciliation" must be judged a relative success. The contrast with the immediately preceding period is striking. But what are we to make of this achievement? Has reconciliation been bought at too high a price? That is the message of the critics, and to these we now turn.

EVALUATION

If the relative calm of the federal-provincial waters is a relief after the storms of the 1970s, some powerful criticisms of the Mulroney approach to federalism have been advanced. Most have been crystallized around the debate on Meech Lake.

Perhaps the deepest rooted are those which suggest the Mulroney model abandons a commitment to the strengthening of the Canadian national community, and to the central role of the federal government in nation-building, and to the articulation a single, cohesive national vision. Mulroney's national unity, it is argued is shallow, based more on disengagement and conflict avoidance, than on a common sense of citizenship and common purpose. Thus, it is argued that under Meech Lake's unanimity and opting-out provisions, the capacity of national majorities to bring about change is severely limited. The sharing of the power to appoint Supreme Court Judges and Senators subordinates these national institutions to provincialist perspectives, and so on. Similarly, it is argued that in deferring, even in a limited way, to the Quebec-centered view of dualism, Mulroney has undermined the national commitment to country-wide bilingualism, and, in Trudeau's view, given legitimacy to one of the basic assumptions of Quebec separatism. Opting-out of potential constitutional amendments or shared-cost programs, it is argued, raises the prospect of a "checker-board Canada," in which the federal role varies from region to region.

These are long-standing, familiar debates. Since they depend so much on underlying views about the nature of the Canadian community, there are no right or wrong answers. Liberal nationalists must reject the model, provincialists and those who take a more communitarian view of the country will support it.

The debate does raise the question as to where, given the character of Canadian society and Canadian history, national unity is most likely to be found. The issue is perhaps not so much nation-building versus provincialism, but alternative forms of nation-building. One, in the Macdonald tradition, most recently exemplified by Pierre Trudeau, seeks to build unity through attempting to articulate a single national vision, and by asserting the federal government's authority to define and implement it. The other — the Laurier tradition — accepts the legitimacy of provincial community and identity and builds unity on this diversity.

The historical record suggests that these two approaches have been in a dialectical relationship since Confederation. Each attempt to pursue the Macdonald model, while achieving important national purposes, has been forced to accommodate provincialist forces. Whether the issue is linguistic dualism or provincial versus national power, no one model of Canadian nationality has been able to prevail. Canadians have embraced both. Only rarely has the federal government effectively been able to represent and encompass all parts of the country, and thus to have the legitimacy to impose its definition of nationhood. In the postwar period, despite the predictions that modernization and new roles for government would inevitably erode provincial interests and identities, and lead to centralization, the reality has been the persistence and reinforcement of provincial differences and provincial powers. It is perhaps more likely that the centralizing thrust of the last Trudeau years — which in any case achieved only partial success — will turn out not to be the thrust for the future, but an aberration. If this is true, the bottom-up accommodative style of Mulroney is indeed more in tune with Canadian realities.

Like all other major constitutional documents, starting with the BNA Act itself, Meech Lake reflects competing tendencies within Canadian community; it does not choose among them. Thus, it encompasses both models of dualism. It accepts Quebec as a distinct society, but goes less far towards institutionalizing special status than any recent Quebec government has sought. It does indeed tilt towards provincialism in many respects: but at the same time it legitimizes the federal spending power, and places fewer limits on other federal powers than many of the proposals discussed in the past. Its ambiguities and inconsistencies are similar to previous constitutional documents, notably the 1982 settlement.

If the debate between Mulroney and Trudeau is a debate about conceptions of Canadian federalism, another kind of criticism is that in so emphasizing accommodation among the traditional cleavages of region and language, the Mulroney approach is hostile to the emergence of newer identities and conceptions of citizenship which cut across these lines. Most important here are identities based on gender, and the increasing tendency to focus on individual rights. This argument is reminiscent of an earlier argument by John Porter and others, who argued that Canadian politics must move from the obsolete, sterile, preoccupation with national unity and federalism, to the more "creative" bases of political mobilization based on class.

Hence the critiques of Meech Lake for undermining — or, more accurately, failing to advance — the Charter of Rights, and for its failure to give adequate recognition to women, native peoples and multicultural groups. Meech Lake is fundamentally about resolving tensions within federalism; these groups argue that political institutions must be redesigned to give greater weight to other dimensions of our existence. They also imply that "progressive" policies with respect to these new issues are more likely to come from the federal government, and thus attack the perceived decentralization in Meech Lake.

The record of the past, however, is that predictions that federalist preoccupations would be "displaced" by new bases of action have always been proven wrong. The lesson rather is that these new divisions have interacted with federalism — they have changed its character, at the same time as federalism has shaped the character of new movements. Federalism has permitted social democratic governments to come to power and introduce policy innovations at the provincial level; at the national level it has slowed and shaped, but not blocked the evolution of the welfare state. Thus it is possible to argue that the complex, relatively decentralized federalism embodied by Mulroney opens opportunities for mobilization and effective action by newer groups, in ways which would not be possible in a more centralized system.

This same group of critics has also mounted a powerful and effective attack on the political style of Mulroney's federalism, especially its reassertion of the elitist, brokerage, or elite accommodation model. The approach elevates "executive federalism" to a central element in decision-making. Again, this is illustrated both by the process and by the outcome of Meech Lake. The process took place largely in secret, public mobilization was carefully avoided, and the decisions were made by 11 first ministers, all men, making a deal, under extra-ordinary pressure, behind closed doors. The result, in turn, is to further institutionalize executive federalism — enshrining annual first ministers conferences on the economy and the constitution, and requiring collaboration in development of shared-cost programs, and appointments to the Senate and the Supreme Court.

The criticisms of executive federalism on democratic grounds are well known (Whitaker, 1983; Smiley, 1980, 1987). Smiley's observations (1979) on intergovernmental relations among consenting adults remains telling: the process freezes out public participation. It places the interests of governments, as governments, at the centre of discussion. It excludes from representation at the table any other interest except those directly linked to governmental actors. More generally, executive federalism is indeed in tension with some of the norms of parliamentary government. Where roles are hidden or blurred, citizens can no longer hold governments clearly accountable; and when delicate deals have been negotiated legislative debate is rendered pointless, because the intergovernmental deal cannot be upset. This has created the most serious disquiet about the legitimacy of the Meech Lake process.

The process is also in tension with newer models of democratic politics which emphasize extensive public consultation and greater public participation in policy-making.

More generally, Albert Breton has advanced a telling critique of cooperative federalism on the Mulroney model (Breton, 1985). Elite accommodation can also be an elite cartel. It can easily degenerate into "collusion, conspiracy and connivence" (Breton, 1985: 492). It transfers to executive and bureaucratic bargaining what should more properly be in the realm of public debate. "The heart of cooperative federalism is secret deals, not the stuff on which a lively democracy thrives" (Breton, 1985: 493).

These are indeed powerful criticisms of the Mulroney approach and its recent results. Again, there are a number of responses. First, it can be argued that given the organizational complexity of contemporary federalism, and indeed of modern government generally, elite bargaining will inevitably be a central part of the policy process. The 1982 constitutional amendment procedure virtually requires it in that field. The task, therefore, is to ensure that the elite bargainers are representative of their constituencies, and can later be held to account for their conduct in the bargaining. In other words, the extent to which intergovernmental bargaining degenerates depends on the vitality of the political processes in each government and legislature. Second, one of the prime justifications for the elite accommodation style is that, given a society deeply divided on fundamental issues, only it can provide the vehicle for compromise. Thus Mulroney would argue: show me another way in which we could have achieved the imperative goal of bringing Quebec in. The point is important: many critics have shown how they would veto Meech Lake, but few have shown an alternative formulation which could command wide support, or, more important, meet the standards for constitutional amendment set out in 1982. Indeed, by most standards of traditional representative government in Canada, Meech Lake has indeed secured a high level of consent.

Finally, it can be argued that many features of Meech Lake, rather than being hostile to a more participatory politics, will encourage it. The opportunities are endless: provinces could hold public hearings on Senate and judicial appointments; they could develop rules for Senate nominations to represent different groups in the society, perhaps even elect their Senate nominees; legislatures could hold hearings and canvass public opinion in advance of the mandated annual first ministers conferences. The procedures set out in Meech lake open up many interstices which activist groups will be able to exploit, though as with any highly fragmented decision-process it opens up more opportunities for veto than for bringing about change. Nevertheless, there is no evidence that the Meech Lake process was more elitist than previous efforts at constitution-making — notably that of 1982 — nor that it prohibits more open decision-making in the future.

The final set of criticisms of Mulroney's federalism is that it further advances processes of decentralization in Canadian federalism which are already far advanced; and that the commitment to collaborative federalism hobbles the future effectiveness of government in Canada. These, it is argued will render Canadian governments increasingly unable to respond to future policy challenges, notably those which flow from the increasing pressures arising from the global political and economic environment, and those, such as day care, responding to changing domestic demands. Such critics suggest that the imperatives of the global and North American environment are that Canada be able to speak with one voice abroad, that it be able to make and enforce international economic treaties, and that it bend domestic policy — including much controlled by provinces — to these requirements.

If it was once said that the growth of the welfare state rendered federalism obsolete, so do, it could now be argued, external challenges. Many of these critics here link Meech Lake and free trade: they see a federal government voluntarily donning a straitjacket, first by devolving power to the provinces, then by devolving it to the United States. Indeed, both are consistent with the Mulroney government's general emphasis on limited government intervention.

But this is much clearer for free trade than for Meech Lake. Meech Lake may reflect the existing balance between federal and provincial power; it may indeed be a "tilt" towards greater provincial power. But it is in itself by no means a radically decentralizing document. Indeed, much greater constraints on federal authority have been proposed and widely accepted before. The declaratory and reservation powers — dead letters, but still in the constitution — remain intact. There is no attempt to restrict interpretations of the general "peace, order" and trade and commerce powers. There are grounds for believing the ambit of both these powers may well expand in the context of a free trade agreement, and of increasing international challenges to provincial non-tariff barriers. The spending power — which is at the moment under court challenge — has been given formal constitutional status for the first time. There is no new transfer of jurisdiction to the provinces.

Hence it is likely, under Meech Lake, as in the past, that it will not be the constitution which limits and constrains federal action. There will still be much in the armory for future activist federal governments.

Breton also argues that the commitment to cooperative federalism also results in important consequences for policy. Insofar as it decries unilateral action by governments, it becomes a shackle on the federal government, and its capacity to act. Cooperative

43

federalism, he argues, conceals either a confederal view of federalism, or a preference which "seeks to reduce the role of the federal
government, indeed, of all governments in society" (Breton, 1985:
493). Insofar as this was indeed a central element of Mulroney's
agenda, Breton may well be right.

On the other hand, federalism, and specifically the commitment
to cooperative federalism, is one factor which has helped to
restrain the Mulroney government from engaging in much more
radical, Thatcherite, attacks on the welfare state, regional development and other policy areas. In other words, both radical conservative, and radical progressive policies are limited by the exigencies
of intergovernmental cooperation, though, as Banting suggests, it
may well be a greater restraint on a neo-conservative federal
government than on a provincial one (Banting, 1987).

In addition, it is clear that a commitment to cooperative federalism and policy innovation are not necessarily incompatible. The
Pearson government of the mid-sixties both presided over the
maturation of modern executive federalism, and over the most
important period of innovation in social policy in the postwar
period.

Most comment on Meech Lake has emphasized how much it is
predicated on, and entrenches for the future, intergovernmental
collaboration. Indeed, many have argued that in the long run, it is
a recipe for deadlock and disagreement, rather than cooperation.
The desire for intergovernmental consensus — and optimism that
it could be achieved — was no doubt the chief motive of the
governments which adopted it. But, in other hands, of course,
Meech Lake creates multiple opportunities for federal-provincial
competition. First, it does nothing to formally restrain governments, federal or provincial, from engaging in unilateral policy
initiatives. Second, it provides many incentives for government, in
pursuing their preferences on Senate appointments, shared cost
programs and so on, to appeal for public support. Third, the holding of annual conferences only requires governments to debate and
consult; it does not require them to agree, or engage in joint action.

As Breton himself suggests, the appropriate model can never be
one of "pure" competition, or of "pure" collaboration. He argues
that the appropriate model is that governments compete in the
shaping of policy purposes; and employ executive federalism to
coordinate implementation. Another view is that the process itself
be open to public view; and that executive agreement is both

preceded and followed by public debate and the mobilization of support by all sides.

More generally, while Breton is correct in his assertion of the benefits for citizens of the competition engendered by federalism, he pays too little attention to the costs of at least some kinds of competition. It seems unlikely the political system could have sustained the levels of conflict engendered in the early 1980s for long. Thus, the Mulroney approach is a welcome corrective. Moreover, cooperation, or more accurately, coordination, is essential, so long as the chief alternatives are unavailable. The political forces of Canadian federalism are such that neither radical centralization, nor radical decentralization are possible. They also ensure that no re-division of powers into a new set of neat, watertight boxes is conceivable. Hence interdependence will remain a permanent feature of the system. Hence, too, national policies will often require complementary action by federal and provincial governments. So executive federalism will necessarily remain a central part of the policy-making apparatus.

CONCLUSION

Brian Mulroney's federalism is, in some respects, an important break with the model pursued by his immediate predecessors. It is not, however, a radical break with the evolution of Canadian federalism at least since 1960. Indeed, in its emphasis on cooperative federalism, its recognition of Quebec as a distinct society, and in other ways, it is consistent with practices which had come to characterize Canadian federalism since about 1960. Meech Lake, too, is less a radical attack on the federal status quo than it is a reaffirmation of tendencies evident for many years. It is a completion, reaffirming classic federalist values, of the constitutional change achieved in 1982. The Mulroney conduct of federalism is not the only cause of reduced conflict, greater harmony and improved collaboration, but it has played a significant role. These — especially the reconciliation with Quebec — are not achievements to be gainsaid. On the other hand, nor has the Mulroney government recast federalism in a mould which cannot be changed. Levels of interregional and intergovernmental conflict, cooperation or competition, are not primarily a matter of constitutions or of intergovernmental machinery. They are a function of

45

the underlying political economy, the issues that arise, the mobilization of interests and the ambitions of federal and provincial leaders.

Indeed, in this sense, the free trade agreement may well have a greater impact on federalism than will Meech Lake.

REFERENCES

Banting, Keith G. (1987). *The Welfare State and Canadian Federalism*, 2nd edition, (Montreal and Kingston: McGill-Queen's University Press).

Breton, Albert B. (1985). "Supplementary Statement." In *Report of the Royal Commission on the Economic Union and Development Prospects for Canada*, Vol. 3, (Ottawa: Supply and Services Canada), pp. 486–526.

Courchene, Thomas (1977). "The New Fiscal Arrangements and the Economics of Federalism," *Options, Proceedings of the Conference on the Future of the Canadian Federation*, (Toronto: University of Toronto Press).

First Ministers Conference, Halifax, November 27–28, 1985.

Graham, Ron (1986). *One-Eyed Kings: Promise and Illusions in Canadian Politics*, (Toronto: Collins).

Hawkes, David and Bruce Pollard (1987). "The Evolution of Canada's New Energy Policy," in Peter Leslie (ed.) *Canada The State of the Federation 1986*, (Kingston: Institute of Intergovernmental Relations), pp. 151–166.

McRoberts, Kenneth (1985). "Unilateralism, Bilateralism and Multilateralism: Approaches to Canadian Federalism." In Richard Simeon (ed.) *Intergovernmental Relations, The Royal Commission on Economic Union and Development Prospects for Canada*, (Toronto: University of Toronto Press), pp. 71–129.

Milne, David (1986). *Tug of War. Ottawa and the Provinces Under Trudeau and Mulroney*, (Toronto: Lorimer).

Romanow, Roy, John Whyte and Howard Leeson (1984). *Canada Notwithstanding. The Making of the Constitution*, (Toronto: Carswell/Methuen).

Savoie, Donald J. (1986). *Regional Economic Development: Canada's Search for Solutions*, (Toronto: University of Toronto Press).

Simeon, Richard (1972). *Federal-Provincial Diplomacy*, (Toronto: University of Toronto Press).

Simeon, Richard (1987). "Federalism and Free Trade." In Peter Leslie (ed.) *Canada The State of the Federation 1986*, (Kingston: Institute of Intergovernmental Relations), pp. 189–212.

Smiley, Donald V. (1979). "An Outsider's Observation of Federal Provincial Relations Among Consenting Adults." In Richard Simeon (ed.) *Confrontation or Collaboration*, (Toronto: Institute of Public Administration of Canada), pp. 105–113.

Smiley, Donald V. (1980). *Canada in Question. Federalism in the Eighties*, 3rd edition, (Toronto: McGraw-Hill Ryerson).

Smiley, Donald V. (1987). *The Federal Condition in Canada*, (Toronto: McGraw-Hill Ryerson).

Whitaker, Reginald (1983). *Federalism and Democratic Theory*, (Kingston: Institute of Intergovernmental Relations).

Through A Glass, Darkly: The Meech Lake Mirage

GERARD BOISMENU

The Constitutional Accord of June 3, 1987 — commonly known as the Meech Lake Accord, despite differences between the agreement in principle of April 30, 1987, and the text of the constitutional document drafted in Ottawa a little over a month later — lends itself to a number of wide-ranging considerations.

I think it safe to say that a new dynamic has now entered federal-provincial relations. Whether we like it or not, it looks as though the rules of intergovernmental politics will have to be changed. Take, for example, the need for negotiation between the two levels of government on the appointment of senators and Supreme Court judges, or, for that matter, recognition in the amending formula of the right to opt out, with compensation, of national shared-cost programs.

The issue can be looked at from another angle, however. Without the Constitution Act of 1982, otherwise known as the Canada Bill, which the Quebec government did not support, there would have been no basis for the negotiations that brought the first ministers to Meech Lake in the spring of 1987. I am going to take a closer look at this aspect by asking the following question: exactly how did the Constitutional Accord of June 3, 1987 make it possible for Quebec to support the Constitution Act, 1982 *"dans l'honneur et l'enthousiasme"*? To begin with, we will have to look very closely at the content of the Meech lake Accord in the light of its potential impact on the Quebec community. Then we will have to determine exactly to what degree the Accord makes it possible to support the Canada Bill.

AN IMPORTANT STEP

Constitutional reforms such as those of 1982 and 1987 (assuming eventual provincial ratification), are very special moments in the history of a country and the various peoples that inhabit it. Such reform redefines who exercises political power and where, as well as shaping the institutional framework of such power and giving preference to a particular form of intergovernmental relations.

It is therefore important not to underestimate the seriousness of this major political step. There is a tendency in Quebec to dismiss it as just part of the political game. Such an attitude is based on a double confusion. In the first place, negotiations to amend the constitutional framework are not just a matter of short-term horse-trading, although this is the view adopted by government. The limited number of changes made to the Canadian Constitution (once all the provinces had been constituted), shows that this is a far cry from routine procedure. More serious still is the fact that, in Quebec, the matter is being debated as though its object and scope were necessarily confined to the juridical dimension. The number of constitutional experts called before the parliamentary commission in Quebec left little room for the non-jurist.

Of course, assessment of the Accord must be based on legal considerations, and this dimension is clearly an important one. Basically, however, we are dealing with a political process. It is a question of defining the framework within which power is to be exercised and political life organized — of determining collective and individual rights, the jurisdictions of the two major levels of government, and the institutions through which democratic rights will be expressed. In this sense, political analysis certainly sheds a useful light on some of the issues at stake.

It might be interesting to speculate on whether changes in the political scene have made a significant difference in bringing about the Meech Lake Accord. The nature of the present political incumbents in Ottawa and Quebec seems to have helped the negotiations. Subsequent turns of the political wheel, combined with delays in the ratification of the Meech Lake Accord, might prove to be its downfall.

Leaving aside conjecture, however, let us recall that between 1985 and 1987 the Quebec government was rarely so accom-

modating or undemanding. Robert Bourassa's objective was to get
Quebec to support the Canada Bill while laying down conditions
that presupposed the other governments' willingness to agree.
Moreover, just prior to Meech Lake, Brian Mulroney made a point
of telling the first ministers of English-speaking provinces that
Quebec's proposals had never been so moderate and that it would
be highly advisable to seize a possibly unique opportunity. On the
other hand, rarely in the course of recent history has the Quebec
government had a chance to benefit from such ineffective parliamentary opposition on the one hand, and general disarray among
groups that might form an extra-parliamentary opposition on the
other. The Meech Lake Accord, to which Bourassa agreed, accurately reflects this combination of factors in its ambiguity, the
dangerous precedents that it sets, and its acquiescence to the
principles of the Canada Bill.

Before proceeding to a closer examination of the Meech Lake
Accord, it is important to bear in mind the five conditions set by
Quebec:

— explicit recognition of Quebec as a distinct society
— guarantee of increased powers in immigration
— limits on federal spending powers
— recognition of a right of veto
— Quebec participation in appointing judges to the Supreme
Court of Canada (Remillard, 1987: 56–57).

DISTINCT SOCIETY: WHAT ARE WE TALKING ABOUT?

The cryptic term "distinct society" can mean a great deal or nothing at all. Some people feel it would be wiser to define the expression clearly whenever it is used. Government and certain jurists
prefer not to be specific, however, since "enumeration in an article
of law always imposes limitations" (Beaudoin, 1987: 80). Nevertheless, two considerations arise regarding the way in which the
term is employed.

The use in a constitutional document of the notion of a distinct
society which has no actual existence in law is, in fact, a rejection
of the notion of people. However, in the words of a group of
Quebec constituents, "practice and international law have clarified
the notion of people as also being defined through culture and

institutions" (Arbour et al., 1987: 169). The provincial Liberals have therefore refused to include in their proposed conditions any reference to recognizing Quebec's right to self determination. The Bourassa government has deliberately banished the notions of people and self-determination from its vocabulary. In his use of vague terminology, Bourassa is hoping that the courts will put muscle into the notion of a distinct society by a wide interpretation that will give the Quebec government greater powers.

Let us look beyond such limitations and hopes as may be vested in the expression "distinct society," however, and consider, as we must, its meaning and scope as given in the official version of the Meech Lake Accord. It is a principle of law that a clause must be interpreted in context, that is to say, in relation to other pertinent clauses. For example, the Meech Lake Accord recognizes that "Quebec constitutes within Canada a distinct society" (s.2.(1)(b)). This second subparagraph must be read in the light of the first, however, which defines Quebec as the place where French-speaking Canadians are "centred" and where English-speaking Canadians are "present" i.e., in the minority. The rest of Canada is defined in similar terms, emphasizing the preponderance of English Canadians "concentrated outside Quebec." The distinct society thus refers to Quebec's internal linguistic duality as well as its French-speaking majority. We therefore have a distinct society defined on the level of language. Linguistic duality is seen as a fact of life in Quebec, but with this difference: its majority language is the minority language in the rest of Canada.

The Accord recognizes that linguistic duality is a "fundamental characteristic of Canada," whereas the distinct society, which seems to be the reverse of the linguistic majority, is not similarly recognized. No matter from what standpoint the distinct society in Quebec is considered, therefore, it can never be a "fundamental characteristic" of Canada. This expression refers only to linguistic duality, a reference that recurs a few lines later: "The role of the Parliament of Canada and the provincial legislatures [is] to pre-serve the fundamental characteristic [of linguistic duality]."

The introduction of this new criterion for interpretation has raised high hopes. The question is worth a closer look. Nicole Duplé, who shares the government's views on this point, has stated that "Quebec will undoubtedly have more room for manoeuvering . . . to protect and consolidate its linguistic and cultural characteristics" (Duplé, 1987: 101). The government has gone so far as

51

to mention possible confirmation of Quebec's role on the international scene.

Is this a reasonable optimism? Let us put it in perspective. It should be noted that a principle of interpretation is not a strict or binding rule. It is therefore difficult in individual cases to anticipate what real impact it might have on judicial decisions. Interpretations in our judicial system tend to restrict rather than extend the scope of legislation. Politicians cannot force the courts to give a decisive significance to a principle of interpretation. Furthermore, the Constitution contains several principles of interpretation and there is no way of knowing how they will adjust to one another in practice (Côté, 1987: 145–146).

On the last point, it is possible to compare in turn the distinct society, linguistic duality, multicultural heritage, and individual liberties. Moreover, any measure that limits freedoms must clearly indicate its reasonable and justifiable nature in a free, democratic society, as outlined in section 1 of the Charter of Rights and Freedoms in the Canada Bill (Woehrling, 1988: 145–146).

This raises several questions. Taking into consideration the fact that the Quebec government has now adhered to the principle of preserving linguistic duality in Canada generally, does the notion that the distinct society is "linguistic duality reversed," so to speak, provide a further, compelling argument for recognition by the Supreme Court of the constitutionality of the Quebec Language Charter? By the same token, we must remember that the whole point of the Meech Lake Accord was to get Quebec to adhere to the Canadian Charter of Rights and Freedoms in the Canada Bill. For all intents and purposes, this document only establishes individual rights, and its main thrust is based on the notion of the individual *per se*. One may wonder, therefore, whether the idea of "collective rights" connected with the notion of the distinct society will have the effect of neutralizing a constitutional charter that only provides for individual rights. In this sense, it must be proven that the promotion and protection of Quebec's distinct character limits individual rights. Take the question of the language of signs, for example. Does the protection and promotion of the distinct society obstruct individual freedom of expression? For the moment it's anyone's guess, although it would be very naïve to think that the distinct society, as a principle of interpretation, could radically change the thrust of the Canadian Charter of Rights and Freedoms, solely on the basis of legal reasoning.

Ironically enough, as the work of the parliamentary commission advanced, the Quebec government came to realize that the first section of the draft amendment to the Constitution proposed by the Meech Lake Accord might well undermine its jurisdiction in cultural and linguistic matters. This article states, in effect, that the interpretation of the Constitution must accommodate not only linguistic duality throughout Canada, but the distinct nature of Quebec society as well. However, in the event of a conflict between linguistic duality and the distinct society as criteria for legal interpretation, linguistic duality would take precedence simply because it is a fundamental characteristic, contrary to the distinct society. Such an outcome could put into question the Quebec political trend toward making French the language of business and daily life, for example.

Faced with threatened erosion of Quebec's jurisdiction over language and culture, Robert Bourassa made sure that an "escape clause," as he called it, was included in the final agreement. It sets out in detail that nothing in the section on linguistic duality and the distinct society "derogates from the powers, rights or privileges of Parliament ... or of the legislatures or governments of the provinces." In other words, the section in question cannot diminish Quebec's powers. This hardly seems to be a major constitutional breakthrough! However, the Quebec delegates cried victory because the their province's jurisdictions would not be reduced. But if politicians must go to these lengths merely to maintain the status quo, we might feel justifiably skeptical about their ability to gain broader powers.

THE BIRTH OF A NEW "FOUNDING MYTH"

The Quebec government claims that the recognition of the distinct society will result in the Supreme Court granting new powers to Quebec or upholding a wide interpretation of present powers. The rhetoric involved implies that we are witnessing the birth of a "founding myth" of Canadian federalism.

The need for fresh constitutional rhetoric should surprise no one. In the course of the last ten years we have watched the destruction of several "founding myths" that struck a responsive chord in Quebec. These included Quebec's political and juridical veto, the two nations pact, and the federal government's inability to act unilaterally. I am speaking of the distinct society in terms of the new "founding myth" because it feeds constitutional rhetoric and claims to make possible what is not. It breeds contention in the name of this new "banner" — a banner whose innocuous nature will be revealed by subsequent defeats in the courts.

The following example is a good illustration of the distortions that can result from this rhetoric about the distinct society. Journalist Jean-Pierre Proulx has written a long article (1987: 131–135) saying, in essence, that even if the distinct society is not defined, the people of Quebec know what it means. He goes into copious detail — citing great editorial writers of the past, the reports of the Tremblay Commission, the Laurendeau-Dunton commission, the Pepin-Robarts Commission, and other documents — in order to demonstrate that continual mention is made, if not of the notion of the distinct society, at least of the reality behind it. This is all very interesting, but not much to the point. One can no doubt say, today, that Quebecers "have at least agreed on the profound meaning of this expression." Only yesterday, however, one could have said Quebecers were agreed on the meaning of the two nations pact. We are indeed in the realm of "founding myths" and the kind of discourse typical of political process.

Proulx is on more relevant ground when, at the very end of the article, he emphasizes that "on the day when Supreme Court judges are called upon to decide what 'society' means," they "will have to judge between the version of the attorney general of Quebec and the attorney general of Canada, if not the attorneys-general of all the provinces." When that time comes, judges are less likely to base their decisions on an editorial or a proposal made by a commission of inquiry whose report is gathering dust in some archive, than on the actual text of the Constitution, which recognizes a "national" federal government in relation to a people composed of citizens enjoying individual rights. There should be no conflict between these rights and an interpretation that acknowledges the fundamental characteristic of Canada — that is, linguistic duality — as well as the existence of a distinct society, and a multicultural heritage.

As a final remark on this question, I should point out that, in the constitutional debate of the past twenty-five years, people have always tended to state the obvious: a special community resides in Quebec — one special with regard to language, culture, history, institutions, and socioeconomic development. While this special quality could be recognized, any attempt to give it political expression by assigning the Quebec government a special role, unusual powers, or some other distinctive mark has been rejected. Trudeau, for example, felt that since francophones live all over Canada as well as being concentrated in Quebec, and since anglophones form part of the Quebec population, it was out of the question to give Quebec a special role of any kind.

Nevertheless, the present agreement reveals a breakthrough in the approach to constitutional matters. Section 1.(3) of the draft amendment states: "The role of the legislature and Government of Quebec to preserve and promote the distinct identity of Quebec . . . is affirmed." As things stand at present, however — and as I have tried to show — the actual effect of this affirmation appears uncertain and limited. Indeed, it might have the opposite effect of what was intended. All in all, the introduction of the notion of a distinct society represents a symbolic breakthrough. It might influence the progress of other negotiations, but it could equally well end up as a durable but meaningless symbol.

POLITICAL OPTING OUT, OR THE VIRTUES OF GOVERNMENT BY JUDGES

Robert Bourassa's method has been to say, in essence: Let's get a principle of interpretation for the Constitution. From this principle will flow, via "juridical reasoning," significant gains in areas where Quebec would fail if it used the normal political process.

Such a method amounts to an abdication of political responsibility. Bourassa is abandoning the fight in the political arena, where the elected representatives control or are at least responsible for their actions, in favour of the courts, which will impose hypothetical decisions on the electorate whether it likes it or not.

Such a proceeding strengthens the system of government by judges introduced in the Canada Bill. It amounts to a subversion of the democratic process. As the jurist Guy Tremblay has mentioned, "the vast majority of Western countries . . . do not submit the policies of the people's elected representatives to the vagaries of judicial confrontation" (1987: 109–110). In the present case, it is carried a step further by introducing a criterion of interpretation designed to push through major constitutional gains in several areas. It is up to the judges to tell us the real meaning of legislation, thus gladdening the hearts of some and satisfying the skepticism of others. From now on, it would seem, the courts will pronounce on Quebec's claims regarding shared jurisdictions, because it is a foregone conclusion that these claims will be rejected in the political arena.

From this point of view, although politicians may be abdicating responsibilities that ought rightfully to be exercised by elected representatives, they are also attempting to avoid probable failure in return for a symbolic, short-term victory. Such a victory does not affect the underlying question; it merely cedes to others the responsibility for decision-making in the hope of hypothetical and improbable gains in an area where elected representatives have no control.

WHAT VETO?

During the last year of the Levesque government, Robert Bourassa campaigned on Quebec's need to recover the right of veto in constitutional matters. He was inflexible on this question, despite the utopian nature of his demands. It was in fact unlikely that the provincial governments, which had been granted legal equality in the amendment procedure of the Canada Bill, would consent to unequal status as expressed in the Victoria Charter, for example, which granted a veto to Ontario and Quebec.

Despite his intransigent rhetoric, Bourassa made sure he had a fall-back position. Quebec Liberal Party documents of 1985 mention that it "would not be easy to regain lost ground," and let it be understood that the formula for "withdrawal with compensation" would be a lesser evil. In this regard, I concluded in an earlier paper (Boismenu, 1985: 58) that Bourassa could always say it was impossible for him to recover the right of veto lost by a careless PQ government.

As one might expect, it was reasonably easy for Bourassa to agree to the formula of withdrawal with compensation for constitutional changes that involve a "transfer of provincial legislative powers to the federal Parliament." Bourassa is an amazing man, all the same. Rather than bow to the inevitable, he converted the withdrawal formula into a right of veto, against all likelihood. Nevertheless, here as elsewhere, erroneous ideas cannot be made true merely by repeating them *ad nauseam*.

Understandably, the right of withdrawal with compensation changes the political dynamic and gives the provinces additional arguments for future negotiations in terms of cold, hard cash. Quebec, like any other province, could oppose a change that might lead to loss or shrinkage of one of its powers, and decide to maintain the status quo for itself alone. However, despite semantic shifts, the ability to oppose a measure is still not synonymous with a veto (see Decary, 1987: 71). The formula was advocated by the Pepin-Robarts Commission and adopted by the Parti Quebecois government and the seven other provinces initially opposed to the Canada Bill. Quebec will probably make the most use of it, but it remains an instrument of negotiation for every province.

There is, nevertheless, another area where constitutional veto is possible. The Canada Bill provides for two procedures to change the institutions of the Canadian federation. Certain limited matters require unanimous consent (the monarchy, provincial representation in the House of Commons, and the composition of the Supreme Court). Other cases require the usual proportionate consent of seven provinces and fifty percent of the population. However, the Meech Lake Accord has, for all practical purposes, retained the rule of unanimity for all institutions. The consequence is clear: each province now has a real veto on changes touching the Senate, the Supreme Court, the creation of a province, or the addition of territory to any province. Commentators one and all remarked on the unwieldiness of this procedure and the added difficulty of making any change whatsoever. Here, too, the general dynamics of intergovernmental relations have been modified. The Quebec government could only acquire a veto if it were granted to all provinces, and so the measure was incorporated into the Accord. In other words, given the rule of unanimity, Quebec has a veto — but so do all the other provinces.

In sum, the initial demand for a Quebec right of veto based on its specificity resulted in legal equality for all provinces in this area. As Lowell Murray wrote, "The requirement of unanimity is just and reasonable. It is reasonable because it respects the principle of provincial equality regarding decisions about our major national institutions. It is just because it offers each of the provinces equal protection on questions touching their place within the federation. There will not be two categories of provinces in Canada" (1987: 386).

57

THE POWER TO SET STANDARDS

In 1964, the Quebec government finally obtained a right of withdrawal with financial compensation from a whole series of shared-cost programs. This agreement provided for a transition period to two to five years during which the programs would remain unchanged. The period was later greatly extended, but more autonomy within pan-Canadian standards was gained. Quebec has always been concerned about occupying areas of jurisdiction that, contrary to the divisions of power set forth in the Constitution, have been taken over by the federal government.

The Meech Lake Accord stipulates that a provincial government which "chooses not to participate in a national shared-cost program . . . in an area of exclusive provincial jurisdiction" must receive "reasonable compensation . . . if the province carries on a program . . . compatible with the national objectives." This acknowledges what all previous Quebec governments had condemned and rejected: the idea that it is normal for the federal government to intervene in the field of exclusive provincial jurisdictions.

This acknowledgment is fraught with consequences. In the first place, it is a major step for a Quebec government to accept the idea at all. Furthermore, the expression "exclusive jurisdiction" no longer means anything. If jurisdiction was at one time exclusive, then a provincial government that rejects federal intervention has a right to withdrawal with compensation within certain limits. But, beyond this compensation "to the initial occupant," to speak of exclusive provincial jurisdiction is in itself an abuse of language. The "functional federalism" which some people have been heartily wishing for has at last been enshrined.

In the final analysis, one may well wonder whether it is simply a question of giving formal expression to past agreements, especially those made since World War II, or whether, on the contrary, jurisdictions have actually changed.

It should be noted that federal spending powers in provincial jurisdictions are "not among our constitutional rights" (Lajoie, 1988: 164), as there is no clear judicial opinion on this subject. This is explained at least in part by the fact that federal and provincial governments have not taken their differences to court in the past. Furthermore, there exist two opposing doctrinal views," one justifying the federal position, the other favouring protection of provincial powers. Each of these views is presently upheld by a judge sitting on the Supreme Court (Judges Laforest and Beetz).

One can argue that the federal government's power to intervene in provincial legislative jurisdictions is offset by the right or withdrawal with compensation. Of course, it is permissible for a provincial government to opt out while obtaining compensation, but only if the province sets up a program comparable to the one from which it has withdrawn — a program that must be "compatible with the national objectives." It means that, in future, provincial legislative jurisdiction may be subordinated to conditions set by the federal cabinet. This prospect moved Andrée Lajoie to write, "The fact that legislative jurisdiction is the only area expressly mentioned means that (the Constitutional Accord) does not aim at maintaining shared executive powers *ante quo*, but, on the contrary, allows for the extension fo federal executive powers at the expense of provincial legislative powers, in what is a new form of oblique transfer" (Lajoie, 1988: 176).

The net result is that the federal government is consecrating both its spending power in federal jurisdictions, and its power to establish the standards of "autonomous" programs. For the provinces, the Accord means that shared jurisdictions limit their initiative in certain areas, while the federal government has the right to intervene wherever it wishes, even in provincial jurisdictions. Speaking as an observer in May 1987, Jacques Parizeau made the following remark: "As a means of limiting the federal government's spending power, it is utterly absurd. Mr. Lesage must be turning in his grave" (Parizeau, 1987: 179).

As a footnote, let me add that the "constitutionalization" of spending power may change the dynamic of federal-provincial negotiations, but certainly less so than some fear. It must be remembered that previous shared-cost programs such as health insurance had few participants initially, and that it took several years for all provinces to become involved. The danger may be, however, that along with a changed dynamic, governments may embark on court battles that they have avoided thus far. Several issues arise in this regard (Lajoie, 1988: 179; Leslie, 1987: 117). For example: When is a program "national," and who decides this? Does the modification of an existing program mean that it is a new program? Are the conditions laid down for financial compensation unduly restrictive? Is financial compensation fair?

WAR WITHOUT TEARS

Since the mid-sixties, the Quebec government has traditionally subordinated constitutional agreements to the results of negotiations on shared jurisdictions. In 1970–71, Robert Bourassa used negotiations on jurisdiction as a test case to show that it was possible to make progress through negotiation. At the time, he sought recognition of provincial supremacy in social security policy. At Meech Lake, although he refrained from symbolic brandishing of this precedent, he attacked the way in which jurisdiction was shared in immigration matters.

The scope and difficulty involved in making gains in immigration jurisdiction were minimal compared to the health insurance negotiations. The latter did indeed set a precedent, given the strongly divergent positions involved. This time, however, Bourassa chose as his ground the constitutional implementation of an existing administrative agreement. He asked that Quebec be guaranteed a minimum proportion of immigrants, and that his province take over services for reception and integration of foreign nationals wishing to settle there. Admittedly these are fairly important gains, but they can hardly be viewed as the result of a prolonged and glorious struggle.

Bourassa's insistence on negotiating immigration matters is no doubt due to the acute problem of Quebec's falling birthrate, as well as to an essentially cultural vision of the Quebec issue. There is another consideration however. The Quebec strategy consisted not in arguing the most strategic points touching the province's jurisdiction, but only those likely to lead to a signed agreement. With the Cullen-Couture administrative agreement in his pocket, Bourassa viewed the matter of immigration, which is by definition an area of shared jurisdiction, as a fairly easy target — much easier, certainly, than claiming exclusive jurisdiction in language matters, for example, or the non-subordination of Quebec jurisdiction in economic policy to the imperative of Canadian economic unity, or of arguing about who has greater jurisdiction in labour policy.

By the same token, there could be little serious objection to giving constitutional sanction to the presence of at least three judges from the Quebec Bar on the Supreme Court. It was merely a question of institutionalizing what had become a traditional practice. While it was not without significance, it could not be called a major break-through. Here again, the strategy of the achievable, so to speak, takes priority. To paraphrase Corneille, "War without tears means triumph without glory."

SWALLOWING THE PILL

In all this discussion of the conditions set by Quebec, we tend to forget the primary object of the Meech Lake Accord, which was to get Quebec to support the Canada Bill. This was the pill beneath the sugar coating. The fact is, however, that none of these conditions makes any significant change to the general thrust of the Canada Bill.

This legislation, passed in 1982, altered the Constitution and put a number of blocks on provincial initiative. Let us look briefly at a few of them. The courts were given the power to watch over government initiatives. The rights of the individual citizen took precedence, thus placing restraints on the recognition and exercise of collective rights, notably for Quebec. Moreover, the federal government is seen as the sole repository of the collective interests of Canadians as a whole. Provincial powers are subordinated to the principle of Canadian economic unity, and the provinces are obliged to conform to precise parameters in language policy.

Quebec envisaged various ways of counteracting this imposed constitutional reform, beginning with a refusal to support to it. Although largely symbolic, this reflected a deep-seated disagreement with the terms of the Canada Bill.

Subsequently, on December 1, 1981, Premier René Lévesque stated in the National Assembly that he could only agree to constitutional change under certain conditions. The Lévesque government based its stand on the right of the Quebec people to self-determination and the fact that no change could be made to the Constitution without its agreement. It asserted that "the two peoples" must be recognized as "fundamentally equal." Moreover, within the Canadian federation, Quebec formed "a distinct society in its language, culture, and institutions, and possessed all the attributes of a distinct national community." Quebec wanted either a right of veto or withdrawal with compensation included in the amendment formula. It would agree to a Charter of Rights and Freedoms that guaranteed unrestricted democratic rights and the use of French and English in federal institutions, as well as equality, the basic freedoms, and guarantees regarding the language of teaching for the minority, insofar as Quebec can "enforce its laws within its own jurisdiction."

In the spring of 1985, the Quebec government proposed a *Projet d'accord constitutionnel* whereby Quebec would support the Canada Bill on condition that the special nature of the Quebec people be recognized, although this would create a constitutional imbalance. Instead of accommodating itself to the Charter of Rights and Freedoms in the Canada Bill, Quebec asserted that the Quebec Charter of Rights and Freedoms should take precedence. This document ensures primacy of Quebec statutes dealing with the language of teaching and the movement of persons and assets. Quebec further asked for a right of veto for constitutional amendments to federal institutions. Regarding amendments affecting jurisdictions, it wanted either a veto or withdrawal with compensation. All in all, about fifteen of the Canada Bill's sixty sections would have remained intact.

Coming from a PQ government, such proposals may have seemed radical. Suffice it to say that they were very nearly what Jean Lesage might have put forward in 1965 (Boismenu, 1988). Looking back, we can see how wide a gap separates them from Bourassa's conditions for adhering to the Charter of Rights and Freedoms in the Canada Bill — conditions that have in common the fact that they make very little change and, in any event, do not address the essential issues. One may wonder at this juncture whether Quebec's political leaders have digested the 1982 defeat — in other words, the Canada Bill — to the point of upholding it without a qualm.

With regard to the Meech Lake Accord and its proposed amendments to the Canada Bill, there is a real possibility that the combined effect of agreeing to unlimited federal intervention (as contained in the section on spending powers) and the hope of favourable interpretations in the courts (bolstered by the subparagraph on the distinct society) will lead to indefinite adjournment of negotiations on the sharing of constitutional jurisdictions. It may well be that, in the years to come, those in Quebec who advocate recourse to the courts and government by judges will be forced to admit — albeit in a suitably dignified and high-minded manner

— their inability to turn the notion of a distinct society to significant advantage. As is customary in Quebec's history, they will retire to lick their wounds and concoct yet another founding myth for domestic consumption. In the meantime, the Canada Bill will have triumphed.

The Meech Lake Accord does not answer the objections made to the Canada Bill, nor does it follow the logic of Quebec's constitutional position since 1960. If it is impossible to resolve the problem of Quebec's adherence to the wide-reaching constitutional changes of 1982, it would be preferable to avoid commitment to something that is, for the moment, off to such a bad start. However, the Bourassa government is determined to settle this nagging issue, come what may. By way of example, it has persuaded the National Assembly to adhere to the Meech Lake Accord. If Quebec is to avoid the consequences of this constitutional blunder, it will be thanks to some English-Canadian government's refusal to fall into line.

Various groups, particularly in Manitoba and New Brunswick, have expressed reservations about the Meech Lake Accord. Some feel it does not cover enough ground. Others want individual rights to take precedence over all collective rights that may result (although this is unlikely) from the Accord. Although it is not immediately apparent, this is a further rejection of Quebec's proposed conditions. The rule of unanimity is the weak point that will make the whole house of cards collapse. There are two conclusions to be drawn from all this. Quebec will be indebted to a government in English Canada for a last-minute reprieve from a cut-rate constitutional undertaking that had very little to offer. Moreover, any such rejection of the Accord (clothed in lofty principles) by one or more English-Canadian governments will amount to a dismissal of Quebec's proposals — proposals that have never been so moderate. One cannot help feeling that the prospect looks pretty bleak for the Quebec-Canada debate.

Translated by Jane Brierley.

REFERENCES

Arbour, J. Maurice et al. (1987). "Press release by eleven experts," in *Le Québec et le Lac Meech*, (Montréal: Guérin).

Beaudoin, Gérald A. (1987). "Brief submitted to the Commission sur les institutions," in *Le Québec et le Lac Meech*, (Montréal: Guérin).

Boismenu, Gérard (1985). "Backing Down or Compromising the Future: Quebec's Constitutional Proposals," in *Canada: The State of the Federation*, (Kingston: Institute of Intergovernmental Relations).

Boismenu, Gérard (1988). "La pensée constitutionnelle de Jean Lesage." Paper given at the Lesage Colloquium, UQAM, April 15.

Côté, Pierre-André (1987). "Brief submitted to the Commission sur les institutions," in *Le Québec et le Lac Meech*, (Montréal: Guérin).

Décary, Robert (1987). "Opinion," in *Le Québec et le Lac Meech*, (Montréal: Guérin).

Duplé, Nicole (1987). "Opinion," in *Le Québec et le Lac Meech*, (Montréal: Guérin).

Lajoie, Andrée (1988). "L'impact des accords du Lac Meech sur le pouvoir de dépenser," in *L'adhésion du Québec à l'Accord du lac Meech*, (Montréal: Editions Themis).

Leslie, Peter (1987). "Opinion," in *Le Québec et le Lac Meech*, (Montréal: Guérin).

Rémillard, Gil (1987). "Allocution prononcée au colloque sur la Confédération canadienne, Mont-Gabriel, 9 mai 1986," in *Le Québec et le lac Meech*, (Montréal: Guérin).

Tremblay, Guy (1987). "Brief submitted to the Commission sur les institutions," in *Le Québec et le Lac Meech*, (Montréal: Guérin).

Woehrling, José (1988). "Dualité linguistique et société distincte," in *L'adhésion du Québec à l'accord du Lac Meech*, (Montréal: Editions Themis).

Atlantic Canada: The Tories Help Those Who Help Themselves

AGAR ADAMSON

According to George Orwell, by 1984 "newspeak" would be well on its way to becoming the accepted official language of "Oceania." Atlantic Canada in 1984, however, heard no "newspeak," nor did the citizens of the region suffer from "double think." Instead, the electorate heard Brian Mulroney's rendition of "oldspeak," which can be loosely translated as "play it again, Sam."

The Federal election campaign for Atlantic Canada's 32 seats in 1984 was very similar to the previous twelve contests. It was one of hope, of rising expectations, of promises of prosperity, and of economic opportunity which, at long last, would end the region's state of "clientism" and dependency upon the federal treasury. In short, the Atlantic electorate was optimistic, despite its innate cynicism, that the promises of 1984 would lead to the end of feudal federalism.

BACKGROUND

In other regions of Canada, politics is a part of life which must be endured, but in Atlantic Canada, politics is the very stuff of life. In the Atlantic provinces, and especially in the three Maritime provinces, politics is followed literally from the cradle to the grave. Furthermore, nowhere else in Canada, with the possible exception of the two Territories, are people so dependent upon government for employment and social welfare assistance.

65

Given the history of the region, including the apathy toward Maritime union, one might expect to find significant political and policy differences among these four provinces. However, the reverse is true. There is a regional political culture which is the basis for this similarity and which was apparent in 1984. Historically, many residents have been tied to a subsistence economy of renewable staples because both federal and provincial governments have consistently been unable to alleviate the region's poverty. Changes in technology, the sea and more developed economies to the south and to the west have served as channels as well as safety valves for dissatisfaction. There has been little, if any, infusion of new blood from immigration into the region since the end of the 19th century. It is true that there has been migration within the region, but this is not the same as is immigration into the region.

When one inspects this history of the region and examines the political culture, one can see why residents of the Atlantic region are interested in politics, but, at the same time, are cynical toward their politicians. Despite the fact that they both distrust politics and politicians and feel incapable of affecting political change, Atlantic Canadians continue to invest in politics with high amounts of physical, intellectual and emotional resources. The result of these tensions is a political culture which is characterized in the word "cynicism."

Basically, the prevailing political orientation of these four provinces has, historically, evolved around the three elements of cynicism, traditionalism and regionalism.

There is some argument as to whether or not Newfoundland and Labrador's political culture should be grouped with that of the Maritimes. Every Newfoundland government since Confederation, and particularly those formed by the Progressive Conservatives, has made it clear that Newfoundland should not be considered as one of the Maritime provinces. There remain many differences between Newfoundland and the other three provinces, particularly in the area of policy development and federal–provincial relations. Since the political demise of former premier J.R. Smallwood, there have been very few occasions when the region has presented a united front at the federal First Ministers' conferences. Furthermore, witness the actions of the Peckford government with respect to the cod fishery, the question of freezer trawlers, Newfoundland's decision in 1983 to withdraw from the Atlantic

Provinces Economic Council, and the current Newfoundland disagreement with Nova Scotia which has surfaced because of the fisheries provision in the Meech Lake Accord. Similarly, John Crosbie sees himself as a defender of Newfoundland, but not of the Maritimes. Nonetheless, the gradual demise of the outports has eroded many of the distinctive aspects in the Newfoundland political culture while integration into the Canadian political community has simultaneously reinforced the pervasive traditionalism and cynicism of Newfoundlanders. It would appear that Newfoundland's political culture is converging with that of the three Maritime provinces.

Historically, Newfoundland has had one of the lowest political participation rates in Canada, while the Maritimes has had the highest. Here, too, one can see a change: voter turnout in the Maritimes is decreasing somewhat, although it is still the highest in Canada, while the percentage of those who exercise their franchise is increasing in Newfoundland.

At the heart of politics and public policy in Atlantic Canada lies the question of economic development. These four provinces have the highest unemployment rates in Canada. Furthermore, they have been economically damaged by technology. It is true that they have not been dependent upon a single crop economy as have the Prairie provinces and, therefore, have not suffered economic catastrophes as the Prairies have from time to time. Instead, poverty in the Atlantic region is of the grinding format: continuous, rather that spectacular.

The economic history of the Atlantic region has been marked by a series of disappointments. If the west is said to have had a handicap, so has the east. Transportation costs coupled with Sir John A. Macdonald's national tariff policies made it not only difficult for Maritime products to be competitive in central Canadian markets, but, at the same time, the region lost many of its pre-confederation foreign markets. Changes in climate and technology, as well as politics, led to the decision to keep the St. Lawrence River open year-round to Montréal, thus harming the economies of Halifax and Saint John. The construction of the St. Lawrence Seaway also damaged the regional economy. The three Maritime provinces did not receive any economic or political benefits from the opening of the northern and western lands.

Each federal and provincial government, no matter what its political colour, has for years endeavoured to end this cycle of poverty by providing jobs through programs of economic development. Furthermore, the electorate constantly demands more jobs from its politicians at both levels. Thus, we have witnessed provincial governments seducing industries to move into the region.[1] Firms refuse to locate in the region without substantial government subsidies.

The region is dependent upon assistance from Ottawa. Indeed, federal money of one form or another (equalization grants, established program financing, DRIE grants, other federal grants, military bases, public works, unemployment insurance, etc.) accounts for more than half of the economy of the region. Thus, Atlantic Canada is deeply influenced by federal policy. For example, it is estimated that, in Annapolis County, Nova Scotia, over 75 per cent of the residents' income is obtained from various sectors of the federal treasury.[2]

It is upon this fertile field that Brian Mulroney speaking in Moncton on July 31 stated: "I have no hesitation in inflicting prosperity on Atlantic Canada."[3]

THE 1984 ELECTION

The electorate, despite the fact it had heard similar promises from politicians before, obviously believed the Conservatives' rhetoric. The Conservatives captured 25 of the region's 32 seats (78 per cent) with 53.2 per cent of the popular vote, tieing Robert Stanfield's 1968 record of 78 per cent of the seats, but only 52.5 per cent of the popular vote. (The maritime record belongs to Mackenzie King and the Liberals who in 1935 won 96 per cent of the seats and 55.7 per cent of the popular vote.) The Progressive Conservatives' 1984 popular vote totals were the highest for any region of the country, and Newfoundland at 57 per cent was second only to Alberta's 69 per cent of the total popular vote. The region had heard Mulroney's message and had "delivered" to the Tory's victory, even though it has only 11.3 per cent of the seats in the House of Commons.

If any region of Canada was optimistic in September of 1984 that better days lay ahead, it was Atlantic Canada. For the first time in years the country had a Prime Minister who was intimately familiar with the region's problems. Not only was Brian Mulroney first elected to the House of Commons in Central Nova (1983), but he had gone to school in northern New Brunswick and university in

Nova Scotia. Robert Stanfield recruited Mulroney to the Conservative Party and he obtained his political baptism of fire in the Nova Scotia election of 1956, Stanfield's first provincial victory (MacDonald, 1984:41).

Some of Mulroney's strongest supporters during the 1983 leadership contest, Elmer MacKay, Robert Coates, Stuart MacInnis and Tom McMillan, were elected in the region. Also, many of his closest advisors, both before and after the 1983 convention, were part of the "St. F.X. mafia"; people like Fred and Gerry Doucet, Pat MacAdam and Paul Cregan were all close to Mulroney and had their roots in Atlantic Canada. They were to be joined later by Charlie McMillan and Frank Moors and, once in office, by the master maritime Tory of all, Dalton Camp.

According to Mulroney's biographer, L. Ian MacDonald, he never forgot his maritime "roots." Following his convention victory in 1983, Mulroney said to Pat MacAdam, "Not bad for a couple of raggedy-ass kids from eastern Nova Scotia" (MacDonald, 1984:21).

Like his three prime ministerial predecessors, Mulroney appointed five Cabinet Ministers from the region. This figure was later to rise to seven if one includes Lowell Murray. True, in 1984 none of these Ministers had the political or administrative "clout" of Alan J. MacEachen, but then in Atlantic Canada, and especially on Cape Breton, Alan MacEachen is *sans pareil*. In 1988, however, Lowell Murray, another Cape Bretoner, is fast closing the regional respectability gap with MacEachen.

Speaking in Halifax on August 2, 1984, Brian Mulroney unveiled the Progressive Conservatives' Atlantic platform. In so doing, he promised "this unique region prosperity and opportunity."[4] The programme was all encompassing and contained five major "planks." These were:

1) regional development
2) the fishery
3) energy
4) transportation
5) shipbuilding

This programme was to be implemented over the life of the Government and was not to be considered as yet another "quick fix" for the region's endemic economic problems. The plan called for regional input and assistance concerning its implementation.

True, the Tory's Atlantic Charter lacked specifics, but, to be fair, it was more detailed than many previous regional political programmes had been.

Regional Development

Under this heading, the platform stated that the Conservatives would provide the Department of Regional Industrial Expansion (DRIE) with the legislative mandate to promote and develop the least developed regions in Canada. Presumably, this meant not only Atlantic Canada, but also the North, the Prairies, and the Manicouagan region of Québec. The Conservatives promised to give DRIE the necessary new policy instruments so that the department could have greater administrative flexibility in assisting the Atlantic and other regions. The final regional development plank pledged a three-point programme to help develop tourism in all four provinces.

The Fishery

Concerning the fishery, which is an important and historic cornerstone of the region's economy as well as that of the Gaspé, the Conservatives promised regional councils within Atlantic Canada to permit fishermen, processors and the provincial governments to have a hand in the formation of federal fisheries policy. The Conservatives also undertook to open talks with foreign countries regarding their fleets' access to Canada's territorial sea, specifically the 200-mile limit. The Conservatives, not surprisingly, wished to gradually reduce the role of Crown corporations in the fishery. The platform also called for research into the possibility of implementing a registered vessel owner's savings plan.

Energy

Mulroney undertook to have Parliament enact the Atlantic Offshore Accord between Newfoundland and Canada which had been unveiled earlier in the year. The Tories would honour the existing Canada–Nova Scotia offshore agreement until a new accord could be agreed upon by both governments. Mulroney reiterated a promise made the previous winter in Calgary which was to remove the "back-in" provisions of the Liberals' National Energy Policy (NEP). However, in August he added a rider to appease Nova Scotians who had approved of NEP's "back-in" provisions. Mulroney promised to compensate any province for revenue lost as a result of the termination of the "back-in" provisions of the NEP.

Transportation

No political party can hope to be successful in the Atlantic region without promising to improve transportation facilities, specifically rail and ferries. The 1984 Conservatives were no exception. They undertook to maintain and, if necessary, to enhance the maritime freight rate subsidy assistance programme. They promised to restore certain VIA rail passenger routes cut by the Liberals, including the Atlantic Limited from Halifax to Montréal by way of Saint John and the state of Maine. The Conservatives also promised to increase the armed forces' search and rescue capabilities.

Shipbuilding

The Conservatives would apply a 25 per cent tariff duty on foreign built fishing vessels over 100 feet in length imported into Canada. They would extend concessionary financing terms to domestic customers of Canadian shipyards, a policy which was previously available only to foreign customers.

Other

Other promises of regional interest included: the continued operation of CFB Chatham (New Brunswick) as an air base, new distinctive uniforms for the three branches of the armed services (a significant promise in Halifax), the increase in size of the armed services from 82,000 to 90,000 persons within three years, to see that a fixed number of ships would be built each year in order to assist steel producers, to protect the future of the region's coal and steel industries, and, finally, to launch an investigation to determine if number 26 colliery at Glace Bay could be reopened following a recent fire. Mulroney promised that a Progressive Conservative government would seek input from the region when implementing all of these policies.

An inspection of the Tories' 1984 Atlantic platform leads one to believe that such consultation had already taken place with the region's four Conservative premiers. Certainly, there were sufficient inducements to bring Premiers John Buchanan (Nova Scotia), Richard Hatfield (New Brunswick), James Lee (Prince Edward Island) and Brian Peckford (Newfoundland) onside during the final month of the campaign. This was important for Mulroney because, in Atlantic Canada, all of the national parties operate on an integrated and united basis with their provincial counterparts. There is only one party machine which is responsible for fighting elections, raising funds and recruiting candidates, not a dual system as is to be found in some other regions. Usually, these machines are controlled by the provincial leader, a fact which is particularly important if he or she is also the premier and, thus, in charge of provincial patronage. Consequently, the national party leaders must placate their provincial counterparts during any election campaign.

Furthermore, because of the relatively high degree of party integration, voters in the Atlantic Provinces are more likely, than are their counterparts in other regions, to support the same party in both federal and provincial elections. This aspect of regional political culture may be breaking down, as is illustrated by the recent provincial election results in Prince Edward Island, but it remains, nevertheless, a fact of political life which must be dealt with by the politicians.

1984–1988: THE TORY RECORD

The question is: Have the Tories delivered and, if so, is the region any better off because of the initiatives undertaken by the Mulroney regime? One of the problems for the Conservative government has been its failure to live up to the expectations created during the election campaign by Brian Mulroney. The Prime Minister would have been well advised to accept John Dryden's aphorism: "But far more numerous was the herd of such who think too little and who talk too much," Instead, Mulroney raised expectations to such a fever pitch that no government could escape the wrath of the electorate for not living up to its election promises.

It is true that the Tories have given the armed forces distinctive new uniforms. CFB Chatham is still operational and Saint John shipyards are building the navy's new frigates. The size of the armed forces has been slightly increased. There has been greater consultation with the premiers than was the case during the Trudeau years.

New offshore energy agreements have been successfully concluded with Newfoundland and Nova Scotia. These agreements give both of these provinces considerably more input into the management of their "offshore" resources than the Liberals had given to Nova Scotia. However, because of the fall in the international price of hydrocarbons, these agreements have yet to be put to the acid test, for the cost of production is greater than the prevailing world price.

The most recent Nova Scotia issue concerns drilling on Georges Bank. The Government of Nova Scotia has buckled to pressure from fishing interests along the province's south shore and has requested that drilling on Georges be prohibited for all time. The final authority on the issue, Energy Minister Marcel Masse, has proposed that no drilling take place before the year 2000. This compromise suits John Buchanan. It also illustrates how he can "swing with the wind." Four years ago he promised Nova Scotia a hydrocarbon bonanza, but that was during the last election campaign.

The Georges Bank situation does illustrate that Nova Scotia, like Newfoundland, has not obtained from the Tories their cherished dream to have their "offshore" resource treated as if they were "onshore." Mulroney did not give these two provinces all they desired in the energy-offshore segments of their economy (Pollard, 1985; Adamson, 1987).

In the area of transportation, the Atlantic Limited is back on the rails and is still losing money. However, subsidies have been removed or drastically cut back from the ferry services which has increased the price of moving goods and voters, particularly from the two island provinces, but also between Nova Scotia and New England. The government has encouraged private interests to undertake the development of a "fixed link" between New Brunswick and Prince Edward Island, something which was not on the 1984 agenda.

The fishery remains a conundrum. It was the basis of the Conservatives' greatest error to date — the *Starkist Tuna* debacle. The political issue in this instance was not whether or not then fisheries minister John Fraser erred in overruling his department's inspectors, but rather the public's perception of the Prime Minister. Mulroney's credibility was put to the test over Starkist, and it has yet to recover. If any one single issue has damaged the Prime Minister's credibility in office it is Starkist. The issue at hand concerned jobs and is another example of governmental attempts to improve the regional economy. The action of opposition politicians and the central Canadian media on *Starkist* was not well received in New Brunswick.

The fishery remains to be properly administered. The talks between France and Canada over St. Pierre and Miquelon have not gone well, as recent events have illustrated. This fact has particularly infuriated Brian Peckford. The licensing of one freezer trawler has similarly pitted Nova Scotia against Newfoundland and the inshore against the offshore fishery. That Ottawa has sided with Nova Scotia, the offshore and modernization, may be the right move for the industry, but it may have been politically imprudent in Newfoundland. The federal government has lived up to one of its promises, and that is to replace government ownership of processing companies with the private sector owners. To date, the two major corporations, National Sea and Fisheries Products International, are making money for their shareholders. However, the rising value of the Canadian dollar has placed a dark cloud on the horizon, and unless the value of the dollar is decreased, these two firms will experience significant decreases in profits.

The fishery is a hornets' nest of squabbles between the inshore and the offshore, between conservationists and processors, between Newfoundland and Nova Scotia, between Prince Edward Island and New Brunswick crab fishermen, between New Brunswick and Québec, between the native peoples and the federal government, between Texaco Canada and those who fish on Georges Bank, and these are only a few of the ongoing disputes within the fishery. Basically, there are just not enough fish to go around and conservationists wish to limit the catch for future generations, but the fishermen need the work now!

However, it is in the area of regional development that one has seen the greatest changes since 1984.

Life in the Atlantic region since the 1984 election has been in a greater state of flux than usual. For instance, Allan MacEachen for years had persuaded his Cabinet colleagues to keep Atomic Energy of Canada's two Cape Breton heavy water plants open, even though there was no market for their product, his argument being that it was cheaper to keep the plants open than to pay the workers unemployment insurance.

In his May 1985 Budget, Finance Minister Michael Wilson brought this Alice in Wonderland situation to an abrupt end: "Continued operation of AECL's two heavy water plants on Cape Breton Island can no longer be justified." To replace these plants Ottawa introduced a number of tax incentives. These included a 50 per cent tax credit to enhance job creation in such Cape Breton industries as farming, tourism, fishing, manufacturing and processing. Finance Minister Michael Wilson predicted that no new enterprise in Cape Breton would have to pay federal income tax for ten to fifteen years because of these tax changes.

The February 1986 budget went even further, establishing the Atlantic Enterprise Program. The budget stated:

> Under this program, guarantees of loans totalling up to $1 billion and interest rate buydowns of up to 6 percentage points will be made available to stimulate and support productive new private investment in the region. To avoid duplication with the existing federal and provincial programs, this program will be limited to term loans of a minimum of $250,000. The sponsors of eligible products will be required to share the risk. The normal level of government guarantees will be set at 85 per cent of the principal amount of the loan. The program will apply not only to manufacturing and processing, but will also complement existing programs in related service sectors, tourism, and primary industries, in recognition of the important role played by these sectors in the Atlantic economy.

This program, which applies to all four Atlantic provinces and also to the Gaspé, is designed to create jobs in the private sector. The government of Canada guarantees loans for business start-up as well as expansion expenses. These are in addition to certain existing income tax incentives. The budget also liberalized some of the specific Cape Breton programs introduced in the May 1985 budget. For instance, the minimum investment required was lowered from $50,00 to $25,000 and some tax credits were raised to 40 per cent from 20 per cent regardless of the size of the business.

The Atlantic provinces, as did the other provinces receiving Established Program Financing (EPF) funds as well as equalization, were damaged by the 1985 budget and Bill C-96, (Adamson, 1987: 46) which curtailed the rate of growth in grants to the provinces under EPF and equalization. This action increased Nova Scotia's deficit in 1986 as it did the deficits of all four provinces.

The provinces also had to incur additional costs because of The Young Offenders Act which had been adopted by the previous Parliament. This federal Act is not in keeping with the theory of interdependent federalism. With the passage of this single piece of legislation, no matter what its merit, the Parliament of Canada unilaterally shifted the cost of incarcerating young offenders from Ottawa's books to those of the provinces.

The history of The Young Offenders Act and of the 1985 budget illustrates a major deficiency in contemporary Canadian federalism: despite talk of reconciliation, there is no intergovernmental machinery, save for First Ministers' Conferences, which scarcely assure amicable resolution of the issues brought before them, to resolve fiscal and other conflicts between the two levels of government. There is no constitutional requirement for any federal government to consult the provinces before Parliament enacts legislation which will have a major, adverse impact upon provincial budgets.

If Ottawa would only consult the provinces more frequently on fiscal matters, it is just possible that the party in power nationally would not see its provincial counterparts defeated so frequently in provincial elections. Also, the nationally disruptive tactics of provincial premiers running against Ottawa might not be as prevalent as they are currently. Despite Brian Mulroney's rhetoric about "national reconciliation," the "fallout" from recent federal fiscal actions has undoubtedly assisted in the defeat of two of the four Conservative governments in Atlantic Canada and has put the remaining two in severe electoral jeopardy. As was pointed out earlier in this paper, the national parties must realize that it is the provincial party which manages the national campaigns in Atlantic Canada. A party in office provincially is a much stronger electoral asset than one in opposition. Yet both Liberal and Conservative governments of Canada fail to take this simple political fact into consideration when dealing with the provinces.

"Free trade" with the United States was not part of the Conservatives' 1984 Atlantic agenda. However, as in the rest of Canada, it is now part of the 1988 agenda and the region, like other sections of the country, is divided on the issue. Initially, support for free trade was higher in the Atlantic provinces than in any other section of the country with the exception of Alberta. (Adamson, 1987). Now that the negotiations have been concluded, support is divided along political and sectoral lines.

The Atlantic Provinces Economic Council (APEC), which is but a mere shadow of its former self and should not be taken as a serious spokesman for the region, is opposed because of the damage the agreement may do to the brewery and textile industries. The fishery, on the other hand, is in favour because those involved in this industry hope the agreement will end the current trade irritants with the Americans over subsidies paid to Canadian fish workers. As a recent study points out, Atlantic Canada could fare badly under free trade because of the various governmental support systems now in place (Adamson, 1987). The Prime Minister has assured the region, and particularly Premier Buchanan, that current governmental assistance programs are compatible with the October 4, 1987 agreement. Only time will tell the accuracy of this promise.

Currently, more than two thirds of the exports of Nova Scotia and New Brunswick, and over half of the exports of the other two provinces, go the United States. Grant Reuber, now Deputy Chairman of the Bank of Montréal, has stated: "The Agreement will allow the Atlantic provinces to take better advantage of their historic trading relationships and to realize more fully their potential in North American and global markets" (Reuber, 1988). Yet, despite the recent growth in the regional economy, one would suspect the region will be divided along partisan political lines on the issue of free trade in the next election, unless John Crosbie can make Atlantic Canadians believe that only those who live in Toronto are anti-free trade.

It has been a major objective of every federal prime minister since Louis St. Laurent to alleviate unemployment and to promote investment opportunity in Atlantic Canada. We have witnessed specific undertakings such as the federal support for the Beechwood Hydro Project in New Brunswick in 1957, the Prince Edward Island Development Plan (adopted in place of the 1960's causeway project), and the Development Corporation (DEVCO) in Cape

Breton. In fact, aid of one form or another has long been a staple of the Atlantic economy.

Despite all the federal money which has been "dumped" into the region, unemployment remains well above the national norm while incomes are below that same national norm. Each prime minister from St. Laurent to Mulroney has pledged to do something about this lingering economic nightmare.

"What is to be done then?" The region is sparsely populated. Only New Brunswick and Newfoundland have any hydroelectric potential while Prince Edward Island has no mineral wealth whatsoever. The fishery, as discussed earlier, is in a constant state of flux and confusion. The pulp and paper industry, though viable, is limited because of the fact that insufficient replacement species have been planted. Also, because of the high cost of production, paper can now be produced more cheaply in other parts of the world. The area is not self-sufficient in agriculture. In fact, its most conspicuous export is its people, either educated or not. It is possible that the only time in which true prosperity could be found in the Maritimes since 1867 was during the period of prohibition. Prohibition was one of the few successful industries which has flourished in this part of Canada.

The region has become dependent upon the federal treasury. This has led to what Simeon and Elkins have called "disaffected societies," Noel refers to as "clientism," and Matthews as "economic dependency" (Dyck, 1986: 4–5). Perhaps all of this can be summarized as "feudal federalism." The Atlantic provinces are vassal states and its citizens villains and both are indentured to the federal treasury. True, this is not the feudalism of the middle ages, yet it remains feudalism nevertheless. The squire is the politician who dispenses the all important gifts of patronage and looks after the social welfare of his people. In return, the residents instead of paying rent are expected to show their respect at the ballot box.

Like individuals who are on welfare, regions can also lose their initiative and desire because they know the state will provide for their future no matter what the circumstances. So, like the social welfare recipients who spend their welfare cheques on beer and fortified wines, the provincial governments spend their federal funds on some rather questionable projects and run up large budgetary deficits knowing that, no matter how peculiar their behaviour, Ottawa will always come to the rescue.

In June of 1987, the Mulroney Government stepped into all of this confusion and dependency with the Atlantic Canada Opportunities Agency (ACOA). The legislation, Bill C–103, to establish this agency is now before Parliament, but, in fact, the agency is in place with new money and its staff is hard at work.

ACOA

There is no doubt that ACOA is a new approach to dealing with the ancient issue of regional disparities in the Atlantic region. The report of the federal-provincial task force on regional development assistance (1987) in calling for a new approach stated, in part:

> We are suggesting that this past experience together with the economic and trade environment and prospect call for a broader based approach to regional development and regionally based strategies — a new agenda. (Government of Canada, 1987:44).

The principal architect for ACOA was Donald Savoie of the University of Moncton, who produced a non-partisan report outlining the needs of the region. Savoie's thinking on regional development may be summarized as, "whatever approach or combination of approaches the Mulroney government opts for, the search for a new regional development strategy should be guided by more realistic expectations of what can be accomplished than was done previously" (Savoie, 1985: 148-149).

The objectives for the Atlantic Canada Opportunities Agency are outlined in Section 12 of Bill C–103:

> The objective of the Agency is to support and promote opportunity for the economic development of Atlantic Canada, with particular emphasis on small and medium sized enterprises, through policy, program and project development and implementation and through advocacy of the interests of Atlantic Canada in national economic policy, program and project development and implementation.

Bill C-103 states that ACOA will be responsible for the Industrial and Regional Development Program (IRDP) and the Atlantic Enterprise Program (AEP) introduced in the 1983 and 1986 federal budgets, respectively. Also included in the legislation is Enterprise Cape Breton which administers the tax and other proposals introduced in the 1985 and 1986 federal budgets. However, the Minister of State for Small Business and Tourism remains responsible for the tourism sub-agreements in the region. The Sydney Steel Corporation remains the responsibility of the Minister of DRIE, who is also responsible for DEVCO which operates the coal mines in Cape Breton. ACOA is intended to be the fulcrum for regional development within the region.

Will ACOA really make a difference, or is it just another shuffle of the ancient cards of regional inequality? Is it, as Senator Lowell Murray recently stated on *The National*, "the last chance" to do something about the Atlantic economy? Or is ACOA just another program by a national political party wishing to gain electoral kudos? Those public servants who have been involved in regional development for some years are enthusiastic supporters of the new agency. This change of attitude is obviously a positive step. However, ACOA must undertake a great deal of public education in order to overcome the existing cynicism and lassitude towards regional development incentives.

One positive step is the fact that the Board of Directors for ACOA is basically non-partisan. Of the first eighteen directors, six are known Conservatives, four are members of the Liberal Party, while eight are politically neutral. The office, including the president of ACOA, Donald MacPhail, is located in Moncton. In spite of fears which have been expressed both politically and in the regional press, there is no political "slush fund" within the ACOA budget. ACOA has been given a public advocacy role so that the agency, including its Board of Directors, can act as proponents for regional development programs.

The emphasis within ACOA is on free enterprise and on existing businesses which might be described as "medium size." Gone, hopefully, is the emphasis on the mega-project which has been replaced by the interest on existing firms. Grant applications can now be processed within two weeks rather than months under former regional development agencies.

Nevertheless, one must contemplate whether ACOA is truly a reform, or just the same old federal programs in new clothing. For example, the Minister still has his hands on the throttle as indicated in sections 6 and 11 of Bill C-103:

In furtherance of the purpose of this part, the Minister may exercise powers and perform duties and functions that affect economic opportunity and development in Atlantic Canada over which Parliament has jurisdiction that are now by or pursuant to law assigned to any other member of the Queen's Privy Council for Canada or to any department, board or agency of the government of Canada.

Originally, this was not to be the case. When ACOA was first announced by the Prime Minister, the Board of Directors with its president resident in Moncton was to have the final say with respect to the operation of ACOA. The Minister was only to report to Parliament in a manner similar to that of the Minister of Transport reporting on behalf of Air Canada or Canadian National Railways. Because of this change in the intent of the legislation, the question remains, will future ministers use the authority of part five of Bill C-103 for purely political purposes. Senator Murray, the current minister, has argued that this section is simply an administrative device so that the minister will remain responsible to Parliament and the Treasury Board for the overall operation of ACOA. It may be accurate to state that this is an administrative procedure, but it is also an avenue for federal patronage.

Already the fight has commenced between the provinces and Ottawa over who is to get the "political credit" for the good deeds of ACOA. The answer to this should be obvious, afterall it is federal money so one would expect the "feds" to get the credit. John Crosbie in answering questions in the House of Commons has made it abundantly clear as far as he is concerned that Ottawa will obtain the political kudos for ACOA actions. However, the premiers have stated they wish to be in on the action.

As stated above, the emphasis in Bill C-103 and on the operation of ACOA to date is on free enterprise rather than on government enterprise. Once again, this should not be a surprise for not only does it fit with the philosophy of the Mulroney administration, but it illustrates the failure of previous regional development programs within Atlantic Canada. It is correct to state that the Mulroney government has kept its regional development promises of August, 1984. The Conservatives have attempted to generate new money and new ideas concerning regional development. However, it is too early to analyze the impact of ACOA on the region.

OBSERVATIONS AND CONCLUSIONS

One cannot discuss the Mulroney government in Atlantic Canada without mentioning the impact of The Hon. Sinclair Stevens, particularly on the island of Cape Breton. It is difficult to ascertain why Stevens took such a dedicated and detailed interest in the economy of Cape Breton. Certainly, it is not the poorest area of the region. Indeed, northern New Brunswick suffers greater economic deprivation than does Cape Breton. Nevertheless, Stevens, until the time of his resignation from the Cabinet, might well have been classified as the minister for Cape Breton and his resignation from the Cabinet under pressure from Liberal and New Democratic MPs was no well received by residents of Cape Breton. Rather, they saw it as another example of central and western Canadian politicians playing politics with the distressed economy of their region.

One can only speculate, but it is quite conceivable that Stevens' interest in Cape Breton was purely and simply to embarrass Alan MacEachen and to show to the citizens of MacEachen's former bailliwick that there were others in Parliament who were as equally interested in the welfare of Cape Bretoners as was MacEachen. Certainly, no other Tory minister, including Lowell Murray, has shown such an all-consuming interest in Cape Breton as did Stevens.

The Maritimes, and particularly Nova Scotia, have been described as the "homeland" of what Gad Horowitz has called "the red tory." For many years, Tory politicians like Robert Stanfield, Flora MacDonald, David McDonald, Richard Hatfield, John Buchanan, Angus MacLean, Joe Clark, Gordon Fairweather and many others have been classified as red tories. To Horowitz, "a red tory is a philosopher who combines elements of socialism and toryism so thoroughly in a single integrated Weltanschauung that it is impossible to say that he is a proponent of either one or against the other" (Horowitz, 1985: 50).

Unfortunately, red toryism is on the decline in the region. The Conservative Members from Cape Breton in the Nova Scotia House are not red tories. It was only the defeat of the neo-liberal Sterling Lyon in the 1981 Manitoba election which prevented these Members from becoming a stronger voice in the caucus.

The current Progressive Conservative philosophy in the region, both federally and provincially, is like a child's teeter-totter. One moment neo-liberalism is on top, the next the red tories are once again in the ascendency. One has a suspicion that the polls are responsible for this turn of events. The Conservatives in the region, like Conservatives everywhere in Canada, live and die with the pollsters. The Progressive Conservatives in Atlantic Canada are driven more by public opinion than by political philosophy. In this respect, they are just like the Liberals.

There are certain differences between the two "old line parties" which have become apparent since 1984. This government, like the Diefenbaker government, is much more willing to be "helpful" to the provinces than were the Liberals. The Beechwood Hydro project in 1957 like the Atlantic offshore agreements of 1985 and 1986 are examples of this attitude. The Conservatives have always stood for the 'rights' of the provinces, as Meech Lake illustrates. Mulroney's national reconciliation has brought about a more harmonious relationship between the Maritimes and Ottawa. Newfoundland is a different situation. Brian Peckford did tone down his anti-Ottawa rhetoric for a time following the Tory's 1984 victory. But, in the last year when he has not received everything he wanted from Ottawa, he has turned the volume up once again. The public arguments between Peckford and Crosbie are a delight to watch — only the English language suffers. It will be interesting to see how supportive Peckford is of the federal party in the next election.

Another difference between the Liberals and the Conservatives is the latter's emphasis on free enterprise rather than government enterprise. An examination of all the programs initiated by the Mulroney government in the area of regional development, including the 1985 and 1986 budgets, Enterprise Cape Breton and ACOA, illustrate this government's desire to help business rather than compete with the private sector. ACOA states that "its principal task is to create and implement development programs for small and medium sized businesses . . . to improve the entrepreneurial climate."[6] Certainly, this is a free enterprise administration. It has emphasized the private sector over the public sector, even though it has not neglected the Tory tradition of using the federal treasury to assist the provinces on specific projects. Yet, under the umbrella of deficit reduction it has curtailed services in the region, particularly transportation, and has cut back increases in EPF grants as it has to all of the provinces. It has also curtailed equalization increases. Because of the economy of the region, the curtailment of growth in such programs as family allowances is having a more drastic impact than is the case in central Canada.

Is the region better off today than in 1984? Real income is up and unemployment is down. For any government this has to be a victory. ACOA, because its emphasis is on the small and medium sized project rather than on the mega-project, has the potential to promote employment and economic opportunity in the region, even after the Mulroney government has left office. Indeed, ACOA may turn out to be the most important and lasting undertaking of this government, at least in the Atlantic region.

Currently, however there are some problems with ACOA. Only the smaller grants are being processed within the promised two-week time frame. A number of grant recipients have been informed not by ACOA officials that their application has been accepted, but by members of the Progressive Conservative Party including, in Nova Scotia, members of the House of Assembly.

Nova Scotia's Minister for Small Business, David Nantes, has complained recently that ACOA is being far too liberal with its funds and is giving some Cape Breton firms 100 per cent equity, thus permitting people to start a new business with literally no personal equity.[7]

The federal-provincial conflict over ACOA must be resolved if the agency is to obtain any credibility in the region. The conflict over who is to obtain political credit is one of longstanding in Canadian federalism, but in this case there should be no doubt that Ottawa deserves the kudos. It is difficult to stamp out patronage, especially in a region where it is part of the political tradition. But, ACOA will become ineffective if it is perceived in the same manner as are the departments of highways in the region, that is, as a mere extension of the party in power. If Senator Lowell Murray is to be true to his word, he must take action to end patronage by ACOA now before it becomes entrenched in the region's political culture.

It is too soon to accurately assess the effectiveness of the Progressive Conservatives' initiatives in Atlantic Canada. The electorate, because they have heard promises from their politicians of El Dorado for years, remains skeptical. Nothing the government has done to date has ended the region's political cynicism, and its attitude toward government remains unchanged. The Conservatives have introduced a philosophy of assisting the private sector which might well be compared to attempting to break the social welfare treadmill. They are not prepared to end the region's social welfare tradition, but rather to change the emphasis from direct "handouts" to individuals and replace them with help for the entrepreneur. If this is neo-liberalism, it is a very mild form of it.

In 1984 one wondered if the Conservatives had a realistic regional agenda. This question has now been answered. ACOA with its budget of $1.05 billion over five years is certainly a move in the right direction. If nothing more, ACOA will stop federal departments and agencies from working at cross purposes. It will have a legislative mandate which can only be amended by Parliament. Thus, it will be safe from future prime ministerial whims unlike past regional agencies. The potential is strong, but the fear of ACOA being turned into a patronage vehicle is real and only a vigilant and attuned citizenry can prevent this from happening.

Feudal federalism still remains a fact of life in Atlantic Canada. It will only be ended when the residents themselves are prepared to come to grips with the situation and to use the tools which have been given to them by government.

The Mulroney government, at least in Atlantic Canada, despite its emphasis on free enterprise and privatization and its neo-liberal rhetoric, is, according to Horowitz's definition, a truly Canadian Conservative government:

> It is possible to perceive in Canadian Conservatism not only the elements of business Liberalism and orthodox Toryism, but also an element of 'Tory democracy' — the paternalistic concern for the 'condition of the people' and the emphasis on the Tory party as their champion . . . (Horowitz, 1985: 49)

NOTES

1 Industrialists are well aware of this situation and will play one province off against the other: in 1986, for example, Litton Systems bargained with each of the Maritime provinces to see which one would give it the best incentive package.
2 This included all forms of social welfare, agricultural and fishing subsidies and salaries for CFB Greenwood and Cornwallis.
3 *Halifax Chronicle-Herald*, August 6, 1984.
4 *Halifax Chronicle-Herald*, August 3, 1984.
5 Council of Maritime Premiers, Press communiqué, February 29, 1988.
6 ACOA information material, Moncton, 1988.
7 *Halifax Chronicle-Herald*, April 21, 1988.

REFERENCES

Adamson, Agar (1987). "Nova Scotia: Optimism in Spite of It All," in Peter Leslie (ed.), *Canada: The State of the Federation 1986*, (Kingston: Institute of Intergovernmental Relations).

Dyck, Rand (1986). *Provincial Politics in Canada*, (Scarborough: Prentice-Hall).

Horowitz, Gad (1985). "Conservatism, Liberalism and Socialism in Canada: An Interpretation," in Hugh Thorburn (ed.), *Party Politics in Canada*, 5th ed., (Toronto: Prentice-Hall).

MacDonald, L. Ian (1984). *Mulroney: The Making of the Prime Minister*, (Toronto: McClelland and Stewart).

Pollard, Bruce (1985). "Newfoundland: Resisting Dependency," in Peter Leslie (ed.), *Canada: the State of the Federation 1985*, (Kingston: Institute of Intergovernmental Relations).

Reuber, Grant L. (1988). "Free Trade And Atlantic Canada." Address given at St. Mary's University, Halifax, 4 February.

Savoie, Donald (1985). "The Continuing Struggle for a Regional Development Policy," in Peter Leslie (ed.), *Canada: the State of the Federation, 1985*, (Kingston: Institute of Intergovernmental Relations).

National Reconciliation and the Canadian West: Political Management in the Mulroney Era

ROGER GIBBINS

Arguably the two most important political initiatives of Prime Minister Brian Mulroney's Progressive Conservative government have been the Meech Lake constitutional accord and the proposed free trade agreement with the United States. While not yet ratified, they both stand out in their potential to reshape the contours of Canadian political life. I would like to begin, then, by noting how these two initiatives were addressed in a recent keynote speech by Premier Don Getty to the annual convention of the Alberta Progressive Conservative party.

Speaking on April 9, 1988, to nearly 2,400 convention delegates in Edmonton, Premier Getty drew attention to Pierre Trudeau's opposition to the Meech Lake accord. "I knew the accord was good," said Getty. "After Mr. Trudeau's intervention I'm certain it's one hell of a deal!"[1] In short, anything that Mr. Trudeau opposed was bound to be good for Alberta. Turning then to the proposed free trade agreement, Premier Getty told delegates that it would ensure that "no one is ever going to shove anything down Alberta's throat again," a phrase unfortunately reminiscent of past western Canadian opposition to official bilingualism. The free trade agreement, Getty implied, was good for Alberta because it would tie the hands of future Canadian governments, ensuring that programs analogous to the National Energy Program would never again be imposed on the West. In the future, Washington would provide the political protection from central Canada, and from the Government of Canada, that parliamentary institutions failed to provide in the past. The agreement, then, is to be welcomed by Albertans not because it protects Canadian sovereignty but because it restricts that sovereignty.

On the surface, Premier Getty's comments suggest that little has changed in the West over the last four years, that Pierre Trudeau is alive and well, that the old battles are still being fought and the old battle lines still being drawn. More importantly, they suggest a continued wariness of national parliamentary institutions despite the massive political change introduced by the 1984 election. (Premier Getty's comments also suggest a certain shallowness of political thought among western Canadian political elites, but this is another matter.)

THE 1984 ELECTION

It is difficult to exaggerate the impact of the 1984 election on the political landscape of western Canada. With the brief exception of Joe Clark's 1979 Conservative government, western Canadians had been all but shut out of the national government since 1972. Although this situation and the consequent alienation were most extreme in Alberta, where the Progressive Conservatives won every seat in the elections of 1972, 1974 and 1980 while the Liberals won nationally, the situation was little better elsewhere in the West. During this period western Canadians confronted national governments dominated by "central Canada" and, more specifically, by Québec Liberal MPs. Not coincidentally in western Canadian eyes, and particularly in the eyes of Albertans, this was also the period marked by the spread of official bilingualism, by regulated oil prices which denied billions of dollars to the Alberta treasury[2] by the reviled National Energy Program, and by the dramatic downturn of the western Canadian economy in the early 1980s.

It was during this period that parliamentary institutions came into general disrepute in western Canada. Admittedly, of course, earlier periods of western Canadian history had also been marked by wide-ranging if not clearly focused critique of parliamentary institutions; during the Progressive revolt of the early 1920s, westerners certainly were very unhappy with the institutional foundations of Canadian political life. I would argue, however, that during the late 1970s and early 1980s there emerged an even more emphatic regional consensus that parliamentary institutions were inherently flawed, that they did not and could not provide western Canadians with adequate or even fair representation in the national government, and that as a consequence national policies would inevitably fail to reflect western Canadian interests and aspirations.[3] It was during this period that political debate in the region became charged with the rhetoric of institutional reform as western Canadians promoted the virtues of Senate reform, electoral reform, party reform, enhanced provincial powers and even separatism.[4]

It is against this backdrop of regional discontent that we must place the outcome of the 1984 federal election, for that election set up an important test for parliamentary institutions. For the first time in a long time, western Canadians faced a national government in which their region enjoyed plentiful representation. In the Alberta case, all MPs found themselves in the unusual position of being on the government side of the House. Moreover, Conservative MPs from the West appeared to control many of the important command posts of the new Mulroney government; certainly Alberta's presence in the federal cabinet, led by Deputy Prime Minister Don Mazankowski and Minister of External Affairs Joe Clark, could not be stronger.

In short, then, western Canadians could now test how well parliamentary institutions worked not in the worst of times, under the Liberal governments of Pierre Trudeau, but rather in the best of times under the Progressive Conservative government of Brian Mulroney in which the West appeared to enjoy full and effective representation. Perhaps, it was argued, parliamentary institutions were not inherently flawed, that given the right party and the right leader, they could indeed deliver public policies which would be well received in the West. Certainly this had been the Conservatives' constitutional message during the late seventies and early eighties, that parliamentary institutions would work just fine if only the right party was in power. The results of the 1984 federal election allowed this important hypothesis to be put to the test.

THE MULRONEY GOVERNMENT

Initially, it seemed that parliamentary institutions in the Mulroney era would pass the test. The Western Accord, admittedly coupled with an abrupt decline in international oil prices, brought to an end more than a decade of acrimonious energy conflict. The NEP was dismantled, and the heavy hand of government regulation lifted from the continental marketing of energy resources; at long last the market rather than Ottawa would set the price of oil and natural gas. Massive financial relief was provided to prairie farmers facing drought and depressed world grain prices. The Prime Minister's efforts to foster more cooperative intergovernmental relations were certainly well-received by provincial premiers in the West, and were likely appreciated by an electorate grown weary with the intense intergovernmental conflict that marked the Trudeau era. Western premiers, and in particular Saskatchewan's Grant Devine, emerged as staunch supporters of both the Prime Minister and his federal party.

On a broader ideological front, the efforts by the Mulroney government to restrain if not actually reduce federal expenditures and to promote both deregulation and privatization seemed to find a receptive audience among western Canadians. Although Petro-Canada was not privatized, the crown corporation seems to have won the hearts of even its most implacable western Canadian opponents through its enormously successful sponsorship of the Olympic Torch Relay. In late 1987, the federal government established the Western Diversification Office (WDO), with its head in Edmonton and regional offices in each of the four western provinces. WDO was given $312 million for the 1988–89 fiscal year with which to promote new economic activity in the region; this money constituted the first installment on the government's August 1987 promise of $1.2 billion over five years to help diversify the western Canadian economy.[5] While there is some dispute whether the WDO money is in fact new money or repackaged old money, the WDO initiative has been generally welcomed in the West.

Thus there is little doubt that the Mulroney government was initially well-received in western Canada, and that there was broad regional support for the policy course being pursued by the Conservative government. At least with respect to western Canada, the

90

national government was delivering on the policy front. However, near the midterm of the Mulroney government some of the bloom was coming off the new Tory rose as the government's political management failed to match its management of public policy. The federal government's decision to award the CF–18 maintenance contract to Montréal rather than to Winnipeg was vigorously attacked in the media across the West, although it is interesting to note that the provincial governments of Saskatchewan, Alberta and British Columbia did not support the Manitoba government. The Prime Minister was accused of spending too little time in the West, and in his preoccupation with the electoral fate of his party in Québec, Mulroney appeared to be little different from his Liberal predecessor.

As the popularity of the Mulroney government began to plummet elsewhere in the country it also fell in the West, although not quite as far or quite as fast. More importantly for the present discussion, regional arguments for institutional reform were also revived. In the West, the Federal government was increasingly harried on its flanks by the supporters of Triple E Senate reform, by Preston Manning's new Reform party which threatened to burrow into the soft underbelly of Conservative electoral support in the West, by the revival of the provincial Liberals in Manitoba and Alberta, and by a more general resurgence of western alienation.

In short, as Mulroney's first term of office continued to unfold, it began to appear that parliamentary institutions were failing the test set up by the 1984 election. To many, although by no means all western Canadians, it seemed that the defeat of the Liberals and the election of a new Conservative government had not dramatically improved the West's fortunes within the national political arena. The new government and the new party seemed just as preoccupied with Québec as their Liberal predecessors had been. Events such as the CF–18 maintenance contract were used as evidence that existing parliamentary institutions could not ensure a fair shake for the West even when there were so many western Canadian MPs in the cabinet and on the government side of the House. Thus the West seemed to be retreating to a mood of sullen alienation as the national Conservative government drifted more and more into Québec's orbit. While it was perhaps too early to conclude beyond doubt that the "great experiment" of 1984 was a failure, western Canadians were once again promoting the merits of institutional reform, and particularly of Senate reform.

I would argue, however, that Ottawa's constitutional and free trade initiatives have, at least temporarily, halted the erosion of its political support in the West. More importantly, they have also forestalled the resurgence of alienation which seemed to be building in the West, and have crippled support for institutional reform. In the West, as in Québec, the Meech Lake accord and the free trade agreement are proving to be important vehicles for national reconciliation.

THE MEECH LAKE ACCORD

It may seem odd to some people that the Meech Lake initiative did anything to strengthen western Canadian support for the national government, given that the initiative was directed primarily to the constitutional aspirations of Québec and to the electoral fate of the Conservatives within Québec. However, while the Meech Lake accord has not enjoyed universal support in the West, it has shored up the support of provincial premiers for the Mulroney government. By universalizing Québec's long-standing demand for a distinctive if not necessarily special constitutional status, the accord has strengthened the position of all provincial governments in the country. Thus western Canadian premiers came away from the 1987 constitutional negotiations with control over Senate and Supreme Court appointments, with greater control over immigration policy, and with greater flexibility with respect to future federal government programs. While the accord did nothing to strengthen the intra-state representation of western Canadians within the institutions of the national government, it did provide additional inter-state protection from those institutions by strengthening the role of provincial governments within the Canadian federal system.

Through the Meech Lake accord, Prime Minister Mulroney was able to forge an impressive coalition between provincialists in the West and nationalists in Québec. The effectiveness of this coalition was demonstrated by Premier Robert Bourassa's April 1988 tour of western Canada. Bourassa's visit came on the heels of the Supreme Court's affirmation of minority language rights in Saskatchewan, and more directly on the heels of the Saskatchewan government's decision to nullify those rights legislatively while at the same time providing enhanced services and limited statutory translation for the province's francophone minority. In statements to the press following meetings with both Saskatchewan Premier Grant Devine and Alberta Premier Don Getty, and to the dismay of francophone groups within the two provinces, Bourassa took the opportunity to support the policy adopted by the Saskatchewan government. Collectively, the three premiers seemed to agree that the spirit of Meech Lake was best expressed through the defence of provincial autonomy rather than through the protection of linguistic minorities. One can only assume that Bourassa's support will be reciprocated by the western premiers should the Québec government act legislatively to ward off judicial challenges to Québec's Bill 101.

While it is true that the Meech Lake accord did not address long-standing western Canadian interests in institutional reform, it did place Senate reform on the agenda for future constitutional conferences. In what may turn out to be a very prolonged interim period, it also gave the plum of patronage control over Senate appointments to the provincial governments. (The chances of any significant reform of the Senate taking place in the future are however severely diminished by the Accord.) Moreover, one could argue that the accord, by enhancing the status of all provincial governments in Canada, has thereby reduced the ability of future federal governments to initiate policies with adverse regional effects.

It is worth noting however that the West has displayed a less-than-solid constitutional front with respect to the Meech Lake accord.[7] Although the accord was quickly ratified in Saskatchewan, it was sharply criticized in public hearing sponsored by the opposition New Democrats before receiving legislative approval. (In the Legislative Assembly, the New Democrats ultimately supported ratification while the Liberal MLAs missed the vote.) In Manitoba, the fate of the accord is very much in doubt following the spring election of a minority Progressive Conservative government; with the opposition parties strongly opposed to the accord, the new Premier has indicated that ratification is not high on his list of priorities. In British Columbia public hearings are still to be completed, while opposition mounts among provincial New Democrats.

This rather confused picture is worth noting if only because it illustrates the growing political fragmentation of the West since the close of the 1981–82 constitutional debates. The political scene both within provinces and across the region has become far less homogeneous with respect to constitutional issues. In this sense, "the West" is falling apart as a political region.[8] However, there is much less regional disagreement with respect to the other dominant issue on the nation's political agenda, free trade.

THE FREE TRADE AGREEMENT

There is no question that the Mulroney government's free trade initiative enjoys broad though by no means universal public support across the West and, with the exception of the recently-defeated NDP government in Manitoba, it has enjoyed the enthusiastic, almost jingoistic support of provincial governments. Interestingly, however, this support does not stem from any compelling argument that free trade will bestow substantial economic benefits on the West. Economic forecasts on the effects of free trade, including ones done by the Canada West Foundation, suggest that Ontario and Quebec will be the principal beneficiaries of free trade. The impact of free trade is likely to be felt only at the margins of the western Canadian economy, in part because the oil and gas industries have already been deregulated, and in part because the great bulk of western Canadian agricultural trade is international rather than continental.

Nonetheless, the free trade initiative draws support from three important sources in the West. The first, and perhaps least important of the three, is the oft-exaggerated ideological conservatism of the West. Free trade in this sense is supported because it promotes a deregulated, market-based economy, one close to the ideological hearts of small–c conservative governments now ensconced across the West. Some evidence for this argument comes from a small survey I conducted in November, 1987, of some 36 Chief Executive Officers in the Calgary oilpatch. All but one of the respondents supported the proposed free trade agreement with the United States. Indeed, almost 80% supported it strongly and without reservation. However, when respondents were asked what impact the agreement would be likely to have on the oil and gas industry generally, and on their own firm in particular, most predicted that the agreement would have little if any positive effect. This suggests that support for the agreement stemmed more from the ideological beliefs of the respondents — their belief that free trade would lift the weight of government from the back of the economy — than it stemmed from any expectation that they themselves, as individuals or as an industry, would benefit.

The second source of support comes from a widespread regional mythology, dating back to the early days of prairie settlement, which maintains that the tariffs of the National Policy imposed a particularly onerous burden on western Canadian agricultural producers. So deeply ingrained is this mythology in the region's political culture that western Canadians assume that any move to reduce tariffs will necessarily benefit the West. Here, of course, Ontario Premier David Peterson's opposition to the free trade initiative reinforces the tariff mythology; if Ontario opposes free trade then it must be good for the West, just as the Meech Lake accord must be good if it is opposed by Pierre Trudeau.

The third source of support stems from the argument alluded to in the introduction to this paper; free trade with the United States is seen as a way of preventing Ottawa from intervening in the national and continental economies to the detriment of western Canadian interests. Free trade provides the guarantee that Ottawa will never again be able to impose a policy such as the National Energy Program. While it is recognized that the free trade agreement may limit the ability of provincial governments to promote economic development and diversification, this limitation on provincial "sovereignty" is seen as a price worth paying to ensure Ottawa's hands are also tied.[9] As I noted above, Washington is looked to for the political protection that parliamentary institutions failed to provide for the West in the past.

As Ian McDougall points out, it is ironic that the western provinces are championing an agreement which will undo ". . . the fruits of decades of provincial argument for more regulatory power over resources."[10] Under the terms of the agreement, provinces will not be able to restrain production to secure higher prices, as former Premier Peter Lougheed was able to do in 1980–81. As McDougall also points out, provinces will not be able to impose minimum oil and gas prices, a power which the natural resources clause in the Constitution Act 1982 was meant to secure. Nor will provinces be able to reduce production in order to prevent future shortages which might adversely affect provincial consumers. In short, the

West may be giving up a great deal for marginally improved access to American markets. However, it appears to be a price that western provincial governments are prepared to pay in order to fend off future raids by the federal government, real or imagined.

To the extent that the proposed free trade agreement continues to dominate the nation's political agenda, it should also shore up electoral support for the Conservatives in western Canada. In part, of course, this is due to the regional popularity of the free trade initiative. That initiative, however, brings two other important payoffs to the conservatives. First, it should mute provincial government criticism of Ottawa in the run-up to the next federal election, although here B.C. Premier Bill Vander Zalm's recent outburst shows that there is no guarantee of this score.[11] Second, it has already defanged the newly created Reform Party, which threatened the right flank of the PC vote in western Canada. Before the free trade initiative was launched, it appeared that the Reform Party might be able to build a viable election platform from the planks of resurgent western alienation, and from a more general unease with the style and mannerisms of the Prime Minister. However, the most likely supporters of the Reform Party are also the region's most ardent free trade supporters. In an election focused on the free trade agreement, they are unlikely to risk the defeat of that agreement by supporting the Reform Party. Moreover, on the most important issue of the campaign, the Reform Party will not be able to draw any useful distinction between its own position and that of the Conservative government. As a consequence, the party's raison d'etre has been thrown into question by the free trade debate.

Therefore in the short term, the Progressive Conservative government is in reasonably good shape in western Canada. Indeed, the short-term prospects look all the more positive when one considers the ongoing disarray within the federal Liberal party in the prairies[12] and the more general disarray on the issue of free trade. If the Conservative government finds itself in a two-way fight with the New Democrats in the next election, it should be well-positioned on the prairies with respect to what is likely to be the dominant issue of the campaign, the proposed free trade agreement. As the above discussion points out, the regional mythology surrounding free trade will handicap the New Democrats in any campaign featuring the proposed free trade agreement. Over the longer term, however, there are clouds gathering on the prairie horizon. The provincial Liberals are clearly on the rebound in Alberta and Manitoba and the provincial New Democrats appear to be regaining some of their fighting trim in British Columbia and Saskatchewan.

Here it is also important to note an important change that has occurred in the character of the Progressive conservative party. In the years of the Trudeau government, the conservative party became the primary vehicle for western Canadian political discontent. As Table 1 shows, western Canadian MPs carried very substantial weight within the PC parliamentary caucus, averaging close to 50% of the caucus in the peak years of regional discontent in the West. To an important extent, the Conservative party had been captured by its western arm; it had become a western Canadian party as much as a national party.

TABLE 1

The West's Contribution to the
Progressive Conservatives' Electoral Coalition

	1972	1974	1979	1980	1984
Western PC MPs as a % of all PC MPs	39.3	51.6	41.9	47.6	27.5
Western PC vote as a % of total PC vote	31.5	35.8	36.8	38.7	28.5

All of this changed dramatically with the 1984 election, which propelled western Canadian MPs into power while at the same time sharply reducing western Canadian influence within the Conservative party. Bluntly put, western Canadians won a government but lost a party. If Québec forms the primary battleground for the next federal election, as is likely to be the case,[13] and if Mr. Mulroney continues to focus his own energies on Québec, which is also likely to be the case, then we can expect the subterranean currents of western alienation to carry prairie voters towards a new partisan home. Whether that home will be the New Democrats, a new party such as the Reform Party or even a born-again Liberal party remains to be seen.

CONCLUSIONS

Using the Meech Lake Accord and the free trade agreement as the thread, Prime Minister Mulroney has stitched together a political alliance reminiscent of the Mackenzie King Liberal alliances in the past. He has brought together the nationalists of Québec and the provincialists of the West in a coalition that should withstand any loss of political support in the Ontario heartland. In this sense, and it is by no means an unimportant sense, Mulroney has clearly succeeded in the politics of national reconciliation by bringing together the economic interests of the west with the constitutional interests of Québec. If he can continue to placate francophone minorities on the prairies without upsetting the jurisdiction sensitivities of provincial governments on the prairies and in Québec, the coalition should carry Mr. Mulroney through the next federal election as it carried Mackenzie King before him.

There is, however, a price to be paid for Prime Minister Mulroney's approach to national reconciliation. First, it is based on two agreements, the Meech Lake accord and the free trade agreement; both of which weaken the national government and thus, potentially, weaken the national community. They are agreements which embody provincialist and continentalist visions, but not national visions in the Canadian sense. Second, Mulroney's alliance draws together the two regions of the country, or at least governmental elites in the two regions, where commitment to the Canadian national community may be the weakest. One can only hope, therefore, that in the near future Mr. Mulroney's vision of Canada extends beyond the politics of national reconciliation to a bolder vision of the Canadian community. If not, the country that has been pulled together by his government may not endure the provincial and continental forces unleashed by the agreements on Meech Lake and free trade.

NOTES

1 Reported in the *Calgary Herald*, April 10, 1988, p. A2.

2 Former Premier Peter Lougheed frequently refers to the $50 billion that Alberta lost when Ottawa refused to let the price of western Canadian oil rise to world levels.

3 It should be stressed that this conclusion was also reflected in the more general body of constitutional literature that emerged in the period between the election of the Parti Québecois in 1976 and the proclamation of the Constitution Act in 1982.

4 As I have discussed elsewhere, there has been much greater consensus in the West on the political problems facing the region than there has been on the appropriate institutional solutions. See Gibbins (1983).

5 *Calgary Herald*, February 24, 1988, p. A1–A2.

6 The March 1988 Globe-Environics poll gave the Conservatives 36% of the western Canadian vote, down 5 points from December 1987. Across the West the Liberals were up 5 points to 28%, while the NDP was down one point to 34%. These figures compare to the national results which gave the Liberals 40% of the decided vote, the New Democrats 30%, and the Conservatives 29%. *The Globe and Mail*, March 29, 1988, pp. A1 and A4.

7 For a detailed look at western Canada reactions to Meech Lake, see Gibbins (1988).

8 For a development of this argument, see Gibbins (1980).

9 Even Peter Lougheed, the West's most forceful defender of provincial rights, has argued that the loss of provincial sovereignty with respect to natural resources is a price worth paying for the free trade agreement, that the degree of provincial control needed in the past will not be needed in the future given the constraints that the free trade agreement will place on the Government of Canada.

10 Ian McDougall, "Energy producers are in for a shock," *The Globe and Mail*, February 23, 1988, p. A7.

11 In his March 15 Speech from the Throne, read by Lieutenant-Governor Robert Rogers, Vander Zalm declared that British Columbians were ready to put Canada's federal system of government on trial. "For too long, British Columbia has been out of sight and out of mind of successive federal governments. For too long the federal vision failed to see beyond central Canada. Even now that vision of Western Canada appears to encompass only prairie grain and Alberta energy." *Globe and Mail*, March 16, 1988, p. A1.

12 Jeffrey Simpson, "Westward how?" *The Globe and Mail*, January 19, 1988, p. A6.

13 Certainly journalists have already trained their guns on Québec in the runup to the next federal election. Note, for example, Jeffrey Simpson's prediction of a "tough, even merciless struggle in Québec." *Globe and Mail*, April 1, 1988, p. A6.

REFERENCES

Gibbins, Roger (1980). *Prairie Politics and Society: Regionalism in Decline*, (Toronto: Butterworths).

Gibbins, Roger (1983). "Constitutional Politics and the West," in Keith Banting and Richard Simeon (eds.), *And No One Cheered: Federalism, Democracy and the Constitution Act*, (Toronto: Methuen), pp. 119–132.

Gibbins, Roger (1988). *Meech Lake and Canada: Perspectives From the West*, (Edmonton: Academic Publishing and Printing).

ECONOMIC RENEWAL

Nowhere is the need for national reconciliation more urgent than in Canada's economic life. Our repeated failure in recent years to achieve our economic potential cries out for correction by a truly sustained, co-operative and national effort . . . .

. . . [T]here are some important initial steps that the federal government can take to help to generate economic renewal . . . . That we must deal urgently with the deficit is beyond dispute. If allowed to continue to grow out of control, it will consume our available financial resources, undermine our capacity to respond to new opportunities, put increased pressure on interest rates, and inhibit investment and growth in our economy.

Second, my government will pursue approaches to improve the efficiency and flexibility of our capital markets; to improve job opportunities for Canada through responsive market-oriented training programs; and to increase investments in research and development to improve our productivity . . . .

Third, my government will introduce . . . proposals to enhance risk taking, innovation and reward among entrepreneurs, especially in the small and medium-sized business sector . . . .

Canada also has a vital stake in the elimination of barriers to trade, commerce and investment on a global basis. In this connection, there is an urgent need for a concerted attack on non-tariff barriers which have become increasingly insidious and more prevalent. Acknowledging that no country, including Canada, is blameless, my government declares its willingness to do its parts in a renewed multilateral effort to remove these obstructions in the international marketplace.

— Speech from the throne, November 5, 1984.

The Canada–U.S. Free Trade Agreement

DAVID LEYTON-BROWN

Free trade with the United States was not a campaign promise in the 1984 election. Nevertheless, it has become the centerpiece of the foreign policy and economic policy of Brian Mulroney and his government. The purpose of this paper is to assess (1) the evolution of trade policy so as to understand the emergence of this priority, (2) the performance of the Mulroney government in the setting of its objectives, the process of negotiations, and the content of the agreement achieved, and (3) the impact of the proposed free trade agreement for relations between Canada and the United States in the future.

EMERGENCE OF THE FREE TRADE INITIATIVE

Unlike some other matters of economic policy on the Mulroney agenda, free trade with the United States was not clearly foreshadowed in the election campaign, though closer relations with the United States were. Indeed in the preceding leadership campaign, Brian Mulroney had argued against the free trade proposal of one of his competitors — John Crosbie, who ironically has been named Canada's minister of international trade in the Mulroney cabinet, with the responsibility of selling free trade to the Canadian public.

However, the commitment of the Mulroney government to free trade is not a policy aberration. It is understandable in terms of the evolution of Canadian trade policy already underway under the previous Liberal government, and in terms of the philosophical preferences of the Mulroney cabinet.

103

Historically various Canadian governments have embarked with more or less seriousness on policies intended to diversify Canada's trade, and to lessen its trade concentration with the United States. The effort by the Diefenbaker government in the 1950s to shift 20 per cent of Canada's trade from the United States to the United Kingdom, and the Third Option policy (Department of External Affairs, 1972) of the Trudeau government in the early 1970s were examples. Despite these efforts, the proportion of Canada's trade conducted with the United States continued to increase, until by the mid 1980s over 70 per cent of Canada's trade was with the United States. It appeared that market opportunities coupled with the preferences of the Canadian business community made trade expansion more likely with the United States than with any other actual or potential trade partner.

At the same time, the Canadian government recognized the importance of trade to the Canadian economy, accounting for over 25 per cent of gross national product. A discussion paper released by the minister of state (international trade) in 1983 reviewed the threats and opportunities for Canadian trade policy in the coming decade, and suggested various initiatives to expand Canadian exports (Department of External Affairs, 1983). The section dealing with the management of trading relations with the United States comprised only six pages out of more than fifty, but soon came to be identified in the public mind as the major theme of the discussion paper. It identified the principal arguments for and against free trade with the United States, and suggested that free trade with the United States on a limited, sectoral basis in such areas as urban mass transit equipment or petrochemicals would not raise the more difficult issues posed by the full free trade option in the absence of a national consensus, and would be consistent with the gradual movement by successive Canadian governments towards free trade (Department of External Affairs, 1983: 45).

This idea of sectoral free trade was appealing to the responsible Canadian minister (Gerald Regan), and was seized upon by the U.S. government as a move in the direction opposite to the rising tide of protectionism. In 1984 a joint work program was agreed upon to examine the prospects for sectoral free trade in four areas — steel, urban transit equipment, agricultural equipment and inputs, and computer services and informatics. In succeeding months, consideration was given to additional possible sectors.

Canada raised the issue of petrochemicals, textiles and clothing, and beef and red meat, while the United States was interested in forest products, cosmetics, alcoholic beverages and furniture.

Though no formal negotiations took place, it became clear in the discussions that sectoral agreements were unlikely to be reached. For one thing, each government had different sectoral priorities. For another, in such arrangements, each sector would have to stand alone as mutually advantageous, with no possibility for tradeoffs across sectors such as would occur in the negotiation of a comprehensive package. Finally, there was concern that even if a sectoral agreement could be reached over the opposition of special interests, it would require approval of two-thirds of the members of the General Agreement on Tariffs and Trade (GATT), unlike a comprehensive free trade pact, because it would be contrary to GATT principles.

As the sectoral free trade discussions rapidly went nowhere, the 1984 election brought the Mulroney government to power. This government's approach to free trade was based on the experience and momentum of the sectoral free trade discussions, and also on a different philosophical assumption about the capability and confidence of the Canadian economy and society.

In a series of public statements shortly after the election, Mulroney and his ministers reiterated the theme of maturity and self-confidence. Secretary of state for external affairs Joe Clark in a speech stressed that because of confidence and accomplishment, Canadians were better able to stand on their own than ever before, and that closer economic relations with the United States could strengthen rather than weaken Canadian sovereignty and independence by helping to build the strong economy which builds respect and allows initiative.[1] Mulroney told a New York audience: "The maturity and self-confidence of our country make it possible for us now to confront issues in a realistic manner, and to examine options that a few years ago produced emotional reflexes that made rational discussion difficult. Nowhere is this more true than the subject of our bilateral relations with the United States."[2] The examination of options in that relationship was done by the new minister of international trade, James Kelleher, in a discussion paper released in January 1985.[3] He suggested that given the importance of the U.S. market for Canada, and the imposing battery of actual or potential barriers to Canadian exports, some form of bilateral trade agreement with the United States should be

105

seriously considered. Four possible options were proposed as a basis for public consultation and discussion:

— that Canada continue as it has in the past, through full exploitation of its rights under the GATT, and through lobbying and coalition building in the United States;

— that the two countries negotiate sectoral arrangements, or functional agreements on such issues as government procurement, subsidization and contingent protection;

— that Canada and the United States negotiate a comprehensive bilateral trade agreement to remove tariffs and non-tariff barriers on substantially all bilateral trade; and

— that a bilateral framework agreement be negotiated that would establish objectives for the improvement and expansion of trade relations, and that would create institutional mechanisms to examine trade issues, make recommendations to governments and resolve trade conflicts.

The discussion paper implicitly rejected the first option as inadequate, the second as unworkable, and the last as insufficiently secure and potentially diversionary. Without explicitly choosing among the options, the paper clearly favoured a comprehensive bilateral trade agreement.

Movement towards trade negotiations was accelerated by the Québec City Summit declaration on March 18, 1985, committing the two governments to reduce existing barriers to trade. The foreign policy green paper released on May 14, 1985, reaffirmed the goal of securing and enhancing access for Canadian exports to the U.S. market, and restated the four options of the Kelleher paper (Department of External Affairs, 1985). The Macdonald Commission report on September 5 as expected recommended a free trade agreement with the United States that would remove all tariffs between the two countries within ten years. The momentum was clearly building.

Finally on September 26, 1985, the die was cast, and Mulroney formally telephoned President Reagan to express Canada's interest in pursuing negotiations on the broadest possible package of mutually beneficial reductions in tariff and non-tariff barriers, and to ask him to explore with Congress their interest in pursuing such talks. Mulroney had gambled the future of his government, and indeed of the country, on the conviction that a closer economic relationship with the United States would yield economic and other benefits to Canada without threat to Canada's independence or interests (Leyton–Brown, 1985).

THE MULRONEY GOVERNMENT OBJECTIVES

The Mulroney government had two types of objectives in the free trade negotiations. The stated fundamental objectives were secure and enhanced access to the U.S. market. Subsidiary objectives ranged from job creation to the protection of Canadian culture and social programs. The unstated objectives were to enshrine certain domestic policy goals so as to bind future governments.

A study prepared in the Trade Negotiations Office at the outset of negotiations focused on the existing and threatened protectionist barriers in the United States (Department of External Affairs, 1986). While the detailed negotiating mandate is not publicly available, this document specifies certain Canadian negotiating objectives:

To secure Canada's market access through:

— new rules and procedures limiting the protectionist effect of trade remedy laws, i.e. exemption from measures aimed at others and a rigorous limitation on the degree and duration of measures which affect Canada; and

— clearer definition of countervailable financial assistance programs (i.e., subsidies) to industry, agriculture and fisheries so as to reduce the threat of countervailing duties.

To enhance Canada's market access through:

— more open entry to the U.S. federal and state government procurement markets; and

— broad trade liberalization, in an orderly manner, through the elimination of tariffs and quotas to be achieved over a reasonable period of time with adequate adjustment transition provisions. Current barriers inhibit full Canadian industry participation in the North American market and in this way prevent Canadian companies from achieving the efficient large-scale production that could enable them to compete

107

more effectively in U.S. markets and other markets around the world.

To enshrine Canada's market access through:

— a strong dispute settlement mechanism to reduce the disparities in size and power and to provide fair, expeditious and conclusive solutions to differences of view and practice;

— institutional and other provisions that maintain Canadian independence of action in areas of national endeavour; and

— a treaty or congressional-executive agreement to enshrine our mutual obligations and accommodate differences in the two government systems (Department of External Affairs, 1986: 3–4).

It is important to note that the language was carefully chosen to specify that, despite public expectations to the contrary, the negotiating objective was limitation on, not exemption from, U.S. trade remedies (apart from safeguard measures aimed at others — the "sideswipe" phenomenon), and a strong (though not explicitly binding) dispute settlement mechanism.

The unstated objectives are harder to specify. They involve the desire to restrict the scope for government intervention and regulation in the economy and to give freer play to market forces. The free trade agreement was used as a device to prevent future governments from retreating from the policy positions preferred and adopted by the Mulroney government on such matters as the open access of foreign investment, and the market determination of energy prices.

THE FREE TRADE NEGOTIATIONS

In pursuit of these objectives, the Mulroney government was remarkably well organized. On no other policy issue was so much official expertise and political oversight deployed, and so much federal–provincial and private sector consultations pursued. The government knew what it wanted, and the current state of negotiations, throughout the process.

Within the bureaucracy, a Trade Negotiations Office (TNO) was created apart from the existing departmental structure. Rather than appoint a serving diplomat or civil servant as chief negotiator, the government turned to Simon Reisman, a retired deputy minister and former negotiator of the Auto Pact. Extensive interdepartmental consultations and working groups ensured bureaucratic coordination, but the activity was clearly centered in the TNO.

At a political level, a special cabinet committee oversaw the content and conduct of the negotiations. This was perhaps the most unusual feature of the decision process, maintaining an unprecedented degree of protracted and concentrated cabinet attention on a single policy issue throughout its development.

Consultation with the private sector was undertaken through the mechanism of the International Trade Advisory Committee (ITAC), which dealt with broad national issues relating to international trade access and marketing matters, and through fifteen Sectoral Advisory Groups on International Trade (SAGIT) to provide a two-way flow of advice and information on sectoral trade matters. Though most major labour organizations like the Canadian Labour Congress refused to take part, these consultations were widely based and useful to the negotiating process.

One of the priorities of the Mulroney government was to bring an atmosphere of reconciliation to federal–provincial relations, and the free trade negotiations were approached in that spirit. At the Halifax First Ministers' Meeting on November 29, 1985, Mulroney promised full provincial participation in the free trade negotiations (without specifying what that meant), though some provincial governments wanted to participate actively in the negotiations themselves, or to have the negotiators operate under the direct instructions and control of the eleven first ministers. These positions were unacceptable to the federal government, but eventually a compromise process was agreed upon. The negotiating mandate was approved at a first ministers meeting, and it was agreed that the first ministers would meet every three months to review the progress of the negotiations. In addition there were continuing meetings of trade representatives and other officials (just about every month), and meetings of designated ministers as required. The provincial governments were kept fully informed through these collective as well as bilateral channels, of all developments throughout the negotiations — as one TNO official said: "The provinces know as much of what is going on as any cabinet minister knows."

THE FREE TRADE AGREEMENT

To assess the content of the FTA, one must first consider how well it achieved the objectives of secure and enhanced access to the U.S. market set for the negotiations. Then it will be possible to assess the deal in certain specific areas of controversy.

In the area of enhanced access, there was a significant gain. Despite the fact that 80 per cent of Canadian exports to the United States currently enter duty free, and a further 15 per cent face tariffs of only 5 per cent or less, tariffs still posed substantial barriers of 15 per cent or more in certain industries like petrochemicals, rolling stock and clothing. The FTA, in perhaps its most notable achievement, provides that all tariffs on all trade between Canada and the United States will be progressively eliminated, depending on the item, by 1989, 1993 or 1998. For some observers, this is the key provision of the agreement, from which Canadian business can hope to derive the economies of scale associated with access to a market of 250 million people which will result in continental and international competitiveness.

Access was also enhanced in a variety of other less dramatic ways hidden in the fine print of the agreement.[4] These include the elimination of U.S. customs user fees, the shielding of energy exports from countervailing duty actions, and the recognition of Canadian whiskey as a distinct product only manufactured in Canada.

However in one important area the enhanced access was far less than had been hoped for. The FTA increases the amount of government procurement open for competition between Canadian and U.S. suppliers in each other's market, but not to the desired extent. In particular, large areas of defence procurement and state government procurement remain closed to Canadians.

With regard to security of access, the success is also mixed. The rise of protectionist pressures in the United States was a powerful motivation for the initiation of the free trade negotiations, and for many Canadians, security of the existing access to the U.S. market was a higher priority than enhancement of that access. Certainly from the perspective of future investment which will provide the "jobs, jobs, jobs" which Mulroney says will flow from the FTA, secure access to the U.S. market is more likely to lead to investment in Canada, while insecurity of access virtually guarantees a greater degree of investment and plant location in the United States rather than in Canada by both foreign and Canadian firms.

Most importantly, Canada was virtually exempted from emergency action to remedy serious injury to U.S. industry caused by surges of imports. When these safeguard actions are aimed at other countries (the sideswipe effect), Canada will be excluded unless imports from it are substantial (i.e. greater than 5–10 per cent) and contribute substantially to the serious injury. If Canadian imports are included in the action because these conditions are met, then there is a limit on the severity of action that may be taken. Imports from Canada may not be restricted below the trend of imports over a reasonable recent base period with an allowance for growth. Thus the insecurity associated with safeguard and escape clause action has been reduced to a minimal level.

A greater source of insecurity was the threat of antidumping or countervailing duty (ADCVD) actions against imports from Canada. Canadian exporters were understandably frightened by the softwood lumber case in 1986, when exports of almost $4 billion a year were threatened with the application of a countervailing duty because of alleged subsidization through stumpage fees set by provincial governments, despite the fact that a similar case just three years earlier had found that no subsidization under U.S. trade law existed (Leyton-Brown, 1987). In this case the Canadian government negotiated a settlement involving a Canadian export tax rather than a U.S. countervailing duty, in order to keep the revenues in Canada, but the lesson was clear — Canadian exports were at jeopardy because of the U.S. proclivity to reinterpret unilaterally its trade laws and its definition of subsidies. Any Canadian export could be next. Canadian negotiators wanted an agreed set of rules defining countervailable subsidies, and a mechanism to apply those rules fairly, without the politicization and unpredictability to which the U.S. trade law system was prone.

Canada didn't get an exemption from U.S. ADCVD laws, but then that was never really the objective. Nor did Canada get what it really did want — an agreed set of new rules to govern ADCVD practices. The FTA however does provide for ongoing negotiations over the next five to seven years to try to achieve such a code. Finally, Canada did not get a binational tribunal to adjudicate ADCVD cases. What it did get was a binational review panel to ensure that the decisions rendered by national tribunals were in keeping with that country's domestic law. That means that after a final determination has been handed down by U.S. authorities (the International Trade Commission, and the International Trade Administration of the Department of Commerce), then the Canadian government may appeal that determination not to a U.S. court, but to the binational review panel.

Supporters of this provision of the FTA argue that the expectation of this review will deter publicization of the ADCVD process, and ensure that laws are interpreted fairly. They contend that if this process had been in effect at the time, the 1986 softwood lumber case would not have resulted in a determination of subsidization. Nevertheless, this review panel addresses only problems in the application of U.S. trade law (and then only after the fact), and not problems with the law itself.

Another aspect of the FTA addresses the difficulty of unilateral U.S. determination of the rules by which ADCVD practices are to be considered, and especially of changes in the rules to alter the outcome of previously decided cases. Once the FTA comes into effect, the United States will still be able to amend its ADCVD laws, but such changes will apply to Canada only if that is specified in the legislation, if Canada is notified of the proposed changes and has the opportunity for prior consultations, and if the changes are consistent with the GATT codes on anti-dumping and subsidies and with the object and purpose of the FTA.

To resolve disputes over ADCVD cases, other trade remedy actions, and any other matters arising under the FTA, Canada sought the establishment of a dispute settlement mechanism. A dispute settlement procedure for ADCVD cases as described briefly above was one of the sticking points in the negotiations, resolved only at the eleventh hour.

A complex and interconnected set of mechanisms and procedures was created by the FTA to avoid trade disputes, and to resolve those that cannot be avoided. These included general dispute settlement provisions and two special procedures for ADCVD cases and for safeguards cases. Four different types of dispute settlement mechanisms were created a high level political body to oversee the implementation of the agreement; binding review for ADCVD cases; binding arbitration (either compulsory or mutually agreed in different circumstances); and expert panels to make recommendations. In some important ways these mechanisms fall short of what was sought, and indeed of what is objectively

112

desirable, but in the aggregate they provide a greater degree of security of access to the U.S. market than is the current situation.

Of course the FTA includes more than just the realization of these Canadian objectives. While it will not be possible here to explore all of the detailed provisions of the 304 page agreement, it is instructive to look at some of the most prominent and controversial additional features. Specifically, attention will be paid to the energy provisions, and to the innovative treatment of investment and services.

The energy chapter bears close scrutiny because of the widely differing interpretations of it within Canada and between Canada and the United States. Clayton Yeutter, the U.S. Trade Representative, has referred to this section as the "jewel of the agreement." Simon Reisman, the chief Canadian negotiator, has said that this chapter is one of the two (the other being automobiles) that he is proudest of as a great deal for Canada. How can they both be right? Clearly they are making different assumptions about future developments in the energy sector, and in consequence come to different conclusions about what matters.

Canadian energy exports are guaranteed unrestricted access to the United States under the FTA, including exports of uranium for enrichment. Since for all but the last 15 years the problem of Canadian energy trade has been to gain greater access to the U.S. market in the face of a variety of quotas and other restrictions, this guarantee of uninterrupted access is the culmination of a historic quest. With the world currently facing a hydrocarbon glut, and the prospect of additional sources of supply coming on stream, supporters of the agreement welcome the market access guaranteed in the FTA, especially for non-hydrocarbon exports such as electricity or uranium.

Others anticipate a world of supply shortages rather than surpluses. Americans among them welcome the guarantee of access to Canadian energy supplies in times of shortage, while Canadians regret the inability to reserve scarce Canadian supplies for Canadian consumption. The FTA provides that in the event of supply shortages and the imposition of production or export restrictions by the Canadian government, Canada must still make available to the United States the same proportion of total production that it had imported during the previous 36 months. Some see this provision as nothing more than the commitment already made under the terms of the International Energy Agreement, but others see it as a massive concession to the United States, denying Canada control over its own resources in time of need.

Another controversial energy issue is the prohibition of a differential export price of energy products higher than the domestic price. Canada will no longer be able to reintroduce some version of the National Energy Program, using a Canadian energy price below world prices as a tool of industrial policy. Here the unstated objectives of the Mulroney government become evident. Once in effect, the FTA will require Canada to adhere to a system of market determination of energy prices. The Mulroney government has willingly pursued such a policy since its election in 1984. It has used the FTA to require all successor governments to be bound by the same policy whether they wish it so or not.

Something similar can be seen in the pathbreaking commitments regarding investment and trade in services. The FTA is the first international agreement to establish obligations in these areas, and it was a priority for the United States in the negotiations to create a precedent which could serve as a model for the ongoing Uruguay Round of multilateral trade negotiations. New principles have been declared in the FTA, but they have not been imposed on Canada by U.S. negotiators. Rather they were embraced by the Mulroney government as affirming and perpetuating policy directions they favour.

The Mulroney government came to office determined to end the discouragement of foreign investment represented by the Foreign Investment Review Agency (FIRA), and to declare Canada "open for business." FIRA was replaced by Investment Canada, with the mission of attracting new foreign investment as a source of jobs and economic growth. The FTA prevents any future Canadian government from moving back in the direction of greater review and control of foreign investment by phasing out review of indirect acquisitions (where one foreign owner sells to another), and by raising the threshold for review of direct acquisitions to $150 million by 1992. Furthermore, the FTA guarantees national treatment of foreign investment once established. In these ways, the FTA can be seen as a legacy of the Mulroney government left for succeeding generations.

The FTA does not however represent a complete renunciation of Canadian investment policy. Investment review is explicitly preserved in sensitive sectors such as oil and gas, uranium, and culture. What is more, for the first time ever, the U.S. government

114

has accepted the legitimacy of another government's review of foreign investment. Similarly, while the FTA limits the ability of the Canadian government to impose certain investment-related performance requirements which affect bilateral trade, the U.S. government for the first time explicitly accepted the legitimacy of other types of performance requirements.

The provisions regarding trade in services also enshrines market principles of right of establishment and national treatment which are favoured by both the U.S. and Mulroney governments.

A final assessment of the worth of the FTA rests on the assumptions made about the nature and future of Canada. The domestic debate about the FTA does not fundamentally address questions about the economic benefits and costs of the reduction of trade barriers, or even the broad questions of enhanced and secure access to the U.S. market. Rather it addresses the question of the relationship between government intervention and the market, and the kind of country Canadians want for the future.

The Mulroney vision given form by the FTA is of an expansion of wealth, economic growth and jobs, resulting from the widest possible play of market forces in a market of 250 million people. Under these assumptions, the enhanced and secure access to the U.S. market represented by the FTA will reduce the incentive for business to move to the United States, thus resulting in more investment in Canada, and will produce the economies of scale necessary for competitiveness in the world economy. However, a full understanding of the implications of the FTA requires the realization that the vision underlying it also entails the commitment of Canada to a course compatible with the philosophical agenda of the Mulroney government.

FUTURE CANADA–U.S. RELATIONS

The most vital but most speculative questions concerning the FTA are about the future of the relationship between the two countries. The text of the FTA alone is an insufficient basis on which to try to answer these questions. Two among the many such questions will be addressed here how symmetrical will be the obligations and constraints, and how likely is it that the FTA will result in irresistible pressures for the harmonization of Canadian policies with those of the United States, and thus the eventual erosion of

Canadian distinctiveness and independence?

The FTA presumes equivalence of the obligations on the parties, such as the requirement for prior notification of proposed changes to legislation affecting the other country. However the differences between the political systems of the two countries suggest that there may be a much greater constraint on a parliamentary system than a system of separation of powers. In the Canadian system, and legislation enacted into law is an emanation of government policy, and as such is long prepared. It will be possible for a Canadian government to notify its counterpart in the United States of its legislative intentions, and accordingly it will be expected to do so. By contrast, much legislation in the United States system results from legislative-executive interaction, and may take its final form only very late in the process. Even if the U.S. Administration notified Canada of its intentions, those intentions may never come to fruition, or may be substantially altered in the legislative process. It is much less possible for a U.S. government to notify its counterpart of its legislative intentions, and accordingly it is less likely to do so. These structural differences, of political system rather than of size, may lead to an asymmetry in the effective operation of the agreement.

Of greatest importance is the question of future harmonization of policy between the two countries. The Canadian government of the day rejected the Second Option of closer economic integration with the United States in 1972, largely because of the conviction that economic integration would inevitably lead to political union (Department of External Affairs, 1972). Mitchell Sharp, the minister responsible for that paper still holds to that view today, as do many others.

A case can readily be made that under the FTA, with free movement of goods between the two countries, investment decisions will be made to minimize costs of production. If firms face higher tax costs in Canada (to finance Canadian social and cultural programs), then many of them are likely to choose to supply the same market from lower cost production locations in the United States. Knowing that, Canadian governments are likely to feel under pressure to change their policies so as to equalize the costs of production, and hence the incentives and disincentives to invest. Of course such cost differentials are supposed to be offset by a lower exchange rate, but there will surely be political pressure to keep the Canadian dollar from falling rather than rising against the U.S.

dollar. The long term result could be expected to be a progressive harmonization of policy.

Nonetheless, it can also be argued that the harmonization pressures are already manifest. The present degree of insecurity about continued access to the U.S. market has itself been a powerful incentive for investment in the United States. Indeed many large Canadian companies have considered it necessary to establish U.S. affiliates rather than to export to the United States, and Canadian investment in the United States is increasing much more rapidly than U.S investment in Canada. The FTA should diminish that incentive to move capital to the United States.

The most important question, however, is whether the degree of harmonization of policy between Canada and the United States will be any different twenty years from now as a result of the FTA than it would have been in the absence of the FTA. That question is of course unanswerable, but it separates critics of the agreement who fear the extinction of the Canadian identity from advocates of the agreement who predict a stronger and more vital Canada as a result (and perhaps from the skeptics who think it doesn't make any difference because the harmonization tide is irreversible in any event). It may be that consciousness of the concept of harmonization, like consciousness of the concept of spillover in the history of Western European integration, can serve to sensitize the Canadian government and public to a danger to be delayed and controlled. At the least, harmonization can be made deliberate and agreeable.

NOTES

1 Joe Clark, address to the Strategic Planning Forum, Ottawa, October 25, 1984.
2 Brian Mulroney, address to the Economic Club of New York, December 10, 1984.
3 *How to Secure and Enhance Canadian Access to Export Markets*, (Ottawa: Government of Canada, 1985).
4 Nineteen different increases in Canadian access are identified by Richard Lipsey (1988).

REFERENCES

Department of External Affairs (1972). "Canada–U.S. Relations: Options for the Future," *International Perspectives*.

Department of External Affairs (1983). *Canadian Trade Policy for the 1980's*, (Ottawa: Minister of Supply and Services).

Department of External Affairs (1985). *Competitiveness and Security: Directions for Canada's International Relations*, (Ottawa: Minister of Supply and Services).

Department of External Affairs (1986). *Canadian Trade Negotiations*, (Ottawa: Minister of Supply and Services).

Leyton-Brown, David (1985). "The Mulroney Gamble," *International Perspectives*, September–October.

Leyton-Brown, David (1987). "The Political Economy of Canada-U.S. Relations," in B.W. Tomlin and M.A. Molot (eds.), *Canada Among Nations 1986: Talking Trade*, (Toronto: James Lorimer).

Lipsey, Richard (1988). "The Free Trade Agreement in Context." A paper presented at the National Conference on the Free Trade Agreement, Osgoode Hall Law School, York University, March 17–19.

Privatization and the Mulroney Government, 1984–1988

W.T. STANBURY

INTRODUCTION

This chapter focuses on the privatization efforts of the Mulroney Government from September 1984 to mid-April 1988. Its approach to privatization has largely taken the form of selling Crown corporations and equity interests in mixed enterprises to private investors.

Privatization on a notable scale has occurred in the past few years in countries from Austria to Zaire.[1] It has been initiated by governments of all ideological bents, although the most extensive program has been carried out by the right-wing government of Margaret Thatcher in the U.K. (Yarrow and Vickers, 1987).[2] It would be quite wrong, however, to assume that the privatization activities of the Mulroney Government are only a sympathetic vibration to a set of forces that are exogenous to Canada. As described below, when they formed a minority government in 1979–80 the Tories proposed to sell several commercial Crown corporations including Petro-Canada. Moreover, the dozen privatizations by the Mulroney government have been accompanied by a variety of other actions designed to make public enterprises more efficient and commercially oriented. At the same time, several provincial governments — notably Quebec, B.C., Saskatchewan, Ontario and Manitoba have sold off some 23 Crown corporations or equity interests in mixed enterprises from 1983 to April 1988 (Stanbury, 1988). The Mulroney Government also came to office after more than a score of studies and reports on Crown corporations over the previous decade raised serious questions about their control and accountability, management, financing, and competitive behaviour. All of this was reinforced by the fact the federal government poured $2.6 billion into Canadair and de Havilland between 1982–83 and 1985–86 (Baumann, 1987), and the Trudeau government wrote off $1.35 billion of Canadair debt in 1982 (Borins & Boothman, 1986: 126). In short, Canada's love affair with public enterprise had soured.

Privatization — even on a modest scale — is of particular importance in Canada because the nation has aptly been described as a "public enterprise country" in contradistinction to the U.S., the quintessential private enterprise country (Hardin, 1974). Factually and mythically, the concept of public enterprise is deeply embedded in the fabric of Canadian society. When the Mulroney government came to power, five of the 100 largest non-financial enterprises ranked by revenues and 11 of those ranked from 101 to 400 were federal Crown corporations. Five of the 50 largest financial enterprises ranked by revenue were federal Crowns (Stanbury, 1986: 66).

The broadest concept of privatization consists of any effort designed to strengthen the role of the market at the expense of the state. This concept, therefore, includes: contracting out government services; shifting from compulsory taxation to a voluntary, user-pay approach to public services; and deregulation in total or in part (particularly the removal of direct or economic regulation). Simply selling off Crown corporations or equity interests to private investors is obviously a narrower definition. It may be done by shifting from 100% government ownership to 100% private ownership, either by sale or by giving away the shares. This may involve "reprivatization" or selling off firms that were formerly privately owned, e.g., Nordair, de Havilland, Canadair. Alternatively, a Crown corporation can become a mixed enterprise in which the government keeps a minority interest or even retains legal control after selling shares to private investors.

NUMBER, SIZE AND SCOPE OF
FEDERAL PUBLIC ENTERPRISES

The Economic Council (1986: 7) indicates that as of the end of 1985 there were 56 parent and 81 subsidiary corporations owned or effectively controlled by the federal government. (Provincial governments owned or controlled 203 parent and 187 subsidiary corporations.) Earlier estimates, which included all federal Crowns, ranged from 306 to 464 government enterprises including subsidiaries.[3]

Official federal figures as of mid-1984 for 57 parent Crowns, their 134 wholly owned subsidiaries, and investments in another 126 companies put their total assets at $77 billion.[4] Fifty parent Crowns were classified as "commercial" enterprises; their assets totalled $49 billion and they had 193,600 employees.[5] Canada Mortgage and Housing had the largest assets with $10.5 billion. The CNR was the largest employer (63,496), while Canada Post employed 62,000 persons. The seven largest non-commercial Crowns had assets of $26.5 billion.

In 1983, 1984 and 1985 at least 17 federal Crown corporations were sufficiently large to rank among the 500 largest non-financial enterprises in Canada (Stanbury, 1988). Six of the 100 largest financial enterprises in Canada in 1983, 1984 and 1985 (measured by assets, but excluding insurance companies) were federal Crown corporations.

Elford and Stanbury (1986: 280) found that the federal government had investments in 92 "first order" mixed enterprises in 1983 and that provincial governments had investments in 167. Subsidiaries or sub-subsidiaries of these mixed enterprises added 34 and 29 investments respectively. In 34 of the total of 126 mixed enterprises, the federal government had legal control, i.e., at least 51% of the voting shares. A handful of these enterprises were in the *Financial Post 500* (Elford & Stanbury, 1986: 280).

EVOLUTION OF THE TORIES PRIVATIZATION POLICY

The Mulroney Government's privatization policy can be traced back directly to the fairly ambitious privatization plans of the short-lived Clark Government of 1979–80.

The Clark Government: In the 1979 election campaign the Conservatives announced that they would privatize Petro-Canada. During the campaign Petro-Canada spent another $800 million to acquire the remaining 52% of Pacific Petroleum it had not acquired in November 1978. Some said this move was designed to make it more difficult for the Tories to privatize the rapidly growing Crown corporation. The task force appointed by the Clark government recommended that Petro-Canada be split into two parts: a profit-oriented, largely privately-owned company; and a government agency focusing on "non-commercial activities" as part of federal energy policy (frontier exploration and high technology development). The former part would be privatized by distributing the shares for free to citizens as had been done for British Columbia Resources Investment Corporation (BCRIC) in 1979 (see Ohashi, 1980). When the government's policy was revealed on the campaign trail in early 1980 it was not well received by the media or the electorate. Peter Foster (1982: 115) has called it a "Frankenstein-monster stitched together from ill-fitting limbs of public policy, political expediency, and a rump of obeisance to the market." The Crown corporation was to be bigger, not smaller! "It would be publicly traded, with half it shares given away, another 20% sold and the remaining 30% held by the government." Under contract, this large mixed enterprise would handle the government's nation-to-nation oil trade, non-commercial frontier exploration and undertake special research and development activities.

During its 259 days in office the Clark Government proposed to sell off several other Crown corporations. Early in September 1979 it announced that a task force had been formed to examine the role of Canada Mortgage and Housing Corp. to determine what aspects of its activities could be placed in the hands of private developers.[6]

The president of the Treasury Board, Sinclair Stevens, announced on September 13, 1979 that "at least five other Crown corporations" would be sold off.[7] They were Canadair Ltd. (a maker of executive jets and aero engines), de Havilland Aircraft (a manufacturer of smaller aircraft including the highly regarded Dash 7 turboprop), Eldorado Nuclear Ltd. (uranium mining and refiner), Canadian Commercial Corporation (a go-between in trade deals between Ottawa and foreign governments), and Defence Construction Ltd. (a builder for the Department of National Defence). Both Air Canada and Canadian National Railways were described as candidates for privatization, but the government claimed they were too big to sell off.

The Clark Government announced in November 1979 that it proposed to reduce its majority holding in the Canada Development Corporation to less than 50% and to encourage the company to take over some of the Crown corporations it had put up for sale.[8] Between 1971 and 1975 Ottawa had invested $322 million in the CDC and 1979 the CDC had assets of $2.5 billion and revenues of $2.0 billion.

Before it was able to sell off any Crown corporations, the Clark Government was defeated on a want-of-confidence motion on its budget in December 1979. The Liberals under Pierre Trudeau won the election[9] and they had little interest in privatization. While they promised to sell the federal government's 48.5% interest in CDC[10] and did sell its 86.4% interest in Nordair, the fourth largest airline, for $31.8 million,[11] the Liberals were preoccupied with bailing out de Havilland and Canadair. They absorbed well over $2 billion of taxpayers money in the early 1980s. The Liberals also established a new Crown corporation, Canada Development Investment Corporation (CDIC), to act as a holding and management company for several Crowns.[12]

Leadership Campaign: Columnist Michael Valpy noted that most candidates for leadership of the Conservative Party in 1983, except Brian Mulroney, "talked much about privatizing public enterprises."[13] Michael Wilson, for example, proposed to sell of a number of Crown corporations, including Air Canada, the CNR, Teleglobe Canada, and Eldorado Nuclear Ltd.[14] In his view, once a Crown corporation ceases to have a public policy function it should be sold to the private sector. All leadership candidates called for stronger accountability to and control by parliament and criticized the Liberals' new Crown, the CDIC.

Valpy suggested that the Tories, before they came to power, were developing an ideology in respect of Crown corporations that was quite distinct from the Liberals. It was seen to have two components: "First, a rejection of the general notion that public enterprise should be used to achieve public policy ends. Second, there (was) a hardening belief that government, in a major way, should divest itself of state enterprise who no longer demonstrably serves public policy ends."[15] It is the latter that became the core of the Tories rationale for divesting Crown corporations.

Task Force: A few months after he was elected leader of the

Progressive Conservative Party in March 1983, Brian Mulroney set up a task force to study federal Crown corporations with a view to identifying candidates for privatization (Gracey, 1985). The co-chairmen were Senator Bill Kelly and John Thomson,[16] MP for Calgary-South. Its members consisted of an MP, three individuals from the private sector, and a former senior public servant, Don Gracey who had worked for several years on policy papers dealing with Crown Corporations.[17] The task force reviewed 115 government owned or controlled corporations, prepared a list of privatization candidates, and designed divestiture strategies. Its report was given to Mr. Mulroney in May 1984. The report was supposed to form the basis of government policy after the Tories came to power, as did the work of Pat Carney on energy policy while in Opposition. While the latter was highly successful (Toner, 1986), the privatization task force report was kept secret by the Prime Minister.[18] It was not given to key cabinet ministers until early November 1984. This was after Sinclair Stevens launched the Tories privatization program on October 30, 1984 with the announcement that the holdings of CDIC were for sale.

The 1984 Election Campaign: Barbara McDougall (1987b: 4), who was Minister of State for Privatization from June 1986 to March 31, 1988, has claimed that "privatization became an integral part of our 1984 election platform." Her memory is imperfect. For example, privatization was not mentioned in the material prepared for all Tory candidates by the Party. Privatization was not an issue in the 1984 campaign as measured by visibility in the media. Frizzell & Westell (1985: 56–57) clipped every item dealing with the election in seven major daily newspapers during the 57 days of the campaign (about 15,000 column inches each, about 80% of which consisted of news stories). Of the 5609 items, a policy issue was the main topic in 1459, and 631 it was a secondary topic.[19] Privatization was not among the 14 issues identified in the analysis. The issues, which in order of importance, included: the economy, 21.5%; national unity, 15.0%; Peace/defence, 11.5%; women's rights, 11.2%; patronage, 10.4%; unemployment, 6.9%; tax reform, 5.4%; energy, 4.2%; social, 4.2%; and change in Ottawa, 3.8% (Frizzell & Westell, 1985: 62). The ranking of issues as a secondary topic was very similar to their ranking as a main topic. It should be evident, therefore, that even if privatization was part of the Tories platform as Ms. McDougall has claimed, it was hardly an issue.[20]

Michael Prince (1986: 7–8) argues very cogently that the Tories election mandate was for a change in the approach of government to making public policy (i.e., process and style), but that the election "did not, however, produce a clear policy mandate for the Conservatives to enact." He notes that in 1984, "policy issues were not important or helpful in distinguishing between the Conservative and Liberal parties. Both parties endeavoured to hug the centre of the political spectrum and evade controversial policy substance." Frizzell and Westell (1985: 103) remark that the Conservative campaign was ambiguous, it "combined the rhetoric of conservatism with a promise to maintain and even improve essential public services."

FEDERAL PRIVATIZATION EFFORTS, 1984–1988

Between September 1984 and April 1988 the Mulroney Government completed 12 privatizations. (On April 12, 1988 the government announced that Air Canada will be privatized in stages. This development is discussed in Section 8.) As table 1 illustrates, nine of the privatizations completed so far were Crown corporations (#1, 3, 4, 5, 8, 9, 10) or parts of Crown corporations (#7, 12); the others consisted of equity interests in mixed enterprises: Canada Development Corporation (48.2%), Fisheries Products International (62.6%) and Nanisivik Mines (18%). One of the sales (Northern Canada Power) is not a privatization as the buyer was another government, namely the Yukon Territory. The largest federal privatization, in terms of its selling price, was Teleglobe Canada which has a monopoly on the provision of telecommunications services between Canada and countries outside North America.[21] Teleglobe, reflecting its previous profitability and the fact it will have a legal monopoly for five years, fetched over $600 million for the federal government. This amount included a special cash dividend of $106 million issued just prior to the closing of the deal. In 1986 Teleglobe had operating revenues of $274 million (i.e., excluding other carriers share of gross revenues) and some $502 million in assets. What was an unregulated *de facto* monopoly owned by the federal government became a legal monopoly (for 5 years) subject to the regulation of the CRTC.

The largest enterprise among the federal privatizations is the Canada Development Corporation. It started as a Crown corporation in 1971, but later became a mixed enterprise when the government began selling shares to the public. In three batches, between 1985 and 1987, the government sold its 48.2% interest for a total of $377 million. The bulk of the shares were sold in a two-stage process in September 1985 and September 1986 in which buyers paid one-half down and the balance a year later.[22] In December 1987, CDC was renamed Polysar Energy & Chemical Corp.

The implementation of the first sell-off by the Tories, Northern Transportation, was, in fact, initiated by the Liberals in March 1984. The Liberals also said in 1982 that they planned to sell the government's shares in CDC.

By far the most controversial federal privatization was the sale of de Havilland to Boeing announced in December 1985 and completed two months later. The sale aroused the ire of nationalists, the two opposition parties and the friends of an activist government industrial policy to create jobs in hi-tech industries.[23] The sale of Canadair to Bombardier, a Canadian company based in Quebec, 11 months later caused much less fuss, in part, because the Tories did a better job of explaining and justifying the sale.[24]

Several other points should be noted about the federal privatizations listed in Table 1. First, several of the deals are small whether measured by the revenue of the enterprise sold or the selling price. Pecheries Canada, Nanisivik Mines (18% interest), Northern Canada Power, and Northern Transportation had sales of only $16 million, $26 million, $19 million and $41 million respectively. These are hardly important enterprises in economic terms. Their collective revenues were less than Canada Post's deficit in 1986–1987 ($129 million).

Second, even the larger privatizations such as de Havilland, Canadair and Teleglobe are well down the list of the largest federal Crowns. De Havilland ranked #255 on the *Financial Post 500* in 1985, while Canadair ranked #189 and Teleglobe, if it had been on the list, would have ranked #280. In 1986 there were seven federal commercial Crowns larger than Canadair, the largest federal firm privatized so far (other than the CDC, a mixed enterprise).

The CDC was something of an anomaly. While the federal government had 48.2% of the voting shares, it manifestly was not able to exercise control over the firm since 1981.[25] In 1985 CDC ranked #28 on the FP 500. In 1986 it ranked #34 after some downsizing (see Olive, 1985). The sale of the CDC shares amounts to something quite different than selling true Crowns such as Canadair, de Havilland or Teleglobe.

126

TABLE 1

Data on Federal Privatizations Completed by the Mulroney Government

Crown Corp./ Asset Sold	Revenues ($mill)	Year[1]	Assets ($mill.)	Employ- ment	Price ($mill.)
Northern Trans- portation (July 15/85)	41	1984	75	389 (1985)	27
Canada Development Corp. (48.2%) (Sept 16/85, Sept. 16/86, June 5/87 Oct. 8/87)	3,257	1985	7,259	17,808	377
de Havilland (Jan 31/86)	300	1985	346	4,405	90 +65 in notes[3]
Pecheries Canada	16	1985	16	575	5
Canadian Arsenals (May 9/86)	103	1985	126	879	92
Nanisivik Mines (18%) (Oct. 28/86)	26	1986	65	195	6
CN Route (1986)	145	1985	40	2,227	29
Canadair (Dec. 23/86)	451	1985	478	5,431 (1986)	205[2]
Northern Canada Power (Mar. 31/87)	19	1986/87	146	34	20 +56 in notes
Teleglobe Canada (March 31/87)	274	1986	502	·1,110	488 +106 dividend +17 redeem prefd.
Fisheries Products Int (62.6%) (April 15/87)	387	1986	224	8,650	104
CN Hotels (Jan. 29/88)[6]	147	1986	161[5]	3,400	264
Total excluding CDC	1,909		2,179	27,295	1,510 (1575)[4]
Total including CDC	5,166		9,438	45,103	1886 (1952)[4]

1. Year for the revenue, asset, employment data.
2. Estimate present value, based on $120 million in cash plus an estimated $173 million in royalties on future sales plus $3 million special dividend plus undisclosed proceeds of a lawsuit plus 1% royal- ty on CF–18 systems engineering contract.
3. The notes are forgiven at the rate of $1 for each $5 of purchases by the buyer for purposes unre- lated to their activities at the time of sale.
4. Including $65 million in notes for de Havilland.
5. Based on value of properties at cost less depreciation — underestimate of total assets
6. Date of public announcement.

Sources: Stanbury (1988)

Third, if we exclude the CDC as a special case, the revenues of the other 11 firms privatized amounted to $1.9 billion. This is much smaller than the revenues of the fifth largest federal Crown, Air Canada, which had revenues of $2.9 billion in 1986.

Excluding the CDC, the 11 federal privatizations disposed of $2.2 billion in assets (at book value). Three sales (de Havilland, Canadair and Teleglobe) accounted for 61% of all assets sold. The $2.2 billion figure should be contrasted to the size of the five largest Crowns ranked by assets as of March 1987: CMHC, $9,588 million; Petro-Canada, 8,329; CNR, 7,806; Export Development Corp., 7,156; and Canadian Wheat Board, 4,583. This list omits Air Canada ($2,923 million assets at the end of 1986) and Canada Post ($2,451 million).[26] In other words, the assets of the five largest federal Crowns are over 17 times the assets privatized to the end of 1987 (excluding the special case of the CDC with assets of $6,324 million in 1986).

Fourth, until it sold Canadair at the end of 1986,[27] the value of assets sold by the federal government was less than the $886 million purchase of Gulf Canada's assets by Petro-Canada in August 1985.[28] Excluding the CDC, the expansion of Crown assets offset 41% of the value of assets sold to the private sector by the Mulroney Government to April 1988.

Fifth, in its privatizations to date the federal government has shown a marked preference for outright sales to a single buyer. Of the 12 deals, only two (CDC and FPI) have involved the wide distribution of shares to the public. (Note that Air Canada is to be sold through wide distribution to private investors — see below) The dominance of the single buyer method may reflect the smaller size of the transactions so far and the particular firms involved. However, one wonders why Teleglobe was not sold as a wide-distribution public offering. Bell Canada Enterprises (#4 on the FP 500 for 1986), which owns Bell Canada, the largest telephone company in Canada, may well have considerable influence over Teleglobe through its approximately one-third ownership of Memotec Data Inc., which owns Teleglobe.[29]

Five of the twelve federal privatizations involved firms that were previously owned: de Havilland, Pêcheries Canada, Canadian Arsenals, Canadair, and Fisheries Products International. With the exception of Canadian Arsenals these firms were created to take over failing private firms (Pêcheries Canada, Fisheries Products International), or to acquire companies from foreign owners anxious to shut down their Canadian operations (Canadair, de Havilland).

Seventh, Table 1 does not include the incremental privatization of part of its activities by Canada Post Corporation (CPC) which became a Crown corporation in 1981. It is the nation's sixth largest Crown corporation and 29th largest non-financial enterprise.[30] Canada Post proposed to establish 50 retail franchises in major cities in 1987, but only four were opened by September. In addition, over the next decade Canada Post plans to convert some 3500 rural post offices to franchise operations and eventually close another 1700.[31]

The Canadian Union of Postal Workers went on strike in October 1987 to protect the "4200 prized day jobs behind the counters of Canada's post offices."[32] While Canada Post offered guaranteed employment with the corporation, albeit with the possibility of having to move to another city, the union has been adamant that these good jobs which do not involve shift work and pay an average $13.43 per hour, must not disappear through franchising. The union stated that it will not fight the creation of franchise locations so long as they are not used to substitute for existing postal stations and provided that none of their present wicket jobs are eliminated.[33] According to a CPC official, "franchising is not a terribly radical situation. It's similar to sub-post stations (which operate in convenience stores, drugstores and other small businesses) which we've been offering for decades."[34]

It is clear that franchising could have several benefits for Canada Post. First, it could greatly reduce its future capital requirements for more retail outlets. Second, franchising may reduce CPC's operating costs at the retail distribution level.[35] Third, by offering greater customer convenience and perhaps more cheerful and helpful across-the-counter service, the post office's abysmal image may be improved. Fourth, franchise operations are easy to adopt, they could impose a useful constraint on the power of the union (CUPW), which has been able to get high wages and restrictive working conditions for its members by exploiting the cracks between CPC administrators, other government departments and the cabinet (see Stewart-Patterson, 1987).

Franchising may be limited by a ruling by the Canada Labour Board on September 1, 1987. The Board ordered the first franchisee, Shoppers' Drug Mart, to pay the same wages and benefits to franchise employees as does Canada Post.[36] Shoppers' was paying its employees from $3 to $8 per hour less. However, Shoppers' dropped its postal franchise a year after it began operation. CUPW has announced it will spend $2 million to defeat Tory MPs and privatization by the Canada Post.[37]

EX POST FACTO RATIONALIZATION

The Mulroney Government was far along its privatization program before it made any significant effort to provide the conceptual basis for the policy or its political rationale.[38] Barbara McDougall has placed the rationale for government's privatization efforts in the context of its electoral mandate and its economic strategy. In her view, the Tories electoral mandate was based on social justice and economic renewal. According to Ms. McDougall (1987b: 3) the message of the election was clear: "Good Government, Yes; Big Government, No." This led to "accelerated efforts" to examine and question the role of Crown corporations — including the returning of the ownership of Crown corporations to the private sector.

When Sinclair Stevens announced the sale of various Crown corporations and other equity interests in the CDIC's portfolio in October 1984, he provided virtually no explanation or justification for the move.[39] One of the reasons why the official rationale for privatization was so ill developed may be the fact that when he was President of the Treasury Board in the Clark government of 1979–80 Mr. Stevens proposed that Petro-Canada and five other Crown corporations would be sold. Three on that list (Canadair, de Havilland and Eldorado) were also on the 1984 list.

In his May 1985 Budget, the Minister of Finance declared that "Crown corporations with a commercial value but no ongoing public policy purpose will be sold." Robert de Cotret, who was given the responsibility for coordinating federal privatization efforts in November 1984, stated that privatization would ensure that the "discipline and vitality of the marketplace will replace the often suffocating effect of government ownership" (President of the Treasury Board, 1985: iv). Yet, in February 1987, over three years after the Tories had launched their privatization program, an investment dealer complained that "the big problem with privatization is there's no economic rationale, ideological or pragmatic."[40] A participant in the process argued that "the thing that is still missing is the policy. Why are we selling these things and what do we want to achieve by selling them?"[41]

However, it was not until May 1987 — after 11 privatizations — that the Minister of State for Privatization provided a fairly comprehensive set of reasons why the federal government was pursuing its privatization policy:

1) *The changing economic environment.* For many Crown corporations, the original objectives behind their creation are no longer valid. Some Crown corporations were created to meet public policy goals that are no longer legitimate. In addition, governments have other options than ownership — taxation, spending, regulation — available to meet public policy needs;

2) *Effectiveness.* There is abundant evidence to suggest that many Crown corporations are not as effective in serving their clients as the private sector. Privatization, but putting corporations under the test of the market place, can improve efficiency . . .

3) *Public Funds.* Public ownership of Crown corporations places enormous demands on government resources to manage and financially support various enterprises . . . On a day-to-day basis, accountability is not always as focussed as it should be. In addition, some Crown corporations cannot expect the infusion of federal funds necessary to expand in the global economy;

4) *Management styles* . . . The recognition that a Crown corporation is responsible for public funds often leads to slow, deliberate decision-making and occasional aversion on the part of management to risk-taking. In a commercial milieu, adaptability to rapid changes in markets and technologies is essential. Successful business leaders use a more flexible, market-sensitive approach to meeting their corporate objectives;

5) *Fairness and Equity.* Many Crown corporations compete directly with the private sector. In effect some businesses see their own tax dollars being used to compete against themselves. This is hardly fair, or conducive to a free enterprise system (McDougall, 1987b).

Charles Dalfen (1987), a former member of the CRTC and an acute observer of telecommunications policy in Canada, has examined the sale of Teleglobe Canada in light of Ms. McDougall's five general reasons for privatization. In his view, Teleglobe was not an obvious candidate for privatization. It was not a burden on Crown — indeed it was highly profitable. It was not competing with private sector — it had a *de facto* monopoly which the government agreed to maintain for five years by legal means. This is hardly conducive to efficiency. Finally, the environment in which Teleglobe has operated for over four decades has been changing and Teleglobe has been responsive to it.

Dalfen's (1987) explanation of the real reasons for the sale is, first, the government wanted to reduce the deficit. However, the sale was closed on April 3, 1987 so the revenue could not be applied to fiscal 1986–87. In any event, the sale reduced the $29 billion deficit by less than $500 million. Second, Dalfen suggests the government has an ideological position in favour of private ownership wherever possible and government ownership is no longer necessary to achieve policy objectives.[42] Furthermore, Dalfen (1987) argues there is plenty of evidence that the government didn't maximize the selling price of Teleglobe: it set a 20% limit on foreign ownership; it could have opted for looser price regulation like British Telecom; and it could have provided more than a five year monopoly including control over bypass via the U.S. The result of this particular privatization is an extension of monopoly and an increase in regulation. This is in contrast to Britain where the sale of British Telecom also resulted in a liberation of regulation of the telecommunications sector. In short, Dalfen found little support for the sale of Teleglobe Canada in the government's general rationale for privatization.

OTHER ACTIONS VIS-À-VIS THE CROWNS

In addition to selling off Crowns, the Mulroney government has eliminated several others. Three Crowns recently created by the Liberals, Loto Canada, The Canadian Sports Pool Corp. and Canagrex[43] were abolished. Uranium Canada, St. Anthony Fisheries and Societa San Sebastino were wound up. The Canada Museums Construction Corp., which was overseeing the building of the expensive new National Gallery and National Museum of Civilization was absorbed into the Department of Public Works. Bercuson et al. (1986: 130) point out that "Most of the crown corporations that the Tories wound up were small, inconsequential, or defunct."

Since coming to power in September 1984 the Tories have made potentially far reaching changes in the federal government's policies toward Crown corporations other than privatization. These include the following:

— In the fall of 1984 Petro-Canada was given a new mandate: "to operate in a commercial, private sector fashion with emphasis on profitability. Petro-Canada is not to be perceived in the future as an instrument in the pursuit of the government's policy objectives. However, the government maintains the right as the shareholders to formally direct Petro-Canada to carry out certain activities in the national interest."[44] Energy Minister Pat Carney was quoted as saying, "All we ask of (Petro-Canada) is that they run a well-managed company. I do not see any difference in my relationship with Petro-Canada and, say, Imperial Oil."[45] The government has made it clear that Petro-Canada must be self-financing. It will inject no more equity capital. This may restrain the growth of Petro-Canada — even if it is quite profitable.

— In *Freedom to Move*, the Tories white paper on transportation deregulation published in July 1985, the Minister stated that Crowns in transportation "will be expected to be effective and efficient while operating as good corporate citizens," and "will be discouraged from non-business-like pricing and in loss-making commercial activities . . . [the government will ensure they] operate as good corporate citizens." In short, the government is placing more emphasis on commercial objectives rather than public policy considerations.

— The government has made it clear to Air Canada that the airline is expected to be self-financing and that it is free to respond in a commercial fashion to full deregulation which came into effect January 1, 1988.[46] Both Tory Ministers of Transport (Mazankowski and Crosbie) have publicly supported privatization of Air Canada and Mazankowski, who became the Minister Responsible for Privatization on March 31, 1988 was able to persuade the Prime Minister to announce the sale of the airline less than two weeks later.

— In June 1987 the federal government broke new ground by deciding to have private investors both finance and operate the third terminal for Toronto's Pearson airport estimated to cost $381 million.[47] Local governments have acted in this capacity in the past for some small airports. However, the federal government has agreed to provide a loan of up to $70 million if the new terminal is not as busy as expected. It will also pay some $4 million for security equipment and roads.

— The government has supported efforts by CN to reduce its $3.5 billion debt[48] (at the end of 1986) and increase its efficiency by reducing employment, selling off non-rail operations (e.g., the money-losing trucking, dockyard and hotel subsidiaries)[49] and shifting CN Marine Inc. (which operates the ferries to P.E.I.) to the federal government in exchange for cancelling $327.6 million worth of common shares. In addition CN sold its Moncton shops employing 1000 to CGE which needs only 300.[50] CN is also attempting to restructure or close down its subsidiary Terra Transport which operates rail, trucking and bus service in Newfoundland at a loss of $50 million annually. It was reported that Ottawa had offered the Province $850 million to close down Terra Transport and upgrade the highways on the island.[51]

—The federal government has sought to reduce its cash budgetary payments to Crowns. Under the Trudeau government they rose from $3.1 billion in 1980–81 to $6.0 billion in 1983–84. Under the Tories they declined from $5.7 billion in 1984–85 to $4.7 billion in 1986–87 (Baumann, 1987).

— The Competition Act, effective in June 1986, was made binding upon federal and provincial Crown corporations engaged in commercial activities in competition with other firms. This provision was enacted to overrule the Supreme Court of Canada's decision in the Eldorado Nuclear case.[52]

— The Tories have tolerated strikes — the first since 1981 — of 19 and 17 days by Canada Post employees in 1987 before legislating them back to work. The Tories, however, were reluctant to raise postal rates to ensure the success of Canada Post's five-year plan to eliminate its deficit by the end of 1986–87. The postal deficit rose between 1983–84 and 1984–85. Michael Warren resigned as president in July 1985 after the cabinet delayed a proposed increase (2 cents for first class letters) in postal rates for six months. Protests by business resulted in the appointment of the Marchment Committee. In November 1985 it described the post office as being "in crisis."[53] In the February 1986 Budget, the deadline for eliminating the deficit was extended to the end of 1987–88. With another increase in postal rates effective January 1, 1988, Canada Post is expected to earn a profit in 1988–89.[54] The minister responsible for Canada Post has suggested that an independent body will be given the responsibility of reviewing proposed increases in postal rates.[55]

THE POLITICS OF PRIVATIZATION

The psychology of privatization would seem to be inconsistent with that of normal politicians. There is usually little personal satisfaction or electoral appeal in either cutting back expenditures or in selling off government enterprises. Margaret Thatcher in the U.K. seems to be an exception.

"Spending [is] more than a simple case of buying votes. It touch[es] on the psychology of politicians. [Politicians] want to be remembered for having built something, for having given something, not dismantling or cutting back" (Graham, 1986: 329–330).

The sale of Crown corporations in the name of greater efficiency or because the enterprise no longer has a policy mandate is unlikely to stir the hearts of many voters, although it may have considerable appeal for a few (see Langford, 1985).

Even left wing governments have found that privatization can be seen as a useful form of "housecleaning" after an orgy of over expansion by the state. For example, 47% of federal government enterprises in existence in 1983 were created since 1970 (ECC, 1986: 11). Moreover the federal state had greatly expanded in the 1970s in terms of direct expenditures, regulation, "tax expenditures" and other types of intervention (Howard & Stanbury, 1984). Times change and needs change, so it is not surprising that the government's portfolio of instruments of intervention needs to be pruned as a reflection of good management. Further, there has been a shift in the composition of the public agenda,[56] but it may have less to do with ideology of a new government than a reaction to the severe recession of 1981–83, the previous government's different agenda (e.g., constitutional reform, a highly interventionist energy program), and the cumulative evidence that the performance of many Crown corporations has left much to be desired.[57]

The political dilemma a government faces when it wishes to sell a Crown corporation to private investors has several facets. First, it is often argued that if the Crown corporation has been profitable, there is no need to sell it since it is meeting the test of the market place. Second, if the enterprise has been incurring losses or is likely to do so in the future, no one will want to buy it, so the argument goes. Moreover, selling the winners eliminates the profits to offset the losses of the unprofitable Crowns. Third, where the government had spent huge sums on the enterprise (e.g., some $2 billion to develop the Challenger aircraft), it should press on to receive the future benefits from this "investment." The obvious inference is that, in political terms, such costs are not sunk. Indeed, there is pressure to make additional investments in the future in order to justify the large outlays of the past. To "write off" such expenditures can easily lead to the inference that they were either the result of poor management or incurred for crassly political reasons. (This is fine so long as the blame falls squarely on the previous government.)

Fourth, to sell Crown corporations to American investors is to rub salt in the nationalists' open wounds. Their worst fears are thereby realized. Graham (1986: 31), for example, has interpreted the sale of de Havilland to Boeing as "throwing in the towel," an admission of failure. The political storm that followed was "as much for the loss of Canadian hopes as for the loss of the taxpayers' investment." In his view the Tories' choice was the classic one of the state versus the United States. The government didn't want to pump hundreds of millions of dollars more into de Havilland and a Canadian buyer could not be found at least on reasonable terms. For Graham (1986: 372), the federal government, in selling de Havilland to Boeing "grabbed a paltry amount of money and sacrificed unknown long-term possibilities in jobs, research, and exports as well as in profits."

Fifth, the sale of a Crown corporation, like the divestiture of a private enterprise, is an occasion for summing up — of counting the cumulative score on the enterprise's behaviour over the years. It brings to an end a long series of incremental decisions which have focused on short run considerations. The market value of the company is determined, not on the basis of all of its past expenditures on plant and equipment, R & D, and manpower training, but on the basis of the expected present value of its future earnings. Those past expenditures ("investments") have value only to the extent that (usually) hard-eyed private investors believe they will contribute to future profits. Moreover, the opportunity cost of capital, the discount rate applied to future earnings is considerably higher than the government's borrowing rate. This means that private investors are rather strongly biased in favour of jam now rather than pie in the sky when they die — to mix a metaphor. For example, under the agreement to sell Canadair to Bombardier, the estimated royalties the latter will pay the government for the development costs of the Challenger jet is $173 million over 21 years. The government has the option of requiring a payment of $20 million in cash within two years of the purchase date in lieu of the future royalties.[58] These facts can be interpreted in two ways. One, the estimated future royalties have either been overstated, or are expected to occur mainly after 15 years, or the buyer and seller have agreed on a very high discount rate. Second, the market value in 1986–1988 of over $2 billion in Challenger development costs in the 1980s was only $20 million.

The Tories, according to Prince (1986: 20), are "making haste slowly" on their economic agenda in order to avoid serious political mistakes, and to indicate a different approach to making policies. (This is evident even with the proposal to sell Air Canada in stages.) They must avoid the impression of holding a "fire sale" of public enterprises. A moderate pace allows the Tories to adapt their privatization policy as it obtains feedback and as circumstances change. For example, in August 1986 the cabinet approved Petro-Canada's purchase of 1800 gas stations and several refineries from Gulf Canada for $886 million. In this case, "Canadianizing" the oil industry was more important than scaling back the state through privatization (see Bercuson et al., 1986: 137). In short, the Tories have had to tack back and forth in the pursuit of economic agenda. The Mulroney Government has had to live with contradictions and find a way of balancing competing interests. The complexity of divesting Crown corporations was indicated by the Minister of Finance in his Budget Speech in May 1985. It was necessary, he said,

. . . to be sensitive to the concerns of management and employees in corporations considered candidates for sale; to consider the impact of privatization on consumers and market competition to consult with provincial governments; to avoid selling at distress prices for the sake of privatization where there may be periods of mixed, private and public ownership; and to examine all related policy and financial considerations on a case-by-case basis before considering the privatization of any given corporation.

MORE PRIVATIZATION TO COME?

As can be seen from Table 1, 11 of the 12 privatizations by the Mulroney Government took place between May 1985 and October 1987. While the sale of CN Hotels for $265 million (to Canadian Pacific) was announced in January 1988,[59] the process had begun in April 1987.[60]

The Situation at the End of 1987

By the end of 1987 it appeared that several events had occurred that would indicate that the volume of privatization activity in Canada is likely to be less in the near future than it was in the period 1985–1987. First, there was the stock market crash of October 1987.[61] It will make it harder to sell Crowns at a good price.[62] Second, the crash cost Canadian brokers who had taken up large blocks of the issue of British Petroleum some $120 million.[63] Moreover, on the last batch of CDC shares, brokers contracted to buy 7.5 million shares at $13.75 on October 8 and on October 27, after the crash, when the sale closed the shares were trading for $9.62.[64] Both events may make underwriters chary of handling further privatizations.

Third, in the case of Teleglobe, the biggest privatization in terms of proceeds, the process has been impugned when an investigation by the Quebec Securities Commission led to charges of insider trading in September 1987.[65] However, one of the persons charged, a lawyer for Memotec and a former president of the federal Conservative Party and a former candidate for its leadership was acquitted in April 1988.[66]

Fourth, newspaper reports suggest that in July 1987 the Prime Minister vetoed the sale of Air Canada when there was widespread support to sell the airline in light of the fact that deregulation in southern Canada was to come into effect on January 1, 1988.[67] It is argued that he did so because he believed his credibility would be further eroded (he was running third in the public opinion polls) in light of his statement in January 1985 that Canada needed a national airline and Air Canada would not be sold (see Stanbury, 1988). The ability to privatize Air Canada even after the next election became problematic following the October crash and a 19-day strike/lockout in November and December 1987[68] which was followed by a period of severe price cutting as the airline sought to regain its large share of the domestic market. The machinists union, which admitted it was fearful of privatization, struck to obtain the principle of indexation of pensions.[69] Although it obtained only partial indexation for retired members, the union succeeded in making the Crown airline less attractive to a private owner and less valuable to the federal government.

While these factors would appear to inhibit future privatizations, the new free trade agreement between Canada and the U.S. will not do so. The agreement signed on January 2, 1988 reduced restrictions on foreign investment in both countries. Canada, however, will continue to be able to impose limits on the holdings by foreigners of shares of existing Crown corporations that may be privatized in the future.[70]

Possible Deals in the Works

There are, however, some indications that more privatizations are to come. First, the executives of National Sea Products, a major fish processing company, are interested in having the federal government sell its 20% interest.[71] In June 1987 the Minister of State for Privatization announced a financial advisor had been retained. On April 14, 1988 the shares were worth $22.5 million.

Second, Radiochemical Co., a subsidiary of AECL, was announced as a privatization candidate in May 1985. At the end of 1987 it was said to be a likely candidate for privatization in 1988. Radiochemical had revenues of $111 million and profits of about $14 million in 1986–87. Analysts suggested it might fetch $150 million.[72]

Third, in April 1987 the Minister of Transport stated that the federal government was willing to transfer ownership and control

139

of 77 airports to local authorities or lease them to private interests.[73] In 1986, federal airports lost some $600 million, but a few such as Toronto, Vancouver and Montreal (Dorval) are profitable. For example, in 1986 Vancouver airport had a profit of $14 million on revenues of $496 million including some $56 million from the tax on all airline tickets.[74] In June 1987 the first bid to acquire one of the federal airports was received. AMS Airport Management Services bid $10 million for a 20 year lease (with an option to buy) Victoria airport.[75]

Fourth, in December 1987 the Minister of Transport announced that all of CN's non-rail assets were to be sold[76] with a view to reducing the Crown corporation's $3.2 billion debt. At its peak in 1952 CN had 131,297 employees but this number had fallen to 41,000 by the end of 1987. In five years the number was expected to fall to 26,000 (Foster, 1988: 40). In addition to the hotels (which were sold in January 1988), the assets for sale include two small telephone companies, the CN Tower, a 50% interest in CNCP Telecommunications, and CN Exploration, an oil and gas enterprise. Terra Nova Tel, which serves 50,000 subscribers in Newfoundland, earned $4 million in profit on $46 millions in revenue in 1987. Northwestel, with 35,000 subscribers in the Yukon, earned $7.6 million on $67 million in revenues in 1987.[77] In 1986, CN Exploration earned profits of $4.5 million versus $30.6 million in 1985 and $15.9 million in 1984. Revenues in 1986 were $33.9 million.[78] CNCP Telecommunications had revenues of $343 million in 1986.[79] At the end of February 1988 CN announced it was seeking a buyer for its subsidiary Grand Trunk Eastern Line which operates in New England.[80] It appears that when all of the non-rail assets of CN are sold they will constitute one of the largest privatizations in Canada.

Fifth, on February 22, 1988 the federal and Saskatchewan governments announced an agreement to merge Eldorado Nuclear Ltd. with Saskatchewan Mining Development Corp. The Saskatchewan government will own 61.5% of the shares of the merged enterprise.[81] The two governments are to reduce their shareholdings by 30% within two years, by 60% within four years, and by 100% within seven years. The rate of sale of shares is to be determined by market conditions.[82] The new corporation will have assets of $1.6 billion, 1000 employees, and sales of about $500 million. Canadian investors will be permitted to hold no more than 25% of the voting shares, while foreigners will be limited to 5%

individually and collectively they will not be able to vote more than 20% of the shares at annual meetings. The new enterprise is expected to issue $600 million to $650 million in new debt to its government shareholders who in turn will pay off part of Eldorado's and SMDC's debt which is backed by government guarantees. The federal government will be reimbursed for only $230 million of Eldorado's $570 million debt. The Saskatchewan government, however, will obtain enough out of the debt refinancing to cover SMDC's debt.[83] The new firm will control over one-half Canada's uranium production which was 32% of world output in 1986.

Sixth, it appears that the Mulroney Government continues to be interested in privatizing Petro-Canada. In late February 1988 the federal Minister of Energy, Marcel Masse, stated that shares in Petro-Canada will be sold when the company needs money for major projects.[84] However, the deputy prime minister announced almost immediately that the Conservatives had made no decision concerning the privatization of Petro Canada. The Tories have blown hot and cold on Petro-Canada, the second largest Crown in terms of assets. While senior ministers did not promise to privatize it, despite the fact public opinion is more equivocal on this issue, they have suggested on more than one occasion[85] that it might be sold (in whole or in part) to private investors (Stanbury, 1988).

Sale of Air Canada Announced

On April 12, 1988, less than two weeks after he became the Minister responsible for Privatization,[86] Don Mazankowski announced that all of Air Canada would be sold to the public as "market conditions permit" with an initial treasury issue of up to 45% of the shares. The Deputy Prime Minister said in an interview that the entire privatization process may take from five to ten years.[87] With assets of $3.18 billion and revenues of $3.13 billion in 1987, the sale of Air Canada represents by far the most ambitious privatization by the Mulroney Government. Mazankowski claimed the announcement as "fully consistent with the Prime Minister's statement to ensure the existence of a national airline . . . " Privatization, he said, was needed to attract new capital to finance the purchase of new aircraft. Opposition Leader John Turner called the move "a clear breach of faith between the Prime Minister and the

Canadian people." NDP leader Ed Broadbent described it as "the triumph of Conservative ideology over good, practical, Canadian common sense" and vowed his party would "do everything it can to stop the Government." Mazankowski argued that "blind devotion to state enterprises would be the only possible reason for not proceeding at this time."[88]

An Angus Reid–Southam News poll in March 1988 indicated 53% of Canadians think Air Canada should not be sold while 35% favour privatization.[89] Liberal transportation critic Brian Tobin argued that the government should sell all the shares in Air Canada or none. Unless there is a guarantee that total control will be transferred to the private sector, the shares will fetch a minimal price, he said. "They've set up a share offering that's not going to get the best return on its money."

The president of the airline division of CUPE said privatization will lead to a deterioration in labour relations and a loss of jobs and threaten the company's pension plan. "What the Government fails to realize," he said, "is that the people of Canada already own Air Canada."[90] Bob White, head of the Canadian Auto Workers Union, which represents some Air Canada employees, declared on CBC television news that he was strongly opposed to privatization. However, several Air Canada employees said they favored it and would buy shares in Air Canada.

The chairman of Air Canada, Claude Taylor, called the Minister's announcement "a giant step towards the realization of a dream I have cherished a long time." President Pierre Jeanniot described privatization as the "financial key to Air Canada's future." It will allow "the airline to plan for fleet expansion and renewal as well as pursue new business opportunities." The head of the machinists' union, which represents 8500 Air Canada employees, described the announcement as "a sad and serious situation." He said, "it's not an economic move. It's a blatantly ideological move."[91] It is a threat to the job security of union members. Deregulation and privatization will result in poorer service for Canadians in his view. The chairman of the Air Canada Employee Ownership Committee, which had 7500 members three years ago, said, "I don't think we're going to have any trouble getting people enthused [sic] again."

Editorially, the *Globe and Mail* supported the proposal, but was worried that Mr. Mazankowski's statement that the policy was "fully consistent" with the PM's January 1985 utterances "suggests a permanent commitment to majority ownership by the Crown."[92] The editorial noted that the Minister had also described CAIL and Wardair as "national airlines," hence "public ownership may not be a condition of 'national' status after all." The paper supported the sale of all of Air Canada's shares to private investors. It noted, however, that the credibility of the government's promise not to interfere with the commercial decisions of the airline after its stake is reduced to 55% "will be critical to buyers of the minority stake." According to the *Globe*, "in denouncing the sale, the New Democrats and the Liberals exhibit a particularly moldy nationalism. Air Canada serves no public policy purpose in our deregulated transportation system." It concluded by saying, "privatization is an entirely responsible move."

The *Vancouver Sun* was more equivocal pointing to the political context of "so many controversies . . . free trade, refugees, abortion, the constitution, tax reform," particularly when selling Air Canada brings the credibility of the PM to the fore. It concluded, however, that in its own terms, the privatization of Air Canada is "on balance . . . probably a good move provided the price is one that is both attractive to investors and fair to the taxpayers who now own it."[93]

Air Canada announced that — despite a 19-day strike in December — its 1987 profits were $45.7 million, up $5.3 million over 1986, but this amounted to 7.6% return on equity. The strike, however, cost the airline some $70 million. Revenues in 1987 were $3.13 billion versus $2.89 billion in 1986. At the end of 1987 only $130 million of the airline's $2.1 billion debt was guaranteed by the federal government. Aggressive use of discount fares following the strike will result in a loss in the first quarter of 1988, but the tactic was successful in recouping Air Canada's previous share of the domestic market. Pierre Jeanniot rejected CAIL's claims that it had increased its market share at the Crown carrier's expense after the strike: "I don't know where our friendly competitor is getting those figures."[94]

The privatization of Air Canada is subject to a number of conditions:

— The headquarters must remain in Montreal; Mazankowski made this clear in his announcement.

— The airline must for the indefinite future maintain its major operational and overhaul centers in Winnipeg, Montreal and

Toronto. Of particular importance is the Winnipeg overhaul base with 400 employees. Its existence is threatened by Air Canada's choice of new aircraft. This requirement was enshrined in the enabling legislation.[95]

— No more than 45% of the share will be sold in the initial offering.

— Employees must be given the first chance to buy shares through a payroll deduction scheme or similar program. (It is not clear whether they will pay a lower price than others.)[96]

— Small shareholders are to be next on the list of preferred buyers, followed by institutional investors and finally, by foreigners.

— The Government's 55% stake will be voted in accordance with the majority of the new private sector shareholders so that there will be "a clear arms-length relationship."[97]

— No individual shareholder will be allowed to hold more than 10% of the shares sold to private investors (hence 4.5% of the initial offering).

— Total foreign ownership will be limited to 25% (or 11% of the initial offering).

Several questions immediately come to mind. First, the 10% limit on individual shareholdings may or may not constitute a serious constraint on the "revenge of the capital market" in the event that management performs poorly. After full privatization five individuals could combine to get control and appoint new managers. However, the federal legislation may follow the unfortunate Alberta precedent. When PWA was privatized in December 1983 the legislation provided that no individual or group of associated individuals could vote more than 4% of the stock.[98] Such a constraint gives management effective control — even though it owns no shares at all. If the 10% rule for Air Canada is similar to PWA's we could have the spectre of Canada's two largest airlines being privately owned but effectively controlled by management. The 10% constraint may be of little consequence if it is possible for private sector interests to buy all or substantially all of the assets of Air Canada.

Second, Air Canada could end up in the worst of all possible worlds, a mixed enterprise (see Economic Council, 1986; Stanbury, 1988). The Tories could sell off up to 45%, but a Liberal or NDP Government could prevent full privatization. This could also occur if the Tories are only a minority government after the next election. A 55/45 mixed enterprise would either involve the exploitation of the private sector shareholders as the federal government uses its 55% to pursue goals inconsistent with profit maximization, or it would result in management exercising effective control where government fails to exercise its rights as a majority owner to remove inefficient management.

It has been suggested that the April 12, 1988 announcement was the result of a clever strategy by Air Canada's top executives.[99] By requesting the government to inject $300 million in new equity capital in January 1988,[100] Air Canada put Ottawa on the horns of a dilemma as the airline needed either more equity or massive loan guarantees to finance over $2 billion to pay for new aircraft which the airline must contract to purchase by 1989. The government's alternative was to sell off the airline and in the process let the private sector provide the capital to permit it to handle the massive purchases of new aircraft. The request for $300 million new equity, predictably, prompted Air Canada's rivals to howl in protest over potentially unfair competition (Stanbury, 1988: Ch. 8).

There is another explanation why the Mulroney Government clearly changed its position between July 1987 — when Mulroney himself blocked the sale of all the shares in Air Canada — and April 1988. The key is Don Mazankowski. As the first Tory Minister of Transport he pushed through deregulation of the transport sector. He was also strongly committed to privatizing Air Canada — he began studies on the issue within weeks of the Tories assuming office. He even persisted after the PM said Air Canada was not for sale in January 1985 (see Stanbury, 1988: Ch. 8). It seems reasonable, in light of Air Canada's "pressure," that Mazankowski made the sale of Air Canada a condition of taking over the privatization portfolio on March 31, 1988. Besides, the PM "owes him one." "Maz" has been a vitally important minister in the Tory cabinet. In my view, Mazankowski moved very quickly to irrevocably commit the Government to this politically ambitious move.

The Government faces a number of important hurdles before the first batch of shares can be sold. The legislation to authorize the sale of Air Canada was introduced on May 19, 1988. However, the bill was to compete for attention with several other major bills before the end of the parliamentary session. Financial analysts and Air Canada officials estimate that after the legislation has been passed it will take at least four months to get the proposed issue ready. This will require some strategic decisions including how much cash from the issue will go to the airline and how much to the government. Moreover, the longer the sale of shares is delayed the greater the likelihood that the issue will come to market during a period of excess capacity, low yields and hence low prices for airline stocks. Both CAIL and Wardair have sufficient new aircraft arriving in 1988 and 1989 that the industry's capacity will be increased by over 20%. If the new capacity comes on line when a recession is underway, a financial "bloodbath" could occur. This could preclude the sale of Air Canada shares for some time. All of these contingencies made it impossible that the shares be sold before the fall 1988 general election.

CONCLUSIONS

Prior to the announcement of the planned sale of Air Canada, the Mulroney Government had made modest progress in reducing the number of Crown corporations or in selling equity interests in mixed enterprises. Of the 12 privatizations completed by April 1988, only a few could be said to be of notable economic significance (de Havilland, Canadair, Teleglobe, CN Hotels and perhaps the equity interests in CDC and FPI). However, their collective economic significance is less than the sale of Air Canada, the fifth largest Crown in terms of revenues in 1986. Other large commercial Crowns such as CNR and Petro-Canada remain quite firmly attached to the federal head, although the government is committed to selling off the considerable non-rail assets of the CNR. Given the fact that CN and Petro-Canada have been told to operate as if they were privately owned, it seems only logical to sell them off. Because they are no longer instruments of public policy, they meet the Mulroney Government's principal criterion for privatization.

Tom Kierans (1985: 5) reminds us that privatization is both a symbolic and a substantive act. It is a symbol of the government's intention to strengthen the market at the expense of the state. He suggests privatization is evidence of the government's "willingness to rethink our mixed economy tradition, a signal which clearly could offend the Canadian psyche." The reactions of union leaders and both opposition party leaders to the proposed sale of Air Canada certainly illustrates this point.

But privatization may be a symbol of a different sort. By selling a few minor appendages privatization may be a cynical ploy to appease right wing interests without alienating the majority of Canadians who retain their faith in a large and benign government. Certainly, one of the senior bureaucrats in charge of the privatization effort has been at pains to play down the ideological motivation for privatization. Stein (1988: 76) describes it as "a pragmatic initiative which fits into Canada's public policy tradition." Privatization is billed as just another bit of bureaucratic fine-tuning, "an exercise in management of government." He goes on, "The environment changes; the objectives change with it; and so do the tools. Pure and simple" (Stein, 1988: 76). It is interesting that pragmatism is being used to explain/justify actions designed to reduce the state, just as it has been repeatedly used to deal with acts of government intervention.

The focus of the Mulroney Government's privatization program has been on selling Crown corporations and equity interests in mixed enterprises. It has made no effort to increase the private production of services financed by government, by, for example, contracting-out. Nor has it shifted more government services to a user-pay approach.

The Mulroney Government has sold 10 of the 12 assets to a single buyer, rather than to the public through wide distribution of the shares. This stands in contrast to the Thatcher Government in the U.K. with its emphasis on increasing the number of individuals who own shares. Given the nature of most of the Crowns sold in Canada (small or in volatile industries with the exception of Teleglobe), this is not surprising.

The Mulroney government has been slow to articulate its reasons for selling Crown corporations, and the explanation has been fairly brief. This stands in sharp contrast to the Bourassa Government in Quebec (see Quebec, 1986). The Tories *ex post facto* approach may be attributable to the fact they proposed a fairly extensive privatization program in 1979, but were not able to carry it out.

Despite reasonable progress on the privatization front, the acid test of the Tories privatization efforts may be yet to come. The emerging political furor over the proposed phased sale of Air Canada will test the Government's resolve. The Tories will have to accord the matter high priority and pray that the health of the airline industry and the stock market will be strong. It would be easy for the Government to make a pro-forma effort but not succeed. Then it would be able to argue that it was on the side of the angels.

The second test will occur when the next severe recession hits Canadair, de Havilland and the others. Will the Government be better able to resist the demands for help in one form or another? The Canadair and de Havilland plants and employees remain where they were when the firms were Crown corporations. Presumably, their political salience has changed little. Will the federal government be able to tolerate large layoffs in the future in what have been treated as marginal ridings in the past?

Although the Mulroney Government's privatization record has hardly gone as far as the Thatcher Government in the U.K. (see Yarrow and Vickers, 1988), given the time it has been in office and the number and economic importance of federal Crown corporations, it is a substantial achievement. If he succeeds in completely privatizing Air Canada Brian Mulroney could legitimately claim that privatization was a major achievement of his first term.

NOTES

1 See, for example, "Privatization — Everybody's Doing It, Differently," The Economist, December 21, 1985, pp. 71–86.

2 Michael Walker (1988) claims that while Milton Friedman proposed privatization in 1976 as "a cure for the British disease," the idea was first implemented when the B.C. government gave away the shares in BCRIC in 1979. The Fraser Institute book on privatization (Ohashi & Roth, 1980) "attracted the considerable attention" of the new Thatcher Government.

3 In 1977 the Privy Council Office published a list of 366 federal "government-owned and controlled corporations." As of August 1979 the number was 401 (Langford and Huffman, 1983). The next year, the Comptroller General (1980) identified 464 federal Crowns, including subsidiaries. Revisions by the Comptroller General (1981) produced a list of 306 corporations "in which the federal government has an interest." This list excluded the subsidiaries or associated corporations of the 22 mixed enterprises, but includes the mixed enterprises themselves.

4 "Ottawa's corporate holdings worth more than $77 billion," *Globe and Mail*, June 27, 1985, p. B11. Grace (1985) notes that in terms of assets, all federal Crowns grew from $6.5 billion in 1958 to $26 billion in 1973 to $45 billion in 1978 to $77 billion in 1983. Baumann (1987) indicates that the assets of federal

Crowns grew from $19.6 billion in 1973 to $33.4 billion in 1978 to $54.1 billion in 1983, to $61.2 billion in 1985 to $59.9 billion in 1987. His figures exclude the Bank of Canada.

5 As of March 31, 1982, the Auditor-General (1982: 57) indicated that 261 federal agency, proprietary and government corporations employed 263,225 persons including 69,457 by Canada Post. By comparison, all federal departments had 221,000 employees while the Armed Forces and RCMP employed another 83,000 and 18,000 respectively.

6 Jack Willoughby, "Government forms task force to examine what portions of CMHC can go private," *Globe and Mail*, September 7, 1979, p. B5.

7 Roger Croft, "Five more crown companies heading for the auction block," *Toronto Star*, September 14, 1979, p. A4.

8 Timothy Pritchard, "Ottawa to reduce holding in CDC," *Globe and Mail*, November 20, 1979, p. B1.

9 Doern and Toner (1985, p. 103) state that "energy taxes, oil and gas prices and the future of Petro-Canada dominated domestic politics, first in the Crosbie Conservative budget in December 1979 and in the subsequent election campaign . . . "

10 See "Ottawa plans to sell its 48.5 percent of Canada Development Corp.," *Toronto Star*, May 28, 1982, p. A3; "Sale of CDC shares will hinge on market," *Globe and Mail*, November 26, 1982, p. B4. The federal government's voting interest in CDC was reduced in 1980 when $300 million in voting convertible preferred shares was issued to private investors.

11 The shares in the airline had been acquired by Air Canada in January 1979 (for $24.1 million) after the previous owners indicated they wanted to sell out (Reschenthaler & Stanbury, 1982). Almost immediately the Minister of Transport announced that Nordair would be sold back to private sector investors within a year. The Minister greatly underestimated the political difficulties involved. Complications arose because various private and public sector (Quebecair — owned by the Province) interests in Quebec and Ontario wanted to buy Nordair, and because the sale could change the structure of the industry, hence influence aviation policy (Reschenthaler & Stanbury, 1982). The short-lived Clark government fared no better than the Liberals.

12 See David Stewart-Patterson, "Reorganization makes CDIC giant holding company," *Globe and Mail*, November 25, 1982, p. B1 and Foster (1983b), Ross (1983).

13 Michael Valpy, "A point of ideology," *Globe and Mail*, July 15, 1983, p. 6.

14 See Michael Valpy, "Selling Air Canada," *Globe and Mail*, April 29, 1983, p. 6.

15 *Globe and Mail*, July 15, 1983, p. 6.

16 His views are described in Thomson (1985).

17 Gracey had a major role in the federal government's White paper on Crown corporations published in 1977 — see Canada, PCO (1977).

18 See Giles Gherson, "For Sale to Caring Buyer: Slightly Used Crown Corporations," *Financial Post Canada Outlook '86*, Winter 1985–86, pp. 79, 84.

19 Coverage of the political process accounted for 2193 items, while "other coverage" including opinions polls and the TV debates, accounted for 1957 items.

20 Finally, even if privatization was an issue in the campaign, it probably had very little impact on the voter's decision. Frizell & Westell (1985: 77) state though specific issues can be much talked about during an election, they rarely become overwhelming in the voter's mind. Surveys from the 1984 election indicate that specific topics, such as patronage, which received much media attention, are mentioned as important by only 2 to 3 percent of voters.

21 The sale was made subject to a variety of conditions:
— Teleglobe will reduce overseas telephone and telex rates by 13.5% and 10% respectively on January 1, 1988.
— Teleglobe management will remain in place, no employees will be laid off and existing collective agreements will continue.
— Teleglobe's head office will remain in Montreal.
— Within six months Teleglobe employees will be offered an opportunity to acquire 5% of its shares at 90% of the price paid by Memotec Data Inc. (See *Globe and Mail*, February 12, 1987, pp. A1–A2.)

22 Unfortunately, when the second payment was due, the shares were selling in the market for about one-half the price set a year earlier. Yet 90% of the 23 million shares were taken up in September 1986. See Patricia Lush, "90% of CDC shares taken up at $11.50" *Globe and Mail*, September 18, 1986, p. B1. The underwriters also lost money on the final batch of CDC shares. They agreed to buy 7.5 million shares at $13.75, but when the sale closed after the crash the market price was $9.62. See Philip De Mont, "Timing still key on CDC," *Financial Times*, November 2, 1987, p. 12.

23 See Bercuson et al. (1986, p. 141) put it this way: "As soon as the announcement was made, former Transport Minister Lloyd Axworthy claimed that although de Havilland was on the verge of profitability, the government was "giving it away, virtually ... the fix (in favour of Boeing) was in from the start. The NDP announced a motion of nonconfidence in the government because of the agreement and claimed that the sale would mean the loss of Canadian jobs. They predicted that Boeing would transfer the manufacture of the Dash 7 and Dash 8 to the United States and close de Havilland down. This, in fact, made little sense ... " Opposition Leader John Turner incorrectly claimed that "Canadian expertise in aeronautics, in space, in short takeoff and landing aircraft (would) no longer belong to (Canada)." Bercuson et al. (1986, p. 143) note that "In the House of Commons, the Liberals and NDP demanded that the government place the agreement before a parliamentary committee and at first the government, led by de Cotret, stonewalled. (Later) it reversed its position when Sinclair Stevens, who had been in hospital, returned to the Commons. The deal was closed on January 31, 1986. See also Doern & Atherton (1987).

24 See *Globe and Mail*, August 19, 1986, pp. A1–A2. See also Doern & Atherton (1987) for a review of the terms of the deal.

25 See Anthony Whittingham, "The seedy assault on the CDC." *Maclean's*, June 1, 1981, pp. 46–47; and Foster (1983a).

26 Data from Baumann (1987), *Financial Post 500* (Summer 1987), and Doern and Atherton (1987, p. 173) for Canada Post, 1985–86.

27 The sale was announced in August. See *Globe and Mail*, August 19, 1986, pp. A1–A2.

28 See Christopher Waddell, "Petrocan will be biggest gas retailer after Gulf purchase," *Globe and Mail*, August 13, 1985, pp. 1–2; Christopher Waddell, "Firms, Ottawa to gain from Gulf deal," *Globe and Mail*, August 14, 1985, p. B1. Petro-Canada acquired 800 service stations in Ontario and Western Canada and four refineries. The purchase made Petro-Canada the largest gasoline retailer in Canada. See Bott (1987).

29 See Ken Romain, "BCE set to acquire one-third interest in Memotec Data," *Globe and Mail*, May 8, 1987, p. A3; Lawrence Surtees, "BCE proposal opens door to major Teleglobe stake," *Globe and Mail*, May 9, 1987, p. B8. "A giant charts its future," *Maclean's*, May 25, 1987, pp. 26–27.

30 In 1986 Canada Post's revenues were $3 billion, its deficit was $129 million and it employed some 63,500 persons. Generally, see Stewart-Patterson (1987). Baumann (1987) states that in March 1987 Canada Post had 52,760 employees, but this figure excludes part time workers.

31 See Graham Fraser, "Liberals attack manual setting out strategy for closing post offices," *Globe and Mail*, October 21, 1987, pp. A1–A2.

32 *Maclean's*, October 12, 1987, p.11.

33 *Ibid.*, p. 11.

34 *Vancouver Sun*, October 3, 1987, p. A8.

35 The expected savings over the next decade were estimated by CPC to be $1.3 billion, mostly wages. See *Maclean's*, October 12, 1987, p. 14.

36 "Postal franchise ruling makes strike less likely, union says," *Globe and Mail*, September 3, 1987, p. A8. However, the ruling, which is being appealed to the Federal Court, may not make franchising infeasible as it was based on the union's successor rights. The franchise in question, in effect, replaced an existing postal station. Where an entirely new outlet is created, the successor rights provision might not apply.

37 Lorne Slotnick, "CUPW will spend $2 million to fight CPs, privatization," *Globe and Mail*, February 22, 1988, pp. A1–A2.

38 In this it was like the Thatcher Government in Britain. Oliver Letwin (1988, p. 50) states that "from the inside we had no coherent policy . . . It came upon us gradually and by accident and by leap of faith . . . As it slowly turned into a success story . . . the whole thing began to look like a coherent policy that was destined to work from the very beginning. It's an illusion."

39 See Patrick Nagle, "Crown firms for sale as CDIC boss fired," *Vancouver Sun*, October 31, 1984, p. A10.

40 Cathryn Motherwell, "Privatization trend faces test over Big 3," *Globe and Mail*, February 28, 1987, p. B1.

41 *Ibid.*

42 This seems consistent with Mcdougall's statement that "our government believes there is one justification for government ownership and it is only one: and that is where ownership is essential to achieve a viable public policy purpose, the supply of an essential public service that cannot economically be supplied in any other way" (McDougall, 1987c, p. 2).

43 In November 1984 the Tories announced that Canagrex would be eliminated effective March 31, 1985 at a saving of $6.7 million annually. See Don Martin, "No tears from West over Canagrex death," *Calgary Herald*, November 12, 1984, p. C1. Canagrex's mandate was to find export markets for agricultural products not managed by the Canadian Wheat Board or the Canada Dairy Commission. It was the favourite godchild of Eugene Whelan, who served as Pierre Trudeau's Minister of Agriculture for over a decade. He endured a great deal of political flak in establishing Canagrex.

44 See *Financial Times*, September 15, 1986, p. 1; Petro-Canada's 1984 Annual Report.

45 *Globe and Mail*, October 3, 1985, p. A6.

46 When it became clear that Air Canada will not be privatized at least until after the next election, the Minister of Transport expressed support for Air Canada's request for $300 million in new equity. See Cecile Foster, "Crosbie backs aid to Air Canada, CN," *Globe and Mail*, February 13, 1988, pp. B1, B4. The money is needed to finance the purchase of about $2.5 billion worth of new aircraft beginning in the early 1990s.

47 Robert Matas, "Airport construction months behind scheduled," *Globe and Mail*, April 19, 1988, p. B9.

48 The chairman of CN has stated that "in excess of one half (of the total debt) can be traced to our obligation to provide uneconomic services in the public interest"; Maurice Le Clair, "The issue is not who owns CN but if anyone would want to" *Toronto Star*, September 22, 1986, p. B10.

49 See CN, *Annual Report*, 1086.

50 *Globe and Mail*, August 20, 1986, p. B7.

51 *Globe and Mail*, February 25, 1988, pp. B1–B2 and February 13, 1988, pp. B1, B4. CN requested that the government take Terra Transport's debt off its hands in 1983. See *Globe and Mail*, August 22, 1983, p. B7. In 1986 Terra lost $41.3 million on revenues of $25.0 million.

52 R. v. Eldorado Nuclear Ltd. R. v. Uranium Canada Ltd. (1983) 4 D.L.R. (4th) 193; 8 C.C.C. (3d) 449.

53 See *Globe and Mail*, November 14, 1985, p. B1; November 19, 1985, pp. A1–A2.

54 See *Financial Post*, March 28, 1988, p. 5.

55 See "New panel suggested to set postal rates," *Globe and Mail*, March 30, 1988, p. A8; and column by Jeffrey Simpson, p. A6.

56 See Prince (1986, p. 4) who concludes that "the Mulroney strategy is to shift federal policies and expenditures in a small–c conservative direction."

57 For a few examples, see Auditor General (1979), Borins & Brown (1986), Canada, PCO (1977), Economic Council (1986), Foster (1986), Halpern et al. (1987), Kierans (1984), Perry (1983), Prichard (1983), Sexty (1979), Stewart-Patterson (1987), Tupper & Doern (1981).

58 See *Globe and Mail*, August 19, 1986, pp. A1–A2.

59 Cecil Foster, "CP beats out 40 other bidders, buys CN hotels for $265 million," *Globe and Mail*, January 30, 1988, pp. A1–A2. CN said CP had agreed to maintain all existing labour contracts and pension benefits and to absorb all employees, about 3400 in total. CP also agreed to continue operating the properties as hotels of similar class and style, to maintain the two hotels in heritage buildings and to complete the renovation of another.

60 Dennis Bueckert, "CN planning to sell its five hotels," *Globe and Mail*, April 4, 1987, p. A2.

61 See "Living With the Crash," *Maclean's*, November 2, 1987, pp. 26–40.

"After the Meltdown of '87," *Newsweek*, November 2, 1987, pp. 14–53.

62 See Cecil Foster, "Ottawa misses the market on privatization," *Globe and Mail*, November 2, 1987, pp. B1–B7; Peter Cook, "Mrs. Thatcher sets sail, but McDougall misses the boat," *Globe and Mail*, November 2, 1987, p. B2.

63 See "Adding to the Wreckage," *Maclean's*, November 9, 1987, p. 45. Wood Gundy is believed to have lost $60 million alone — see Peter Foster, "Scrambling for cover after BP," *Financial Post*, November 9, 1987, p. 16.

64 Philip De Mont, "Timing still key on CDC," Financial Times, November 2, 1987, p. 12.

65 Karen Howlett and Robert Gibbens, "Memotec insiders face charges on trading," *Globe and Mail*, September 26, 1987, pp. B1, B13. See also "The Memotec affair," *Maclean's*, October 5, 1987, p. 38; *Globe and Mail*, January 20, and 21, 1988, pp. A3; A5.

66 Patricia Poirier, "Former president of federal PCs cleared on insider-trading charge," *Globe and Mail*, April 6, 1988, pp. A1–A2.

67 See Cecil Foster, "Air Canada sale won't fly," *Globe and Mail*, August 22, 1987, pp. B1, B4.

68 Patrick Poirier & Lorne Slotnick, "Air Canada halts services, locks out groundworkers," *Globe and Mail*, November 17, 1987, pp. A1, A5; "Returning to the air, *Maclean's*, December 28, 1987, p. 49.

69 Robin Schiele, "Sale of Air Canada is eye of dispute," *Financial Post*, December 7, 1987, pp. 1–2. It should be noted that the union settled with Canadian Airlines International just before the strike started for 4%, 4% and 5% over three years without any indexation of pensions.

70 See "Ownership of privatized firms may be limited," *Globe and Mail*, December 12, 1987, p. B5.

71 "National Sea Products wants Ottawa to sell its 20% holding," *Toronto Star*, May 7, 1987, p. C9.

72 David Hatter, "Crown selloff decisions get harder to make," *Financial Post*, December 28, 1987, p. 6.

73 Christopher Waddell, "Ottawa is ready to get out of the airport business," *Globe and Mail*, April 10, 1987, pp. A1–A2.

74 Vancouver Sun, April 10, 1987.

75 Gavin Wilson, "Bid to buy Victoria airport a first," *Vancouver Sun*, June 11, 1987, p. A10.

76 "CN's non-rail assets for sale, minister says," *Vancouver Sun*, December 2, 1987, p. F5.

77 Nancy Begalki, "Native groups link to pursue Norwestel," *Globe and Mail*, February 1, 1988, p. B8.

78 CN, *Annual Report*, 1086, p. 26.

79 Canadian Pacific Ltd. has the right of first refusal with respect to CN's 50% interest in CNCP. See Fred McMahon, "CP sees bright future in bid for CNCP control," *Financial Post*, January 4, 1988, p. 5.

80 Cecil Foster, "CN considers closing Newfoundland unit," *Globe and Mail*, February 25, 1988, p. B1–B2.

81 Geoffrey York, "Eldorado–SMDC merger 'world-beater,' " *Globe and Mail*, February 23, 1988, pp. B1–B6. The merger follows a turn-around for Eldorado. It had profits of $12 million in 1987 versus losses of $64 million in 1986 and

$57.2 million in 1985. SMDC paid a dividend of $15 million in 1986 and had a profit in 1985. See Jane Becker, "Crown owned Eldorado Nuclear posed for return to the private sector," *Globe and Mail*, January 28, 1988, p. B13.

82 Philip De Mont, "The emerging uranium giant," Financial Times, February 29, 1988, p. 13.

83 David Hatter, "Merger leaves Ottawa with Eldorado's debts," *Financial Post*, February 29, 1988, p. 7.

84 "Petro-Canada shares will be sold to public," *Globe and Mail*, February 24, 1988, pp. B1–B3.

85 See Bercuson et al. (1986, p. 137); *Financial Post*, February 22, 1986, pp. 1–2; *Globe and Mail*, March 2, 1987, p. B4; *Toronto Star*, June 25, 1987, p. E4; Bott (1987); Foster (1986).

86 Barbara McDougall, who had been the Minister of State for Privatization and Regulatory Affairs from June 1986, was made Minister of Employment and Immigration on March 31, 1988.

87 Christopher Waddell, "Ottawa to begin selling off Air Canada," *Globe and Mail*, April 13, 1988, pp. A1, A9.

88 Ibid., p. A9.

89 "Critics slam sale of Air Canada," *Vancouver Sun*, April 13, 1988, p. E1.

90 For a more detailed critique, see Val Udvartely, "Why should public buy shares in something it already owns?" *Globe and Mail*, April 14, 1988, p. A7. This particular assessment contains numerous errors of fact and logic, but does assemble in one place all of the bad arguments against privatizing Air Canada.

91 Waddell, *Globe and Mail*, April 13, 1988, p. A9.

92 "Selling Air Canada," (editorial) *Globe and Mail*, April 13, 1988, p. A6.

93 "Air Canada sale on odd flightpath" (editorial) *Vancouver Sun*, April 13, 1988, p. B2.

94 "Shutdown hurts Air Canada's profit," *Globe and Mail*, April 13, 1988, p. B1.

95 See "Air Canada won't be deserting Winnipeg, Mazankowski says," *Financial Post*, April 26, 1988, p. 3; Paul Koring, "Ottawa moves to protect Air Canada bases," *Globe and Mail*, May 20, 1988, pp. B1–B2.

96 Waddell, *Globe and Mail*, April 13, 1988, p. A9.

97 Generally, see Waddell, *Globe and Mail*, April 14, 1988, pp. A1, A10.

98 Note the Alberta legislation still applies to PWA Corp., the holding company of Canadian Airlines International. The new name was adopted after PWA paid $300 million for CP Air early in 1987.

99 Cecil Foster, "Slick Air Canada move forced sale decision," *Globe and Mail*, April 14, 1988, pp. B1, B4.

100 See Cecil Foster, "Crosbie backs aid to Air Canada, CN," *Globe and Mail*, February 13, 1988, pp. B1, B4.

REFERENCES

Auditor General of Canada (1979). *Report to the House of Commons*, (Ottawa: Minister of Supply and Services) Ch. 8, "Control and Accountability of Crown Corporations."

Baumann, Harry (1987). "Between Ideology and Ad Hocery: A Pragmatic Approach to the Management of Energy Crown Corporations," (Notes for a seminar presented at the Faculty of Commerce, University of B.C., November 26, mimeo).

Bercuson, David, J.L. Granatstein and W.R. Young (1986). *Sacred Trust?*, (Toronto: Doubleday Canada).

Borins, Sandford F. and Lee Brown (1986). *Investments in Failure: Five Government Corporations that Cost the Canadian Taxpayer Billions*, (Toronto: Methuen).

Bott, Robert (1987). "Would You Buy a Piece of This Company?", *Report on Business Magazine*, September, pp. 56–64.

Canada, Privy Council Office (1977). *Crown Corporations: Direction Control Accountability-Government of Canada's Proposals*, (Ottawa: Supply and Services Canada).

Comptroller General of Canada (1980). *Government of Canada Corporations in Which the Government Has an Interest*, (Ottawa: Minister of Supply and Services).

Dalfen, Charles M. (1987). "Deregulation and Privatization in the Canadian Telecommunications Sector: The Case of Teleglobe Canada," (Paper presented to the International Colloquium on Privatization and Deregulation in Canada and the United Kingdom, Gleneagles, Scotland, November 2–4, mimeo).

Doern, G. Bruce & Glen Toner (1985). *The Politics of Energy*, (Toronto: Methuen).

Doern, G. Bruce and John Atherton (1987). "The Tories and the Crowns: Restraining and Privatizing in a Political Minefield," in M.J. Prince (ed.), *How Ottawa Spends, 1987–88: Restraining the State*, (Toronto: Methuen), pp. 129–169.

Economic Council of Canada (1986). *Minding the Public's Business*, (Ottawa: Minister of Supply and Services).

Elford, Craig and W.T. Stanbury (1986). "Mixed Enterprises in Canada" in D.G. McFetridge (ed.), *Economic and Industrial Structure*, (Toronto: University of Toronto Press), pp. 261–303.

Foster, Peter (1982). *The Sorcerer's Apprentices: Canada's Super-Bureaucrats and the Energy Mess*, (Toronto: Collins).

Foster, Peter (1983a). "Battle of the Sectors," *Saturday Night*, March, pp. 23–32 (re: CDC).

Foster, Peter (1983b). "Strong Politics," *Saturday Night*, August, pp. 17–23 (re: Maurice Strong, CDC and CDIC).

Foster, Peter (1986). "The Empire Builder," *Saturday Night*, June 1986, pp. 17–24 (re: Bill Hopper of Petro-Canada).

Foster, Cecil (1988). "The Rule of Lawless," *Report on Business Magazine*, February, pp. 38–44 (re: CNR).

Frizzel, Alan and Anthony Westell (1985). *The Canadian General Election of 1984: Politicians, Parties, Press and Polls*, (Ottawa, Carleton University Press).

Grace, William D. (1985). "The Case for Implementing Privatization," Speech to the Conference *Implementing Privatization*, Ottawa, June 25, mimeo.

Gracey, Don (1985). "Privatization in Ottawa," *Insight*, Winter, pp. 6–8.

Graham, Ron (1986). *One Eyed Kings*, (Toronto: Collins).

Halpern, P., A. Plourde and L. Waverman (1987). *Petro-Canada, Its Role, Control and Operations*, (Ottawa: Minister of Supply and Services).

Hardin, Herschel (1974). *A Nation Unaware: The Canadian Economic Culture*, (Vancouver: J.J. Douglas).

Howard, J.L. and W.T. Stanbury (1984). "Measuring Leviathan: The Size, Scope and Growth of Governments in Canada" in George Lermer (ed.), *Government and the Market Economy*, (Vancouver: The Fraser Institute), pp. 87–110, 127–223.

Janisch, Hudson and Richard Schultz (1985). "Teleglobe Canada: Cash Cow or White Elephant?" in T.E. Kierans and W.T. Stanbury (eds.), *Papers on Privatization*, (Montreal: Institute for Research on Public Policy), Ch. 13.

Kierans, Thomas E. (1984). "Commercial Crowns," *Policy Options/Options politiques*, Vol. 5(6), pp. 23–29.

Kierans, Thomas E. (1985). "Privatization: Strengthening the Market at the Expense of the State," *Choices*, (Montreal: The Institute for Research on Public Policy, April).

Langford, John (1985). "Privatization: A Political Analysis" in T.E. Kierans & W.T. Stanbury (eds.), *Papers on Privatization*, (Montreal: The Institute for Research on Public Policy) pp. 55–74.

Langford, John and Kenneth J. Huffman (1983). "The Uncharted Universe of Federal Public Corporations" In J.R.S. Prichard (ed.), *Crown Corporations in Canada: The Calculus of Instrument Choice*, (Toronto: Butterworth), Ch. 4.

Laux, J.K. and M.A. Molot (1987). *State Capitalism: Public Enterprise in Canada*, (Ithaca, N.Y.: Cornell University Press).

Letwin, Oliver (1988). "International Experience in the Politics of Privatization" in Michael A. Walker (ed.), *Privatization: Tactics and Techniques*, (Vancouver: The Fraser Institute), pp. 49–68.

McDougall, Hon. Barbara (1987a). "Excerpts from Statements Made by the Honourable Barbara McDougall on the Reasons for Privatization," (Ottawa: Ministry of State for Privatization, May 1, mimeo).

McDougall, Hon. Barbara (1987b). "Luncheon Address to the B.C. Politics and Policy Privatization Conference," Vancouver, May 21, mimeo.

McDougall, Hon. Barbara (1987c). "Privatization in an Information Age," speech to The Institute for Political Involvement, Toronto, September 21, 1987, mimeo.

Ohashi, T.M. (1980). "Privatization in Practice: The Story of the British Columbia Resources Investment Corporation" in T.M. Ohashi and T.P. Roth (eds.), *Privatization: Theory and Practice*, (Vancouver: The Fraser Institute).

Ohashi, T.M. and T.P. Roth (eds.) (1980). *Privatization: Theory and Practice*, (Vancouver: The Fraser Institute).

Olive, David (1985). "Turnaround Travails at the CDC," *Report on Business Magazine*, May, pp. 28–43.

Perry, Robert L. (1983). "The CDIC: Jobs for the Boys or Jobs for the Country?'', *Financial Post 500*, June, pp 46–56.

President of the Treasury Board (1985). *Annual Report to Parliament on Crown Corporations and Other Corporate Interests in Canada*, (Ottawa: Minister of Supply & Services Canada).

Prichard, J.R.S., ed. (1983). *Crown Corporations in Canada: The Calculus of Instrument Choice*, (Toronto: Butterworths).

Prince, Michael J. (1986). "The Mulroney Agenda: A Right Turn for Ottawa" in M.J. Prince (ed.), *How Ottawa Spends, 1986–87, Tracking the Tories*, (Toronto: Methuen, 1–60).

Privatization Secretariat (1986). "The Privatization of Crown Corporations," (Ottawa: Privatization Secretariat, Treasury Board, June, mimeo).

Quebec (1986). *Minister Responsible for Privatization of Crown Corporations: Orientation and Prospects*, (Quebec: Minister of Finance, February).

Reschenthaler, G.B. & W.T. Stanbury (1982). *Canadian Airlines and the Visible Hand*, (Vancouver: Faculty of Commerce, University of B.C., unpublished book manuscript).

Ross, Alexander (1983). "Strong Medicine," *Canadian Business*, April, pp. 38–41, 107–112 (re: CDIC and Maurice Strong).

Sexty, Robert W. (1979). "Direction, Control and Accountability of Crown Corporations: Review and Analysis of Government Proposals," *Osgoode Hall Law Journal*, Vol. 17(1).

Simpson, Jeffrey (1980). *Discipline of Power*, (Toronto: Personal Library).

Stanbury, W.T. (1988). *Reducing the State: Privatization in Canada*, (Montreal: The Institute for Research on Public Policy, in press).

Stein, Kenneth C.C. (1988). "Privatization: A Canadian Perspective" in Michael Walker (ed.), *Privatization Tactics and Techniques*, (Vancouver: The Fraser Institute), pp. 69–76.

Stewart–Patterson, David (1987). *Post Mortem: Why Canada's Mail Won't Move*, (Toronto: Macmillan).

Thomson, John (1985). "Politics and the Process of Privatization" in T.E. Kierans and W.T. Stanbury (eds.), *Papers on Privatization*, (Montreal: Institute for Research on Public Policy), Ch. 5.

Tupper, Allan and G. Bruce Doern (eds.) (1981). *Public Corporations and Public Policy in Canada*, (Montreal: The Institute for Research on Public Policy).

Walker, Michael A. ed. (1988). *Privatization: Tactics and Techniques*, (Vancouver: The Fraser Institute).

Yarrow, George & John Vickers (1988). "Privatization in Britain" in Paul Mac-Avoy et al., *Privatization and State–Owned Enterprises; Lessons from the United States, Great Britain and Canada*, (Boston: Kluwer Academic Publishers).

Government Participation in Investment Development

ARPAD ABONYI

The enactment of the Investment Canada Act of 1985 closed a controversial ten year chapter in the country's business history. During this period the Federal Government regulated the inflow of foreign direct investment into Canada through the Foreign Investment Review Agency (FIRA), an instrument specifically designed to extract significant benefits from international investors. The abolition of FIRA and the establishment of Investment Canada under the new Act also propelled the Federal Government into more active participation in investment development activity. While Ottawa was involved in specific industrial development projects (usually through large subsidy or grant programs) in the past — e.g. Bell Helicopters or Fleet Aerospace — the lion's share of investment development activities — making proposals to investors abroad and courting specific companies to invest in a particular region — had been performed by the provinces for a considerable number of years.

The transition from a regulatory to a proactive role ushered in a new era in Canada, but internationally the country was catching up to the major changes being made in other jurisdictions. In a number of countries around the world regulation of foreign investment was being replaced by new promotional strategies. In the turbulent business environment of the 1980s there were a number of reasons why FIRA had to go. This chapter examines the factors which led to the abolition of FIRA. It also reviews the mandate and operations of Investment Canada, the Agency which the Mulroney Government created to facilitate the flow of international investment into Canada. Finally, it outlines a number of strategic factors in the promotion of investment which increasingly bear upon the success of initiatives in today's more volatile and complex business environment.

WHY FIRA HAD TO GO

An Orphan of 'Would Be' Industrial Strategy

An agency to screen foreign direct investment was originally proposed in the 1972 review of Foreign Direct Investment in Canada, usually referred to as the Gray Report (GC, 1972). In addition to the many recommendations that were made with regard to the objectives and operations of such a screening mechanism, the Report advised that, depending on the nature of those objectives, the ability of such a screening agency would ultimately depend on the effectiveness of general economic policies (GC, 1972:452). In fact, if the government chose to employ the review process to protect Canadian entrepreneurship, as it did in many cases over the ten year period, the Report suggested:

> this should be done only where an industrial strategy exists under which areas are identified where Canadian ownership and control could be of significance, otherwise this approach should be avoided because it could involve costs that are not justifiable (GC, 1972:452)

As Richard French (1980) pointed out in his review of policy-making in Ottawa during the 1970s, an industrial strategy, indeed sectoral strategies, did not materialize for a number of reasons which we do not have to analyse here. Moreover, the relative merits of an industrial strategy are not at issue here either. The point is that FIRA, the screening agency which the government established in 1973 in response to the recommendations of the Gray Report, was originally intended to function in conjunction with an industrial strategy that had a complementary set of policy objectives (GC, 1972:452).[1] The strategy failed to materialize and the Agency was stillborn.

The Agency's effectiveness was questionable from the outset. Dewhirst and Rudiak (1986: 154–155) recently suggested that FIRA was operating at the margin and for this reason its impact on total

159

Canadian investment activity was probably limited. The authors are conditional because the quantitative impact of the Agency is not easy to measure. However the operational problems and adverse business reaction has not been hard to gauge. Left to dangle in a policy vacuum and poking around at the margin, FIRA became a lightning rod for criticism for the way it handled reviews. Despite the fact that the Agency only dealt with a minor share of all foreign investment in Canada, it gave the country a hostile image in a changing business environment.

FIRA and the Procedural Problem

There are several aspects to the review process which ultimately necessitated change. From the business perspective the major problem was a lack of transparency in FIRA's dealing with investors. This was precipitated for several reasons. First, for commercial reasons, the Agency was required by law to keep information confidential in its dealings with business and could not provide basic information to interested parties. Second, since all decisions about investment under FIRA were made by Cabinet, the decision-making process was also secret and the Agency was not allowed to reveal how or why such decisions were reached. As a result businesses did not know what they were up against.

Moreover, each investment proposal was evaluated on its own merits rather than according to general guidelines. This process, though it provided flexibility for the Agency in its bargaining with companies, created uncertainty for the investors. (And this was quite apart from the general issue that government officials, for a host of reasons, may not be able to effectively evaluate the opportunity cost and significant benefits of each investment.) Terms could change and prior decisions could not be relied upon as a guide to the policies and direction of the Agency. As will be outlined later, this aspect of FIRA's operation was in sharp contrast to the increasingly volatile business environment of the 1980s. The one thing investors were searching for, of course, was certainty.

The review process also required changes for administrative reasons. The process was ill-conceived. Every case reviewed by FIRA was brought before Cabinet for approval — no matter how small or large. By the early 1980s it took up approximately 20% of all Governor in Council Orders each year. It was an administrative burden. At the same time, the multi-step process enabled the Minister responsible for the Agency as well as other Cabinet members to politicize the decision-making process. Under some ministers negotiations could drag on for more than six months, while at the Cabinet table other ministers were able to get the Cabinet to place conditions on investors which primarily served non-commercial objectives — thereby making some investment less viable. This clearly made a firm's investment decision-making process more problematic with Canada than with other industrial countries.

FIRA and the Perceptual Problem

FIRA, and later the National Energy Program, created a negative perception of Canada in the international business community. While many of the international corporations continued their operations in the country, the Agency represented an aberration in Canadian business history. Canada had largely been viewed by international business as a hospitable environment, and the type of operations conducted by FIRA were not in keeping with historical precedent. In international business, perceptions about the environment are, in most cases, reality — and by the early 1980s Canada was viewed as hostile towards foreign business. The degree to which there was unanimity on this issue is revealed by the World Economic Forum's annual scoreboard on competitiveness which registers the views of international business on a range of environmental indicators. In 1984 Canada was ranked last by this prestigious group.[2] It was considered the least hospitable to foreign investors among twenty-two advanced industrialized countries of the world. While this view was certainly reinforced by the National Energy Program, FIRA contributed in a major way.

Unfortunately, however, during the fifteen years that it took Canada to navigate its way down to the bottom of this international list, the world of international investment changed. International investment became important to industrial restructuring and technological change all over the world (OECD, 1985). It became an important conduit for networking and international market access. Instead of regulating the inflow of investment, many nations turned to actively pursuing it.

The Changing International Investment Environment

The procedural and perceptual problems associated with FIRA became important obstacles in the evolving world of foreign investment. FIRA and the Gray Report from which it sprang, were based on Canada's experiences with foreign direct investment and corporate behaviour, especially those of Multinational Enterprises (MNEs), during the 1960s and very early 1970s. This was an era dominated by American foreign investment and U.S. MNEs. By the 1980s, these corporations were challenged by the development of Japanese and European MNEs as well as by some from newly industrializing countries (NICs) such as Brazil, South Korea and Hong Kong.

Moreover, the continued pressures for new, creative forms of competition and market access ensured that the era of foreign investment dominated by U.S. MNEs had changed considerably. Not only are MNEs larger and more global in their operations, but the volatile and uncertain nature of today's business environment has forced them to equip themselves with new corporate strategies and approaches to international investment. In this endeavour they are complemented by an increasing number of small and medium sized firms that are internationalizing their operations much faster than similar firms did twenty years ago. Simply put: the determinants of international investment *are* changing and, as a result, the nature, destination and sources of investment *have* changed (OECD, 1985).

The Determinants of Investment Today

The transformation of corporate behaviour during the last fifteen years has been precipitated by the need to maintain competitiveness in a highly volatile environment. Strategies, in large as well as smaller firms, have changed in response to a number of factors, including the emergence of new competition in NICs and elsewhere, differential rates of growth in productivity and labour costs around the world, greater technological intensity of production, fluctuating exchange rates, and new forms of protectionism.[3] With NICs developing a competitive edge in most of the standardized production techniques used to manufacture consumer durables and the stiff competition between European, Japanese and U.S. firms in advanced technologies — the monopoly position enjoyed by MNEs has eroded. According to Drucker (1986, 1987), most companies in developed countries are equally capable of doing everything, doing it equally well and doing it equally fast. Both technology and product cycles have become shorter so that even the most sophisticated advances provide only a short term lead. With access to instant information, companies can compete, just about anywhere, the moment economic conditions give them an advantage. In this environment, firms have increasingly relied on new organization and product strategies, global markets, knowledge intensity and new locational advantages for their competitive edge and, as a result, for their investment priorities as well.

Knowledge-base is a growing source of competition as firms are pushed up the technology ladder to compete in new products and processes. The move to knowledge intensity applies across industries. Technological innovation is not limited to emerging sectors, but also affects traditional areas of production. Automobiles today are made by robots and contain an increasing amount of composite plastics as well as microprocessors. Tomorrow they will run on ceramic engines. Textiles are made by supra efficient computers and agribusiness is being augmented by biotechnology. Not only do firms need more R&D programs and large reinvestments to commercialize technologies, they also require the critical mass of talent that it takes to work on the newer technologies which incorporate several streams of science. As a result, not even the largest firms today can hope to do all the R&D they require. Companies such as Sony, Phillips, General Electric, IBM and Seimans develop joint ventures and strategic alliances, create R&D joint ventures or join consortia, and subcontract to universities to gain access to markets and technology (Porter, 1987; Mytelka, 1987; OECD, 1987).

With this trend toward knowledge intensity, many firms are operating differently than they were fifteen years ago. In attempting to corner research, infrastructure and new human resources across the world, they are interested in developing or accessing more than just technology in the traditional sense. They are reaching out for the capability and ingenuity that a society has developed. Moreover, they are doing it in different ways. For example, they externalize some activities through joint ventures, rather than continuing them internally. At the same time, greater competition among firms has produced shorter technological and product life cycles. In order to stay competitive, they must not only innovate but also get their new product to the largest possible market as quickly as possible or risk obsolescence.

The pressures of competition have created a greater need for organizational flexibility and specialization as companies strive for innovation, efficiency, and better use of human resources. Their operations are becoming rationalized through horizontal rather than vertical management as well as through greater decentralization of certain functions to exploit know-how and other advantages. In terms of innovation the stress is on entrepreneurship and smaller units rather than vertically integrated multi-layered companies (Drucker, 1986; Behrman and Fischer, 1982).

Specialization has been adopted by many corporations, not only because of the efficiencies it provides, but also because it enables firms to capitalize on competitive capabilities and knowledge endowments of one subsidiary as opposed to another. There is a transition from the typical branch plant operation which merely duplicated production methods originally introduced in the parent company. MNEs are rationalizing operations on a global basis, with integrated affiliates in various countries producing parts of a final good that is marketed worldwide.

This organizational environment, as well as the need to commercialize more costly knowledge intensive products in as large a market as possible, has also contributed to the development of new global product strategies. Global marketing enables firms to standardize products on a world scale. At the same time, with computerized inventory, design, and manufacturing systems, niche products can be developed for the global market. GM's world car and the Sony Walkman are two examples. As part of these strategies corporations assign to their affiliates, missions to specialize in the production of one component, product or type of research. In Canada, for example, a certain type of jet engine is made for Pratt and Whitney and a specific turbine is made for Westinghouse. Secondly, on the marketing side, it provides a capability to market homogeneous or standardized products on a global basis.

Several developments are facilitating the emergence of global product and marketing strategies. First, in the course of product development, it is becoming practically impossible to recover investments solely from sales in the domestic market. Second, a high standard of living has emerged in North America, Europe, and Asia. Third, the emergence of common "westernized" tastes and lifestyles in a "TRIAD" market of about 650 million people (Ohmae, 1987). In today's environment, if manufacturers rely on spreading new products slowly, they may seriously jeopardize their competitive advantage. They must move quickly from domestic to overseas markets to capitalize on proprietary know-how.

Not surprisingly, in many cases investment decisions now revolve around the issue of how to maintain and/or enhance competitiveness. The advantages that one location provides in relation to another has become an important factor in strategically positioning operations of firms. Gone are the days when companies could rely only on their monopoly position in the market place. With increased pressures to access markets, as well as knowledge-based resources around the world, a location has to help maintain or enhance a firm's competitive advantage in order to attract technology intensive investment. As a result, market proximity, quality workforce, technological excellence, stable operating costs and conditions, and quality of life have become more important factors in location considerations (Wilson, 1987: 23).

While not all of these considerations are new they are being assessed within the context of a new competitive environment. For instance many firms are implementing computer-integrated manufacturing (CIM) to cut cost and improve product quality. By doing so they are increasing their reliance on skilled engineers and technicians. Subsequently, one of the determinants of site location is proximity to educational institutions that can offer a steady supply of quality CIM engineers, technicians and operators. The effects of automation in the work place are making the availability of skilled workers more important. In some instances, qualitative considerations are dominating cost factors.

Certainly macro issues do play a role in site selection, but they are not sufficient criteria for making location decisions today. In a world where three-fourths of the foreign direct investment dollars go to advanced industrial economies — economies which have similar demand structures and in which the traditional basis of comparative advantage have narrowed — other factors such as advanced technology have grown in importance. Enterprises, whether located in high technology or traditional sectors are relying on production processes utilizing advanced technologies. In this sense, the locational factors cited as critical to the producers of high technology goods are becoming increasingly important to the low technology producers: (1) computing and communications infrastructure; (2) technology supply; (3) reliable electric power and air services; (4) higher education, technical training facilities and quality workforce; (5) quality of life considerations such as a 'clean air' environment (keeping the quality worker satisfied) (Wilson, 1987: 88; Henry, 1987: 36-7).

The Nature of Investment Today

In today's more globalized and knowledge-intensive environment, the nature of investment has changed. First of all, in the past foreign investment and trade were seen as substitutes because investment would usually be considered after exporting became too costly. Investment was also a way to overcome protectionist barriers around a market, often starting with local distribution of the product, then moving production for the domestic market. Many branch plant operations in Canada developed this way. But today investment and trade are more complementary. A recent McKinsey (1987) study of fast-growth U.S. companies showed that most enter foreign markets simultaneously, in a number of different ways, including through exports, greenfield investments (new investment in plant and equipment), joint ventures and mergers and acquisitions. In many cases investments are specialized and are intended to serve export markets rather than just domestic needs.

Secondly, the elements of international investment have also changed. Investment has expanded to include commitment of not only tangible resources (capital, equipment, etc.) but also non-tangible resources (production know-how, management talent, etc.) with the intention of earning future benefits or advantages.

The Direction of Investment

Since the early 1970s, there have also been some important changes in the sources and destination of international investment. These changes are a reflection of the shifting behaviour of firms and indicative of an erratic, yet highly competitive and integrated, global economy. The instability has been brought on by a number of factors; the most prominent ones being continuing high interest rates in the 1980s, changing exchange rates, and the introduction of various forms of protectionism among OECD countries.

In this environment the deceleration in the growth of international investment, which started about twenty years ago, has continued (OECD, 1987:9). Since 1975, foreign direct investment (FDI) has been characterized by new sources of investment and greater balance between Europe and the United States, and increasingly, Japan (which has recently displaced the U.S. as the number one net exporter of capital). Two decades ago the United States and Britain accounted for about 77 percent of all FDI. By 1986, five other countries (France, Germany, Japan, Canada and Holland) accounted for over 50 percent of all such investment (IMF, 1987) Since the beginning of the 1980s, the newly industrializing countries (NICs) of Asia, most notably South Korea, Hong Kong, and Taiwan, have also emerged as new sources of direct investment.

The impact of these changes is gradually being felt in Canada. Since 1977 portfolio investment has become the dominant form of foreign investment in Canada. By 1987, it represented 63.4% of total foreign investment in the country, while direct investment accounted for 36.6% of the total (Statistics Canada, 1988). Meanwhile, from 1976 to 1985, the U.S. share of the stock of direct investment in Canada fell by almost 4 percent, while the French, Swiss, Dutch and West German share increased. Most of the increase in the book value of U.S. investment comes from reinvested earnings by subsidiaries already located in Canada. At the same time, Japan has had the fastest growing rate of direct and portfolio investments among major economic powers. Its standing as an investor in the Canadian economy rose by more than 500 percent between 1976 and 1985. Other Asian investors have also significantly increased their position in Canada over the same period.

The Competition for New Investment

The new determinants and shifting direction of international investment, coupled with the slowdown in economic growth during the early 1980s, has heightened competition for growth generating investment and has developed a new approach toward FDI. Investment, including FDI, has become more important in enhancing industrial competitiveness. Accumulation of investment, particularly in technology-intensive products and production processes, at the level of the firm, is an important source of competitive advantage (Porter, 1985). At the national level, knowledge-based infrastructure, has become a major contributor to comparative advantage. (Zysman & Tyson, 1983: 29; Zysman, 1983: 39-40).

As a result, the competition for direct investment has become intense. Countries that previously regulated foreign investment now actively promote it. Over 35 countries, 500 states and provinces and 6000 municipalities actively and aggressively compete for new investment. Government participation has ranged from reactive — responding to unsolicited enquiries — to complex promotional programs based on well-defined goals and targeted investors, as in Ireland, Britain and New Zealand. Strategies by Belgium, Holland, France, and others, have also included forward-based industrial development activities in foreign countries, in order to facilitate investment from the industrial and technological centres of the world.

The Streamlining of FIRA

In the face of these international realities the Liberal government started to make modest changes to FIRA. In 1977 it introduced shorter forms and simpler procedures for investments involving businesses with gross assets of less than $2 million and fewer than 200 employees. In June 1982 several new administrative measures were introduced to simplify procedures. They included increasing the ceiling for review under the abbreviated small business procedures from $2 million in gross assets and 100 employees to $5 million and fewer than 200 employees. In addition a new ceiling for small business procedures of $15 million in gross assets and 600 employees was set for indirect acquisitions. Measures to clarify the administration of the FIRA Act were also introduced at this time.

In 1984 the Liberal government also accepted a GATT ruling — that resulted from a protest by the United States — to stop requiring undertakings for domestic sourcing. The U.S. questioned FIRA's right both to impose such undertakings and to impose export performance requirements on foreign investors. While GATT rules did not cover export performance, the international body found that Canada had contravened the GATT by obtaining commitments on domestic sourcing. In accepting the ruling the government decided to cease requiring such undertakings. The establishment of Investment Canada (IC) in 1985 went beyond minor adjustments and fine tuning. It marked a philosophical transformation about the relationship of foreign investment to the economy. It involved major organizational and managerial changes, which served as a fitting testimonial to a new international reality.

INVESTMENT CANADA AND THE PURSUIT
OF BENEFICIAL INVESTMENT

Goals

In terms of philosophy, Investment Canada (IC) is predicated on dealing with the benefits rather than the costs of non-Canadian investment. It is based on the notion that a more open policy toward international investment will present new opportunities for growth and spur Canadian entrepreneurship in a very competitive world. In today's environment new investments can provide access to important technology and marketing networks. The Investment Canada Act, which gave birth to IC, assumes in Section 2 that increased capital and technology benefits Canada and sets as its goal "to encourage investment in Canada by Canadians and non-Canadians that contributes to economic growth and employment opportunities . . . ." In order to achieve this goal the Act is considerably different from the Foreign Investment Review Act that it replaced. The key features of the two Acts are compared in the Appendix I (following this chapter).

In pursuing its goal, IC and its Minister have a proactive mandate. Sections 5(1) and 5(2) outline ministerial responsibilities to encourage and facilitate investment. For example, subsection 5(1) states that the Minister shall "encourage business investment . . ."; "assist Canadian businesses to exploit opportunities for investment and technological advancement"; "carry out research and analysis relating to domestic and international investment"; "provide investment information services and other investment services to facilitate economic growth"; and "assist in the development of industrial and economic policies that affect investment in Canada." As a result, IC can work with investors to assist them with their investment plans.

In stark contrast to FIRA's secrecy and isolation, the Act also provides for collaboration with others in the public and private sectors. Subsection 5(2) states that, in carrying out his or her duties, the Minister shall ". . . make use of the services and facilities of other departments, branches or agencies of the Government of Canada"; ". . . with the approval of the Governor in Council, enter into agreements with the government of any province . . . for the purposes of this Act"; and ". . . consult with, and organize conferences of, representatives of industry and labour, provincial and local authorities and other interested persons." In this context IC was to pursue a practical approach, using the vast network of contacts and resources already available to the Government of Canada in both the public and private sectors — and in many instances it has.

The subsections dealing with the positive mandate are not very elaborate in the Act. It was felt that IC needed flexibility in developing its proactive initiatives in consultation with other departments of the government, the provinces and the private sector. Moreover, programs are required to be adaptable so that they can be adjusted to changing economic circumstances and conditions.

The Review of Significant Investments

In addition to its proactive mandate, IC is also charged with the review of "significant" investments in Canada by non-Canadians in order to ensure "benefit" to Canada. In administering the Act, IC has two requirements for investments by non-Canadians — notification for certain investments and review for others. The notification requirement applies (1) to all investments by non-Canadians establishing new businesses and (2) to all acquisitions by non-Canadians of non-Canadian businesses with assets below the review thresholds. In the case of direct acquisitions, the review threshold is Canadian businesses with assets of $5 million or more, and in the case of indirect acquisitions, resulting from the merger or acquisition of control abroad of the parent company of a Canadian business, the review threshold is $50 million in assets. This will change further with the proposed Canada-United States Free Trade Agreement. As Appendix II (following this chapter) indicates, the review threshold for direct acquisitions will rise in stages to $150 million by 1993. The review of indirect acquisitions will be abolished by 1992 under the Agreement. As part of the notification requirement investors are required to file a notification of their investment within 30 days of making the investment.

If the review requirement applies, an application has to be filed with IC prior to the investment taking place or, in the case of indirect acquisitions, within 30 days of the investment taking place. IC submits the application to the Minister, together with other information or written undertakings given by the investor and any representations by a province likely to be significantly affected by the investment. The Minister then assess the proposal to determine whether or not it is likely to be of net benefit to Canada by reference to the information provided and the factors of assessment. In contrast to FIRA which required significant benefits from investors, that were hard to prove from a bureaucratic point of view and at times impossible to demonstrate from a small business perspective, IC assesses an investment on the basis of "net benefits". It is basically a no detriment test based on the assessment factors presented in Appendix I and implies that the expectations of benefit will be scaled according to the size and nature of the investment.

Sensitive Industries and New Assessment Factors

IC also has the authority to review acquisitions below the thresholds and investments by non-Canadians to establish new businesses in culturally sensitive sectors which impact on the country's heritage and national identity. As a result, special consideration was given to firms in economic activities such as publishing, film production and film distribution. This is defined under reserve powers in Section 15 so that investors in other sectors will be assured that their notified investment cannot be subject to review. This was an attempt to deal with the problem of transparency which plagued FIRA. Under this section investments will be reviewed if the Minister considers it in the public interest to do so and if the Governor in Council issues an order to that effect within 21 days of the date when a completed notification of the investment was filed.

The factors of assessment, on which the Minister's decision to allow or disallow an investment must be based, are similar to those specified in the Foreign Investment Review Act as indicated in Appendix I with two exceptions. A cultural policy component has been added to the fifth factor so that it reads:

the compatibility of the investment with national industrial, economic and cultural policies, taking into consideration industrial, economic and cultural policy objectives enunciated by the government or legislature of any province likely to be significantly affected by the investment.

The other difference between the factors of assessment under the Investment Canada and the Foreign Investment Review Acts is the addition of a sixth factor, which is:

The contribution of the investment to Canada's ability to compete in world markets.

Process

The review process also differs under IC. By giving decision-making power to the Minister, one level in the process is eliminated. There is also a definite limit on the time which the Minister has to make a decision under the Act: 45 days, unless the applicant agrees to a 30 day extension. Under FIRA no such limit existed and reviews could drag on indefinitely.

The Act also introduced new rules for determining Canadian control of a corporation. Under Section 26 it takes into account the extent of Canadian ownership. It uses new presumptions to encourage non-Canadian controlled enterprises whose investments might be subject to review, to take steps to increase ownership and participation by Canadians. Finally, it changed penalties from criminal to civil, except for breach of confidentially.

ORGANIZATION

The current Investment Canada organization was designed to integrate three activities: (1) encouraging and promoting investment in Canada including policy development and research; (2) determining the retrievability of investments, assessing proposals and monitoring conformance; and (3) administration. This will probably change with the advent of free trade as Canada puts greater emphasis on attracting and retaining investment. This will increase the need for marketing and strategic planning and will require less resources for the review function.

The Agency has five operational divisions: Investment Development, Investment Review, Investment Policy and Research, Corporate Secretary, and Corporate Services. The responsibility of each division is outlined in IC's main estimates report, the document which also shows that the estimated cost of the total IC program for 1987-88 was $10,018 million — modest by international standards. (GC, 1987:22)

The federal effort in investment development has required close co-ordination among three organizations — Investment Canada, the Department of Regional Industrial Expansion (DRIE) and the Department of External Affairs (DEA) — and a clear definition of their respective roles. IC offers services to facilitate investments and complements the activities of the other departments through the preparation and co-ordination of promotional material and advertising. It is also responsible for the regulatory requirements of the Investment Canada Act.

Federal investment promotion activities are coordinated by means of an inter-departmental committee consisting of officials from IC, DRIE and DEA. DEA, with its extensive representation abroad, has had responsibility for international investment promotion activities; DRIE, with its network of regional offices, has had responsibility for sectoral and regional investment activities in Canada and abroad and for specialized policy and research targeted at specific regions. However, with the proposed transformation of DRIE into the new Department of Industry, Science and Technology (DIST), this relationship may change as the new department may well undertake a more extensive role in identifying and targeting technology intensive international investment.

IC has launched several initiatives at home and abroad in pursuit of its goal of encouraging investment by Canadians and non-Canadians. The objectives of these undertakings have been:

- to ensure that Canada's environment for investment is attractive compared with the many formidable competitors, and that it is recognized as attractive by potential and prospective investors, both Canadian and non-Canadian;

- to carry out a sustained campaign, supported by all levels of government and the private sector, to increase investment in Canada by Canadians and non-Canadians; and

- to complement and support the promotion initiatives of the provinces, territories and the private sector (GC, 1987:10).

While more initiatives were added, the initial thrust has been on marketing and promotion rather than strategic targeting and policy development. This is in part explained by the fact that under FIRA, Canada had developed a poor image and refrained from promoting itself. It is also a consequence of IC being a small agency by Ottawa standards with modest resources. A number of promotion activities were undertaken around the world, but the question is how effective were these initiatives and how did they affect the flow of investment to Canada?

PERFORMANCE AND EFFECTIVENESS

The Flow of Investment

IC's effectiveness can be evaluated in both quantitative and qualitative terms. However, it is important to note that a number of factors impinge on a country's ability to attract a specific quantity and quality of investment. Therefore the success which is achieved cannot be attributed to a specific entity such as IC. For example, there have been several complimentary initiatives by the government — in the areas of deficit control, energy policy, deregulation, privatization and general business confidence building — to make Canada a more hospitable location for investment. Canada's favourable exchange and interest rates have also acted as incentives for investment. This is in addition to industry and firm specific factors which may provide an automatic locational advantage. These are all determinants over which IC has no control. More importantly, other government agencies such as DRIE/DIST, DEA, as well as Employment and Immigration with its Entrepreneurial Immigration Program, actively contributed to the investment development initiative. Finally, provincial governments and municipalities have also been very prominently involved in promotion around the world.

With such a collective effort underway it is not surprising that, in quantitative terms, the encouragement investment has been wildly successful. The gross flows of foreign direct investment into Canada more than doubled between 1984 and 1987, rising from $3.7 to $8.9 billion during the period (Statistics Canada, 1988). Portfolio investment has also increased. Between 1984 and 1987 it grew 67 percent from $114.8 to $178.9 billion, representing 63.4% of total foreign investment[4] in the country (Statistics Canada, 1988).

However, Canada, like other industrial countries, has been faced with less opportunities to attract new "greenfield" investment into business plant and equipment. Investment development activity of this kind has encountered very stiff international competition. Many OECD countries are aggressively seeking foreign investment

174

in an attempt to recover from the sagging domestic investment levels of the late 1970s and the early 1980s, while increasing the technology intensity of their economies.

OECD (1987) studies show that since the 1970s a decline in "greenfield" investment has taken place in tandem with a trend toward mergers and acquisitions. In part, this is a normal development that follows when companies gain experience and information after their initial foreign investments have been established. Market growth is then often accommodated by expanding existing operations, while local knowledge makes the task of identifying possible acquisitions much easier. On the other hand, in cases of slower growth, successful companies have employed conservative strategies, increasing their market shares by acquiring existing capacities of less successful competitors. Greater instability and volatility in the market has also heightened sensitivity to costs. Where cost considerations are more important to strategic decisions there has tended to be increased risk aversion and a preference for reduced time frames for an investment's payback period. According to the OECD (1987:23) these forces have acted to divert a considerable proportion of investment away from new plants and towards rationalization of existing capacity and acquisition.

In Canada's case, business reluctance to support R&D or become involved internationally in joint ventures or technology intensive strategic alliances has hindered efforts to attract greenfield investment.

There are, of course, other factors involved. The large investments in pulp and paper plant and equipment in 1988, for example, reflect an appreciation of Japanese and European currencies vis-à-vis the Canadian dollar as well as specific resource advantages. The depreciation of North American currencies will serve to increase new investment, but even here the problem continues. In many cases it is simply cheaper to buy a company than it is to build one, particularly when the lower price-to-earning ratios of Canadian companies make them such attractive takeover targets. As we indicate later, a more strategic approach to investment development could help to direct it toward corporate needs in other areas.

A More Positive Image

The period between 1984 and 1988 also witnessed the transformation of the country's image as a place to do business. Under FIRA

175

and the National Energy Program, whether deserved or not, Canada developed a poor reputation internationally. By 1986 this situation was turning around. Canada was ranked 6th in international competitiveness by the World Economic Forum (WEF) and it moved up to 15th position among the OECD countries in welcoming foreign investment (EMF, 1986). These views were echoed by a high level Japanese business delegation visiting Canada in 1986, which reported a "new" Canada with more opportunities and openness for international business.

Costs

Higher inflows of investment were achieved through modest expenditures by IC, when compared with its international competitors. With an allotment of 127 person-years, IC has nine individuals less than FIRA. Though IC's annual budget is approximately $10 million, only about $1 million goes to advertising and promotion. The rest goes toward salaries and wages, administration and research. Of course promotion outlays are also augmented by activities in both DEA (geographically) and DRIE/DIST (sectorally), but these are not generally considered part of IC activity.

By way of comparison it is interesting to note that in 1985-86, the United Kingdom, with twice the population, $8.5 million was spent on advertising and promotion through Invest Britain, the Scottish Development Agency and the Welsh Development Agency. During the same year Ireland's Industrial Development Authority, which is working on behalf of 3.5 million people, spent $10 million dollars for promotion. The Netherlands with 14.4 million people spent $3.8 million for the same activity.[5]

With the Mulroney Government's budgetary restraints in effect, future expenditures for investment promotion are not likely to increase substantially. At the same time the increasing competition for new international investment, the changing and more sophisticated patterns of corporate behaviour — as well as the greater complexity of technology intensive investment — all pose challenges for government investment development in the years ahead. With the trend toward greater niche marketing, specialization in production and globalization of corporate strategies a more focused approach to investment development is now required.

A STRATEGIC APPROACH TO
INVESTMENT DEVELOPMENT

Why does investment promotion need to be focused? Canada, as other countries, is faced with greater international competition for a slower growing investment pie, which is now composed of a smaller proportion of new "greenfield" investment. In this environment international investors have more options and are attracted by a location's strengths. Not only must investment development efforts be based on a strategic understanding of corporate operations and technological position, they must also be based on an appreciation of how those corporate production activities can be enhanced by the strengths of a Canadian location. A strategic approach to investment development marries locational advantage to corporate competitiveness.

Investment and trade promotion are different sides of the same coin. There are considerable differences in the types of capabilities and outlooks that make them successful. Investment promotion is based more on strategic business intelligence than is trade promotion.

Because of corporate preoccupation with competitiveness, attracting new investment, especially in technology intensive sectors, requires an ability to determine the strengths of Canadian locations in relation to that of international competitors. While this process may be complex, it is necessary for an understanding of which plants and industries will thrive in the local economic environment. Relevant goals and action plans for investment development can then be formulated. Specific prospects can be identified and approached. Sponsors of the numerous investment seminars and presentations designed to provide information on how to do business have to keep in mind that *companies are looking for new forms of advantage* — not just general information. In today's aggressive environment, economic jurisdictions must capitalize on their strengths and be willing to develop new ones by restructuring their economies.

Facilitating the flow of investment into Canada also necessitates the development of a corporate intelligence and analysis capability. This is necessary if Canada is to understand company goals and strengths, appreciate technical complexities, and assess international operations. This enables intermediaries and government officials to tailor persuasive approaches when targeting the investor. Today, even mid-sized companies are becoming internationalized and have to be appraised with regard to their needs so that we can show why a Canadian location can enhance their international competitiveness.

When we look at giant multinationals — firms such as Seimans, Phillips or Thyssen which are several times larger than the largest Canadian controlled firms — it is critical that intermediaries have an up-to-date appreciation of what these firms, or their Japanese and U.S. equivalents, produce and where these products are assembled. These international giants own numerous companies and produce a wide range of products around the world.

Shreveport, Louisiana is testimony to the fact that strategic corporate intelligence pays off. It lost thousands of jobs as the community's largest employer, IT&T, moved part of its phone production to Singapore. Local officials and suppliers formed a committee to analyse IT&T's global operations and the role of its facilities in Singapore. In this way they came to understand their community's advantages in relation to IT&T's international network. They developed a strategy to approach IT&T and convinced the company to invest in a new facility that could be more competitively operated from Shreveport, thus winning back most of the jobs that were lost (Morrison, 1987).

In order to secure investment for new businesses an up-to-date investor database offering timely and specific information is required. Investment developers need to differentiate their message from that of competing jurisdictions. A persuasive investment development strategy can no longer be based solely on traditional industrial development information. It should, for instance, deal with innovative financing capacity. Changes in markets, in technology, and in business practices demand that economic development authorities enjoy immediate access to complete, reliable and current strategic intelligence in order to provide it to prospective investors. In a highly competitive global economy, this information should be both homogeneous and comparative. Remember: Asian and European business cultures are more concerned with details than image. Japanese businessmen always have an appetite for more specific information than Canadians have ready for them.

A strategic approach to attracting investment into new business has to be reinforced by a commitment to increasing domestic investment. Foreign investment is attracted by a dynamic, innovative and technology oriented business community which is willing to develop new opportunities and has the confidence to invest in the future. For example, Ireland has had great success in luring companies to establish operations in that country, but it has lost several firms because their investments were not sufficiently complemented by domestic investment initiatives, especially the development of an adequate supply network.

In view of the increasing role of technology and specialization in investment, the Government's new Department of Industry, Science and Technology may emerge as the natural base from which to generate a strategic investment development program. With sector expertise, support for technological innovation and development of business and corporate intelligence, it will have the necessary ingredients for more strategic corporate targeting. Meanwhile the Department of External Affairs has the experience to continue to promote investment abroad. Together, they are better equipped to take the next steps: developing new data base instruments, business environment products and software packages which target strategic corporate decision makers and planners who are making comparative locational choices.

DEA should use its overseas network to monitor and constantly gather business intelligence on factors important for Canadian Business dealing in the international arena. DIST for its part could increase its role in the gathering of business intelligence on the domestic industrial activities and structure and the dissemination to Canadian business of the relevant intelligence gathered.

The relationship between these two departments should also be complemented by more focused cooperation between Business, Government and Universities in the development of new programs to facilitate the growth of strategic investments tht will make Canada more competitive.

STEPS TO BE TAKEN

There are at least four steps that have to be integrated into any new investment promotion program to be undertaken by the government.

(1) *Development of strategic goals that take into account.*
— the current and future corporate environment, at the international level
— Canada's position vis-à-vis its competitors.
— industry and technology needs in a global context.
— the impact of changing technology and corporate specialization.

(2) *Investment attracts investment. Focus on the linkage between investment development and the domestic economy.*
— nurture technology intensive domestic and foreign investment that develops knowledge-based infrastructure and increases productivity.
— encourage domestic industry to think globally and benefit from joint ventures and strategic alliances. These can provide technology windows, marketing networks and enhanced learning curves of Canadian firms.
— in traditional industries, encourage and facilitate investment in strategic technologies (biotech, advanced materials, micro-electronics).

(3) *Promote investment that matches locational advantages with corporate strengths*
— identify locational strengths
— identify and target key companies and their international deployment
— focus on specialization

(4) *Develop strategic marketing methods*
— determine benefits and present opportunities in a competitive context
— introduce software to communicate business environment advantages
— develop interactive systems to exchange information on opportunities

CONCLUSIONS

With the abolition of FIRA and the creation of Investment Canada, the Mulroney Government ended a controversial decade of Canadian business history. The actions of the Government only confirmed the development of a new international business reality which had eclipsed FIRA; an Agency rooted in a world that no longer existed. Today, Japan, rather than the United States, is the dominant international source of investment. American multinationals have been challenged, in many cases successfully, by dynamic European and Japanese firms which are more favourably disposed to alternative forms of international investment. These firms have also increased the technology intensity of investment.

Such developments, and the increased pressures of international competitiveness today, have led to new corporate organizations and strategies that give impetus to investment. Decentralization of R&D capabilities in many firms, such as IBM, enable Canada to attract research intensive investment. Corporate rationalization, on the other hand, provides opportunities for supplier industries to grow and develop forward linkages, as larger companies focus more narrowly and subcontract more work. This has been the case in the automobile industry where a company like Magna International has moved into new areas.

These examples simply highlight the opportunities which exist for Canada and Canadian business when knowledge and understanding form the basis of efforts to develop a vibrant and productive economy. The knowledge is available. Now, with the Government's attention fixed on new trade and investment initiatives, it is time to examine its investment priorities and develop the organizational tools and promotional strategies needed to create the kind of investment that will carry Canada into the next century.

181

Appendix I: Comparison of Foreign Investment Review Act and Investment Canada Act

Key Features	Foreign Investment Review Act	Investment Canada Act
Purpose	Level of foreign control a matter of national concern	Investment by Canadians and non-Canadians presumed to be of benefit to Canada
Scope of Review		
• New Businesses	All	Not reviewed
• Direct Acquisitions	All	Reviewed if $5M or more
• Indirect Acquisitions	All	Reviewed if $50M or more, or $5M or more if Canadian subsidiary is more than 50% of total transaction
Scope of Notification	No separate provision as all investment reviewed	All new businesses and acquisitions below thresholds indicated above
Reserve Power to Review	None required	Any investment regardless of size in prescribed culturally sensitive sectors
Benefit Test	Significant benefit to Canada	Net benefit to Canada
Assessment Factors	Impact on: • economic activity • Canadian participation • efficiency and technology • competition • compatibility with federal and provincial economic and industrial policies	Impact on: • economic activity • Canadian participation • efficiency and technology • competition • compatibility with federal and provincial economic and industrial policies • compatibility with cultural policy • international competitiveness
Review Process		
• Consultation with	• Provinces affected • Departments affected	• Provinces affected • Departments affected
• Cabinet	In sensitive cases	In sensitive cases
• Decision by	Governor in Council	Minister
• Time frame	60 days with unlimited extension by Government	45 days with extension beyond 75 days only with agreement of investor
Definition of Foreign Investor	Complex rules based on control-in-fact with presumptions biased against investor. No incentive for investors to Canadianize.	Simpler rules which take account of extent of Canadian ownership and employing more balanced presumptions. Modest incentive for investors to Canadianize.

Key Features	Foreign Investment Review Act	Investment Canada Act
Penalties	Criminal penalties	Civil penalties except for breach of confidentiality
Positive Role	None	Specific mandate to: • encourage investment for growth • provide information services • advise on opportunities and contacts

Appendix II: Investment Provisions Under the Canada–U.S. Free Trade Agreement

Under Chapter Sixteen of the Agreement, the two Governments:

— agree to extend national treatment to each other's investors, including the establishment of new businesses, and the operation, conduct and sale of those businesses;

— agree not to require minimum equity holdings by nationals of the host country;

— agree not to require performance requirements of each other's investors in the form of export levels, local content, local sourcing or import-substitution requirements. Performance requirements linked to government subsidies and incentives are not prohibited.

— agree to further liberalize conditions for cross-border investment and provide greater assurance regarding the flow of capital, profits and other earnings;

— agree to grandfathering of existing laws, regulations and published policies and practices not in conformity with the above obligations;

— agree that Canadian provincial governments and American state governments will be subject to the provisions of the Agreement relating to investments;

— agree that Canada reserves the right to review U.S. investments in Canada's cultural industries, irrespective of the size of the investment and, in the case of privatization, retains the right to restrict the sale of shares of Crown corporations to Canadians.

— agree that domestic laws governing trade activities will continue to apply. U.S. anti-trust laws will continue to govern all businesses operating in the

183

U.S., while Canadian competition laws will continue to govern all businesses operating in Canada;

— agree that the review thresholds under the Investment Canada Act will be raised in accordance with the following schedule.

For Direct Acquisitions

Effective January 1, 1989	Cdn$ 25 million
Effective January 1, 1990	Cdn$ 50 million
Effective January 1, 1991	Cdn$ 100 million
Effective January 1, 1992	Cdn$ 150 million
Effective January 1, 1993	Cdn$ 150 million

in constant dollars, adjusted annually using the Canadian Gross National Product Deflator.

For Indirect Acquisitions

Effective January 1, 1989	Cdn$ 100 million
Effective January 1, 1990	Cdn$ 250 million
Effective January 1, 1991	Cdn$ 500 million
Effective January 1, 1992	no review.

Canada also agrees that the thresholds described above will apply to the acquisition by third-country investors of Canadian firms controlled by U.S. investors.

NOTES

[1] For instance, development of entrepreneurial, financial technological and managerial areas and general competitiveness of the Canadian economy, (see: GC, 1972:462)

[2] The World Economic Forum, previously the European Management Forum, represents 800 of the top international businesses. The Forum meets annually in Davos, Switzerland in late January to discuss changing issues confronting business.

[3] These changes have been outlined in detail by a number of OECD (1981, 1983, 1985, 1987) reports.

[4] By this is meant portfolio plus foreign direct investment, excluding other liabilities in Canada's international investment position.

[5] Data collected by the author.

REFERENCES

Behrman, Jack and William Fischer (1982). *Overseas R&D Activities of Transnational Companies*, (Oelgeschlager: Gann and Hain Publishers).

Dewhirst, Gordon and Michael Rudiak (1986). "From Investment Screening to Investment Development: The Impact of Canada's Foreign Investment

Review Agency (FIRA) and Investment Canada in Canada's Technological Development," *Canada–United Law Journal*, vol. 11, pp. 154–155.

Dewhirst, Gordon and Michael Rudiak (1987). "The Transnational Economy," *The Wall Street Journal*, August 25.

Drucker, Peter (1986). "The Changing Multinational," *The Wall Street Journal*, January 15, p. 25.

Drucker, Peter (1987). "The Transnational Economy," *The Wall Street Journal*, August 25.

European Management Foundation (EMF) (1986). *World Competitiveness Report*, (Davos: EMF Foundation).

French, Richard D. (1980). *How Ottawa Decides*, (Toronto: Canadian Institute for Economic Policy).

Government of Canada (GC) (1972). *Foreign Direct Investment in Canada*, (Ottawa: Minister of Supply and Services).

Government of Canada (GC) (1987). *Investment Canada, 1987–1988 Estimates Part III*, (Ottawa: Supply and Services Canada).

Henry, Donald (1987). "How Japanese Executives Select U.S. Sites," *Area Development*, (August).

International Monetary Fund (1987). *Balance of International Payments*, (Washington: IMF).

McKinsey and Company Inc. (1987). *Winning the World Market*, (Washington: American Business Council).

Morrison, Edward (1987). "Cities in a Global Economy," *Issues in Science and Technology*, (Summer), pp. 42–51.

Mytelka, Lynn (1987). "Political Economy of Strategic Partnering," A Study prepared for Investment Canada.

OECD (1981). *Recent International Direct Investment Trends*, (Paris: OECD).

OECD (1983). *International Investment and Multinational Enterprises: Recent International Direct Investment Trends*, (Paris: OECD).

OECD (1985). *Structural Adjustment and Multinational Enterprise* (Paris: OECD).

OECD (1987). *International Investment and Multinational Enterprises: Recent Trends in International Direct Investment*, (Paris: OECD).

Ohmae, Kenichi (1987). "The Triad World View," *The Journal of Business Strategy*, (Spring), pp. 8–13.

Porter, Michael (1985). *Competitive Advantage: Creating and Sustaining Superior Performance*, (New York: The Free Press).

Porter, Michael (1987). "From Competitive Strategy to Corporate Strategy," *Harvard Business Review*, (May–June).

Statistics Canada (1988). *Canada's International Investment Position*, (Ottawa: Supply and Services Canada).

Wilson, Reese (1987). "Strategic Positioning of High-Tech Enterprises," *Area Development*, (June).

Zysman, John (1983). *Governments, Markets and Growth*, (Ithaca: Cornell University Press).

Zysman, John and Laura Tyson [eds.] (1983). *American Industry in International Competition: Government Policy and Corporate Strategies*, (Ithaca: Cornell University Press).

Regulating Conservatively: The Mulroney Record, 1984–1988

RICHARD J. SCHULTZ

Although it may be somewhat presumptuous to designate the first and possibly only term of the Mulroney Conservative Government as an era, at least in the standard sense of a "period of time characterized by a notable historical change," nevertheless 1988 is an apposite time to review the Government's record in the area of regulation. It is apposite not only because it is the fourth year of the Government's mandate which provides a good time to assess its performance in a number of policy arenas. Perhaps more significantly, 1988 is the tenth anniversary of the emergence of regulation as a significant public policy issue in Canada. It was in 1978, at a First Ministers' Conference, that Prime Minister Trudeau joined with his provincial counterparts in a call for a reduction in "the burden of government regulation on the private sector" and the elimination of "the burden of overlapping federal and provincial jurisdictions" (Economic Council of Canada, 1979: Appendix A). Consequently, we have an opportunity not simply to assess the Conservative record but to engage in a comparative exercise, to see if there are any significant differences in the approaches of the two Governments to a common set of issues. Such an approach would appear to be particularly appropriate in order to assess the extent to which the Conservative strategic policy objectives over the past four years constitute an embrace of neo-liberalism for Canada. While a comparison in a single issue area over a ten-year period can only permit us to draw some tentative conclusions, in conjunction with the other issue areas covered in this book we should be able to develop a more comprehensive appreciation of the nature of the impact of the past four years of a Conservative government on the definition of the role of the Canadian state.

This essay is divided into four parts. The first develops a general perspective on the nature of economic regulation as employed by the Canadian state. Part two reviews the record of the Trudeau governments from 1968 to 1984 from the vantage point of the general approach of the Liberals to regulatory issues and to the role of regulation as an instrument of governance as well as initiatives taken in several individual sectors. Part three then reviews the Mulroney government record from a similar perspective. In the concluding section, I shall attempt to draw out the implications of the record of the past four years in the regulatory sector for our understanding of the role of the Canadian state with particular reference to the claim that Canada may have adopted, or alternatively had imposed on it, some variant of neo-liberal ideology.

REGULATION AND THE CANADIAN STATE

By way of an introduction to our assessment of the Mulroney record on regulation, it is important that we clearly specify what I mean by the term "regulation." We employ a traditional definition that is restricted to what is commonly labelled "economic regulation": such regulation entails a governmental role in restricting or restraining the economic behaviour, that is the choices, of individuals or firms in three areas — the terms of entry into, or exit from, a specific economic activity; the prices economic actors may charge for their products or services; and finally the conditions or standards governing relations between firms which are regulated and their customers (Schultz and Alexandroff, 1985:4)

For the purpose of this essay there are three general points that need to be made about the historical role of regulation in Canada.[1] The first is that there has been an extensive reliance on economic regulation to pursue public policy objectives in Canada. The second is that a primary reason for such extensive reliance is the flexibility of the instrument of economic regulation. It is an instrument which has proven to be multi-functional and multi-dimensional and consequently very adaptable for the pursuit of many public goals. Thirdly, and I will argue most significantly in terms of the current debates, the traditional heavy reliance on regulation and its adaptability have led, I contend, to fundamental misunderstandings about the very nature of the instrument and especially its potentialities. The following summary discussion will attempt to clarify what I mean by these three points.

Although it is somewhat facile to describe Canada as a "regulated state," it is undoubtedly true that regulation of economic activity is an enduring Canadian tradition and a tool which has been central to successive governments' attempts at nation-building and the promotion of economic development. This is shown by its regular employment on its own or in conjunction with other public policy instruments. The early history of the building of our first trans-continental railway, the Canadian Pacific, entailed both substantial public subsidization and regulatory control over competitive entry through the grant of a monopoly, albeit short-lived, to the CPR in the western provinces. From its creation in 1932, and especially after 1936, until 1958, the Canadian Broadcasting Corporation was not only a state-funded broadcaster it was also the regulator of the private sector radio and television. Similarly, the dominant characteristic of the development of air transport in Canada was the route protection granted to Air Canada for almost thirty years from competition. In short, economic regulation has played a central role in the development of both sectors of the Canadian economy and specific public and quasi-public policy instruments.

One of the major reasons that accounts for the extensive use of economic regulation is its multi-functional, multi-dimensional nature. The traditional view is that regulation is introduced as a corrective for market failure. More specifically, regulation is thought to be imposed to protect consumers against the abuse of monopoly power to charge excessive prices or to discriminate amongst customers. Much of the research and policy attention, particularly in the United States from the 1950s to the 1970s has stemmed from a concern that regulation has either been an ineffective corrective or worse has been "captured" by the very interests whose unacceptable behaviour it was expected to control. The focus on this aspect of regulation has prevented, however, a deeper appreciation of the many facets of regulation and the broader roles for which it has been employed.

As I have argued at length elsewhere, the traditional initial assumption that regulation is a "negative" instrument of government to prevent or correct unacceptable economic conduct through the policing of individual monopolistic firms must be supplemented with an understanding of the more positive, pre-scriptive regulatory roles. One such role has been to promote or protect individual firms from competition deemed to be "unheal-thy." The protection granted to Air Canada is the outstanding Canadian example of such a positive use of regulation. A second, more expansive positive role for regulation is found in its use, often in conjunction with other instruments such as public enterprise or subsidies, as a planner for a specific sector of economic activity. When used to plan, regulatory authorities establish goals and coor-dinate relationships among individual economic actors. The goals of planning regulation are usually much broader than simple economic efficiency; indeed efficiency considerations are normally assigned a low priority when regulation is employed as a planning instrument. In the period 1964 to 1970, the federal government sought to employ regulation of air competition in an attempt to plan the air sector. Perhaps the most obvious example of regula-tion as planning is found in the broadcast sector where first with the introduction of television, then cable systems and more recent-ly pay television and satellite systems, the scope of the regulator was expanded to envelop and stipulate the roles and relationships of the individual members of the "single system" as broadcasting has long been described.

The traditional recourse to regulation as either primary or sup-plementary instrument combined with the multiple goals sought through its use have led, I would contend, to fundamental mis-understandings about the very nature of regulation as an instru-ment of government. Such misunderstandings are often at the heart of the current ideological disputes over the efficacy of regula-tion.

Economic regulation, at its core, involves the use of the state's coercive powers to impose restricted choices on economic actors to obtain, or seek to do so, socially-desired objectives. Although regulatory authorities, be they individual ministers, cabinet as a collectivity or independent agencies such as the Canadian Radio-television and Telecommunications Commission or the National Energy Board, may have other powers at their disposal such as suasion or subsidization, coercion — the power to impose obliga-tions on economic actors and to enforce those obligations if neces-sary — are the cornerstone of regulation. It is in this sense that regulation is described as a "command and control" instrument of governance (Schultze, 1977; Lowi, 1985). Although some find the terms coercion or "command and control" to be unsettling or even worse "derogatory" or "pejorative," they are not meant to be but are used in a strictly neutral sense.[2] Regulation, particularly as policing but also as promoting and planning, is premised on the Weberian definition of the state and its concomitant, that coercion is a part of all state action.

Aside from the intellectual stigma that may inappropriately be tied to the concept of coercion in a democratic state, there are other reasons why the coercive core of regulation is often ignored. One simple reason is that our support for a "good" end may lead us to ignore or underemphasize the characteristics of the specific instrument for its attainment. Doing "good" be it promoting Canadian culture or air service to small communities is allowed to take precedence over any concerns with the means we use. Another, and perhaps more important, reason for devaluing the role of coercion is that in too many instances the presumed object of coercion is the actual beneficiary of the regulation. Theories which emphasize regulatory capture of that "regulation is demanded by the regulated" lead to an emphasis on the winners in the regulatory "game" and if they are the regulated firms, as they all too often are, it is all too easy to be sceptical of the role of coercion in the regulatory system.

To deny the reality of coercion, especially for the latter reason, is to adopt a very narrow view of the regulatory regime. Our definition of economic regulation advanced above did not restrict the restriction of choice only to the choices of so-called regulated firms, or suppliers of regulated goods and services. To appreciate that there are other objects of restricted choice, it is necessary to have a comprehensive understanding of the identity of all the players or participants who may have a stake in any individual system of regulation. Aside from the firms or companies whose behaviour may be regulated, it is also the behaviour of consumers as well as alternative suppliers which may be restricted to the specific or range of choices established by the regulatory authorities. From this wider perspective, it is not only the pricing alternatives of a monopolist that are restricted as they are in policing regulation but also the choices of consumers, be it the prices they must pay or service providers they must use, that can be restricted. In the case of airline regulation, for example, the control over entry both into the industry or on specific routes, restricted the available choices for air passengers. Similarly, the decade-long refusal by the CRTC to licence pay-television in Canada restricted the range of choices available for Canadian viewers, or at least those without access to satellite dishes.

It is important to emphasize that at no point in the preceding discussion have I questioned the appropriateness of the state imposing such restrictions. Nor do I wish to enter into a discussion of the "rightness" or soundness of such public policies. My purpose here is much more specific. As a result of the traditional heavy reliance on regulation as an instrument of governing, particularly given the attractiveness of its multi-functional nature, it is all too easy to ignore questions about its effectiveness. More specifically, it is too easy to ignore the conditions or prerequisites that underlie the utility of economic regulation. My discussion of the centrality of coercion to economic regulation is an attempt to open this issue to discussion. I will argue later that, if regulation indeed rests on the coercive power of the state, then regulation as an instrument of governing is only as effective as the capacity of the state to impose its range of choices on those whom it seeks to regulate. If it cannot control excessive profit-making or acts of discrimination by monopoly firms, or entry into previously closed sectors of economic activity, or, and this is perhaps the most interesting dilemma of all, the exit of those economic actors, be they companies or consumers, from regulated sectors generally or at least from the regulators, prescribed set of choices, then the state's capacity to regulate will be undermined. To my mind, this issue of capacity, of effectiveness, of the state regulatory instrument is perhaps the most crucial variable in determining the future of the use of regulation by the Canadian state. I will return to this question in the concluding section.

THE LIBERALS AND REGULATION

To provide a useful base for an evaluation of the Mulroney record on regulation it is instructive to examine that of its immediate predecessor, the Trudeau Liberals. It is particularly important to do so because, as mentioned earlier, it was Trudeau who helped put regulation on the public agenda by his request to the Economic Council to undertake the comprehensive "Regulation Reference" from 1978 to 1981. Furthermore, lest one too easily falls into the trap of thinking that regulatory reform is essentially a "neo-liberal"/conservative issue, it should be recalled that long before Ronald Reagan and Margaret Thatcher began their assaults on the roles and powers of their respective states, the government of Lester Pearson introduced the first comprehensive act of regulatory reform. The 1967 *National Transportation Act*, although somewhat of a misnomer because it was in essence a revised *Railway Act*, fundamentally reduced the regulation of Canadian railways with the introduction of a banded pricing system consisting of a regulated floor and ceiling for rates with railway freedom to price within this band.

Despite his apparent championing of the cause of regulatory reform by adopting the rhetoric of "regulatory burden" on the private sector and the concern that growing regulation "might be having serious adverse effects on the efficiency of Canadian firms and industries" and his request that the Economic Council undertake a series of studies and develop a set of proposals to "improve government regulation," Trudeau's Liberal governments from 1968 to 1984 were at best tepid reformers.[3]

This is not to suggest that no reforms were introduced. Entry controls on foreign banks were relaxed in the 1980s and most significantly, the venerable Crow's Nest Pass legislation which held a number of important agricultural rates at their *1898* levels was replaced thereby ending an historic instance of economic regulatory rate-setting. Perhaps the most significant departure was the initiative to reduce airline regulation undertaken by Lloyd Axworthy, Trudeau's Minister of Transport, in the final months of the Liberal regime in 1984. I shall return to this issue below.

Despite the preceding examples, it is abundantly clear that when it came to the use of regulation to accomplish public policy objectives, Pierre Trudeau was in the mainstream in his government's high belief in the capacity and the appropriateness of regulatory instruments. They held the prevailing view that economic regulation can and should be used not only to protect consumers but to "micro-manage" sectors of the Canadian economy in order to promote either individual firms or broad sets of policy objectives.

The evidence in support of this assessment can be found in at least four major policy initiatives, two of which were implemented. The first was the proposed, but never enacted, series of telecommunications laws in 1977–78. This legislation, I have argued elsewhere, constituted an attempt by the federal government to transform its traditional, narrow policing approach to telecommunications into a planning system for the attainment of a *mélange* of objectives including national unity, contributing to the flow of regional and cultural information and safeguarding, enriching and strengthening "the cultural, political, social and economic fabric of Canada" (Schultz and Alexandroff, 1985:11, 86–91). What was particularly revealing about the Liberal approach was that, at a time when competition was being introduced in the United States, the Canadian government enunciated a set of proposals that declared that its objectives "can *best* be achieved by . . . regulation . . . ." [emphasis added]. Similarly the Trudeau government's proposals during the election of 1980, which were included in the subsequent Speech from the Throne, to empower the Foreign Investment Review Agency to undertake performance reviews of foreign-owned companies already operating in Canada, would have entailed, if they had been implemented, a significant extension in the ambit of economic regulation.

The third initiative of the Liberal government that clearly indicated its predisposition to employ regulation, and if possible to buttress regulatory regimes under threat, was the 1981 Air Transport Policy. This initiative sought to reassert the government's power to plan the air industry by assigning areas of operation for different segments (Schultz and Alexandroff, 1985:47–61; Reschenthaler and Stanbury, 1983). What is rather noteworthy of this initiative was its timing — just after the United States had deregulated its air sector. In the same year the Economic Council of Canada had recommended in the Regulation Reference significant liberalization of air regulation for Canada.

The final example which I suggest is the clearest expression of the Trudeau Liberals' belief in the efficacy of regulation in the face not only of domestic but worldwide pressures was the unveiling of the National Energy Program in 1980. This program was not simply regulatory in nature as it entailed the use of almost every policy instrument in the government's arsenal such as grants, subsidies, taxes and tax expenditures and public ownership as well as enhanced regulatory controls on development and oil and gas pricing and export licensing.[4] Doern and Toner have described NEP regulation as constituting a move from traditional public utility pricing under the National Energy Board to a much broader conception of "developmental bargaining" (1985:398–450) To use the terminology I have used elsewhere, from my perspective the set of regulatory instruments including the NEB, the Canadian Oil and Gas Lands Administration and the Office of Industrial and Regional Benefits combined with the broad goals of the NEP constitute a paradigmatic case of the use of regulation as a planning tool.

The only major exception — and I would argue that it was both major but an exception — to the overall pro-regulation thrust of the Trudeau Liberals was Lloyd Axworthy's to reform air transport regulation in 1983–84. His efforts to liberalize both the rate setting and route allocation processes to allow for greater consumer choice and carrier freedom were important precursors to the actions taken by the Mulroney Government (Axworthy, 1984; Stanbury, 1988). In my view, Axworthy's reforms did not represent an intellectual or even ideological proclivity on either his part or more significantly that of the Liberal government of the day to place less trust in regulation as a social control device. I would suggest that a more persuasive explanation is that it was a case of entrepreneurial politics by a minister both to salvage his own, and perhaps his government's electoral prospects as well as possibly to create a reputation as an "activist minister" for a future leadership contest much as John Turner had once done himself in the consumer protection area.

Support for my general assessment of the Liberal approach to regulation is also provided by Trudeau's treatment of the Economic Council's recommendations in the Regulation Reference which he mandated and by his limited efforts, despite his proclaimed concern for regulatory reform, to undertake any structural initiatives to encourage such reform. With respect to the former, although the Council in its two reports articulated a fairly consistent strategy, approach and set of reform proposals (Economic Council of Canada, 1979:143–174), none of the major proposals, aside from the Axworthy air policy, was taken up by the Liberal government. Nor did Trudeau make any but the most token of efforts to institutionalize regulatory reform within the federal government. His only significant step was the creation of a position of "Coordinator of Regulatory Reform" within the Treasury Board. The office, however, had limited staff resources, even less of a mandate to promote regulatory reform within Ottawa and not surprisingly was largely ineffectual as a result.

To conclude this section, the period immediately prior to the election of the Mulroney government saw in Ottawa a government in the Canadian historical mainstream with respect to the use of economic regulation. Prime Minister Trudeau might muse about the failures and weaknesses of the market place, as he did in his end-of-year interviews in 1975 and in his government's blueprint for the post-wage and price controls period in *The Way Ahead*, but he and his ministers had no apparent equivalent concern about the efficacy of government intervention. Although it would be incorrect to argue that the Liberals under Trudeau were ideologically driven in their approach to state intervention in general and the use of economic regulation in particular — after all while individual politicians may be ideological, Canadian parties and especially Canadian governments are not — nevertheless, it is clear that Mulroney's predecessor had little faith in market forces and much trust in the capacity of economic regulation, as well as other instruments of public policy, to achieve a wide range of public goals.

THE MULRONEY RECORD ON REGULATION

Having reviewed what I believe to be the major characteristics of the Liberal government's approach to regulation, I am now in a position to describe the actions and proposals of the Mulroney government in this field from 1984 to the present. The description can be easily undertaken; what will be more difficult is to assess whether or not the Mulroney approach constitutes a fundamental shift in philosophy and practice so as to merit the designation "neo–liberal" similar to that bestowed on Margaret Thatcher and Ronald Reagan.

As we shall shortly see, the Mulroney record in this area is substantial especially given the limited number of years in which it was amassed. What is particularly interesting is that few specific promises were made in the 1984 election involving regulatory issues except, of course, those more specific commitments to dismantle the NEP and to "open Canada to business" by the elimination or radical restructuring of FIRA. The government's first Throne Speech is also largely devoid of any discussion of regulatory proposals. The one specific regulatory reference in it was to introduce changes in the regulatory framework of the financial services industry.

195

For all the limited advance indications that the Mulroney government would place a high priority on regulatory reform, the last four years has seen the implementation or consideration of a considerable number of reform initiatives. One of the first acts of the new government was to abolish, as promised, FIRA and to substitute a new agency, Investment Canada, which is far more of a national "Welcome Wagon" than regulatory agency. Secondly, the National Energy program was dismembered and the parts sent for disposal, thus ending a short-lived attempt to use regulation to plan the energy sector. As part of this undertaking crude oil marketing and pricing were deregulated, there was also a reduction in the regulatory role of the NEB with respect to the price and volume of oil product exports, as well as in the regulation of natural gas exports and finally domestic natural gas products were deregulated (see Toner, 1986). In the financial services area, the government has issued a policy paper entitled "New Directions for Financial Institutions" which, if implemented, will see the regulation of banks and trust, loan and insurance companies substantially revised particularly the removal of restrictions on the types of activities each set of entities may undertake. As these restrictions were originally introduced as both a means of protecting consumers as well as some of the components of the financial service industry from competition from other parts, the result will be to lessen the industry protective or promotional role of regulation. The government's proposals are premised on the assumption that the individual parts no longer need protection and that increased competition among the different types of financial institutions will benefit consumers. Ironically, one of the obstacles to the implementation of the proposals is the controversy over new regulations governing ownership (Stanbury, 1988:30).

The single most extensive set of fundamental changes in a regulated sector are those enacted in the transportation area.[5] The Mulroney government decided that the industry was mature enough and that regulatory planning was both inappropriate and ineffective to build on the Axworthy initiative to virtually deregulate the air transport sector by removing traditional rate and entry controls.[6] It is important to note, however, that some regulatory protective devices were left both for the area designated as northern Canada and for consumers in the south. The legislation also included a provision for direct public subsidies to guarantee "essential" air service anywhere in Canada.

As for railways, the new legislation matched in many respects, although not all, the American deregulation that had occurred a decade earlier. What is particularly notable about the railway sections were that they were not solely deregulatory in nature. The legislation abolished the railways' existing freedom to engage in collective rate-making and also, through a provision governing "Collective Line Rates" introduced a new form of regulatory control over the railways.[7] Finally, the federal government resolved a twenty year dispute over the delegation of federal powers to the provinces to regulate interprovincial trucking in the new Motor Vehicle Transport Act. Although the federal government had to accept provincial demands for a longer phase-in period than it originally wanted, the new legislation provides for entry and rate deregulation for the interprovincial trucking industry after a five-year period.

The new transportation legislation is clearly the cornerstone of the Mulroney government's regulatory reform initiatives. Whether or not one agrees with the substance of the initiatives, it is undoubtedly an impressive achievement given the scope of the changes especially when one considers the inability of the previous government during the 1970's and 1980's to legislate even the partial changes that had been proposed. It is also impressive for the several innovative provisions that are introduced as alternatives to traditional regulatory measures. In particular the legislation provides for binding arbitration and mediation for disputes between regulated firms and their customers instead of using traditional regulatory procedures such as public hearings which were not only time-consuming and expensive but largely ineffective (Heaver and Nelson, 1978:237–238). The section that permits payment of subsidies to ensure "essential" air service where necessary is also imaginative. It discourages existing carriers from applying for a subsidy because there is no guarantee that if the Minister agrees a subsidy is warranted a specific carrier will be the successful recipient. The law requires that the Minister "ascertain by public tender the most economical and efficient method by which service can be provided." Finally the new legislation provides for a systematic comprehensive review of the operations of the legislation and its effectiveness five years after its introduction. Such a review must be done by independent commissioners and must be tabled in Parliament.

The Mulroney government, in addition to the very substantial sectoral reforms, has also gone much further than previous governments to institutionalize a regulatory review process. Although a separate central agency has not been created, there is now an Office on Regulatory Affairs that is also responsible for privatization attached to, but distinct from, the Treasury Board. Perhaps more importantly the new Office has its own minister whose responsibility is to ensure that any proposed regulatory initiatives by individual departments are in accordance with the government's announced "regulatory reform strategy" and consistent with the principles enunciated therein. The fact that the Minister responsible for regulatory affairs is also a member of the powerful Cabinet Operations Committee gives the Office and its staff influence in policy debates within Ottawa that its predecessor never had.

The record of the Mulroney government does not consist solely of examples of reduced or reformed regulatory regimes. There are significant gaps and inconsistencies that must be taken into account in any overall evaluation. Telecommunications policy is a major area where the Mulroney government has displayed little reforming zeal. Indeed, its actions in this sector could easily have been introduced by the Trudeau Liberals. The privatization of Teleglobe, for example, offered a unique opportunity. Teleglobe as a crown corporation was both unregulated and did not have a statutory monopoly to provide overseas telecommunications services yet when privatized was given such a monopoly for a minimum of five years and subjected to traditional rate of return regulation by the CRTC (Schultz, 1988). No serious consideration was given during the process of privatization either to opening up the sector to competition because of the fears that this would drive down the sale price or, once a decision was taken to grant a private sector Teleglobe a monopoly even for a limited period, to employing a non-traditional method of regulation such as the price caps as was done in the case of British Telecom. The sale of Teleglobe was a clear instance where privatization did not result in any "downsizing of the state."

An even more traditional approach is evident in the current federal proposals to introduce a new regulatory regime for telecommunications that would classify carriers and service providers into two categories, Type I and Type II. The underlying premise of this approach is that the federal government can use its power to regulate entry into the Type I category to plan the development of the telecommunications system or at least its most important segments. To use regulation in this manner is reminiscent of the various Liberal planning proposals in the late 1970s. In addition the proposal calls for the federal Cabinet to issue licenses to enter the Type I category, a method similar both to the pre-1906 regulatory system and to that employed by the Liberals with FIRA.[8]

The Conservative approach to broadcasting regulation is somewhat mixed but not one which to date justifies its inclusion on the reform side of the ledger. Advocates of reform in this sector were unenthusiastic when the first Tory Minister of Communications, Marcel Masse, appointed Gerald Caplan and Florian Sauvageau, hardly two "neo-liberals," to chair a review of broadcast regulation. Nor did the potential for reform increase when the Task Force criticised the record of the CRTC and recommended not a different approach to promoting Canadian content but simply more "effective" regulation. Although Masse's successor, Flora MacDonald, initially endorsed the recommendations, subsequently she qualified her support somewhat and proposed that alternative methods be examined to obtain the same goals. The result has been a new Broadcasting Act tabled in the House of Commons on June 23, 1988. The legislation does not end the traditional planning regulatory role for the CRTC inasmuch as the Act continues the longstanding but by now meaningless definition of the broadcasting system as a "single system" and declares that the objectives of public policy "can best be achieved by providing for the regulation and *supervision* of the Canadian broadcasting system by a single independent public authority" [emphasis added] which is almost verbatim from the 1968 *Broadcasting Act*. The only major innovation, and it is potentially very significant, is to empower the CRTC to develop and enforce a system of performance incentives to encourage the provision of Canadian programming. Such a measure indicates a willingness to consider new regulatory techniques but the overall approach continues to depend on regulation to obtain a wide variety of public goals in this sector.

THE MULRONEY RECORD AND NEO-LIBERALISM

In light of the preceding, it is now possible to ask whether Canada has, under the Mulroney Tories, embraced the neo-liberalism of other conservative governments in the western world, notably Margaret Thatcher and Ronald Reagan? Despite what some perceive to be the assault on regulation mounted by the Mulroney government, my answer to this question is in the negative. Mulroney and his government are not neo-liberals in the sense that they are dedicated to, and have sought to impose, a fundamental reduction of the role of the state and the substitution of market forces as the dominant social control instrument in areas of economic activity. Despite this conclusion, I do wish to suggest that under the Mulroney Tories a significant revision in the regulatory role of the state in Canada has occurred. Such a revision, I will argue, has been consistent with Tory objectives but not caused by their actions.

It is undoubtedly the case that in the energy, foreign investment and transportation sectors and potentially in financial services, Mulroney has reduced the role of regulation in determining the allocation, production and consumption of goods and services. The key point, however, is that his government has brought about a reduction, not an elimination, of state controls in these areas.

Regulation, it must be recalled, is a device for social control of economic decision-making. From one perspective, that of regulation as a means of policing areas of economic activity where market forces are thought to work poorly or not at all, regulation is an instrument to protect consumers from unacceptable forms of behaviour or conduct by economic actors. But regulation, I have argued, has also been used, alone or in combination with other state instruments, as a positive instrument of direction for such actors in an effort to accomplish a wide range of economic and social policy objectives.

Economic regulation in Canada has routinely been employed to perform this latter role either to promote individual firms such as Air Canada or Petro-Canada or, even more expansively to plan whole sectors, as in the broadcasting, air transportation and, with the NEP, in the energy sector. The Mulroney government's approach, at least in all but the telecommunications and broadcasting

200

sectors, has been to reject the use of regulation as a positive tool of government for the most part. It has provided in each of these sectors, however, where it was deemed to be necessary, important safeguard mechanisms to protect consumers from the potential abuse by firms of their power. Indeed, as with the railways, the Tories have introduced new regulatory tools to accomplish this objective. Similarly in the financial sector, the ownership restrictions proposed are new.

The Mulroney Tories have not practised, in Daniel Moynihan's phrase, "heavily ideological radicalism" in the regulated sector comparable to what he alleges the Reagan Administration has attempted (Moynihan, 1988). They have, I would argue, albeit inconsistently, sought to move regulation back to its more traditional, limited policing role in the economy. In contrast with the Trudeau Liberals, the Tories have been much more sympathetic to the market place and less convinced about the effectiveness or appropriateness of government as an instrument for the attainment of positive economic goals. Yet they have not rejected, in principle or in practice, the need for, in their own words, ". . . improved and even intensified regulation where public protection requires it" (Office of Privatization and Regulatory Affairs, n.d.:4). In short, I would conclude that the Mulroney Tories have not been ideologically driven in their approach to regulatory reform in the sense of having sought to impose a conscious, coherent and consistent vision or blueprint on the regulatory apparatus of the federal government.

Although I do not believe this was their objective, the Tories initiatives have been consistent, however, with the profound transformation that is occurring in the role of the Canadian state in the area of regulation. In my judgement, the power of regulation as an instrument of government is in decline. This is particularly true with respect to its use as an instrument for industrial promotion or planning. Although the Mulroney government's actions may have anticipated such a decline, I do not believe that they are the root cause. The cause is found in those economic and social forces which are undermining the capacity of regulatory instruments to be used to restrict the choices of those economic actors whom the state would control.

When regulation is used to police the behaviour of individual firms by price regulation, or to restrict entry into specific sectors by licensing, these are tasks which can be accomplished, albeit crudely perhaps and with some difficulty. On the other hand when the state seeks to restrict the choices of thousands of economic actors, that is the consumers of the goods and services, which is what in fact is attempted in promotional and planning regulation, the prerequisites for effective control are no longer tenable. The most important reason is that the regulated systems are increasingly porous and penetrated by those who are non-regulated to offer the same or equivalent services as the regulated firms. But they seek to do so and in many instances have been successful, at prices or conditions more attractive than those offered by the regulated firms.

In my view, Canadian air passengers who opted out of the Canadian regulatory system to use American carriers were the real deregulators. Similarly, Canadian shippers with access to American railway companies were the deregulators of the railways. For many of the same reasons, I believe that Canadian broadcasting regulation is increasingly irrelevant except, of course to the private broadcasters whose profitable base is protected, because of the freedom of choice that Canadian viewers have acquired and will not agree to surrender. The telecommunications policy of the Mulroney government, I suggest, will be the last gasp for regulatory dominance in this sector and in the not too distant future will have to be extensively revised.

My basic point is that the power of government to coerce, or to restrict the choices, of consumers in many regulated sectors has been or will be eroded. The use of such regulation for these ends requires an extremely closed system where the goods and services are necessary and/or otherwise unavailable from other "exit" from the system and yet satisfy their demands, the core of regulation is threatened, if not undermined.

I conclude with this point because there is a very real danger that, given the ideological nature of the debate surrounding neo-liberalism, the real forces at work in Canada will be ignored or misunderstood. The Mulroney government has amassed an impressive legislative record in the area of regulatory reform. The Mulroney government is not responsible, however, for undermining the power of regulation in Canada. Those who advocate continued state intervention for legitimate causes such as the promotion of Canadian culture or universal telephone service should take care that they do not sacrifice their cause through a defense of a governmental instrument that may have lost its utility. They would also be well advised to consider the following words of Alfred Kahn:

> One of the most fascinating aspects of the public policy disputations I have participated in during the last few years is the widespread acceptance of the notion that the burden of proof rests always with the advocates of change — that even if one is dealing with manifestly irrational, if not idiotic, arrangements, the advocate of moving in the direction of rationality is called upon to predict exactly how the process will work out and to prove beyond all doubt that it will work perfectly. (1978:27).

The author would like to thank Alan Bartley for his helpful comments on the first draft of this paper.

NOTES

[1] For an encyclopaedic review of developments, both federal and provincial, in economic and social regulation covering the past two decades, see Stanbury (1987 and 1988).

[2] Michael D. Reagan, for example, finds the term "command and control" to be derogatory and pejorative but does not explain why. See his otherwise illuminating *Regulation: The Politics of Policy* (1987: 133).

[3] See the text of the Prime Minister's letter to the Chairman of the Economic Council, July 12, 1978 in which he requests the Council to undertake the "Regulation Reference" printed as Appendix A to the Council's final report entitled *Reforming Regulation* (1981).

[4] On the National Energy Program, see G. Bruce Doern and Glen Toner (1985) and Peter Foster (1982). For a defense of both the energy and the foreign investment initiatives, see Stephen Clarkson (1982).

[5] The relevant legislation is the National Transportation Act, C–18, Statutes of Canada, 1987, and Motor Vehicle Transport Act, C–19, Statutes of Canada, 1987. For useful background information and summaries of the essential elements of both statutes, see Hon. Don Mazankowski (1985 and 1986).

[6] The single best comprehensive overview of the airline segment of the new National Transportation Act is found in W.T. Stanbury and Michael Tretheway (1987).

[7] For an extremely informative guide to the provisions of the new legislation with particular reference to those affecting the railways, see Western Transportation Advisory Council (1988).

[8] For a negative critique of these proposals, see Richard Schultz (1988b).

REFERENCES

Axworthy, Lloyd (1984). *New Canadian Air Policy*, (Ottawa: Department of Transport), May 10.

Clarkson, Stephen (1982). *Canada and the Reagan Challenge,* (Ottawa: Canadian Institute for Economic Policy).

Doern, G. Bruce and Glen Toner (1985). *The Politics of Energy,* (Toronto: Methuen).

Economic Council of Canada (1979). *Responsible Regulation,* (Ottawa: Supply and Services Canada).

Economic Council of Canada (1981). *Reforming Regulation,* (Ottawa: Supply and Services Canada).

Foster, Peter (1982). *The Sorcerer's Apprentices: Canada's Superbureaucrats and the Energy Mess,* (Toronto: Collins).

Heaver, T.D. and James C. Nelson (1978). *Railway Pricing Under Commercial Freedom: The Canadian Experience* (Vancouver: Centre for Transportation Studies, UBC).

Kahn, Alfred E. (1978). "Applying Economics in an Imperfect World," *Regulation,* November–December.

Lowi, Theodore (1985). "The State in Politics: The Relation Between Policy and Administration," in Roger Noll (ed.), *Regulatory Policy and the Social Sciences,* (Berkeley: University of California Press).

Mazankowski, Don Hon. (1985). *Freedom to Move: A Framework for Transportation Reform,* (Ottawa: Supply and Services Canada).

Mazankowski, Don Hon. (1986). *Freedom to Move: The Legislation,* (Ottawa: Transport Canada).

Moynihan, Daniel Patrick (1988). *Came the Revolution,* (San Diego: Harcourt Brace Jovanovich).

Office of Privatization and Regulatory Affairs (n.d.). *Regulatory Reform Strategy,* (Ottawa).

Reagan, Michael D. (1987). *Regulation: The Politics of Policy,* (Toronto: Little Brown and Co.).

Reschenthaler, G.B. and W.T. Stanbury (1983). "Deregulating Canada's Airlines: Grounded by False Assumptions," *Canadian Public Policy,* vol. 9, no. 2, pp. 210–222.

Schultz, Richard (1988a). "Teleglobe Canada: Selling the Jewel in the Crowns," in Allan Tupper and G. Bruce Doern (eds.) *Privatization, Public Corporations and Public Policy in Canada,* (Montreal: Institute for Research on Public Policy).

Schultz, Richard (1988b). "Forward to the Past: The Canadian Approach to the Telecommunication Reform," *Working Paper* 1988–42, (Montreal: Centre for the Study of Regulated Industries, McGill University).

Schultz, Richard and Alan Alexandroff (1985). *Economic Regulation and the Federal System,* (Toronto: University of Toronto Press).

Schultze, Charles L. (1977). *The Public Use of Private Interest,* (Washington: The Brookings Institute).

Stanbury, W.T. (1987). "Direct Regulation and Its Reform: A Canadian Perspective," *Brigham Young University Law Review,* no. 2, pp. 467-539.

Stanbury, W.T. (1988). "Reforming Direct Regulation in Canada," in K.J. Button and D. Swann (eds.), *The Age of Regulatory Reform,* (Oxford: Oxford University Press).

Stanbury, W.T. and Michael Tretheway (1987). "Analysis of the Changes in

Airline Regulation Proposed in Bill C–18," paper presented to the House of Commons Standing Committee on Transport on behalf of the Consumers' Association of Canada, March 12. Mimeo.

Toner, Glen (1986). "Stardust: The Tory Energy Program," in Michael J. Prince (ed.), *How Ottawa Spends — 1986–87: Tracking the Tories*, (Toronto: Methuen).

Western Transportation Advisory Council (1988). "The National Transportation Act, 1987: Digest: General and Rail Provisions" Westac *Newsletter*, vol. 14, no. 1 (January).

The Myth of Tax Reform: The Mulroney Government's Tax Changes

HAROLD CHORNEY and ANDREW MOLLOY

One of the first laws of public finance is that taxation reveals much about the character of a regime. After all, revolutions and other such political upheavals have been fought over taxation. The history of tax reform in Canada since the ill fated attempt of the Carter Commission to introduce serious progressive restructuring of the tax system has been a consistent record of evasion, retreat, and betrayal (McQuaig, 1987: 93–122).

To its credit the Mulroney administration has actually changed the tax system in ways that are quite consistent with its ideological orientation. Along the way to doing so the Government has also undertaken certain measures which form part of the agenda of those who have been interested in reforming the tax system to make it more equitable and less prone to loopholes to shelter upper income tax payers and special interests. But because of the government's neo-conservative bent in economic policy matters, the beneficial impact of its measures to close loopholes and convert exemptions to credits are for the time being outweighed by the changes that it has introduced in terms of flatter rates, the reduction in corporate rates and the impending introduction of consumption taxes. The Government has cleverly donned the mantle of reform and used it to hide the clear benefits it is introducing on behalf of upper income tax payers. In doing so it is, of course, not only following the ideological dictates of its political conscience but also the faddist belief that now predominates in public policy circles.

In order to make sense of the Mulroney Government's tax package it is useful to break it down into four basic sections: the reduction of tax brackets or the "flatter" tax system; the closing of loopholes; the move from exemptions to credits; and the objective of revenue neutrality and the shift to consumption taxes. From the perspective of social democratic policy analysts looking to the future not all of what the Government has done is unwelcome. Indeed, with some pruning and adjustments and the re-introduction of genuine as opposed to bogus notions of reform it ought to be relatively easy to improve our taxation system in the future.

Of course, the question of taxation is not just about matters of revenue and expenditure and equity considerations. It also involves important questions of economic policy. We intend to discuss these as well in the course of this paper.

One of Canada's better known tax specialists, Professor Neil Brooks of Osgoode Hall Law School has described the criteria for evaluating tax measures as follows: is it simple?; it is equitable?; is it economically efficient? (Brooks, 1987). Of these three criteria only the first is unlikely to be a matter of controversy. Prior to the return of the right wing mythology of Freidrich Von Hayek to political legitimacy in establishment circles there would have been in the past relatively little controversy about the second as well. Now, however, in the light of the "oppressed circumstances of our wealthiest citizens" it would seem that one has to admit controversy about this criteria. The question of economic efficiency has always been controversial. Furthermore, there are inevitable conflicts between economic efficiency, particularly when it is defined in neo-conservative terms and equity. Nevertheless, we propose to evaluate the Mulroney Government's tax measures by these criteria. We also will trace the origins of the tax reforms in the American tax reform package that the Government has so clearly copied in its own legislation.

THE ORIGINS OF FLAT TAXATION

Let us begin with the question of "flatter taxation." The Mulroney Government's tax measures reduces the number of tax categories from the existing ten brackets to three. These are 17% on the first $27,500 of taxable income, 26% on the next $27,500 and 29% on taxable income in excess of $55,000 (Wilson, 1987). It is interesting to compare these rates with the rate structure that the Americans adopted under Reagan's tax legislation. The American rates are 15% and 28% with a phantom surtax on upper incomes (Birnbaum and Murray, 1987: 294–5). The lower rate applies to incomes up to $29,750 U.S. for joint filers and $17,850 U.S. for single filers. The 28% rate applies on incomes above that level. The phantom rate of 33% comes into play gradually for incomes in excess of $71,900 U.S. or joint returns and for individuals in excess of $43,150 U.S. For individuals with incomes above $89,560 U.S. and joint filers with incomes above $149,250 U.S. the effective rate on every dollar of taxable income is 28% (U.S. Government, 1988: 4–6; Boidman and Gartner, 1987: 202 ff).

In Canada, then the top rate at the federal level has been dropped form 34% to 29%. It is worth noting in this respect that as recently as 1981 the top rate was 43% in Canada for taxable incomes above $118,000. In the United States the top rate for individuals was 50%. In the 1987 tax year in the United States there is a transitional rate structure that preserves five tax categories ranging from 11 to 38.5%. In Canada the new tax system will be introduced for the 1988 tax year.

In the area of corporate tax rates the comparison with the U.S. tax act is also revealing. The U.S. has lowered its top rate from 48% to 34%, while four lower rates on incomes less than $100,000 U.S. have been collapsed to two on incomes under $100,000 (Birnbaum and Murray, 1987: 296; Boidman and Gartner, 1987: 19). In the Canadian case the tax rate except for manufacturing and small business income is being lowered from 36% to 28%. In the case of manufacturing the rate is dropping from 30% to 26%. In both cases these rates are net of the 10% points of provincial abatement. If one factors in the typical provincial tax after deducting out the abatement the overall rate has dropped from around 51% to 43% (Wilson, 1987). In addition to these rate changes there are a number of other changes that involve the closing off of loopholes and broadening of the base. We will discuss these in more detail below.

The Federal Government's proposal to reduce the existing ten individual Federal tax brackets to three is the culmination of a campaign against progressive taxation that has its roots in American neo-conservatism. For a number of years leading up to the introduction of tax reform as a major initiative by the Reagan administration in 1984, the neo-conservative critique of progressive taxation as a barrier to savings and enterprise had been promulgated in various think tanks and institutes (Walker and Bloomfield, 1983; Hall and Rabushka, 1983, 1985; Birnbaum and Murray, 1987).

In order to appreciate the philosophical orientation that lies behind the flatter tax package (akin in some ways to the flat earth theory) we must trace the roots of the argument for a flatter tax system to the writings of certain key American neo-conservatives and, in particular, their obsession with discrediting the concept of progressive income taxation.

Nothing is more appealing than a simple idea. Nowhere is this truer than in the area of tax reform. Neo-conservatives have been quick to learn this lesson. The proposal for a flat-rate system of (income) taxation is an idea that was first suggested in its modern form in the writings of Milton Friedman, the guru of neo-conservative economics.

In *Capitalism and Freedom* Friedman argued that "all things considered, the personal income tax structure that seems to me best is a flat-rate tax on income above an exemption, with income defined very broadly and deductions allowed only for strictly defined expenses of earning income" (1962: 174). Not surprisingly, Friedman introduced this proposal in the context of a polemic directed against progressive taxation: "I find it hard as a liberal, to see any justification for graduated taxation solely to redistribute income. This seems a clear case of using coercion to take from some in order to give to others and thus to conflict head on with individual freedom" (1962: 174).

For a long period of time this kind of ideological opposition to progressive taxation lay buried in the subterranean passage ways along with similar ultra-conservative sentiments about society that were beyond the pale of the post-war liberal consensus. The receding tide of liberalism however, laid bare such ideas as the general terrain of neo-conservatism came into view and dominated the political landscape in the late 1970s and the early 1980s.

Thus predictably when in December 1981 in the *Wall Street Journal* there appeared a major article "A Simple Case For Tax Reform," by Robert Hall and Alvin Rabushka of the conservative Hoover Institute of Stanford University, the media response was swift and largely approving. A flurry of articles, letters and positive editorials appeared in rapid succession. Within a few months nearly a dozen "flat-tax" bills were introduced in the American Congress (Hall and Rabushka, 1983). These bills influenced the character of the final American tax reform package that was passed in the fall of 1986.

Friedman himself acknowledges that the current popularity of the flat-tax proposal can be traced to the work of these particular writers. After the traditional short period time lag, the flat-tax idea made its appearance in Canada. True to form, the right-wing Fraser Institute took up the case for flat-taxation after a series of articles appeared about the American debate in *The Financial Post*. During the Conservative leadership race which resulted in the selection of Brian Mulroney, the neo-conservative businessman Peter Pocklington championed the cause of flat-taxation.

Like most simple ideas there is more to flat-taxation than meets the eye. But before we examine this proposal in detail it is important to bear in mind the strategy that lies behind the concept. In sum, flat-taxation cannot easily be separated from its neo-conservative casing.

When Friedman first broached the idea of flat-taxation he argued that a simple rate ought to be levied on taxable income broadly defined after appropriate personal exemptions were allowed. Friedman argued that deductions and shelters such as the oil depletion allowance, the special treatment of capital gains and other such special exemptions be eliminated in order to simplify the system. He further argued that the program of flat-taxation be combined with the abolition of corporate income tax and "the requirement that corporations be required to attribute their income to stockholders, and that stockholders be required to include such sums on their tax returns" (Friedman, 1962: 11). Friedman also suggested that if a rate of twenty three percent on taxable income were chosen, subject to the then prevailing laws and deductions, the yield would be as great or even greater than under the current prevailing system.

This rather optimistic result supported by no more than the back of an envelope kind of numerical calculation led Friedman to argue that the flat-rate system would actually increase revenues because the incentive to find legal means to avoid taxation would be diminished and therefore reported incomes would be greater and the "disincentive effects" of the graduated tax would be diminished. This would produce more "efficient" allocation of resources and therefore higher income. Furthermore, the elimination of loopholes would eliminate wasteful activities such as tax avoidance which produce no positive economic benefits and actually reduce overall productivity. The result is a predictably rosy world of incentive, simplicity and virtue. Friedman pays no attention however, to the transfer of the tax burden disproportionately on to the shoulders of the lower income tax payer whose tax burden would have risen under his proposal.

In their 1981 article and subsequent books, R. Hall and A. Rabushka have attempted the same sort of economic sophistry as Friedman. They decried progressive taxation as a complex system of waste which has bred distrust in the minds of taxpayers. This in turn, has led to a number of distortions which had reduced the efficiency of the market place. The culprit was the state which had introduced graduated tax rates which over the years had risen to an "unfair" level. The business community was spending most of its time obsessed with getting advice on how to exploit tax-based opportunities rather than thinking about producing goods and services and improving productivity (Hall and Rabushka, 1985). Conversely, the burden of taxation had fallen on the working poor and middle class, "because the existing system was severely biased against wages and salaries" (Hall and Rabushka, 1985: 76).

Since middle and low income earners' taxes were paid at the source, there was a much more accurate reporting of wage and salary income. Other groups were paying less tax because their earnings were harder to trace and therefore carried a lighter portion of the tax burden. The result of this excessive government intervention according to Hall and Rabushka, had been the creation of the petty-delinquent who hid his income within the burgeoning underground economy. This underground economy involved billions of dollars each year in unreported income.

The resulting unfairness of the tax system the authors claim led to a major shift in public opinion over the last two decades away from support of progressive taxation to a critique of the supposedly "worrisome" disincentives of the double rate of taxation of wealthy businesses, i.e. taxes on profits plus taxes on interest, dividends and capital gains. "With fifty-percent top marginal rates, it was alleged that many high-income people felt they could not afford to reveal any significant income to the IRS (Hall and Rabushka, 1985: 89).

In short, those who are unwilling to pay will not pay. Hence nothing short of a virtual tax amnesty will do for them. Hall and Rabushka's solution was deceptively simple. A uniform taxation rate of nineteen percent would replace the current range of rates.

All business would be taxed only once at its source. The wealthy, buttressed by large amounts of after-tax income on interest, dividends and capital gains would turn back to maximizing and investing more of their income. Tax shelters, subsidies and credits would be abandoned in favour of a first year tax holiday on all business investment (Hall and Rabushka, 1985: 90). They also argued that the flat-tax would bring down high interest rates because it would permit no deduction for interest paid and put no tax on interest received. The implication was that with no special tax burden on deductions for interest income, the rate charged would no longer have to reflect this burden. This in itself begs a number of serious questions about how interest rates are determined for which Hall and Rabushka offer no answers. This argument is further evidence of the supply-side mythology which has developed around the flat-tax. In reality, interest rates have as much to do with the policies of the central bank as with the expectations of private capital.

Interestingly, Hall and Rabushka differ from Friedman on the question of the deficit. They argued that with the implementation of a flat-tax to engender more investment, the debt would continue to remain a small part of the overall U.S. economy until a balanced budget could be reached in the 1990s (Hall and Rabushka, 1985: 89).[1]

To rectify the "biases" against wages and salaries, a comprehensive tax would be imposed to include cash wages and salaries, the market value of fringe benefits and contributions to public and private pension plans. As a result the economy would benefit from the growth of an increased tax base which would probably produce more revenue than the government needed to maintain existing programs! Implicit in this argument is the notion that no spending on new programs would be envisioned. In other words, the flat-tax proposal goes hand in hand with a political program to limit the welfare state. Finally, a simplified tax with low marginal rates would help restore confidence in government and would support the basic honesty of the American people.

As always with this type of analysis, one is faced with complex phenomena disguised as programmable solutions. Clearly, a taxation system in the real world can bear no close relation to that conceived in a utopian dream world. There is a strange kind of moral paradox in assigning equal weight to government concessions to the business community (tax shelters, capital gains, exemptions, tax credits) with income maintenance programs for socially disadvantaged groups. This is not to deny that the business community performs a critical function in a mixed capitalist society and would continue to perform such a function in a social democratic society. Rather, it is to point out that tax expenditure subsidies to business are an inefficient method of trying to alter the pattern of private market driven investment. It is far better to intervene directly where there is evidence of market failure in allocating investment and therefore employment than to waste public funds through unproductive transfers to private interests. There is simply no comparison either in terms of morality or in terms of effectiveness in accomplishing objectives between subsidies to the private sector and tax expenditures on social programs. Hall and Rabushka never gave any thought to this distinction nor to developing more efficient methods in order to tighten up the existing tax system.

Rather it is assumed that the only alternative is to tax upper income earners and the wealthy at a much lower rate and hope they will contribute their fair share. Their own evidence however offers nothing to support this optimistic conclusion. Indeed, defenders of the flatter tax structure that was introduced in the U.S. point to greatly increased receipts from upper income taxpayers as proof that the system is already living up to its promises. They ignore however the impact of the boom in stock prices that was reflected in the increased capital gains revenues and the closing of loopholes. The real question is — was the rate reduction necessary as a political tradeoff to permit the closing of loopholes? We think the answer is obvious. The backers of flatter tax will unequivocally argue that it was. But that conclusion is at least debatable. Furthermore, although the Americans have for the time being laid aside the introduction of a consumption tax, here in Canada the Mulroney Government seems determined to convert the federal sales tax into a broader based consumption or value added tax.

While Hall and Rabushka were quick to point out that their proposal would raise almost an equivalent amount of revenue as the current system; they failed to specify how much the burden of taxation would increase on low income taxpayers. Milton Friedman confronts this criticism directly in one of his most recent works, *The Tyranny of the Status Quo* (Friedman and Friedman, 1986). According to Friedman the flat-tax is one of those remarkable innovations typical of neo-conservatives — it benefits everyone:

[T]he, poor, middle class, and rich would all gain from the substitution of a true flat-rate tax for the present income tax. The poor would pay less tax because of higher personal exemptions. Many in the middle class would pay less tax because of a lower rate. Others in the middle class, as well as the rich, would pay more tax to the government, yet they would be better off. They would pay more because the lower rate would render present costly tax shelters unattractive. And they would be better off because the gain to them from being free to use their assets in the most productive way would be greater than the gain from tax avoidance (Friedman and Friedman, 1986: 66).

As Friedman puts it "the flat-tax is clearly a splendid idea" (Friedman and Friedman, 1986: 67). Splendid, no doubt but for one minor problem. Friedman introduces no data to back up his claim, and for that matter the data that Hall and Rabushka introduce is not detailed enough to be able to reach Friedman's conclusions.

The overall thrust of Hall and Rabushka's argument is very close to that of the original intention of Friedman. The progressive taxation system, they argue, because it includes such high marginal rates, acts as a major break upon entrepreneurial incentive and retards both savings and therefore investment. In this sense the flat taxers support the supply side and anti-Keynesian notions of Arthur Laffer, George Gilder and other neo-conservative thinkers. The problems of the modern capitalist economy, according to this view, lie with inadequate savings and excessive interference by the state with private initiative which is after all the engine of economic growth and prosperity for all. Let us say simply we do not agree. Most of our current problems in Canada stem from excessive savings and inadequate investment opportunities because of the drag on the economy from this excessive pool of privately hoarded wealth. The suggestion by Hall and Rabushka that the flat tax system restores true progressivity is rather disingenuous. The only progressivity that exists under the flat tax system stems from the larger percentage of income that is exempt for lower income filers. A truly progressive system would combine this feature with graduated rates and the elimination of loopholes to ensure that it actually collected the taxes that it was supposed to. In addition to taxing income it would tax wealth and inheritance. More about this later.

CANADA AND THE FLAT-TAX

In the realm of honesty the Canadian variant of flat-taxation ranks higher. Michael Walker of the Fraser Institute not surprisingly supports the flat-tax rate idea. But to his credit Walker admits that lower income tax-payers would bear a heavier burden under flat-taxation (1983: 28). Walker, nevertheless makes the case for flat-taxation on the usual grounds. He declares that progressive taxation reduces the incentive for people to work harder. He claims that a progressive tax system penalizes additional income so severely that rational taxpayers will simply choose to work less under such a system (1983: 8).

Yet curiously, Walker also argues that the progressive tax system because of the operation of tax loopholes effectively does not impose significantly higher taxes on many upper income earners (1983: 10). Clearly the system cannot do both simultaneously. Nevertheless, let us assume for the moment that a progressive tax system could be designed in which loopholes were closed and the upper income groups thereby paid proportionately more of their income in tax. How convincing would Walker's argument be in these circumstances?

As far as Walker is concerned he presumes that people make decisions about work based on after-tax income (1983: 8). For the upper income professional there may be some truth in this but for the average income earner it is more likely that they do not have the luxury of choosing how much to work. Furthermore, most people pay, at least as much if not more attention, to the status and prestige attached to a job and to its pre-tax salary, as they do to the after tax income. The psychic income they derive from the status and minimal income increase associated with the job is what drives people up the ladder of success.

On the other hand, even if it were true that high progressive tax rates discourage effort on the part of high income earners, can we be so certain that all that much is lost. It is part of the neo-conservative mythology that the hard-driving upper-income entrepreneur creates additional wealth. Perhaps. But it is equally plausible that he or she creates reduced social welfare by increasing the numbers of workaholics in society with all their unhealthy and costly side effects.[2] Perhaps the increased leisure that is involved here represents a net gain in societal wealth rather than a reduction. Furthermore, even if additional wealth is created, how is that wealth distributed.

In general, Walker operates with the assumption that the market and private unimpeded behaviour always yield the best outcome. But as we know from bitter experience this is not always so. Market failure and its consequences are pervasive in Canadian society.

Of the four specific proposals discussed by Walker, the Pocklington Plan was the most generous toward the wealthy. The former leadership candidate for the Progressive Conservative Party in 1984 advocated a flat-tax of twenty percent, with a total exemption from tax for individuals earning less than $7,500 a year. (For a family of four this exemption would rise to $12,000.) By the Fraser Institute's own figures, this would mean an average tax increase of $388 for those in the $10,000 to $14,000 range (Walker, 1983: 24). The highest income earners with incomes above $200,000 would receive a tax-cut of $39,915. Pocklington's justification for giving the wealthy the biggest tax break rested on the happy nostalgia of keeping money in the hands of those who know how to use it. Anyone remotely familiar with Canadian economic history might raise their eyebrows at this statement. Certainly, the high unemployment Canada suffered from during the 1980s suggests that perhaps some of our business leaders are not as all knowing as Pocklington presumes.

The dual flat-tax was another variant. This proposal would exempt the very poor ($1–5,000 of annual income); the working class would be taxed at seventeen percent (for incomes below $30,000); and middle and upper income earners would pay a twenty-four percent rate (for incomes above $30,000) (Walker, 1983: 28). It was argued that by removing all tax shelters and incentives, the wealthy would end up paying the same or more than under the current progressive system. Under the current system, tax expenditures and shelters benefit upper income groups the most. So there appears to be some justification for this claim. But when one actually calculates the tax incidence, the results are not quite so unambiguous as Walker claims.

Alan MacEachen's November 1981 budget contained a move in the direction of flat-tax. In keeping with the Friedman-Hall-Rabushka-Walker scenario, MacEachen attempted to broaden the tax base by closing a number of important tax shelters belonging to upper-income groups (i.e. the repeal of the capital gains tax, the repeal of deductions for income-averaging annuities, the reduction of the federal dividend tax credit, etc.). At the same time there was to have been a substantial reduction in the maximum tax rate from sixty-five to fifty percent. Those making over $30,000 would also have experienced a federal tax saving.

This political compromise should have had a happy ending according to Friedman, Hall et al. Instead wealthy special interests with the help of the media brought pressure upon the Liberal government. In the end only the top rate-reduction was implemented as the government withdrew its opposition to tax shelters favouring the rich. This perverse result was symptomatic of what occurs when a simple idea which examines the role of wealth uncritically is presented for public scrutiny. The lobbies which protect the interests of the wealthy were quick to spring into action to defend their interests. As a consequence of this miscarried reform, the tax base was not widened but the progressivity of the system was lessened.

The third proposal, suggested by then Liberal MP John Evans called for a flat-tax of thirty percent for those above a level of $11,120 per year (Walker, 1983: 30). Those below would still be under the then prevailing system. The wealthy would experience a drop of twenty points below the top marginal rate of fifty percent. Evans conceded that such a scheme would not be able to produce the same amount of revenue as under the current progressive system.

In defense of some of the obvious difficulties raised by the above proposals Walker suggested that larger burdens on lower income taxpayers were less onerous because close to two-thirds of such taxpayers were either under thirty or over sixty-five years of age. Hence, he suggested that the natural life cycle of earning ensured that no single group of taxpayers would be permanently burdened. This however would seem to be an inadequate defense of this kind of inequity. A large proportion of those taxpayers over the age of sixty-five had already spent much of their best earning years at low income levels. Many of those under the age of thirty increasingly are victims of high unemployment and have a higher degree or risk of suffering permanently lower income levels during their peak earning years. The fact then seems inescapable: those with lower incomes would pay more.

As we suggested at the outset, the flat-tax proposal is part and parcel of the neo-conservative policy shrine. It grows out of a fundamentally ideological opposition to progressive taxation. As Reagan's former Attorney-General Edwin Meese has put it, the progressive income tax is criminal.

THE TORY TAX REFORM

The Mulroney Government's tax reform seeks to compromise on flat-taxation. While it refuses to endorse the single or dual flat-tax, it does propose a somewhat watered down variant of this plan. This three level version involves significantly reduced taxes for those earning above $100,000 *per annum* and much more modest reductions for those earning under $30,000. Furthermore, when one takes into consideration the impact of the proposed new sales tax, the result is even more regressive. In this respect, the White paper and the resulting legislation, despite certain improvements in eliminating exemptions and closing loopholes is a failure.

The neo-conservative nostalgia for a simpler world ignores the inescapable complexities of modern capitalist society and yearns for a world that never was. Flat-taxation would benefit the rich. There is no doubt. As well, because of its inherent revenue limitations it would help the neo-conservatives advance the goal of placing a cap on potential state expenditures. Flat-taxation would also be no blessing for hard pressed middle-income earners. The Mulroney Government's proposals because they strive to be revenue neutral in the end do not avoid this problem.

The Mulroney tax initiative is about more than just flatter rates of taxation. Supposedly it is also about closing some of the more outrageous and unproductive tax loopholes that currently exist in the system. In the area of corporate tax income these loopholes are particularly costly to the government in terms of lost revenues. We leave aside for the moment the rather important question of whom actually pays the corporate income tax — the corporation being taxed or the consumer of the goods produced by the corporation?

Most analysts of the Canadian corporate tax system suggest that a combination of accelerated capital consumption allowances, deferred taxes, depletion allowances, and other diverse tax incentives cost the federal government over ten billion dollars a year. In other words, if we were to adjust the existing federal government deficit for inflation and the unnaturally high rate of unemployment the economy has been suffering from since the 1981–82 recession, virtually all of the structural deficit that remains would be accounted for by these tax expenditures.[3] One measure alone, that of permitting corporations to defer the payment of taxes arising out of differences in book value of assets as compared to their depreciated value accounts for some 28 billion dollars of accumulated unpaid taxes.

The Mulroney tax changes with regard to closing corporate tax loopholes barely scraped the surface. In fact, by the government's own calculation the total increase in tax revenues due to closing corporate tax loopholes will amount to an additional 2.2 billion dollars in the 1988–89 fiscal year. However, the rate reductions in corporate income tax rates that accompany these base broadening measures will result in a loss of 1.6 billion dollars of revenue. The net impact therefore is an additional 700 million dollars in 1988–89. This is hardly an impressive accomplishment for a government that likes to portray itself as a major reformer of the tax system. It should be said that the measures the government are enacting are good measures insofar as they go. The problem is that they do not go far enough. These measures include changes in the treatment of corporate investment income, greater inclusion of corporate capital gains into taxable income, reduction in the rate of accelerated capital cost allowances; reductions in the rates of investment tax credits for research and development; increases in the tax liabilities of financial corporations and insurance companies. It is revealing that after successful lobbying pressure the Government supported by none other than the NDP backed away from changes it had proposed for tougher treatment of flow through shares — a tax incentive particularly favoured by doctors, lawyers, dentists and other such professionals (Wilson, 1987: 72 ff; Tax Probe, 1986).

Since the early 1950s there has been a steady erosion of the contribution that corporations make to the total tax revenue of the federal government. In 1951 direct taxes on corporations accounted for more than 100% of personal direct taxes. By 1984 that percentage had been reduced to less that 33% (Canada, 1985). This erosion is important because it has undermined the equity of the tax system and also contributed to the revenue pressure that the Government has experienced and that middle income taxpayers feel.

But perhaps the real solution to the corporate tax problem is to recognize that the real beneficiaries of corporate profits are the shareholders and it is they and not the corporate entity that should pay their fair share. In order to accomplish this we would have to

ensure that all corporate profits were either distributed to shareholders or invested in the firm. Distributed profits then would be
subject to the ordinary taxable treatment of income. Of course,
there would be problems dealing with foreign-held corporations
and the inevitable uproar by the lobbyists on behalf of the wealthy
interests that own most of the shares in the country. There would
also be inevitable complications involved in shares held by pension plans and similar public institutions. Nevertheless despite
these obstacles it is a proposition worth considering.

One final point about corporate taxation that merits attention is
the fact that in recent years because of the extensive nature of tax
incentives and allowances in any given tax year the majority of
corporations pay no tax despite profitable activities. For example,
Tax Probe, the N.D.P.'s tax commission reported that in 1983 a total
of 79,196 corporations with book profits paid no taxes. Of the top
20 corporations on the Canadian Business 500 list six, General
Motors, Chrysler Shell, Hudson's Bay, Nova and TransCanada
Pipe Lines ltd. paid no tax for at least one year between 1980 and
1985, while reporting positive profits (Tax Probe, 1986: 35–40).

The Government in its supplementary information about tax
reform tabled in the House in December reported that in 1983 that
out of 320,000 profitable corporations, 110,000 paid no taxes in
1983. It then argued that once the new corporate tax measures were
put in place an additional 50,000 would pay taxes leaving 60,000
non taxable either because of previous losses or because of receiving as income previously taxed dividends or because of ongoing
tax incentives. It suggested that in more than half of these cases
prior losses were the explanation. The remaining firms largely had
"such low profits that a small amount of the incentives remaining
after tax reform can result in them being non taxpaying" (Wilson,
1987: 52–3). On the basis of this logic the government concluded a
minimum tax on corporate profits was counter-productive. It
would seem that this conclusion adds support to the suggestion
that moving away from taxing corporate profits and taxing the distributed dividends might be a desirable policy option.

Let us now turn to other measures that the Government is enacting with respect to individual taxpayers. Here on the whole the
record is somewhat more favorable. For example, the conversion
of exemptions to credits in the area of personal exemptions, disability deductions and pension income are welcome changes. It
should be pointed out however that the government has continued

the partial de-indexation at rates below 3% inflation of the tax brackets. In the years to come this will result in a considerable increase of the tax burden on middle and lower income tax payers.

TABLE 1

Impact of Tax Changes Selected Years 1982–1988

Single Individual — No dependents

Year	(A) Gross Income Adjusted for Inflation	(B) Taxable Income	(C) Federal Tax Owing	"C" as % of "A"
Part I				
	LOW INCOME			
1982	15,808	11,106	1,341	8.5
1984	17,448	12,141	1,500	8.6
1987	20,030	14,217	2,095	10.5
1988	20,858	*20,858	2,005	9.6
Part II				
	HIGH INCOME			
1982	49,047	44,319	8,581	17.5
1984	54,139	448,833	9,415	17.4
1987	62,150	56,337	11,761	18.9
1988	64,718	*64,718	11,373	17.5

Part III

IMPACT OF TAX CHANGES UPON HIGH INCOME INDIVIDUAL WHO TAKES FULL ADVANTAGE OF RRSP TAX SHELTER

Year	(A)	(B)	(C)	"C" as % of "A"
1982	49,047	38,119	7,651	15.6
1984	54,139	43,333	8,067	14.9
1987	62,150	48,837	19,882	15.9
1988	64,718	57,218	9,643	14.9

* This category no longer has the same meaning with the introduction of a system of tax credits.

TABLE 2

Impact of Tax Changes on a Married Couple
with Two Children under 18

Year	(A) (Includes Family Allowance) Gross	(B) Taxable	(C) Federal Tax	(D) "C" as % of "A"
Part I				
LOW INCOME ONE EARNER				
1982	16,456	7,404	0	0
1984	18,167	8,070	0	0
1987	20,806	9,993	416	2.0
1988	21,534	*21,634	320	1.5

This category no longer has the same meaning with the introduction of a system of tax credits. The above table assumes that the spouse earns 0 income and receives the full child tax credit which is deducted from the husband's taxes.

Year	(A) Gross	(B) Taxable	(C) Federal Tax	(D) %
Part II				
HIGH INCOME ONE EARNER FAMILY				
1982	49,695	40,516	7,428	14.9
1984	54,858	44,562	7,426	13.5
1987	62,926	52,293	19,713	17.0
1988	65,494	65,494	10,576	16.1

Note: Above assumes taxpayer does not take advantage of RRSP's and does not have pension plan deductions from all high income levels except for a token $9 reduction for first 1982.
* This category no longer has the same meaning with the introduction of a system of tax credits.

The changes made to the child tax credit also appear to move in the right direction although the taxation of family allowances will begin at the rather low level of $26,000 at the rate of 9%. Many would argue that this is unfair to moderate income families. On the whole, these changes, coupled with the new tax rates, represent important benefits for moderate income families with children. It is significant that single individuals receive considerably less relief and in some cases will pay more taxes. (See table 1).

In fact the amount that a childless one earner family will receive back from the government because of these changes at the $30,000 level (some $680) is significantly less than the close to $1200 that an upper income family will receive back at the $75,000 level. And of course a poor family at the $15,000 level receives only $425.

The differences in the impact of the tax changes upon individuals and families is strikingly illustrated in Table 1. The table assumes that tax payers at various income levels are able to protect their gross income from erosion by inflation over the period 1982 to 1988. The tables show what these taxpayers owe in federal taxes in the years 1982 and 1984 when the Liberals were in power and 1987 and 1988 when the Mulroney Conservatives have been the government.

It is important to understand the significance of protecting gross incomes for inflation in order to assess the true impact of the tax changes. The results are very clear for single individuals. Low income earners who we have defined as having earned $15,808 in 1982 and have been protected from inflation over the years so that in 1988 they earn $20,858 will pay a higher percentage of their income in taxes in 1988 than they did in 1984 — 9.6% in 1988 versus 8.5% in 1984. The percent of income paid in taxes rises sharply from 1984 to 1987 from 8.6% to 10.5%. This is because the Mulroney government increased taxes in 1985 and 1986 and lowered them somewhat in the 1987 tax reform. The flatter tax system does nothing to lower the burden on low income tax payers when the base of comparison is the 1984 tax year rather than the 1987 year after taxes had already been raised. It may strike the Government as clever politics but it is not likely that too many tax payers will be fooled.

The picture for high earner taxpayers is somewhat more comforting at least as far as individuals are concerned. We define a high income taxpayer as someone who in 1982 had a gross income of $49,047 and managing to keep pace with inflation earned $64,718 in 1988. In 1984 such a taxpayer would have paid 17.4% of their income in taxes, while in 1988 they would pay 17.5%. However because the table makes the unrealistic assumption that high income tax payers purchase no tax shelters such as RRSP's and flow-through shares their actual taxable income would be much lower. And since the flatter tax rates involve substantial reductions in the tax rate for these individuals the effective rate would decline significantly.

In order to illustrate this we recalculated the taxes owed by the high income individual making the additional assumption that they purchased the maximum amount of R.R.S.P's in each tax year. In 1982 and 1984 this amounted to $5500. In 1987 and 1988 this amount was raised to $7500. The impact of this purchase upon tax liability is shown in table 1 part III. Taxes owed as a percentage of gross income is 15.6% in 1982, 14.9% in 1984, 15.9 in 1987 and drops back to 14.9% in 1988. In effect the Mulroney tax changes narrows the gap in effective rates of taxation between low and high income taxpayers. Whereas single individual taxpayers will pay a higher percent of their income in taxes to the federal government, compared to either 1982 or 1984 upper income taxpayers will pay virtually the same percentage, both in comparison to the base year of 1984 or a smaller percentage in comparison to 1982.

The situation for one earner families with two dependents under the age of 18 is similar although the tax burden is considerably less. In the case of the low income family the child tax credit system and the child exemption virtually eliminate federal taxes for the taxfiler. For example, in 1982 such a taxpayer would have still paid no taxes. After the 1984 budget this taxpayer, again assuming full protection for inflation would have still paid no taxes. In 1987 they would have paid 2% and 1988 1.5%. Clearly the improvements in the child tax credit work heavily in this family's favour. In the case of the upper income taxpayer the child tax credit has no impact. Here the taxpayer would have paid 14.9% of gross income in 1982, 13.5% in 1984, 17.0 in 1987 and 16% in 1988. Again, of course, this table assumes that the high income taxpayer does not take advantage of the RRSP deduction. If they were to the result would be quite similar to that obtained for the high income individual.

In general then the tax changes confer much bigger cash benefits to upper income taxpayers. In addition, once the new revamped VAT style tax is introduced whatever reductions the tax changes do introduce for families will vanish as the consumption tax quietly soaks back up the illusory benefits. The only way this will not occur is if the Government introduces a refundable tax credit linked to income to return to low and moderate income families a substantial portion of the consumption tax. With a broad based tax set at 8% this rebate will have to be set at a very substantial level if the consumption tax is not to be regressive.

In this respect it is also important to note that the government is eliminating the employee expense deduction as well as the $1000 interest income deduction. In the area of base broadening the Mulroney changes also include a reduction in the totally regressive capital gains lifetime exemption down from $500,000 to $100,000 for all but qualified farm property and the shares of small business corporations. It should be noted that this lifetime exemption was introduced by the Mulroney government in the first place. It also increased the proportion of capital gains to be included in income from 50% to 75% by 1990. The government also maintained the dividend gross-up and tax credit system for corporate dividends, again maintaining the bias in favour of income from capital. The government tightened up slightly on home offices, automobile expenses, business meals and entertainment expenses. The last of these would seem to be the least defensible and the most often likely to be abused. Finally the Government has extended the period before the phase out of Multiple Unit Residential Buildings to 1994 by which time undoubtedly pressure by the real estate lobby will probably find a way to continue this particular incentive. All of these personal tax measure changes will result in a net reduction of some $4 billion in revenues. This however will be offset by an additional $700 million in corporate tax revenues net of rate reductions. This will be further offset by increases in the sales tax and other selected taxes to the tune of $1300 million and an additional $1.1 billion through acceleration of source deductions and quarterly instalment payments. The final impact in the 1989–90 tax year is an increase in the deficit of $1.3 billion.

CONCLUSION

By emphasizing savings and protecting upper income groups and shifting in the future to broader consumption taxes the government risks worsening an already fragile economic system in which the problem is not too little saving but too much hoarding. If one analyses the secular rise in unemployment rates in Canada over the past fifteen years and compares them with changes in the tax system that have favoured upper income savings there is a strong correlation between these two phenomena. There can be no doubt that biasing the tax system in favour of upper income groups, contrary to the mythology of neo-conservative economics, worsens rather than improves overall economic performance.

The goal of equity and progress in a mixed capitalist economy has always been elusive. But turning away from the fundamental problem of excessive concentrations of wealth and poverty can offer no answer. Those who wish to tax in the name of justice and efficiency must confront this problem directly.

NOTES

1 For a different view on the question see Eisner (1986) and Chorney (1988).

2 For an ironic confirmation of this fact, see the remarkably unself-reflexive column by Peter Cooke on "overworked and underappreciated" millionaire businessmen in the "Report on Business" section of the Globe and Mail, July 5, 1988.

3 Obviously the rate of unemployment chosen as the full employment rate and the assumptions one makes about the impact upon tax revenues of a percentage point fall in the unemployment rate as well as the impact of removing these tax incentives upon employment have a major effect on this kind of calculation. As such, it must be seen as only a crude estimate. Nevertheless, it is a fairly safe bet that at least a significant part of whatever structural deficit that exists is explained by these tax expenditures. For further discussion of these issues see Chorney (1988: 53 ff) and David Wolfe (1985).

REFERENCES

Birnbaum, J.H. and A.S Murray (1987). *Showdown at Gucci Gulch: Lawmakers, Lobbyists and the Unlikely Triumph of Tax Reform*, (New York: Random House).

Boidman, and Gartner (1987). *U.S. Tax Reform — The Canadian Perspective*, (Toronto: CCR).

Brooks, Neil (1987). Discussion of the White Paper on Tax Reform at a Conference sponsored by the Canadian Study of Parliament Group, Ottawa, November 4 and 5.

Canada (1985). *Economic Review*, (Ottawa: Department of Finance).

Chorney, Harold (1988). *Sound Finance and Other Delusions: Deficit and Debt Management in the Age of Neo-Liberal Economics*, Working Papers in Public Administration and Public Policy, (Montreal: Department of Political Science, Concordia University).

Eisner, R. (1986). *How Real is the Federal Deficit?*, (New York: Free Press).

Friedman, Milton (1962). *Capitalism and Freedom*, (Chicago: University of Chicago Press).

Friedman, Milton and Rose Friedman (1986). *The Tyranny of the Status Quo*, (New York: Harcourt, Brace, Jovanovich).

Hall, Robert and Alvin Rabushka (1983). *Low Tax, Simple Tax, Flat Tax*, (New York: McGraw Hill).

Hall, Robert and Alvin Rabushka (1985). *The Flat Tax*, (Stanford: The Hoover Institution Press).

McQuaig, Linda (1987). *Behind Closed Doors*, (Toronto: Penguin).

Tax Probe (1986). *The Canadian Corporate Income Tax System: Towards Reform. An Interim Report*, (Ottawa: Tax Probe).

U.S. Government (1988). *Budget of The United States Government. Fiscal Year 1988*, (Washington D.C.: Executive Office of the President, Office of Management and Budget).

Walker, Charles E. and Mark Bloomfield (1983). *New Directions in Federal Tax Policy for the 1980s*, (Cambridge, Mass.: The American Council for Capital Formation, Centre for Policy Research).

Walker, Michael A. (1983). *Focus: On Flat-Rate Tax Proposals*, (Vancouver: The Fraser Institute).

Wilson, Michael (1987). *Supplementary Information Relating to Tax Reform Measures*, (Ottawa: House of Commons).

Wolfe, David (1985). "The Politics of the Deficit" in G. Bruce Doern (ed.), *The Politics of Economic Policy*, Research Study No. 40, Royal Commission on the Economic Union and Development Prospects for Canada, (Toronto: University of Toronto Press).

The Mulroney Government and the Deficit

EDWARD A. CARMICHAEL

It is conventional wisdom that fiscal policy in the Mulroney years has focused single-mindedly on reduction of the budgetary deficit. In spite of this emphasis, the budget deficit is still too high, according to this view, and can only be brought under control in future through tough actions to cut spending on social programs or through further tax increases, probably in the form of a value-added tax.

I say that this is conventional wisdom because I hear it so frequently. My purpose in this paper is to demonstrate that much of this conventional wisdom is only partially correct and to put the Mulroney government's efforts to cut the deficit in some perspective.

The deficit certainly has not gone away in the Mulroney years. Indeed, at $29.3 billion in the fiscal year just ended, in 1988 the deficit is just $3 billion or 10 percent lower than it was in the last full fiscal year in which the previous Liberal government was in office. In the 1984–85 fiscal year, in which the Liberals set the budget but the Conservatives took over half way through the year, there was really no one at the fiscal controls. The Liberals were spending on Special Recovery Capital Projects when the recovery was already well on its way without government assistance. In the election campaign both party leaders avoided the deficit issue like the political plague that it is. Mr. Turner announced at one point that his target would be to cut the deficit in half — that is, by $15 billion, over seven years but his political handlers quickly advised him to "low-bridge" the deficit issue and he made no further such announcements. Mr. Mulroney, on the other hand spent most of the time during his campaign telling voters in the East about his plans for expensive new initiatives and voters in the West about his plans to dismantle the National Energy Program — a federal policy which generated sizable revenues from the petroleum sector.

One demonstration of the vacuum within which the deficit issue existed during the 1984 election was the reception accorded to a C.D. Howe Institute publication entitled *Tackling the Federal Deficit*, which was released about four weeks before the election. The study was covered on the front page of the *Globe and Mail*. This generated many media interviews and follow-up editorials. The reaction in my view was not so much the result of the study being the definitive statement on this important issue but rather of it being the only statement on the issue. Still, it did not have the effect we hoped it would — namely, of getting the party leaders to address the issue.

Thus, the Mulroney government did not enter office with a clear set of targets and/or proposals for cutting the deficit. Indeed, it is my view that it took the government eighteen months — that is, until the February 1986 budget — to enunciate clear targets and approaches to deficit reduction.

Finance Minister Michael Wilson's Agenda document of November 1984 represented a recognition of the magnitude of the deficit problem that the Mulroney government had inherited. The accompanying expenditure restraints announced by Treasury Board President Robert de Cotret were important stop-gap measures which helped to reverse the rise in the deficit but this did not represent a strategy. The bungled Universality debate at Christmas 1984, the disappointing effort to build consensus on the need for fiscal restraint at the National Economic Conference of February 1985, and the retreat from partial deindexation of Old Age Pensions in the May 1985 budget all represented costly dead-ends for a government groping for deficit-reducing strategies for which the electorate had little or no appetite.

It was not until February 1986 that the government clarified its fiscal targets and put in place a credible medium-term fiscal strategy for achieving an ambitious yet politically acceptable and economically sound approach to reducing the deficit.

FIGURE I

FEDERAL DEFICIT PROJECTIONS
FISCAL YEARS 1985-86 TO 1990-91

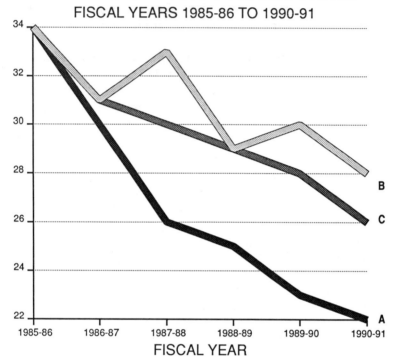

A **FEBRUARY 1986** Based on February 1986 *Fiscal Plan*.
B **FEBRUARY 1987** Excluding February 1987 budget measures.
C **JUNE 1987** Including February 1987 budget measures and the first-stage tax reform measures.

Source: C.D. Howe Institute, based on Department of Finance, *The Fiscal Plan*, (Ottawa, February, 1986); idem, *Budget Papers* (Ottawa, February 1987); and idem, *Economic and Fiscal Outlook* (Ottawa, June 1987).

Let me sum up to this point my first challenge to the convention-al wisdom. That is, far from having deficit reduction as a clearly defined priority before coming to office, the Mulroney campaign avoided the issue. Then, once in office, it took the government 18 months to settle on deficit reduction objectives and instruments which, in the view of most mainstream economists, were both feasible and desirable.

Following the February 1986 budget the C.D. Howe Institute issued a commentary entitled "Paying by the Installment Plan" in which the government was deemed to have gotten its fiscal act together. The reason for this conclusion was the following: the government had laid out a medium-term fiscal plan that would see the deficit fall from over $34 billion in 1985–86 to about $22 billion in 1990–91. This would involve sizable but manageable reductions in the deficit in each of the next five fiscal years. These reductions would be sufficient to slow down the growth of the federal public debt so that it no longer exceeded the growth of the economy, that is, the growth of GDP. This latter target meant that the ratio of federal public debt so that it no longer exceeded the growth of the economy, that is, the growth of GDP. This latter tar-get meant that the ratio of federal debt to GDP, which had risen from 17 percent in March 1975 to 49 percent in March 1986 would stabilize at about 55 percent in March 1991 and then begin to decline.

This objective of stabilizing the ratio of public debt to GDP has been accepted by most mainstream economists and most indus-trial country governments as a minimum target for prudent fiscal policy. To do less invites ever-increasing public debt charges and a self-perpetuating spiral of deficits and debt as Nobel economist James Tobin pointed out in an influential paper in 1985. For a small country like Canada, which has no choice but to accept interest rates set in highly integrated world financial markets, allowing our federal debt-to-GDP ratio to move above 50 percent toward 60 per-cent greatly increases our vulnerability to upward movement in world interest rates. At the current federal debt level of $300 bil-lion, a one percentage point rise in world interest rates quickly results in a $2–3 billion increase in unavoidable public debt char-ges. To put this in perspective, one could say that to offset the impact on the deficit of a one percentage point rise in world inter-est rates it would be necessary to either cut spending by an amount equivalent to the entire cost of the Family Allowance program or to raise taxes by an amount equivalent to an increase of about 15 percent in the average effective corporate income tax rate.

The Mulroney government couldn't avoid this vulnerability which was already inevitable given the size of the budget deficit that the government inherited when it took office; it could only hope to limit and eventually stabilize the extent of the vulnerability. The February 1986 budget was important because it appeared to achieve this important objective.

I say appeared to achieve the objective because, even as the ink was drying on the budget, events were making its targets virtually impossible to achieve. In particular, the collapse in crude oil and grain prices in early 1986, immediately knocked the government off the deficit reduction path that it had laid out in the budget.

The drop in the price of crude oil from U.S. $28 per barrel to U.S. $10 per barrel in the space of four months led to an immediate reduction in energy tax revenues and, by September 1986, to an announcement by Michael Wilson that he would immediately terminate the still lucrative Petroleum and Gas Revenue Tax.

The drop in grain prices was the result of the U.S. Farm Bill passed in December 1985 which replaced direct price supports for U.S. grain farmers with farm income supports. Without U.S. grain price supports, world market prices for wheat and other grains dropped sharply. This necessitated the introduction in December 1986 of a Special Grains Program involving additional payments to farmers of $1 billion.

The combined impact of the oil and grain price collapse was to increase the federal budget deficit by about $2 billion in 1986–87 and $5 billion in 1987–88 and thereafter, an increase which the federal government did not attempt to offset with spending cuts or higher taxes in other areas of the budget.

At this point let me state my second challenge to the conventional wisdom. That is, that rather than focusing single-mindedly on deficit reduction as some would have it, the Mulroney government permitted the pace of deficit reduction to slacken markedly when faced with serious economic problems in the petroleum and agricultural sectors of the economy. The federal assistance provided to individuals working in these sectors was generous and appropriate, but it forced a lower priority on deficit reduction.

The February 1987 budget was another disappointment to those who preferred to see a faster pace of deficit reduction. In it, Finance Minister Michael Wilson announced that the government had decided that a "breathing space" was necessary prior to the tax reform expected later in the year. Rather than launching new initiatives to restrain program spending or raise taxes, the government began to indulge in less painful yet more temporary methods of keeping the deficit on a downward track. For example, the $2.4 billion reduction in fiscal year 1986–87 was made possible only by the last minute sale of Teleglobe Canada for $450 million and by delaying $700 million in special payments to grain farmers until after March 31, 1987. The government reserved its neatest trick for fiscal year 1987–88, when it gained $1.2 billion in additional revenue by accelerating remittances of income taxes and unemployment insurance premiums.

In a C.D. Howe Institute review of the February 1987 budget, I made the following observations:

> In the face of increasing difficulty in maintaining the appearance of a downward deficit track, the government has resorted to asset sales and fiscal tricks to fulfill its principles. This is not the way to reduce the underlying imbalance between spending and revenues; it is merely a way to finance it. The underlying budget deficit is stuck at about $30 billion.

The February 1987 budget was a clear signal that the Mulroney government had lost its appetite for tough deficit reduction measures. It sought solace in the fact that Canada's federal budget deficit was slightly smaller than that in the United States — a comparison which demonstrated nothing more than the fact that Canada could pile up public debt at a world-class rate.

In the June 1987 tax reform, the government argued that such reform should be deficit neutral and thereby rejected the use of a potentially potent weapon for reducing the deficit. Finally, the February 1988, "pre-Olympic" budget contained only two face-saving adjustments — a one cent per litre gasoline tax and an unspecified $300 million cut in non-statutory programs — which were necessary to obtain a modest reduction in the deficit to $28.9 billion in the current fiscal year from $29.3 billion in 1987–88.

To summarize, while the Mulroney government has achieved some progress in reducing the federal budget deficit, its approach to deficit reduction can hardly be described as zealous or tough. Indeed, one can speculate that had Mr. Turner and the Liberals won the 1984 election, they would not have made less progress than the Mulroney government in tackling the federal deficit. It is possible, however, that the Liberals might have gone about deficit reduction by different methods which leads me to the second question about the Mulroney government's deficit reduction record: How has the deficit been reduced?

In one considers the federal deficit as percentage of the GDP (Figure II), one notices that the ratio has declined since 1984–85. In fact, in the last fiscal year, the ratio was actually below the average for the period 1977–84. To be sure, future declines may be anticipated, but they are based mainly on the government's assumption that the economy will not experience recession or higher interest rates over the next five years.

But to what extent have revenue increases and spending cuts been responsible for the relative reduction of the deficit? The ratio of federal revenues to the GDP has increased by 1.5% during the Mulroney years (Figure III). This is quite significant. The apparent plan of the government seems to be to stabilize federal revenues around 17% of the GDP which is equal to the average ratio of the 1970s but substantially higher than the 1977–84 average. On the expenditures front, Figure IV indicates that the ratio of federal expenditures to the GDP has fallen since 1984–1985 but still remains at 1.0% higher than the 1977–84 average. Again, the sharp decline which is projected after 1988–89 should be treated with some scepticism as these projections are largely the result of economic assumptions rather than actual expenditures cuts.

In light of the preceding observations, it seems that modest deficit reduction actions by the government combined with strong economic growth have permitted a sizable decline in the deficit relative to GDP to a level which is now below the average of the eight year period prior to the Mulroney years.

It is important to note however that this deficit reduction has not been accomplished by a sharp reduction in government spending which remains well above the levels associated with the previous Liberal government. Rather, it has been accomplished by restoring federal revenues to the share of GDP experienced in the 1970s.

The above analysis however does not tell the full story. While some people may find encouragement in the relative decline of the deficit, a consideration of the public debt situation should provide a more sobering picture. The public debt in Canada has risen steadily from 17% of the GDP in 1973–74 to 53% today, and it is still rising (Figure V).

234

FIGURE II

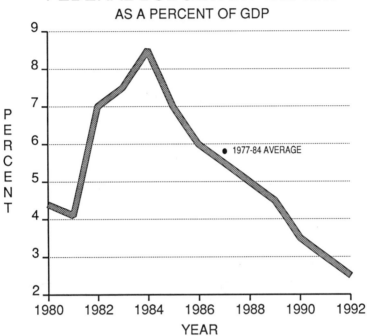

FEDERAL BUDGETARY DEFICIT
AS A PERCENT OF GDP

FIGURE III

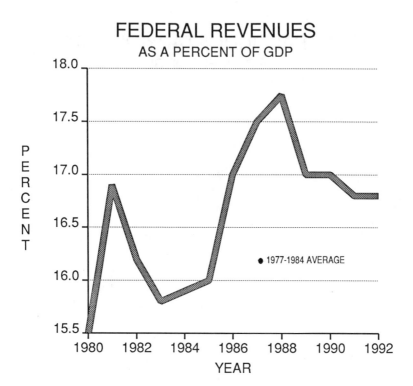

FEDERAL REVENUES
AS A PERCENT OF GDP

FIGURE IV

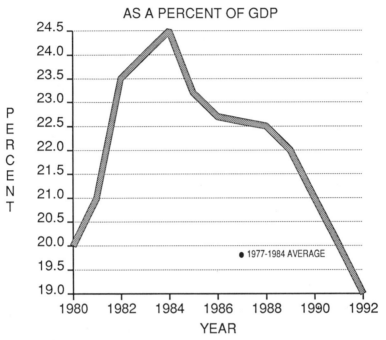

FEDERAL EXPENDITURES
AS A PERCENT OF GDP

● 1977-1984 AVERAGE

In the process, public debt charges have increased from 2% to 5% of the GDP. There are two major consequences to this phenomenon:

1) Public debt charges have crowded out program spending which by 1989–90 could be down to shares of GDP not seen since the early 1970s.

2) The government of Canada has become highly vulnerable to either an unexpected economic downturn or an unexpected rise in interest rates. If either of these events occur within the next few years, the climb of Canada's debt-to-GDP ratio could reaccelerate eventually forcing the next government to take deficit reduction actions that will be much more painful than anything seen during the Mulroney government's first term.

CONCLUSIONS

The conventional wisdom is correct in asserting that Canada still has a serious federal deficit problem. Few people recognize, however, that, as a percentage of GDP, the deficit is already lower than it was during the eight years preceding the Mulroney government's election. The point is that deficits have been too high since the mid-1970s and further steps need to be taken in the years ahead to bring the deficit down further.

The conventional wisdom is wrong to the extent that it claims that the Mulroney government came to office with clear deficit reduction objectives, that it made deficit reduction the only real objective of fiscal policy and that it used deficit reduction to significantly reduce the size of government. As I have tried to point out, the record of the Mulroney years is that it took eighteen months in office to devise a credible deficit reduction strategy, that it backpedaled on deficit reduction when oil and grain prices caused hardship in Western Canada, and that it has presided over a period when federal spending has been a higher percentage of GDP than at any other time in Canada's post-war history.

FIGURE V

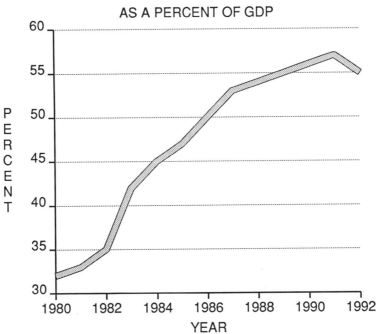

FEDERAL NET PUBLIC DEBT
AS A PERCENT OF GDP

Finally, the main lesson to be learned from an examination of the Mulroney government's record in tackling the deficit is that the task was made doubly difficult by the accumulated public debt of the previous Liberal government. It is the size of the debt, not the deficit, which has become the issue. Looking ahead, a major challenge facing the next government of Canada will be how to cope with the continuing vulnerability to fiscal crisis posed by a federal debt that is almost 60 percent of Canada's annual national income.

Labour Policy and the Labour Market

GINETTE DUSSAULT

In addressing the labour policy of the Mulroney government, there are two essentials: one to place the Conservative government's record in a historical context, and the other to examine it as a reflexion of the neo-conservative thinking that has gained a widespread following in various parts of the world since the early 1980s. Before attempting to evaluate the Conservative government's record, first in macroeconomic policy and then in manpower and unemployment insurance policy, I shall therefore quickly review the precepts of neo-conservative theory with respect to labour.

The coexisting problems of inflation and unemployment beginning in the mid 1970s and, even more, the worldwide job crisis in the early 1980s have stimulated a global resurgence of conservatism. Analysis of contemporary economic problems has led certain economists to attribute the difficulties attending a resumption of growth without inflation to inflexibility in the economy in general and most of all in the labour market.[1] For these economists, the inflexibility can be blamed on a multitude of interventions in the economy by the State and on the power of labour unions. For them, the solution must therefore be found through a return to the free-market discipline that alone can force adaptation to changing economic conditions. This means allowing the market to select both the winners and the losers. Necessarily, there will follow a certain increase in income inequalities. This last precept envisages especially a reduced tax burden on the highest income brackets and therefore a lessened redistributive role for governments.

Regarding employment, neo-conservative precepts call more

241

specifically for better adjustment between the conditions governing the profitability of each company and the number of jobs it provides and/or its total wage bill. This calls into question the rules of job security and determination of wage levels. Social and income security programs are also questioned, partly because of their impact on State budgets (and indirectly on the tax burden for business) but also because of their presumed work disincentive effect. Certain provisions of unemployment insurance plans are associated with downward rigidity to wage adjustment because the plans allow the unemployed to be choosy over accepting new employment. In the labour sector as in others, neo-conservative precepts may be summarized thus: less state and more market.

In order to analyze the Conservative government's policies and record regarding labour and the job market, we must identify the discernible policy trends and place them in a historical context. Western governments became aware that they had some responsibility in achieving full employment only after World War II, following the depression years of the thirties and the spread of Keynesian theories. In Canada,[2] the division of constitutional powers among the various levels of government hardly gave the federal government a predisposed responsibility for achieving full employment. Nonetheless, under the heading of "national interest," that is a responsibility it claimed. The implementation of the unemployment insurance plan under federal jurisdiction even needed a constitutional amendment. The division of powers in fact explains the unique form that the applications of Keynesian policies takes in Canada. Aggregate demand management, a key element in any Keynesian stabilizing policy, operates almost solely through the use of macroeconomic instruments (monetary and fiscal policy), in contrast to more focussed interventions, leaving the market to decide allocation of resources among sectors and regions. Fiscal policy, for example, has been exercised largely through income security programs, and expansionist policies have taken effect through upgrading of the various programs. This particular configuration of Keynesian teaching has produced an effect that was observed only long after the Keynesian heyday: it does not easily reverse and bears the seeds of inflationary pressures.

Second thoughts about this line of economic policy predated the accession of the Conservatives to power in Canada, where the break in the direction of thrust in macroeconomic policies may be situated around 1975. Indeed, this was the year in which the prime policy objective became the fight against inflation. The Conservatives have maintained this orientation, adding the second objective of deficit reduction. Deficit control and reduction have even become the dominant themes in Conservative budget speeches. Tax increases and cuts in expenditures (particularly restraint of expenditure increase, through deindexation for instance) have been features of the period. The content of budgets has been determined by the state of the deficit, not that of the job market. Tax increases have complied with neo-conservative precepts, that is, they have fallen more heavily on low and middle incomes and spared high incomes. With the introduction of very substantial capital gains exemptions and reductions in marginal tax rates in the highest brackets, the income tax system has become much less progressive, leaving intact a greater proportion of profits for those with high incomes. Since the aborted attempt to deindex old age pensions, cuts in expenditures have not really been directed at the substance of social programs. Among the areas of concern that the cuts have affected, however, are federal transfers to the provinces via the adoption of new rules for equalization and calculation of the federal share of existing programs (Government of Quebec, 1984, 1985). This has allowed the federal government to reduce its deficit but has forced on the provinces the unpleasant choice of cutting back services themselves or seeing their financial situations deteriorate, unless they raise their taxes. This is a good illustration of the degree to which federal deficit reduction has dominated the Conservatives' economic policy. All other policies with economic impact adopted by the Conservatives must also be seen in this context, which is to say, a context in which employment is not a major objective.

More specifically regarding manpower policies and the job market, the federal government has traditionally used these tools: job creation, manpower training, and unemployment insurance. The objectives of the first two have been both counter-cyclical and structural. Over the years, even before the Conservatives came to power, there has been criticism from within the public apparatus itself (Economic Council of Canada, 1983; Government of Canada; 1981a, 1981b). Several aspects of traditional federal intervention have been called into question. Doubts have been raised over the effectiveness of temporary job creation programs, with the observation that they draw an inactive part of the work force into the labour market, create needs that too often bring subsequent pressure for permanent government intervention, and do not in the long run lead to the addition of any new, unsubsidized, permanent jobs. With respect to training programs, the critics have deplored the heavy emphasis on institutional training (as opposed to in-house or on-the-job training), and have noted that political pressures lead to a regional distribution of funds that depends more on local unemployment levels than on manpower training needs, and that consequently federal funds have been used for training in regions and job categories where there are no job openings.

In response to this criticism, the Conservatives created the Canadian Job Strategy. In its *Annual Report* of 1985–86, Employment and Immigration Canada introduced the new strategy as follows:

> The Canadian Job Strategy is a new approach to training for Canadians. It involves a major modification of federal employment programs and a fundamental change in the way in which, through our investments, we develop our most important resource: Canadian workers.
>
> After a period of intensive consultation by the government with its economic partners in late 1984 and early 1985, it was generally accepted that the range of job creation and training programs did not adequately meet the need for the kinds of skill and experience that would enable Canadians to face a rapidly changing labour market.
>
> The programs of the Canadian Job Strategy have attacked this problem by linking training to current economic activity and real jobs. These programs ensure the necessary flexibility to meet constantly evolving regional and local needs because the budgets assigned to them are determined according to criteria defined on a regional scale (1986: 20–21).

The Department's *Annual Report* of 1986–87 stressed that "[the Canadian Job Strategy] marks a clear departure from previous programs, which were directed toward short-term solutions for fluctuations in the labour market" (Employment and Immigration Canada, 1987: 21). These two quotations clarify the nature of the Conservatives' response to the criticism of federal manpower policies. Primarily, despite high unemployment rates but consistent with the direction taken at the macroeconomic level, the objective of manpower policy is no longer to counter cyclical unemployment; the emphasis is now on structural unemployment. Short-term job creation programs have virtually disappeared. Almost all interventions have a manpower training aspect whose content is defined by employers themselves. This is the era of made-to-order training cut to fit the needs of business. The Institut canadien d'education des adultes stressed at a recent conference (*Refaire le casse-tête autrement*, Montréal, April 1988) that there are dangers in this new orientation: new dependence on private teaching institutions; training that is too focussed, adhering too closely to the short-term needs of business; loss of control over the transferability of the training.

The accent on countering structural unemployment is evident also in the choice of target clientele. Almost all the programs address a clientele in difficulty, meaning persons long unemployed, and there is a real effort to integrate four target populations, namely women, the handicapped, native peoples, and young people.

Emphasis on the structural is also apparent in the greater importance placed on training in skills in which there are shortages of qualified manpower. Here too, the initiative is left to employers. According to the Department, the Skill Shortages Program "offers financial assistance to employers who need support in providing their personnel with training for skills in which there is a shortage of specialized labour" (Employment and Immigration Canada; 1987: 21).

This has two effects. First, the regional allocation of funds depends on employer initiatives and manpower shortages, and second, the program applies mostly to workers who already have jobs in dynamic sectors. It will be noted that the first effect is one that fits the government's objectives. It is an answer to a chronic complaint about federal programs, namely the high level of uniformity they have imposed across the country. The Department explains the system as follows:

> Employment Planning offers the flexibility necessary to meet the changing needs of the regional labour market. The regions receive a lump sum along with certain guidelines concerning national priorities but they may spend the money as they see fit according to the most pressing needs (. . .).
>
> In most of Canada's regions there are also Local Advisory Councils which advise on the needs of the labour market. The Advisory Councils are composed of local business people, community group representatives, local government officials, and others. In regions where the level of unemployment is

high or rising, emphasis will be placed on the Job Development and Skills Investment Programs. In others where manpower shortages are a high-priority concern, the emphasis will be on the Skill Shortages Program (1987: 22).

The effects of this philosophy on the regional distribution of funds are very apparent. In 1986–87, Ontario received almost half the money allocated under the Skill Shortages Program while Quebec received less than 10%. Another effect worth mentioning concerns the proportions of men and women benefiting from this program. Almost all the beneficiaries are men. This is the program that does least to meet the objective of reaching the target groups. But these effects were to some extent intended by the Conservative government. With decentralization, it was envisaged that each province would use the programs which best fulfilled its special needs.

As for the mechanism of decentralization, while great effort has gone into setting the system in place, a rather surprising degree of unity remains. Indeed, the Local Advisory Councils correspond to federal electoral ridings rather than to an approximation of local job markets. The local member of Parliament is a central figure in each of the Councils. It is he or she who appoints the members of the Council. The Canadian Labour Congress has pointed out that only 7% of the members of the Local Advisory Councils were union representatives (1988). In short there seems to be a considerable distance between the principle to pursue and the reality. This reality furthermore applies in provinces other than Quebec, where the advisory structure described was declined since it would have duplicated an existing provincial structure, the Commissions de formation professionnelle.

The federal government's other special tool of intervention in the labour market is of course unemployment insurance. Since 1975 there have been many changes in the plan. The most important are as follows. In 1976 the penalty period after quitting one's job was lengthened. In 1977 the entrance requirement was modified, increasing from eight weeks of work to a variable requirement of ten to fourteen weeks, depending on the regional level of unemployment. The maximum benefit duration was reduced to fifty weeks. The use of unemployment insurance funds for innovative application (shared work, job creation, training) was declared permissible. In 1979 the benefit rate was reduced to 60%. The entrance requirement was made more stringent for workers entering or re-entering the labour market. The federal share of financing was reduced, the prolongation of benefits on the basis of the length of prior employment was now to be paid from the unemployment insurance fund. A regulation was introduced requiring reimbursement of 30% of benefits received by high-income individuals.

A clear trend toward a less generous plan was therefore well under way. Given the neo-conservative view of the role of such programs in the inflexibility of the labour market, still more drastic measures were to be expected. In July 1985 the Conservative government created the Commission of Inquiry on Unemployment Insurance, which submitted its report in November 1986. This was the Forget Commission.

The recommendations of the Commission coincided very closely with theoretical precepts that favour allowing market logic to allocate resources in the labour market. The two principal recommendations called for annualization of benefits and elimination of the regional dimension for determining the benefit duration. The Commission's objective with these two recommendations was to scale down the protection available to workers (and employers) who make too frequent use of benefits, and to give the system the means to encourage mobility, both professional and geographical. But despite the close correspondence of these recommendations to theoretical neo-conservative thinking, the Conservative government has implemented none of them. The only change it has made to the plan predated the creation of the Commission and dealt with the treatment of severance pay and retirement income. These can be considered minor changes in comparison with all the others put into effect since 1975.

What then has the Conservative government accomplished since 1984 in this domain?

This analysis of the Conservative government's policies since 1984 leads to the conclusion that, where employment and the labour market are concerned, this government has followed the same direction taken by previous governments since 1975 rather than moving in any fresh, new direction. Its labour market policies do show a trend toward decentralization and flexibility favouring regional priorities, but there are really no new departures. In the realm of manpower, federal governments have always striven for effectiveness in their policies, and none have really succeeded. Critics of the system have all found the same faults and this Conservative government seems to have genuinely intended to respond. With respect to the pivotal question of unemployment insurance, however, this government has not gone ahead with the reform proposals which most closely match its own theoretical reasoning, namely those put forward by the Forget Commission. What it has done is merely more of what the previous government was doing before, whereas the Forget Report was proposing an important rethinking for the plan.

This policy has had an effect on the labour market which is worth noting. Employment increased between 1984 and 1987, although this is much more to the credit of the American economic recovery and a worldwide easing of inflationary pressures. The proportion of jobs relative to population rose from 57.4% in 1984 to 60.3% in 1987, matching and even slightly surpassing th pre-recession peak of 59.9% in 1981. The unemployment rate consequently fell from 11.3% to 8.9%. A large majority of the new jobs (86%) were full-time jobs.

However, these figures obscure a regional disparity that can be viewed as a consequence of the neo-conservative outlook: 45% of the new jobs created were in Ontario, 25.5% in Quebec, and 26% in the rest of the country. As a result, Ontario's economic preponderance increased from 1984 to 1987, the number of jobs in that province standing now at 39.4% compared to 38.6% in 1984. The same disparity is seen in other indicators. In Ontario the ratio of jobs to population has risen from 61.3% to 64.7%; the unemployment rate has dropped from 9.1% to 6.1%; nearly 90% of new jobs created are full-time, while in the rest of Canada the proportion is 82%. Ontario is the province which has by far benefitted most from the economic recovery since 1984. The most visible effect of the new Conservative approach in manpower and the labour market is perhaps here. The lesson appears to be that when market forces are given a greater role to play in the allocation of resources, regions already favoured are favoured even more, and regional disparities grow larger.

Translated by Patricia Claxton.

NOTES

1 For an overview of neo-conservative thought, see L. Jalbert and L. Lepage (1986).

2 For a more detailed analysis of Keynesian policy development in Canada see D. Bellemare and L. Poulin-Simon (1986).

REFERENCES

Bellemare, Diane and Lise Poulin-Simon (1986). *Le défi du plein emploi. Un nouveau regard économique, (Montréal: Albert Saint-Martin).*

Canadian Labour Congress (1988). *Mémoire présenté au comité parlementaire permanent du travail, de la main-d'oeuvre et de l'immigration sur le Programme canadien de planification de l'emploi,* 19 January.

Economic Council of Canada (1983). *On the Mend,* 20th annaul review, (Ottawa: Supply and Services).

Employment and Immigration Canada (1986). *Annual Report 1985–1986,* (Ottawa: Supply and Services).

Employment and Immigration Canada (1987). *Annual Report 1986–1987,* (Ottawa: Supply and Services).

Government of Canada (1981a). *Labour Market Development in the 1980's.* (Ottawa: Employment and Immigration).

Government of Canada (1981b). *Work for Tomorrow, Employment Opportunities for the 1980's.* Report of the Task Force on Labour Market Development, (Ottawa: Supply and Services).

Government of Canada (1986). *Report of the Commission of Inquiry on Unemployment Insurance,* (Ottawa: Supply and Services).

Government of Quebec (1984). *Budget 1984–1985,* (Quebec: Department of Finance). 1

Government of Canada (1985). *Budget 1985–1986,* (Quebec: Department of Finance).

Jalbert, Lizette and Laurent Lepage (eds) (1986). *Neo-conservatisme et restructuration de l'Etat,* (Montreal: Presses de l'Université du Quebec).

SOCIAL JUSTICE

My government is determined to ensure that social justice in Canada keeps pace with changing needs and circumstances of our people. In this respect the most significant development of recent years is the greater participation of the women of Canada and their rightful claim to equality with men everywhere in our society . . . .

Economic equality is the vehicle through which women will come to full partnership and participation with men in our society. Parliament has committed the federal jurisdiction to equal pay to work of equal value. My government agrees that this concept is one of the keys to the achievement of economic equality for women . . . .

Canadians value and support the comprehensive social security system that has been put in place over many years by the federal and provincial governments. Many areas of this system must be strengthened to respond to the changing nature and needs of our society.

— Speech from the throne, November 5, 1984.

The Status of Women Under the Mulroney Government

LOUISE DULUDE

Because of the minority status that is all too often theirs, because of frequent discrimination that characterizes different aspects of their life, the status of women should be a central policy concern for any democratic regime claiming to be committed to the promotion of social justice.

During the campaign leading up to the 1984 election, and particularly at the leaders' debate on women's issues organized by the National Action Committee on the Status of Women, the Progressive Conservative Party Leader identified a number of policy options he would pursue as head of the government. Mr. Mulroney's promises considerably increased the expectations of women's groups and their constituents.

What became of these promises? This paper will show that the Mulroney government failed to follow up on its election rhetoric and that in some cases it even reduced some of the modest gains of the previous decade achieved by the Canadian women's movement. In short, the expectations of greater social justice for women, raised with such fanfare in 1984, are a long way from being met.

THE STATUS OF WOMEN IN 1988

To understand the policy demands of the women's movement and to prepare the way for workable policy responses to the genuine needs of Canadian women, one must first have a clear grasp of the many problems and handicaps faced by women in our society on a daily basis.

I. Poverty

Far too many women in Canada live below the poverty line. The main reason for the economic plight of Canadian women is that fewer of them hold paid jobs and those who do have paying jobs earn substantially less than their male counterparts.

Table 1, which is drawn from the 1986 Census, shows that 44% of all women aged 15 and over, compared with only 23% of the men, had no employment income at all in 1985. The proportions of men and women holding paid part-time jobs were the same, at 33%.

TABLE 1

1985 Employment Status and Income of Women & Men Aged 15 and Over

	Women	Men
With full-time, full-year paid jobs	23%	44%
With full-time, full-year unpaid jobs	1%	1%
With part-time paid jobs	33%	33%
Not employed or with part-time unpaid jobs	43%	22%
TOTAL:	100%	100%

Table 2 further develops this picture by comparing the median earnings of women and men in similar situations: in 1985, women in full-time, full-year jobs made 67 cents for every dollar earned by

254

a man; in part-time occupations, the female/male ratio was 64%. Many studies have shown that while part of this earnings gap can be attributed to legitimate factors such as differences in age and experience, there still remain large unexplained differences that can only be due to discrimination.

TABLE 2

**1985 Median Employment Income of
Women and Men Aged 15 and Over**

	Women	Men	Female/ Male Ratio
	$	$	%
With full-time, full-year paid jobs	$18,845	$28,209	67%
With part-time paid jobs	5,695	8,863	64%

The inevitable result of the above, as shown in Table 3 by figures provided by the National Council of Welfare, is that with the single exception of children, females are significantly more likely to become poor than males at every stage of their lives.

The two sub-groups of women with the highest poverty rates are female single parents and unattached elderly women (mainly widows); the incidence of poverty among them were 56% and 46% respectively in 1986.

TABLE 3

Poverty Rates By Sex and Age, 1986

	Female	Male
Children	18%	18%
Adults Aged 16 to 64	15%	12%
Elderly (65+)	24%	13%
ALL AGES	17%	13%

This is an ominous sign for the future since these are the two fastest growing categories in our population at the present time.

The women's movement has been particularly concerned about the widespread poverty among women and has been vigorously advocating policy options to correct this deplorable situation. Its main demands are:

A. *Improved Income Security:* Higher family allowances and other benefits for parents; higher social assistance payments (cost-shared by the federal government under the Canada Assistance Plan); a national income supplementation program for the working poor; and a better pension system providing higher minimum guaranteed incomes, a doubled (50%) income replacement rate under the Canada/Quebec Pension Plan, the inclusion of homemakers in the C/QPP and reformed employer-pension plans providing benefits protected against inflation.

B. *Better jobs and better pay for women* through measures such as mandatory affirmative action programs, contract compliance, more training of women for non-traditional occupations through large increases in the minimum wage, equal pay and benefits for part-time workers, and vigorous implementation of equal pay for work of equal value.

C. *Improved family law provisions:* Over the last fifteen years, pressures from women's groups have succeeded in bringing about changes in the family law provisions of all provinces and territories to protect the family home during the marriage and to effect a more equitable division of family property upon separation or divorce. While this was being achieved, however it has become increasingly obvious that property division can only do so much and that on-going support/maintenance provisions — which are mainly ruled by the federal Divorce Act — must be strengthened and enforced.

WOMEN AND SOCIAL SERVICES

Women have a crucial stake in social services not only because of the unfair burden of poverty that they have carried for so long. Women have a crucial stake in social services because they are the ones who have babies and are expected to be the primary care-givers to children and all other dependent family members. Without adequate social supports, mothers of young children and other women with sick or disabled family members are gravely handi-capped compared to men in the labour force.

As a result, it is not surprising that issues such as better mater-nity/parental leave and benefits and the provision of universal, accessible, quality child care services remain among the most cur-rent and strongest demands of the women's movement. As long as childcare continues to be perceived as a personal responsibility to be borne mainly by mothers — who must often spend more than half of their earnings on that item alone — the principles of equal pay and equal opportunity for women will remain a cruel joke.

Decent support for the elderly, including home support services, comprehensive health care and dependable institutions, are also extremely important; without them, aging parents can impose a crushing burden on their middle-aged daughters, effectively pre-venting them from having professional lives of their own. These services are also essential for elderly wives, who spend years caring for their ailing husbands and are then left without anyone to take care of them when they can no longer manage on their own.

Other special services must also be made widely available for women in crisis situations. These include shelters for the homeless, transition houses for battered wives and their children, as well as rape crisis centres. All these services are chronically under-funded now, and remind women, as they should all, of the policy neglect of successive governments.

Government and social services are also extremely important for women because they are the main source of relatively good tradi-tionally female jobs. As well as affecting the quality of the services offered, therefore, any cutbacks or privatization in sectors such as education, health and social services have devastating effects on the female teachers, nurses and social workers who make up the bulk of the employees working in these areas.

WOMEN AND HUMAN RIGHTS

It has been widely documented that women are more often the vic-tims of human rights violations than men, and that this has been the byproduct of centuries of discrimination. Most affected by human rights violations are women who suffer from double handicaps, such as the Native, the poor, pregnant women, women who are immigrants and/or from visible minorities, lesbian women, disabled women, young women and prostitutes. Specific recommendations to improve their situation have included: reinstating the rights of Native women who married non-Native men; entitling immigrant women to the same language training programs as immigrant men; and many amendments to the Human Rights Act and Charter to strengthen their anti-discrimination and affirmative action provisions.

Other broad human rights issues of particular concern to women include reproductive rights and protection against the abusive and/or exploitive depiction of women in the media and in pornographic material. In the first area, women's groups want the abolition of all criminal legislation on abortion, a much greater emphasis on sex education, and a large-scale public review and control of new reproductive technologies. On pornography, feminists are calling for new criminal legislation concentrating on violence and exploitation, rather than on sexuality.

Finally on human rights, because women are still largely absent from the main political, judicial and economic decision-making spheres of our society, it is important (a) that the government make a special effort to appoint women to senior positions; and (b) that women be able to continue to express their views and exercise pressures through the medium of women's groups. For this to be possible, the federal government must not only continue but increase its financial support to organizations whose activities are devoted to improving the status of women in Canada.

CONSERVATIVE PROMISES IN THE FIELD OF WOMEN'S RIGHTS

During the campaign preceding the 1984 federal election, the Conservative Party made a number of promises to women. These included:

I. Income Security Programs

In the course of the leaders' debate on women's issues, Mr. Mulroney categorically stated that "No social program at all, affecting anyone in need, shall be touched by a Progressive Conservative government." In addition, he and his party promised to "eliminate poverty among retired Canadians," to reform all pension plans, to include homemakers in the Canada Pension Plan, and to extend Spouses' Allowances payments to all widowed people in need aged 60 to 64.

Within a year of taking office, however, the PC government did "touch" social programs affecting people in need by attempting to partially de-index old age security payments, even for the poorest elderly. Following massive outcries by seniors, this proposal was soon dropped, but the government did go ahead with its plan to partially de-index family allowances.

As promised, legislation was passed to extend Spouses' Allowance benefits to all poor widowed people aged 60 to 64. Although this was supported by everyone, it was criticized for discriminating in favour of the widowed while leaving other poor people of the same age — mainly women — without benefits.

The following year, the government amended its pension legislation. This brought about some positive changes to employer-sponsored pension plans to shorten the vesting period, increase the portability of their benefits, forbid different benefits for men and women, and make the option of surviving spouses' benefits mandatory. In the absence of any inflation protection, however, these measures provide dubious benefits.

After consultations with the provinces, changes to the Canada Pension Plan were also passed to increase disability benefits, reinforce the provisions relating to credit-splitting on separation or divorce and substantially raise the contribution rates. The issue of homemakers' coverage was delayed indefinitely. It was generally felt that by agreeing to raise contributions without insisting on a major improvement in the benefits provided by the only pension plan that covers all Canadian earners (only about a third of employed women are in employer-sponsored plans, and about half of the men), the federal government had failed to protect the Canadian public.

The other major federal government initiative in the area of retirement benefits was its endorsement of the Liberal proposal to triple the maximum level of deductible Registered Retirement Savings Plans (RRSP) deposits. This is a regressive step that will only benefit better-off taxpayers.

Finally on income measures, following the U.S. tax reform

exercise the Canadian government proceeded with its own so-called tax reform in 1987. As a result, the better-off now pay lower taxes and the benefits of middle and upper-income parents are reduced, while the poor are more or less in the same situation as before. Increased sales taxes, which would also have a regressive effect, have also been announced for the future.

The overall impact of all the above changes, combined with the continued increase in the proportion of single-parent families led by women, has been an increase in the poverty rate of families with young children over the last four years. On the other hand, the rate of poverty among seniors has steadily diminished, mainly as a result of the increases in the federal Guaranteed Income Supplement introduced by previous Liberal governments.

II. Employment

While the economic upturn following the recession of the early 1980s, reduced the level of unemployment, the average rate of 8.5% for men and 9.4% for women in 1987, is still quite high. Studies of real incomes (in constant dollars) show that while the incomes of Canadian households rose between 1984 and 1986, they had not yet caught up with their 1981 pre-recession levels.

Conservative promises to women in the area of employment included: vigorous enforcement of equal pay for work of equal value; mandatory affirmative action in jobs under federal jurisdiction, with contract compliance for all those receiving federal contracts; legislation to give equal benefits to "regular" part-time workers; and job training programs to encourage women to enter non-traditional fields and retrain those displaced by technological change.

The reality of what was done by the Conservative government is as follows:

— equal pay for work of equal value is still largely unenforced at the federal level; the Human Rights Commission issued a statement in 1987, declaring that the present complaints-based federal law is almost useless and should be changed to a proactive law that would force employers to act. Almost a year later, the federal government has yet to react to this recommendation.

— mandatory affirmative action. Although the Employment Equity law passed by the government states that employers under federal jurisdiction should set up affirmative action programs, the only sanctions it imposes are on employers who fail to release statistical information on their employees on a regular basis. The obligations imposed on federal contractors are more stringent in theory — they must present affirmative action plans before they can obtain a contract — but no mechanism has been set up to verify that the plans are carried out.

— equal benefits for part-time workers have not been introduced, probably because of strong business opposition to any tampering with their main source of cheap labour.

— the job training programs introduced by this government have been assessed as inadequate, largely misdirected and of little use to women.

But the one single Conservative policy that would have most effect on women's employment is free trade. The bulk of the manufacturing jobs that are expected to disappear as a result of free trade with the United States are in industries employing mainly women, such as textiles and food processing.

Perhaps even more important for the long-term prospects of women is the failure of the present free trade agreement to specify which social programs would and would not be considered "unfair subsidies" giving rise to countervailing duties. If Canadian social programs such as medicare and old age pensions were to be challenged because they lighten the burden of Canadian employers and make them more competitive, the whole safety net which took decades to build in this country could be unravelled. If this happened, women would be the prime losers.

Free trade with the United States was definitely not a Conservative election promise. On the contrary, during the Conservative leadership race, Mr. Mulroney had said that he was opposed to such a free trade pact because it would compromise Canada's sovereignty.

III. Changes in Family Law

As promised, the Conservative government did pass changes to make divorce easier and to give provincial enforcement officials access to federal data which will facilitate the collection of maintenance payments. At the same time, however, the Divorce Act was also amended to make it more difficult for ex-wives to obtain support payments, and the federal government backed out of its promise to set up a national system of maintenance and custody enforcement.

IV. Childcare

Before the 1984 elections, the Conservatives promised "to find solutions to the urgent problems of child care." Once in office, Mr. Mulroney made the more specific commitment of introducing "a comprehensive national system of childcare." As a result, when the long-awaited federal childcare proposals were unveiled last December, they were a major disappointment.

Far from providing a comprehensive national system, the proposals are a hodge-podge of measures whose central component is the provision of large tax deductions to better-off parents. The second largest component, consisting of cost-sharing of provincial and territorial childcare expenses, imposes no national standards at all as a condition of receiving federal funds. Worst of all, it has been estimated that the federal funds promised under these proposals could end up being lower in the long run than those which the federal government would have had to pay under the current system of cost-sharing under the Canada Assistance Plan.

The lack of national standards in the federal childcare plan highlighted the diminished capacity of the federal government to introduce any new Canada-wide social programs if the Meech Lake accord came into force. This is because the accord would modify the federal government's spending power by providing that henceforth, whenever the federal government wants to introduce a national shared-cost program, it will be obliged to provide compensation to any province that wishes to opt out of it by setting up "a program or initiative that is compatible with the national objectives."

Women's groups have asked that this portion of the accord be modified to clearly establish that opting out and compensation will not be allowed unless the provincial programs in question meet minimum standards of universality, portability and quality.

V. Other Services

Before the election, the Conservatives promised to take "moral and financial leadership" in the area of services for victims of family and other violence. Much talk and numerous studies have followed, but precious little in the way of concrete financial support. Services to the elderly have also been the subject of a great deal of rhetoric and few real commitments.

The one area in which changes have been visible is the steady reduction in federal financial contributions toward the cost of social housing. In spite of Conservative pre-election promises to "improve housing," the number of new social housing units decreased from an average of 25,000 a year in the 1970s and early 1980s to 18,000 new units in 1986 for all of Canada.

VI. Human Rights

Conservative promises included the reinstatement of the status of Native women who had married non-Native men; the introduction of better pornography legislation; increased access to training and information for immigrant women; and increases in the appointment of women to boards, commissions and other positions to a level reaching at least 30%.

Shortly after the election, the Indian Act was amended to allow the reinstatement of Native women who had lost their status. Implementation has been very difficult and even impossible in many instances, however, since the federal government has failed to give Indian bands the funds required to cope with the resulting increased needs for housing and social services.

In other areas, the federal government has not changed its language training programs to give equal access to immigrant women. It has, on the other hand, passed a new prostitution law (actually an anti-solicitation law, since prostitution is technically not illegal in Canada) that severely increases the police harassment of prostitutes, and introduced pornography legislation that focusses on sexuality rather than on exploitation and violence. Most women's groups have denounced both of these initiatives. The record of the government on its human rights policy initiatives on behalf of women is meagre to say the least. As in the preceding areas, promises were made and expectations raised as part of an electoral strategy — the government of Brian Mulroney, once elected to office conveniently ignored some of the key demands of Canadian women.

CONCLUSIONS

As this summary indicates, the only two areas in which the Conservative government has respected its promises to women are the amendment reinstating Native women and the increase in the Spouses' Allowance for the widowed aged 60 to 64. Even these measures are flawed, however, since the first cannot be implemented without additional expenditures and the second introduces a new discriminatory feature.

In many other areas, such as divorce, retirement benefits, affirmative action and contract compliance, childcare, services to victims of violence and to the elderly and pornography, the federal government's initiatives have been a skillful exercise in smoke and mirrors. In each case, the government has done little or has actually harmed women, while engaging in major public relations exercises to convince the public that it had done a great deal.

Most important of all have been the government's large-scale projects such as tax reform, free trade and the Meech Lake accord. Every one of these major initiatives is bound to have very negative effects on the long-term situation of Canadian women and their children.

Canadian Social Services Beyond 1984: A Neo-Liberal Agenda

ANDREW F. JOHNSON

During the election campaign of 1984, the Progressive Conservatives produced a spate of quick-fix promises to redress the immediate concerns of electors. Their promises were not linked to a long-term strategy designed to cure Canada's economic and social ills. Apparently, they had finally discovered the Liberal recipe for success at the polls — quick solutions and short-term thinking[1] — to which they added, once safely elected to office, a long-term agenda for economic renewal.

The agenda, clearly governed by principles endemic to neo-liberalism, sought as its main objective economic growth and, in turn, productive jobs for Canadians (Wilson, 1984b). Moreover the agenda identified "four thrusts essential to economic renewal": first, to get the budget deficit under control; to give business a new boost; to make government more efficient in its own operations and less obstructive to the work of the private sector; and to bring about these changes with a sense of equity and openness that characterize Canadian society.

Two years after the agenda was tabled, Finance Minister Wilson asserted that its objective "has not changed . . . and it will not change" (Wilson, 1986b:1). Significantly, he went on to sing the praises of deficit reduction and expenditure restraint, two sides of the same coin, as the primary means to realize the objective. Thus, the administration and delivery of social services, for which the provinces are almost entirely responsible, have been greatly affected by the Conservatives' determination to curb spending. After all, social spending consumes well over one half of federal

265

expenditure, most of which is transferred to the provinces. In addition, provincial social services have been greatly affected by the Conservatives' neo-liberal designs to boost the private sector while, simultaneously, maintaining social justice.

The purpose of this paper is to assess the impact of the Mulroney government's neo-liberal agenda, particularly as it relates to social spending, on provincially administered and delivered social services. Subsequent sections analyze the impact of these principles on provincial financial requirements for social services, in general, and on the development of health care, social assistance and day care services, in particular.

A NEO-LIBERAL AGENDA:
ECONOMIC GROWTH AND SOCIAL JUSTICE

For the most part, neo-liberalism has been imported from the United States. It is a somewhat eclectic perspective which seeks "realistic" alternatives to traditional liberal economic growth and social justice in the modern welfare state. Indeed, proponents of neo-liberalism frequently describe themselves as "nonideological", as "pragmatic," or as "tough-minded" (Dolbeare and Medcalf, 1988:66). In this sense, Mr. Mulroney, who describes himself as "a pragmatic individual and a realistic one," appears to be of a neo-liberal ilk.[2]

Mr. Mulroney and the Conservative leadership can ill-afford to be otherwise because the main principles of neo-liberalism effectively mitigate and obscure ideological cleavages within the rank and file of the party and lessen similarly antagonistic predispositions within the electorate at large (Johnson, 1988). The party has long been divided into two divergent ideological factions, identified as business liberalism and Toryism (Christian and Campbell, 1983:83–131). Both factions promote economic growth as a means to achieve social justice but they differ on the extent to which the state should intervene to generate economic growth as well as on the meaning of social justice.

On the one hand, business liberals contend that individual initiative, unhindered by state intervention, especially in the realm of social services, stimulates economic expansion, creates jobs, reduces unemployment, and, in the end, reduces poverty. Individuals are rewarded in proportion to their initiative; and if, by virtue of individual initiative jobs are plentiful, then society as a whole benefits and social justice prevails. On the other hand, "organic" conservatives advocate state intervention, when and where necessary, to direct economic growth and to ensure that its rewards are distributed, if not evenly, at least equitably; social justice is not the justice of the marketplace but the justice of restrained intervention. From this perspective the economic health of the whole society is only as good as the vitality of each of its parts and, ultimately, the sum of its parts.

Hence, the principle of economic growth is held sacred by both factions as it is by adherents to neo-liberalism. Indeed, Charles Peters, purportedly speaking on behalf of the faithful, asserts that economic growth is "essential to almost everything else we want to achieve" (1983:10). The primary agent of economic growth is individual initiative or, to borrow Peters' phrasing, "the risk-taking entrepreneur who creates new and better products." PC Finance Minister Wilson could not agree more in that he identifies one of his government's principal tasks as providing "an economic environment that encourages private initiative and risk-taking . . . " (House of Commons, 1986:3574).

However, in the context of neo-liberalism and within the perspectives of senior ministers in the Mulroney cabinet, this notion of individualism is tempered by the principle of community which derives from an organic view of society. Neo-liberal theoretician, Lester Thurow points out that society is "more than a statistical aggregation of individuals" (1985:24). He explains that "it is a community, a society, where socially organizing to help each other leads to a more attractive society, a more equitable society, and a more efficient society than one where each individual is left to make it on his or her own." National Health and Welfare Minister, Jake Epp, has expressed similar sentiments:

> Canadians attach a great deal of importance to individual accomplishments and to individual freedoms. At the time, Canadians are a caring people: we hold it to be a fundamental aspect of our national character that we will help our neighbours who are in need . . . Reconciling these two aspects of our national psyche means that we must never, in our haste to help those in need, forget that they are individuals (1988:5–6).

From this perspective, individualism, as a propellant of economic growth, is intertwined with the notion of a community that shares the benefits of growth. Amitai Etzioni aptly formulates this neo-liberal tenet as "shared wealth will rise as that of individuals does" (1984:56). Individualism, but not the selfish and un-restrained individualism advanced by business liberalism, must be encouraged to generate economic growth. But the state must spread the costs and benefits equitably among the various groups of society as a whole. This conceptualization of social justice is most compatible with organic Toryism; and it is a conceptualization that neo-liberal spokesman, Robert Reich, lucidly amplifies:

> Policies that spread the benefits and the burdens of economic change more equitably among our citizens are superior to those that widen the gap between rich and poor . . . People who feel themselves to be respected work more productively within it than are those who feel that the dice are loaded against them (1983:20).

Individualism qualified by social justice has culminated in the view that the state should intervene to help individuals to help themselves. In this view, self-sufficiency, self-reliance and produc-tivity are terms which are generously sprinkled throughout neo-liberal rhetoric and the public pronouncements of the Mulroney government. Individual incentive is the means by which the econ-omy will grow, by which particular social programs will be made more "efficient." Paul Tsongas puts the case succinctly:

> . . . it is actually the nurturing of incentive that is the essential condition for achieving justice. The reason is that if we maxi-mize "justice" we destroy the conditions for economic growth. In more specific terms, if you maximize all your "just" social programs, the cost would be so burdensome as to cripple the economy, leading to sharply reduced governmental revenues, and the collapse of those very programs as a result (1981:135).

In practical terms, this means that the state must create condi-tions that provide incentives for the entrepreneur to invest and, concomitantly, to create productive jobs. What better way to do so than by curtailing its economic intervention especially in relation to social services? The $45 billion that the federal government currently disburses on social services (broadly defined) amounts to a substantial tax burden on the private sector, and, is said to discourage investment and private sector job creation. However, the state must also maintain "just" social programs while reducing their financial burden. What better way to do so than by maintaining some programs while modifying and designing others in order to sustain the needy and to reduce the dependency of the not-so-needy?

The Mulroney government has not divined better ways to balance economic growth and social justice. It has reduced spending on social services in general. However, it has retained the basic financial structure of health care services in order to spread the fruits of economic growth albeit in a more limited manner than in the past. In conjunction with the provinces, it has begun to redesign social assistance services in order to promote a sense of self-reliance among recipients. Finally, it has begun to mix public funds with private initiative in order to deliver day care services.

Hence, the Mulroney government's neo-liberal approach to social services reconciles the divergent views of business liberals and organic Tories as they pertain to the relationship of the individual to the state in generating economic growth and in distributing its subsequent benefits. Its neo-liberal approach attempts to integrate and balance four different social service strategies which stem from the two ideological traditions. As such, the approach and the strategies are inherently inconsistent and, as might be expected, have produced inconsistent results in relation to social services. At least, that is what the record of the Mulroney government demonstrates.

TRIMMING GOVERNMENT: THE BUDGET, TRANSFERS, AND EQUALIZATION

In the government's first fiscal statement of November 1984, grave concern was expressed about the rising deficit and about the need to put "our own fiscal house in order" (Wilson, 1984:1). However, by all appearances the government, in its first budget, had not seen fit to take drastic action to allay these concerns because spending was increased by 7.3% in relation to the Liberal budget of the previous year.[3] But budgets can rarely be judged by appearances. The 1985 budget was shaped by the neo-liberal approach to trim government by way of reducing its largest component of expenditure, social spending (Prince, 1985:7–9 and 1986:32–34). Old age security and family allowances were to be partially de-indexed so

that benefits could be "targeted to those most in need and funds
... freed for other social priorities (Wilson, 1985:12). However, the
Conservatives were ill-prepared for the public ire that was subsequently stirred by the "universal-selective" debate. Therefore,
they withdrew their selective initiatives with respect to old age
security payments and the Prime Minister admitted that "a mis-
take" had been made.[4]

The controversy was something of a "red herring" which dis-
tracted attention from the Conservatives more subtle determination to effect a global policy of restraint with respect to social
services by reducing transfers to the provinces. In the same budget,
the growth of transfers was curtailed in order to save $2 billion
annually by the end of the decade. And in the 1986 budget, the
Finance Minister applauded his government's success in having
reduced these payments. Furthermore, the government, in the context of its fiscal plan, changed the formula used to determine Established Program Financing (EPF) arrangements so that, in fiscal
year 1986–1987, the indexation factor was reduced by two percentage points per annum (Wilson, 1986c:20). In 1986, the government
passed legislation to this effect (Bill C–96) and, as a result, recent
estimates hold that the provinces are likely to lose over $8 billion
between 1986 and 1992 (Quebec, 1986:11).

More to the point, Bill C–96 added to the burden imposed on the
provinces to make up the shortfall in EPF transfers previously imposed by the Liberal government.[5] However, the current government has continued to provide supplementary equalization payments to provinces whose benefits have been appreciably reduced
by cutbacks to the EPF as well as by cutbacks effected by the 1981
alterations to the equalization formula. As a matter of fact, in its
1986 budget the government proudly indicated that it had provided "supplementary equalization payment for all six equaliza-
tion-receiving provinces in 1985–86 and for Manitoba in 1986–87
(Wilson, 1986a:11). Furthermore, in March 1987 the government
introduced Bill C–44 which, like Bill C–96, amends the EPF. Bill C–
44 permits the federal government to provide and additional $175
million, or an increase of approximately 5%, in equalization payments over a two year period. However, these funds hardly make
up for the withdrawal of supplementary equalization payments
enacted in April of 1987. Moreover, the funds do not make up for
provincial losses incurred under Bill C–96.

Hence, the provinces have begun to bear the impact, but not the full impact, of the 1981 changes to the equalization formula and of the various changes to the EPF throughout the 1980s. The value of federal transfers began to increase slightly in 1987 but are not likely to increase sufficiently to compensate for previous losses.[6] The erosion in the amount of revenues that the provinces derive from the EPF and equalization, has directly weakened their ability to withstand current and rising costs in their health and educational programs. It has also exerted considerable pressure on their fiscal capacity to shoulder increasing costs in their social service budgets as a whole. Indeed, the Government of Quebec, for one, admits that the slow growth in federal revenues will force a further "rationalization" in spending, a euphemism for further cutbacks in spending.[7] The province strongly hints that these rationalizations will be applied to social service programs.

In addition, the federal government's present proposal for tax reform may accentuate pressure on provincial social service budgets (Wilson, 1987:77–79). The proposal asserts that payments via equalization will grow but that the amounts involved will be substantially smaller than increased payments expected via the EPF. It also promises accelerated payments, initially to offset reductions in personal income tax revenues to the provinces. However, it has been argued that losses in revenues from tax reform as a whole will eventually put pressure on the federal government to further shrink transfers (Battle, 1987: 15–18).

However, all of this is hypothetical because white paper proposals are not written in stone. In the meantime, Conservative budgets, especially as they have affected EPF and equalization payments, suggest that the federal government is disposed towards trimming, but not dismantling, social services.

The disposition is entirely consistent with a neo-liberal strategy for economic renewal. But the maintenance of social service programs, perceived as not interfering with individual initiative, is also compatible with neo-liberal thought. Health care services fit this requirement and, as such, have been well-defended by Conservatives in Opposition as well as in a governing capacity.

MAINTAINING SOCIAL JUSTICE: HEALTH SERVICES

The Conservatives cautious approach to health services can be best understood against the backdrop of the Canada Health Act of 1984,

271

which they, in opposition, fully supported along with the New Democratic Party and its sponsors, the governing Liberals. The Act was passed in order to thwart provincial attempts to shift some responsibility for health services from their treasuries to individual users, a subject which requires amplification.

The Canada Health Act essentially focuses on two major principles of the health care system: universality of benefits and accessibility to services. According to these principles, the entire population is entitled to a full range of health care services. However, prior to 1984, several provinces had begun to violate this provision by permitting user-charges and/or extra-billing. The Act was passed to thwart these initiatives by permitting the federal government to withhold $1 in transfer payments for every dollar directly paid by patients for health services; the money is to be held in escrow but refunded, if extra charges are eliminated within three years.

During the 1984 election campaign, the Conservatives were compelled to recognize the shortcomings of the Act mainly because their long-standing allies in Alberta, New Brunswick, and Ontario were most adversely affected by the financial penalties. There is little doubt that the governing parties of these provinces were, at that time, ideologically disposed towards extra-billing. But the harsh reality of underfunding justified their ideological inclination to encourage a modest measure of individual self-reliance via user charges.

However, the Act did little to alleviate underfunding because the government of the day was unwilling to concede that such a problem existed. The Liberal Minister of Health and Welfare, Monique Bégin, pointed out that health care spending, as a portion of national income, had been nearly constant over the decade prior to the introduction of the Act (Bégin, 1983: 13). Furthermore, she contended that the provinces had received more from block-funding EPF arrangements than they would have from the previous cost-sharing arrangements (Bégin, 1983b: 6). Her arguments were supported by subsequent studies (Grenier, 1985: 264–274). However, other studies have also demonstrated what the provinces then realized: that the costs of health services were rising (about 14% per annum) due to investments required for new medical technology and increasing demands of an aging population (Economic Council, 1986: 39–41). In addition, the provinces have had to contend with increasing salary demands of health care professionals. Thus, the Act placed the provinces in a "no win" situation:

if they allowed extra-billing and/or user fees, they could alleviate some of the strain of rising health care costs but they would also lose an equal amount in federal monies.

In Canada's electoral tradition of quick-fix solutions and short-term thinking, the Conservatives promised to repair the financial damage inflicted on their provincial stalwarts by the Act. Mr. Mulroney agreed to inject an additional $100 million into provincial health care systems during his first fiscal year in office and $150 million during his second year; these amounts were roughly complying with the Act at the time.

As it turned out, the Conservatives were never required to deliver the promise. The offending provinces, faced with electors overwhelmingly opposed to user fees, eventually complied.[8] However, once elected to office, the Conservatives did not ignore the underfunding issue. Rather, in their long-term agenda for economic renewal, the Finance Minister proposed consultations on funding for health care with the provinces but cautioned that "the answer is not simply more money" and offered "to look for new approaches within the limits of budgetary realities" (Wilson, 1984b: 81).

The Conservatives have stuck to the Finance Minister's word. As has been pointed out, additional funds have not been pumped into the system; and studies have been conducted to investigate "privatization," a means of controlling public costs by shifting responsibilities for delivering services to the private sector and some costs to individual consumers. As early as June 1985, Bud Sherman, a former Manitoba health minister, submitted a report on privatization (Association of Health Planners, 1985). Sherman endorsed the publicly-funded health system but recommended that governments consider contracting out non-medical services such as housekeeping, dietary and laundry services. More importantly, he acknowledged provincial dissatisfaction with current funding arrangements but merely urged governments to do what they claimed they were already doing: to engage in "an exchange to consider the proposed changes in Federal health financing legislation . . . (and) to encourage wider address of current needs" (Association of Health Planners, 1985: 14). Six months later, a report issued by the Nielsen Task Force expressed broadly similar views (Task Force on Program Review, 1985a: 33). However, the report fully recognizes that cost pressures are mounting. It therefore, urges both levels of government to pursue an "evolution option" which, in so many words, enjoins governments to consider current needs in light of establishing a new relationship between the EPF and the Canada Health Act.

Jake Epp claimed that he thought that the Sherman Report would have "put privatization to a large extent to bed."[9] However, the Nielsen Report subtly re-opened the issue. More importantly, the Minister of National Health and Welfare refuses to let it rest. He continues to advance the idea that health policy should "provide for the fullest expression of our individual talents, abilities and preferences" (Epp, 1988: 6) or, in other words, that volunteer services — individual initiative — should be used to slow the growth in health care costs (Epp, 1986). Yet, he also continues to affirm the need to maintain the system, given one condition: economic growth. According to the minister, "we cannot maintain the system as Canadian, if we don't get the economy generated. It is as simple as that."[10] The same neo-liberal condition is attached to the ongoing viability of social assistance services in Canada.

REDESIGNING FOR SELF-SUFFICIENCY:
SOCIAL ASSISTANCE SERVICES

The Canada Assistance Plan (CAP) only constitutes about one-tenth of federal disbursements on social programs but it represents about one-half of provincial spending on social assistance services. Naturally, CAP expenditure is highly sensitive to economic growth or the lack thereof, namely unemployment, because it is fueled by demand which cannot be denied by law to persons in need.

The level of spending on CAP is not controversial, although it climbed steadily throughout the 1980s to slightly over $4 billion at present and is expected to increase to approximately $8.5 by the end of the decade.[11] The increase is largely due to a decade long series of amendments to the Unemployment Insurance Act which transferred much of the responsibility for the unemployed to provincial regimes of social assistance. Moreover, the CAP caseload remains high because unemployment, despite recent reductions, still remains high. Finally, spending on job creation programs has actually declined since 1984 and has, therefore, not make a major dent in the overall number of cases. Indeed, it has been pointed out that present spending on the Canadian Jobs Strategy program would have to be increased from $1.7 billion to $2.5 billion just to maintain 1984 funding levels (House of Commons, 1987: 4352).

Despite rising costs, the Conservatives have not streamlined CAP disbursements in the short-term. However, it is certainly not safe to assume that the same will hold in the long-term. The Nielsen Task Force claims that CAP funds are well spent but is also quick to point out that "if the cost of CAP becomes intolerable, the federal government might limit its expenditures" and "the burden would be shifted to the provinces or simply ignored (Task Force on Program Review 1985b: 14).

The provinces have maintained low benefit rates to ensure that the costs do not become intolerable.[12] Moreover, low benefit rates are appealing to neo-liberals at the federal level; low rates make social assistance unattractive to the alternative of productive employment and, therefore, ostensibly promote individual initiative among recipients. Social assistance rates vary from province to province and, although, several provinces have recently increased benefits, benefits as a whole are not realistically related to the costs of purchasing goods and services needed to support and adequate individual and family budgets. Indeed, the National Council of Welfare reports that, by its calculations, welfare incomes ranged from a low of 23% of the poverty line to a high of 85% in 1986. More to the point, welfare recipients are not much better off than they were in 1984 (National Council of Welfare, 1987: 63).

Neo-liberal strategists within the federal government have also been instrumental in keeping costs to a minimum by redesigning CAP, in conjunction with the provinces, to reduce the caseload. In September of 1985, the Minister of National Health and Welfare announced the Canadian Jobs Strategy program which is essentially designed to encourage employable welfare recipients to return to the work force (House of Commons, 1985: 6790–6795).

According to the Minister, roughly 30% of social assistance recipients are employable. Thus, funds, which would have been spent on social assistance for employables, have been channeled into job training, counselling, and job creation opportunities, provided under the program. The Minister indicated that the program should not be considered as an attempt to transform the welfare state into a workfare state but as an attempt to promote self-sufficiency at no cost. "The idea is simple," he claimed in the House of Commons, "the effect on the client will be vastly increased opportunities for self-sufficiency. There is no coercion, simply increased opportunity. There is no increase in cost, simply a more creative and positive use of funds" (House of Commons, 1985: 6792).

To be sure, the main intention has been to save money. However, the root of the new approach to welfare is to promote individual initiative or, to put it otherwise, self-sufficiency. And the notion has been accepted by most of the provinces. In March of 1987, the federal government signed an agreement with the provinces which will direct $600 million over the next three years into the program. British Columbia, Saskatchewan, Manitoba, New Brunswick and Newfoundland have already agreed to provide voluntary programs on the 50–50 cost-sharing arrangement with the federal government.[13] Quebec has recently tabled a green paper which promotes the work-not-welfare concept (Quebec, 1987b). Ontario, which has implemented such programs in twenty-three communities, has commissioned a comprehensive study of its social assistance system; and the commission is expected to be favourably disposed to a wider implementation of such programs.

It is too early to judge the success of the program. Its success will depend on the quality of the jobs created, on the quality of the counselling available, and on the marketability of skills that are acquired as well as on the nature of the persuasion used to encourage those eligible to take advantage of the various opportunities. However, the signs are not encouraging because the success of the training component of the strategy, the essential ingredient, depends on the responsiveness of the private sector. Private enterprises can hardly be expected to respond effectively because, as the Forget Commission notes, "with the pressure of the bottom line, (they) may find it difficult to provide much training to the disadvantaged unless they are given contracts for that purpose" (Canada, 1987b: 89).

Finally, the success of the Canadian Jobs Strategy will also depend on the quality of support services available. However, the quality of support services proffered by the federal government to date leaves little room for optimism. Day care services are a case in point.

MIXING PUBLIC FUNDS WITH PRIVATE INITIATIVE:
DAY CARE SERVICES

During the 1984 election campaign, Mr. Mulroney went on record as supporting government funding of day care. He repeated his pledge at the federal-provincial first ministers, conference held in Vancouver in November of 1986. The Prime Minister kept his commitment but his government's program for day care falls far short of the universal, publicly-funded, and non-profit, quality services promoted by day care activists.

The "National Strategy on Child Care" is the first major and new social service initiative of the Mulroney government (Epp, 1987). All of its previous initiatives have been to streamline or redesign existing programs in order to make them more compatible with a neo-liberal strategy for economic renewal. However, the widespread demand for day care services provided the government with and opportunity to virtually give birth to an original package of social services.[14] The government seized this opportunity albeit within the rather restrictive parameters of a neo-liberal approach to social services.

From the outset of the Conservative mandate, the Finance Minister made it clear that the twin litmus tests for social programs were to be fiscal responsibility and social responsibility (Wilson, 1984: 71). The former has referred to limiting costs while the latter has referred to directing funds to those most in need. It may be of little consolation to a majority of working parents but the proposed day care program successfully passed these tests.

Fiscal responsibility is expressed in the current day care strategy by virtue of the relatively limited funds to be made available. The Cooke Task Force recommended a package of universal and publicly-funded day care services which carried an estimated price tag of $2.9 billion annually in the "medium term" and an additional $6.3 billion spread over the "longer term" (Canada, 1986: 339). Clearly, the government took more comfort in a House of Commons committee report which advanced a more modest program and, concomitantly, a more modest financial role for government: the estimated costs were between $767 million and $966 million annually by 1989 (Canada, 1987a: 133). In the current proposal, $5.4 billion is to be spent over a seven year period. However, $140 million of the $5.4 billion is already spent annually under CAP on cost-shared day care services for social assistance recipients; in other words, only $4.4 billion is new money.

In relation to social responsibility, the program does provide additional funds to those in need, at least in the short-term. The $140 million, provided for day care services under CAP, is to be increased by over 300% annually. However, CAP's open-ended provision for day care services will be terminated. This means that there may be no federal cost-sharing funds beyond that amount, despite rising costs for day care service.[15]

However, one-half of the new funds ($2.3 billion) will be spent by way of tax credits and deductions for child care expenses. By spending one-half on the funds through the tax system, the government has demonstrated that it is only willing to assume partial involvement in providing day care spaces. It is using tax expenditures to provide parents and guardians with the financial wherewithal to demand additional day care spaces but it expects the private sector to respond to increased demand. In short, the government's intention is to mix public funds with private delivery of day care services. Indeed, the Minister of National Health and Welfare declared that this was his "obligation" (House of Commons, 1987: 11496).

At the same time, he also claimed that it was his government's intention to create 200,000 new spaces over the seven year period. However, the end result may be that tax incentives will simply ease the cost burden of day care services on many parents without increasing the number of spaces at the same rate as in the past and without enhancing the quality.

But all of this is speculation. It is incumbent on the Minister to demonstrate whether the funds designated for tax breaks will or will not increase the number of spaces and whether the funds will or will not stimulate the growth of quality spaces. To date, the Minister has neglected to do so. After all, the neo-liberal strategy is an embryonic and long-term strategy, sustained by little experience but by lots of faith, that, with a modicum of public assistance, private initiative and self-reliance will be re-activated to generate economic renewal and its by-product, social justice. At best, he redressed these criticisms by adding $1 billion to the package in July of 1988. However, it is still not clear how the funds are to be spent.

ERRATA

Page 279

Paragraph 2, from line 12 onward, should read:

than they were in 1984 but not much better off. To put it another way, there is still as much need for social services as there was when the Conservatives took office. But their inconsistent response to the need has had negative, positive, and questionable effects.

Page 280

Starting on line 9, the following should be deleted:

... The basic financial structure of national health care has been maintained but the government has neglected to take measures through the EPF to redress underfunding crises which persist in many provincial medicare systems.

CONCLUSION: 1988 AND BEYOND

There is more evidence to confirm the faith of neo-liberals in their strategy for economic growth than there is to strengthen their faith in their strategy for social justice. As is well known, the Conservatives, as a government, have succeeded in shrinking the deficit as a proportion of GDP; the economy has expanded steadily since 1984. Unemployment has declined from 11.1% of the labour force in 1984 to 8.1% in 1987. A boom is suggested by all of the broad economic indicators. It also seems that the neo-liberal intention to promote social justice, largely by providing jobs, has been realized. Has it? Not quite.

Despite the falling jobless rate, Canada has the dubious distinction of having the third highest unemployment rate among OECD nations. Still, according to one recent report, there were 1.3 million more jobs in 1987 than there were in 1980 and 78% of these have been created since 1984. But 27% of the jobs created since 1984 have been part-time jobs and, in 1987, one-fifth of these jobs were held by workers who wanted full-time work. Furthermore, average wages have not kept pace with inflation since 1984. And there has been little income redistribution except in an upward direction (Canadian Council on Social Development, 1988). In short, the broad social indicators reveal that Canadians are slightly better off than they were in 1984 but not much need for social services as there was when the Conservatives took office. But either inconsistent response to the need has had negative, positive, and questionable effects.

On the negative side of the ledger, cutbacks to the EPF and equalization, on top of previous Liberal cutback, have placed a considerable strain on provincial social budgets. It is estimated that federal alterations to the EPF and equalization since 1981, combined with the financial implications of the Canada Health Act, will amount to $23 billion in revenue losses for all provinces between 1982 and 1992 (Quebec, 1986: 21). Thus, the provinces have become increasingly hard-pressed to meet social service needs as a whole.

Furthermore, in the future the poorer provinces will not be able to absorb reductions in transfer payments as easily as richer provinces because of the unsatisfactory role that equalization is expected to perform. The richer provinces possess a higher fiscal capacity which gives them more latitude to levy taxes. Yet the richer provinces have less social needs to support because they have had and continue to have lower rates of unemployment than the poorer provinces.

On the positive side, the basic financial structure of national health care has been maintained but the government has neglected to take measures through the EPF to redress underfunding crises which persist in many provincial medicare system. The basic financial structure of national health care has been maintained but the government has neglected to take measures through the EPF to redress underfunding crises which persist in many provincial medicare systems. The basic financial structure of CAP also remains much as it was in 1984. In addition, a program for training and employment has been devised to make it easier for welfare recipients to re-enter the labour force. Of course, the program can only be regarded as a step forward if participants are provided with long-term, skilled and better paying jobs, unlike the jobs created by governments in the past.[16]

Finally, the Conservative response to the apparent need for day care services is highly questionable. There are no guarantees that the meagre funding provided will enable the public or private sectors to address current of future needs. In effect, the federal government has transferred much of the financial responsibility for providing day care services to the provinces. However, the provinces are financially ill-equipped and, in several instances, appear to be ideologically ill-disposed to providing suitable day care services.

In the final analysis, the social justice component of the neo-liberal strategy has largely been shifted to the provinces while the Conservatives concentrate on the economic growth component. The Meech Lake Accord sanctions, and will likely accelerate, this shift.[17] However, wide variations in the financial and ideological circumstances of provincial governments provide little assurance that social services will fully develop according to neo-liberal expectations of social justice for all beyond 1988.

NOTES

1 See Clarke et al. (1984: 77–99) for a thorough discussion on this point.
2 *Montreal Gazette*, June 29, 1985.

3 *Toronto Star*, February 27, 1985.

4 *Montreal Gazette*, June 29, 1985.

5 The Federal government intervened to alter the EPF arrangements on two occasions between 1982 and the enactment of Bill C–96 in 1986. First, the Canada Health Act (Bill C–3) was passed in April 1984. The Act provides for financial penalties for provinces which permit extra-billing or apply user fees. Second, Bill C–92, also passed in April 1984, imposed a 6%1 and 5% threshold on transfers for 1983–1984 and 1984–1985, respectively.

6 A fuller explanation is provided in Appendix B and Appendix F of the Quebec 1987–1988 Budget (Quebec, 1987: 6 and 24).

7 The Quebec Finance Minister remarks that "in light of the government's high-priority financial objectives and the impossibility of increasing the burden of Quebec taxpayers, in the coming years and government will have to compensate for slow growth in federal transfers by further rationalizing spending." (Quebec, 1987: 6).

8 For example, in May of 1984, a Gallup Poll reported that 83% of Canadians were opposed to extra-billing. See *Montreal Gazette*, May 10, 1984.

9 *The Ottawa Citizen*, February 20, 1986.

10 *The Ottawa Citizen*, February 20, 1986.

11 A Study Team Report to the Task Force on Program Review (1985b:81–90) discusses in detail three controversial themes that have been prevalent in discussions on social assistance: "unemployed unemployables," fiscal restraint, and federal-provincial friction.

12 David P. Ross (1988) reports that, between 1980 and 1986, the annual increase in real terms averaged $45.00 per beneficiary. Of course, increases vary from province to province. For example in Nova Scotia and British Columbia average benefits actually decreased during the same period; in Saskatchewan and Newfoundland, benefits remained unchanged.

13 *Toronto Star*, March 22, 1987.

14 Public opinion polls suggest that there has been considerable demand for government-funded, quality day care services. During July 1986, a survey, undertaken by the Canadian Union of Public Employees, indicated that three of four Canadians regarded the provision of such services as important. See *Globe and Mail*, July 29, 1986. During January of 1987, two-thirds of Canadians surveyed by Southam agreed "that governments should provide funding to ensure that everyone who wishes to use quality day care can do so." See *Montreal Gazette*, January 24, 1987.

15 See *Action: A Bulletin From the National Action Committee on the Status of Women*, February 1988, for a succinct financial analysis of the government's child care program.

16 Two recent reports have criticized government job creation projects as having been largely of the short-term "make-work" variety. (Task Force on Program Review, 1985c: 17–20; Canada, 1987a: 91).

17 The impact of the Meech Lake Accord on social programs remains a subject of considerable debate. See *Perception*, 12, 1 (Winter 1988), 16–23 for a synopsis of the debate.

REFERENCES

Association of Health Planners (1985). *Management by Private Contract: A Study for the Minister of Health and Welfare Canada*, (Winnipeg: Association of Health Planners).

Battle, Ken (1987). "Broader Base/Lower Rates: A Formula for Fair Tax Reform?" *Perception*, vol. 11, no. 2 (November–December), pp. 15–18.

Bégin, Monique Hon. (1983a). *Preserving Universal Medicare: A Government of Canada Position Paper*, (Ottawa: Minister of Supply and Services).

Bégin, Monique Hon. (1983b). Statement by the Hon. Monique Bégin, Minister of Health and Welfare, to the Conference of Provincial Ministers of Health, Halifax, September 7, 1983.

Canada (1986). *Report of the Task Force on Child Care*, (Ottawa: Supply and Services Canada).

Canada (1987a). *Report of the Special Committee on Child Care (Sharing the Responsibility)*, (Ottawa: House of Commons).

Canada (1987b). *Report of the Commission of Inquiry on Unemployment Insurance*, (Ottawa: Supply and Services Canada).

Canadian Council on Social Development (1988). "Communiqué," February 10.

Christian, William and Colin Campbell (1983). *Political Parties and Ideologies in Canada*, 2nd edition, (Toronto: McGraw-Hill Ryerson).

Clarke, Harold D. et al. (1984). *Absent Mandate: The Politics of Discontent in Canada*, (Toronto: Gage Publishing Inc.).

Dolbeare, Kenneth and Linda J. Medcalf (1988). *American Ideologies Today: From Neo-politics to New Ideas*, (New York: Random House).

Economic Council of Canada (1986). *Changing Times*, (Ottawa: Supply and Services Canada).

Epp, Jake Hon. (1986). *Achieving Health for all: A Framework for Health Promotion*, (Ottawa: Supply and Services Canada).

Epp, Jake Hon. (1987). *Sharing the Responsibility: Federal Response to the Report of the Special Committee on Child Care*, (Ottawa: Government of Canada).

Epp, Jake Hon. (1988). *Notes for the Honourable Jake Epp, Minister of National Health and Welfare, on the Occasion of the First International Symposium on Research and Public Policy on Aging and Health*, (Saskatoon).

Etzioni, Amitai (1984). *An Immodest Agenda: Rebuilding American Before the 21st Century*, (New York: McGraw Hill).

Grenier, Gilles (1985). "Health Costs in Canada: Past and Future Trends." In François Vaillancourt (research coordinator), *Income Distribution and Economic Security in Canada*, (Toronto: University of Toronto Press).

House of Commons (1985). *Debates*, September 18.

House of Commons (1986). *Debates*, February 26.

House of Commons (1987). *Debates*, December 4.

Johnson, Andrew F. (1988). "Federal Policies and the Privatization of Provincial Social Services." In Jacqueline S. Ismael and Yves Vaillancourt (eds.), *The Privatization of Social Services in Canada: Policy, Administration and Delivery*, (Edmonton: University of Alberta Press).

National Council of Welfare (1987). *Welfare in Canada: The Tangled Safety Net*,

(Ottawa: Supply and Services Canada).

Peters, Charles (1983). "A Neo-liberal's Manifesto," *The Washington Monthly*, May.

Prince, Michael J. (1985). "Social Policy in PC Year One," *Perception*, vol. 9, no. 1 (September–October), pp. 7–9.

Prince, Michael J. (1986). "Federal Budget, 86: Social Policy Through the Tax System," *Perception*, vol. 9, no. 5 (May–August), pp. 32–34.

Quebec (1986). *1986–1987 Budget Speech and Additional Information*, (Québec: Gouvernement du Québec).

Quebec (1987a). *1987–1988 Budget: Budget Speech and Additional Information*, (Québec: Gouvernement du Québec).

Quebec (1987b). *Pour une politique de sécurite du revenu*, (Québec: Gouvernement du Québec).

Reich, Robert B. (1983). *The Next American Frontier*, (New York: Times Books).

Ross, David P. (1988). "A Review of Poverty, Income Distribution and Income Security Policies in Canada," *Perception*, (forthcoming).

Task Force on Program Review (1985a). *Improved Program Delivery: Health and Sports, a Study Team Report*, (Ottawa: Supply and Services Canada).

Task Force on Program Review (1985b). *Service to the Public: Canada Assistance Plan, a Study Team Report*, (Ottawa: Supply and Services Canada).

Task Force on Program Review (1985c). *Service to the Public: Job Creation, Training and Employment Services*, (Ottawa: Supply and Services Canada).

Thurow, Lester C. (1985). *The Zero-Sum Solution: Building A World Class American Economy*, (New York: Simon and Schuster).

Tsongas, Paul (1981). *The Road From Here: Liberalism and Realities in the 1980s*, (New York: Alfred A. Knopf).

Wilson, Michael Hon. (1984a). *Economic and Fiscal Statement*, (Ottawa: House of Commons).

Wilson, Michael Hon. (1984b). *A New Direction for Canada: An Agenda for Economic Renewal*, (Ottawa: Department of Finance).

Wilson, Michael Hon. (1985). *Securing Economic Renewal: The Budget Speech*, (Ottawa: Department of Finance).

Wilson, Michael Hon. (1986a). *Securing Economic Renewal: The Budget Speech*, (Ottawa: Department of Finance).

Wilson, Michael Hon. (1986b). *Notes for an Address by the Hon. Michael Wilson to the Canadian Club*, Toronto, September 18, 1986.

Wilson, Michael Hon. (1986c). *The Fiscal Plan*, (Ottawa: Department of Finance).

Wilson, Michael Hon. (1987). *The White Paper on Tax Reform*, (Ottawa: Department of Finance).

Between Income Security and Family Equalization

GUY LACHAPELLE

A government is never defeated because it has run out of ideas,
but because it can no longer give effect to the ideas it has.
— *Jean Francoeur* (1984: 10)

Politically and socially speaking, the nineteen eighties have been
particularly intense in Canada and many other industrialized
countries. After decades of sustained economic growth, governments have been obliged to face rising interest rates, persistent
inflation, and slowing internal growth rates. These phenomena
have all taken their toll. Many employers have been forced to lay
off workers whose only salvation is the Welfare State which half a
century of reforms have sought to place on firm foundations
(OECD, 1981; Gillespie, 1980; Vaillancourt, 1985; Pelletier, 1982;
Banting, 1982).

With the election of the New Right in many countries, however,
the Welfare State was before long being seen as both the cause and
effect of our economic woes. The hour of bottom lines had come.
Income security programs were targeted for revision inasmuch as
there was increasing doubt regarding their continuing adequacy
to fill the needs of families and individuals. At this juncture, the
Reagan, Thatcher, and Mulroney brand of neo-conservatism/neo-
liberalism was bound to appeal to many, particularly since the
economic crisis was not being blamed on private enterprise but on
the burdens imposed by an overly interventionist state that had
failed to respect free market and other principles. With reduced
revenues, the state could no longer meet the urgent demands of

the underprivileged, the poor, and the unemployed without jeopardizing its efforts toward economic revitalization and rebuilding. Social-democratic policies of more state intervention as the solution to unemployment (full-employment policies), for example, had lost their appeal because they offered no short-term prospect of a better standard of living to those already without jobs. The crucial question facing the New Right was therefore how to redistribute wealth without increasing the fiscal burdens for both citizens and state.

In the wake of its election on September 4, 1984, the Conservative government of Brian Mulroney fully intended to meet this challenge. The exercise was to prove difficult but necessary, and also useful in that it forced all interested groups in Canada to evaluate the effect of all the federal programs, benefits, and fiscal measures affecting the income of Canadians (see Table 1). In other words, interested groups were forced to look carefully at all the state's redistribution techniques together, those involving direct payments to families and individuals as well as those using the tax system. The role of the federal government was to be studied in the well-defined context of "fiscal expenditures."[1] The debate was therefore to bear not just on the social impact of income security programs but on the cumulative, progressive, or regressive effect of the various programs together with that of federal taxation on the real income of Canadians.[2]

The principal hurdle to be faced by the Conservative government was to be first and foremost a political and ideological one. While the Mulroney government's political philosophy is clearly Reaganist and Thatcherist, it also has characteristics of its own. Although certain of the neo-liberals held that fiscal expenditures were at the root of the economic crisis,[3] the Conservative Party hesitated to endorse this stance because it has always recognized a certain government role in the equitable redistribution of resources among the various regions of the country (Stanfield, 1982: 325–327; Preece, 1977). But all Canadians were apprehensive over the latent internal conflict in the party between the hawks (the "blue tories"), who insist that any government intervention must give way to market imperatives, and the doves (the "red tories"), who believe that government has a role of economic engine to play by creating a social climate favourable to growth and investment. Moreover the principle that income security is an individual rather than social responsibility did not seem to be unanimously espoused by the Conservative Party. Party strategists therefore decided that the issue of social policy and income security would not be faced head on in the election campaign lest it should eclipse all other issues and cause dissent (Canadian Press, 1984; Descôteaux, 1984b).

TABLE 1

**Federal Programs, Benefits, and Tax
Measures for Income Security**

Programs and Benefits	Tax Measures[3]
1. Financial Benefits for the Elderly	
a. Old age security (universal)[1]	a. elderly exemption
b. Guaranteed income supplement (selective)[2]	b. pension income deduction
c. Spouse allowance (selective)	
2. Financial Benefits for Children	
a. Family allowance (universal)	a. child tax exemption
b. Child tax credit (selective)	
3. Unemployment Insurance Program	
a. Unemployment insurance	
4. Financial Benefits for Veterans	
a. Disability pensions for veterans and civilians	
b. War veterans' allowance for veterans and civilians	

1. Universal — for all Canadians regardless of income — benefits taxable and indexed to the cost of living
2. Selective — level of benefits depends on family income
3. Tax measures are among a government's "fiscal expenditures."

Canadians smelled something fishy and well they might, especially when the Conservative party succeeded finally in making its bed midway between the "neo-liberal" and "neo-democratic" elements in its ranks. There was reason to foresee that the same divided views on social policy and income security visible in European rightist parties would spell trouble for the Conservative

Party.[4] Before long there was conflict between the champions of financial and budgetary policy, for whom debt and deficit reduction came first and who included the Minister of Finance, Michael Wilson, and the bards of social and family policy, for whom the needs of Canadian families must not fall victim to accounting exercises. The Prime Minister felt obliged to rebuke his Minister of Finance several times during the first months of the Conservative government's mandate, insisting that his government would never reconsider the principle of universality in family allowances and old age pensions.

It will therefore be interesting to examine the overall picture of measures of income security improvement offered to Canadians by the Conservative government. Next we will look more closely at the thorny problem of universality versus selectivity for certain federal programs and benefits, along with the parameters of fiscal reform. Finally, we will try to discern the present state of what this government has done for income security and consider whether we are moving toward a more integrated system of "family equalization."

FROM AMBIVALENCE TO CONFUSION . . .
OR, THE MAD HATTER'S TEA-PARTY

From the time of its first speech from the throne on November 5, 1984 and the publication of Finance Minister Wilson's paper, *A New Direction for Canada*, which came three days later on November 8, the Conservative government was committed to certain income security reforms.

In the speech from the throne, the Mulroney government tried to reassure Canadians by showing genuine interest in social questions and income security. First, it indicated that there was no intention to reconsider existing income security programs, but rather to bring forward reforms to improve them, since it recognized that "Canadians like the vast social security system that the federal government and the provinces have established over the years" (Desrivières, 1984). Three priorities were identified: equal pay for women, improvements to child care services, and revision of old age pension regulations. Regarding the first, the government was committed to respect of the principle of "equal pay for work of equal value," which Parliament had adopted in the course of seeking to improve employment prospects for women in the federal civil service.

Regarding child care services, a parliamentary committee was set up to examine all aspects of the question and continue the work of a task force of non-elected persons created by the previous government. Four years later, in January 1988, The Minister of Health and Welfare, Jake Epp, tabled his National Strategy on Child Care. The principal components of this new policy were to be embodied on the one hand in fiscal measures, in the form of an increase in the child care deduction and a child tax credit supplement for low-income families, and on the other in the creation of a joint federal-provincial program to increase the number of day-care spaces and reduce their cost to families.

But the more pressing short-term preoccupation for the newly-elected government seems to have been old age pension reform. Two promises were made: all widows and widowers from age 60 to 64 would be made eligible for the spouse allowance regardless of the age of the deceased spouse at the time of death or the financial situation of the surviving spouse; the standard of living for veterans would be improved. The Conservative government also promised to open discussions with the provinces with a view to harmonizing pension programs, both public and private (old age pensions, guaranteed income supplements, pension plans). Subjects on the agenda would include portability, benefits to the surviving spouse, the inclusion of women in various plans, and the introduction of measures to encourage saving in anticipation of retirement.[5] The Mulroney government intended thus to answer the concerns of many that the increasing number of retired persons in Canada would mean less generous treatment from public pension coffers.

The Conservative government's initial intentions set forth in the speech from the throne had given hope of beneficial changes for low-income families and the retired, but the Minister of Finance's paper to a large extent confirmed the fears of many Canadians regarding the Mulroney government's real objectives. Indeed, the government's concern for social justice and income security appeared to be paling, since the principal objectives according to Mr. Wilson were to bring order to public finances with a view to reducing the budgetary deficit and the national debt, to redefine the role of the government in order best to bring about renewed economic growth, and to adopt policies to encourage increased investment in Canada. And all without penalizing a single citizen. The minister promised, among other things, not to weaken "the basic income support programs that have served Canadians well" (1984: 3), and even to be pretty generous if Canada's economic performance improved. A formidable challenge, and it left many Canadians perplexed since it was to "downsize government, while entering maintenance of the social safety net" (1984: 85).

Regarding income security programs and benefits, Mr. Wilson's paper put forward the principle that government policies should be better adapted to the needs of Canadians and that a reexamination of the various programs was necessary. It therefore proposed a national debate on the twofold theme of a sense of social and financial responsibility for everyone. It was vital henceforth to direct the limited resources of government toward needy families and individuals, Mr. Wilson stressed, noting "that the best income security is a job, and that government expenditures must be allocated to provide immediate employment opportunities and insure better sustained income growth" (1984: 71). The financial health of the State was therefore clearly being given priority over improvements in income security programs and benefits. No one was fooled by this manifestly neo-liberal attitude, particularly since all the minister's proposals for families with children, benefits for the aged, unemployment insurance, and housing policy were contained in the chapter entitled "Restoring Fiscal Flexibility."

The paper also questioned the efficiency of existing programs and benefits for families with children, particularly family allowances, the repayable child tax credit, and the child tax exemption. It advanced three suggestions: elimination of the child tax exemption; continuation of universality in family allowances while reducing the amount paid to high-income families; and/or reductions in both family allowances and the child tax exemption while increasing the child tax credit for low or average-income families.

Regarding benefits for the elderly, the Minister questioned the pertinence of sums expended for old age security and guaranteed income supplements, and of fiscal expenditures in the form of old age exemptions and pension income deductions. His intentions became even clearer when he declared that the government would have to consider "whether these federal transfer payments should continue in their present form or whether they need to be redesigned to increase fairness, assist those in greatest need, and reduce the burden on the federal government" (1984: 74). The document proposed a number of hypothetical courses of action: a reduction in old age security benefits to high income retired persons by taxing these benefits at higher than average rates or some other fiscal recapture mechanism; gradual elimination of the old age exemption and pension deduction, making the system more progressive; and reduction or elimination of old age security indexation, along with compensatory measures favouring the needy. In Mr. Wilson's mind, the idea behind all these propositions was to encourage retirement planning by Canadians themselves rather than have them leave this to the State.

The final item of the proposed reform involved unemployment insurance. On this point, the objective set by the Minister was to adapt the system more closely to economic and social change. He also proposed modification of the rates of benefits paid, reduction of the term of payment, reexamination of costs relating to job creation, shared employment, and maternity benefits, along with enhancement of beneficiaries' employability by obliging them to participate in training and recycling programs. The entire matter was later to be handed over to the Forget Commission with a mandate to study the various alternatives. The idea of abolishing unemployment insurance along with all income security programs and substituting a new guaranteed minimum income program, as proposed by the Macdonald commission in 1985, was not judged worthy of priority consideration.

Mr. Wilson's paper was therefore suggesting to Canadians avenues of reform that would substantially modify the existing income security programs and benefits and move away from the principle of universality, adopting a decidedly more selective approach. Many organizations raised their voices to protest a change of direction that would mean a break with the traditional approach of preceding governments, seeing it as reversion to a system in which beneficiaries would be subjected to means tests.[6] Thus, universality for income security programs and benefits roused passions in many breasts and dominated the debate in Parliament for the Conservative Government's first three months in office. It must be said, however, that the Liberals and New Democrats, vying for the spotlight as effective opposition in the House, nourished the debate and succeeded in showing the ambivalence of Conservative pronouncements.

Faced with such widespread protest, the Mulroney government was forced to define its intentions. The task fell to the Minister of

National Health and Welfare, Jake Epp, who tabled a document entitled *Child and Elderly Benefits* in January 1985, in which the government set forth its guidelines respecting income security. First, universality in family allowances and old age security would be maintained. Second, the idea of a financial means test to determine eligibility for selective programs was unequivocally set aside. Finally, if there were savings realized as a result of changes in income security programs and benefits, the money would be used to create new programs and not to reduce the deficit.

In the case of benefits and tax advantages for children, Mr. Epp proposed two options: 1) abolition of the child tax exemption, an increase in the child tax credit (from $367 to $595), and a reduction in the eligible family income ceiling (from $26,330 to $20,500); 2) a reduction in the child tax exemption (from $710 to $240), a reduction in family allowances, an increase in the child tax credit, and a reduction in the eligible family income ceiling. With the first option, the federal government would save $80 million and the provinces $330 million. With the second, the federal savings would be $130 million and the provincial $150 million. As for old age benefits and advantages, the document merely reiterated the federal commitment announced in the speech from the throne and by the Minister of Finance in his paper with respect to payment of allowances to surviving spouses, both widows and widowers aged 60 to 64, which, he announced, would come into effect as of the autumn of 1985.

The speech from the throne and the Epp and Wilson documents all rightly noted that the Canadian income security system was not merely a matter of federal and provincial transfers to families and individuals but also a system of taxation. They also raised the question of universality in family allowances and old age security, and whether these programs should be considered a system of social insurance or assistance.

UNIVERSALITY IN FAMILY ALLOWANCES AND OLD AGE SECURITY

The speech from the throne set off a debate over universality in family allowances and old age security that, for the Canadian electorate, confirmed the ambivalence of the Conservative Party's ideology regarding income security. Although the Mulroney government kept repeating to anyone who would listen that only these two programs were involved in the discussion over universality, in the eyes of many such a breach would mean the creation of a dangerous precedent that in the long term could jeopardize existing health programs. Others whose convictions were more in line with Conservative party ideology reproached the Mulroney government for its timidity in failing to reexamine the entire Canadian Welfare State (Descôteaux, 1984b).

In fact, the fundamental question raised by the Conservative government was whether family allowances and old age security payments could really be considered universal benefits. These programs do not, indeed, apply to all Canadians but rather to well-defined target groups, to families with children and persons past the age of retirement. Moreover, these benefits being taxable, the sums received after taxes are not uniform since they vary with each beneficiary's marginal tax rate. Families and individuals in high-income brackets retain less than those with low incomes and the benefits can therefore be considered progressive in nature.

However, the reality is more complex because the intricacies of taxation make it impossible for a program like family allowances to achieve its objectives. For example, as shown in Table 2, using 1985 benefits and tax provisions for children, a family of two working parents and two children with an annual income of less than $10,000 retains less than an identical family with an annual income of $33,000. As the National Council rightly stressed, "the overall effect of the three child benefit programs is illogical from both the social and fiscal points of view" (National Council of Welfare, 1985a: 8). The problem is that the tax exemption for dependent children totally cancels out the progressive nature of the two other measures.

Throughout the debate on universality there have been two rather different definitions of the concept. The first and more "traditional" of these defines a universal program as one whose target group members all receive the same pre-tax sum. The second, which might be called "realist," accepts the variability of universal benefits after taxes although the target group as a whole remains eligible for those benefits. But when we realize that since the early 1960s, by taxing and by partially or totally de-indexing family and old age security payments, successive governments have relentlessly whittled down the benefits that some citizens receive, can we really continue to talk about universality in the

1980s? In my opinion, the first definition merely perpetuates a certain "social illusion" by allowing the belief that these benefits are universal when in fact they are clearly selective. The second definition at least has the virtue of shifting the debate into its true context, meaning that one cannot discuss universality without involving taxation in the discussion. In short, Canada is equipped with income security programs in which the principle of "selectivity in universality" is applied.[7]

TABLE 2

**Child Benefits, Two-Income Family with
Two Children, by Family Income, 1985**

Family Income	Net Family Allowances	Child Tax Credit	Tax Credit for Dependent Children	Total Benefits per child
10,000 and under	$ 750	$ 734	$ 0	1,484 $
15,000	560	734	356	1,650
20,000	550	734	378	1,662
25,000	539	734	399	1,672
30,000	539	734	407	1,680
33,000*	528	734	420	1,682
40,000	528	414	469	1,411
50,000	482	0	525	1,007
60,000	472	0	525	997
70,000	472	0	601	1,073
80,000 and over	417	0	630	1,047

* income and benefits are approximately equal to the median for families with two children ($35,000)

Source: National Council of Welfare, (1985: 8)

FIGURE 1

UNIVERSALITY/SELECTIVITY
IN GOVERNMENT BENEFITS

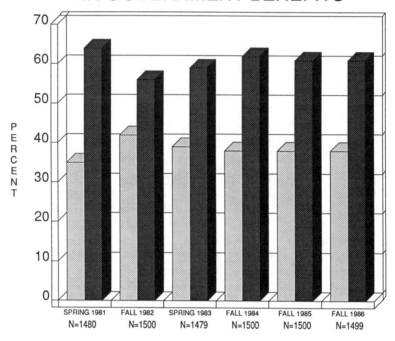

PERSONS IN NEED ONLY

EVERYONE

QUESTION: Do you believe that only people who have a financial need should be elibigle for government benefits, such as family allowances, or that everyone should receive such benefits?

Source: Decima Research. Persons expressing no opinion are not included in this table.

It must be recognized that the Conservative government has demonstrated a degree of political courage, for all its neo-liberal convictions, in questioning whether it is fair to continue paying family allowance and old age security benefits to families and individuals in high-income brackets. Making the existing system more selective was of course what was under consideration. Such a measure might help the least fortunate families if the savings thus realized were passed on to them. Canadians seemed to agree with the Mulroney government's thinking when, in a poll conducted by Goldfarb Consultants between May 18 and 26, 1984, before the height of the debate over universality, 86% of Canadians declared themselves in favour of reductions in certain social benefits paid to high-income taxpayers if this would help reduce the national deficit. However, once the allusion to the deficit had been removed from the question, the number of respondents favourable to such a measure fell to 67%, suggesting some concern over the use to be made of the money saved. Furthermore, 63% of respondents were in favour of eliminating social benefit payments to families with income over $40,000, and 75% liked the idea of a guaranteed income for all Canadians (Descôteaux, 1984a). Data from Decima Research covering the period from Spring 1981 to Autumn 1986 shows remarkable stability in the replies of Canadians when asked if they believe that only people in financial need should be eligible for certain benefits (Figure 1). Over the period, an average of 60.5% of respondents declared themselves in favour of some selectivity in benefit payments. The debate over universality has not changed their thinking.

It may be surprising to learn that the most vociferous defence of universality came from the middle class. Members of this group apparently saw a threat to their own benefits in a measure of greater selectivity. Indeed, Table 3 shows that in 1981 this group received a major portion of family allowances paid. Nearly 45% went to families with incomes of $20,000 to $40,000. In the case of old age pensions, it will be seen that a majority of eligible persons were living on incomes of less than $20,000. This is hardly surprising considering the fact that in 1981 61% of persons living below the poverty line were aged 65 and over, and three quarters of them were women.

TABLE 3

Family Allowances and Old Age Pensions
by Income Category in 1981

FAMILY ALLOWANCES

Income Category $	Number of recipients	%	Total payments ($ millions)	%
Under $10,000	704,909	19.0	348.5	18.3
10,000-20,000	1,047,066	28.3	512.6	26.9
20,000-30,000	1,095,103	29.6	567.1	29.8
30,000-40,000	522,458	14.1	287.6	15.1
40,000 and over	333,961	9.0	187.0	9.8
Total:	3,702,497	100.0	1,902.8	100.0

OLD AGE PENSIONS

Income Category $	Number of recipients	%	Total payments ($ millions)	%
Under $10,000	1,165,354	48.8	3,634.7	49.0
10,000-20,000	788,047	33.0	2,455.3	33.1
20,000-30,000	236,414	9.9	719.5	9.7
30,000-40,000	88,357	3.7	267.0	3.6
40,000 and over	109,848	100.0	341.2	4.6
Total:	2,388,020	100.0	7,417.7	100.0

Compiled from Revenue Canada, Fiscal Statistics, 1983 edition, Table 2, and from Statistics Canada Cat. 86-509.

Source: Langlois, (1984: 9)

Nevertheless, in that year the federal government paid a total of $187 million in family allowances and $341 million in old age pensions to families and individuals with incomes over $40,000 a year. While some may consider this $528 million a drop in the bucket in comparison to the size of the federal deficit at the time (Langlois,

1984), for others maintaining these benefits in their present form means perpetuating a system that is increasingly inequitable and does not achieve its primary purpose, which is to help people with inadequate incomes. Family allowances are an eloquent example from this point of view because of their decreasing effect on family income; furthermore they do nothing to make women in the home more financially independent.

The attitude of certain organizations, the middle class, and even the New Democratic Party has been rather disturbing because in their determination to preserve hard-won benefits they seem to be totally impervious to the idea of better redistribution of wealth in Canada, particularly toward families and individuals living below the poverty line. The National Council of Welfare notes that, "if the universality of programs like old age pensions and family allowances were abolished, the middle class majority might prove to be less willing to finance improvements to selective social programs addressed to people with low incomes, or even to maintain these expenditures at their present level" (1985: 19). According to the Council, the middle class is not at this time prepared to reconsider the principle of universality, and any attempt to do so by the federal government would inevitably bring major political consequences. But beyond a certain class interestedness, an inconsistency must be recognized in the stance taken by Messrs. Wilson and de Cotret who, when they insist that the money saved in this way will not be rechanneled to the poorest families, are merely clouding the question of why we have an income security policy in the first place.

We should not be taken in by this political dickering, for a great many Canadians would undoubtedly rather trade the present system for a guaranteed minimum income or a negative income tax. For this to come about, not only universality but all existing income security programs, and unemployment insurance in particular, would have to be put on the bargaining table. Ironically, the very people who oppose the idea of more "selectivity in universality" are often those who favour a guaranteed minimum income, which would also be selective.

While the whole debate over universality in family allowances and old age security has on many counts been beside the point (Fancoeur, 1984: 10), it must be recognized that the contradictions evident in the Mulroney cabinet have only increased the confusion. The debate has probably allowed a consensus to emerge, however, to the effect that our tax structure is highly regressive and any income security reform would have to begin with tax reform.

SOCIAL PROGRESS AND TAX REFORM

In the wake of the public's reaction to the issue of universality, the Conservative government began late in 1984 to look more closely at the Canadian tax system. In December Prime Minister Mulroney declared, "we are prepared to examine the possibility of recourse to the tax system to make these programs more equitable toward the least fortunate without violating the principle of universality" (Descôteaux, 1984b: 1,10). For many observers, this meant that the government had resolved to take income security benefits away from high-income taxpayers. Back in April 1984, the Prime Minister had indicated that in his thinking social progress would be achieved through a tax reform that would allow better redistribution of wealth among Canadians. The first hurdle to be crossed when talking of tax reform, however, for Conservative Party supporters as well as for specialists on the subject, is to define the extent of such reform. If it means evaluating taxation at all levels for individuals and corporations, scrutinizing all federal and even provincial expenditures, and also looking more closely at all transfer payments to citizens (Auld & Miller, 1984: Ch. 15), also looking more closely at all transfer payments to citizens, the job will without doubt be an enormous one.

The Nielsen Task Force on Program Review, which was formed in 1984 and published its report in 1986, evaluated 989 programs and noted the complexity of government activity. The Task Force declared that the federal government had lost all control over its expenditures and the Department of Finance was incapable even of evaluating the cost of the various fiscal policies. Thus the government had such a limited notion of the effect of its expenditures that it could not evaluate precisely the tax impact of any new program. Of the $92 million represented by the programs studied, the Task Force noted that $36 million were tax expenditures, or subsidies disguised as tax exemptions, $37 million were legislative expenditures provided for by federal laws, and $20 million were non-legislative, the only segment over which the government could exercise a degree of control. The Nielsen report was also strongly critical of the manner in which governments had granted "universal subsidies" to solve all social problems — a panacea that only served to hide the inability of government to project the exact tax cost of its policies (Descoteaux, 1986).

Regarding income security, the Nielsen Task Force dwelled longest on pension plans, in particular the Canada Assistance Plan. In its report, the Task Force recognized that this program does contribute appreciably to the reduction of poverty in Canada (Task Force on Program Review, 1986: 19). Overall, the Committee applauded the measures introduced by the Conservative government in its budgets and urged the government to pursue and augment its cooperation with the provinces.

But prior to the publication of its White Paper on Taxation in June 1987, the Conservative government had already implemented certain budgetary measures in compliance with its election promises. In his 1984 mini-budget first of all, the Minister of Finance extended surviving spouse benefits to widows and widowers aged 60 to 64 and substantially improved the veterans' pension plan. But apprehensions were roused anew when Mr. Wilson announced in December 1984 that new unemployment insurance regulations would come into effect in January 1986, under which some 34,000 Canadians approaching retirement would lose their eligibility for unemployment benefits in the year preceding their retirement. However, the Minister of Employment and Immigration informed employers of this measure only a month before it came into effect, which prejudiced many people who had planned an early retirement. This also affected members of the armed forces, whose retirement after 20 or 25 years is compulsory and many of whom had been counting on receiving these benefits while seeking new employment. Since the average age of retirement from the armed forces is 50, the measure was a source of considerable difficulty.

In its May 1985 budget, its first full budget, the Mulroney government roused further controversy by announcing only partial indexation of old age pensions, beginning in January 1986. This new assault on the elderly drew such a storm of protest that Mr. Wilson was obliged to reverse the decision a month later (Battle, 1986). The child tax credit was increased to $70 per child and the income ceiling was lowered from $26,330 to 23,500, still fully indexed. For 1987, the ceiling was $23,760. The Conservative government was therefore forging ahead with the policy proposed by Jake Epp, who had anticipated four years for replacement of the tax exemption for dependent children by a tax credit (National Council of Welfare, 1985b).

When it presented its 1986 budget, the Conservative government was much more cautious. Families whose income in 1985 had been less than $15,000 received advances of $300 per child against the child tax credit. A new federal sales tax credit also' gave these families $50 for each adult and $25 for each child. Finance Minister Wilson further announced an increase of $200 in the disability deduction, continuation of the spouse allowance for widows and widowers, and the creation of a new program to assist elderly workers seeking employment, into which the government would inject $125 million a year for four years. Finally, the government promised to study the recommendations of the Forget and Macdonald Commissions to enable it to incorporate more substantial reform of both social expenditures and the tax system in its next budget (Rice, 1987).

With the February 1987 budget, however, the long-awaited tax reform was postponed to a later date. Counting on this reform still to come, Mr. Wilson introduced no major changes. The publication of the White Paper on Taxation on June 18, 1987 opened new avenues of discussion to Canadians. Mr. Wilson was proposing to reduce income taxes for individuals and corporations while extending the federal sales tax to many new sectors and converting income tax exemptions and deductions into tax credits. The idea of extending the sales tax to food products was undoubtedly the measure most deplored and criticized because it would penalize all low-income families. While he proposed initially to tax prescription drugs, he decided not to do so. He also proposed replacing full indexation of tax exemptions with partial indexation. To date little has been done to evaluate the overall impact of all these suggested measures. In the light of comments by the Nielsen Task Force, it appears that such an evaluation would be extremely difficult (National Council of Welfare, 1987 b; Battle, 1987).

Clearly, the federal government will need the support of the provinces, particularly if it intends to implement a national sales tax (Maslove, 1987). Wholesale revision of the tax system is inconceivable without measures to harmonize federal and provincial policies in order to end overlapping of programs and at the same time meet the needs of Canadian families. It is to be hoped that such a reform will make it possible to address the problem of disparities, individual and regional, with respect to income security.

Resolving the disparities will certainly be a major challenge for the new federalism proposed by Prime Minister Mulroney.

It must be recognized that there are limits to any tax reform. No tax system can be totally faire and equitable. If income tax increases faster than incomes, the burden of taxation will fall even more heavily on the buying power of Canadians. The major goal of the reform may be to fix a maximum rate of taxation, down to 29% from 34%, but it must also fix a threshold income below which a family or single person will pay no tax. In 1967 the Carter Commission discussed at length whether the amount of family allowance should be calculated on the mother's, father's, or family's income. The National Council of Welfare considers that tax reform could play an invaluable role if it paves the way for an eventual guaranteed minimum income (1985). Other groups, such as the Canadian Council on Social Development, call for outright replacement of family allowances, child tax credits, old age security, guaranteed income supplements, and surviving spouse allowances by a new programme designed to redistribute resources to the most needy, and a more progressive tax system as well (1986). However, a judgement on the Mulroney government's tax reform will have to await announcement of the final plan, when an evaluation of all the implications can be made.

The present economic climate is relatively favourable to the Conservative Party and the moment could be ripe for such a reform. Presently available data shows that during the year 1985 the number of families and single persons living below the poverty line fell by a substantial 1.3%, from 17.3% to 16.0% of the population, or 263,000 fewer poor people. This was the first decrease since 1981 (National Council of Welfare, 1987a: 2). Consequently, the federal government's contribution to the average Canadian family's income decreased from 10.9% to 10.6% for 1985, also the first decrease since 1981 (Statistics Canada, 1985). Unemployment has decreased as well, from 10.7% in December 1984 to 7.9% in December 1987. In this kind of context, a tax reform that would benefit the most disadvantaged and also the middle class would be financially and politically attainable by the Mulroney government.

TOWARD A SYSTEM OF "FAMILY EQUALIZATION"

If we define "family equalization" as an equitable spreading of taxation for families and single persons, along with implementation of transfer programs that answer the needs of Canadians and take account of variations in cost of living, it can be said that this is the thrust of the Mulroney government's policies respecting income security. While these policies are rather incremental, as indeed were those of its predecessors, the present government must be given credit for trying to break with tradition in proposing, rather than simply a revision of certain programs, an appraisal of the impact of fiscal measures on the incomes of all Canadians. However, clumsiness and inconsistencies on the part of certain cabinet members have blotched the Conservative Party's image and shown that the "hawks" perhaps rule the roost in this government. This has been enough to show doubt in the minds of Canadians, particularly among the elderly, who in the Mulroney government's actions perceive confirmation of its neo-liberal tendencies.

The current rethinking of welfare state philosophy in Canada and other industrialized countries has brought an awareness that traditional income security programs do not provide families and individuals with an unbreachable shield against all economic misfortunes. Nevertheless, if the recession seems to have been less severe in Canada than elsewhere, particularly the United States, the reason is undoubtedly the effort since the early sixties in Canada to improve the structure of our welfare society. There remains much to be done. Other countries with neo-liberal governments, the Federal Republic of Germany for example, have followed the same course and today are seeking to recast their income security programs in the framework of a real family policy. In the FRG, proposals being debated at present are an increase in family allowances and education premiums for dependent children (Grosskopff, 1986).

If the government of Prime Minister Mulroney intends to implement a better system of family equalization and at the same time lay to rest certain fiscal illusions related to and perpetuated by exemptions and subsidies for families, individuals, and corporations, a number of principles hitherto considered inviolable will have to be revised to allow satisfactory guarantees and better redistribution of economic and social resources through the modalities of tax reform. But Canadians must be constantly watchful and sagacious to ensure that the welfare society in which we live not only provides families and single persons with adequate income but also responds better to their needs.

Translated by Patricia Claxton

NOTES

1 Fiscal expenditures are all the exemptions, deductions, credits, deferrals, and preferential tax rates that reduce income tax payable by corporations and individuals. While statistics of this kind are available in the United States, Canada unfortunately has no precise data on the cost effectiveness of these measures.

2 The National Council of Welfare has recognized the rationale of this approach, albeit with reluctance and some harsh criticism for the policies of the Mulroney government. See National Council of Welfare (1985a).

3 The Economic Council of Canada declared in 1984 the principal cause of the drop in the federal government revenues since the early seventies was the increase in its "fiscal expenditures" — especially individual income tax exemptions, but above all business exemptions.

4 On the role and impact of European political parties, see F.G. Castles (1982); J. Corina et al. (1982).

5 At the first meeting with provincial ministers responsible for income security, which was held in Toronto in December 1984 after the election of the Mulroney government, all the provinces agreed with the principle of compulsory eligibility of all employees for their employer's private pension plans, compulsory payment of a pension to a surviving spouse, and stipulation of minimum employer contributions. A question which remained unresolved, however, was that of private indexation plan. See C. Beaulieu (1984).

6 The Social Policy Reform Group, a coalition of the National Action Committee on the Status of Women, the National Council of Welfare, the Canadian Association of Social Workers, the National Anti-Poverty Organization, and the Canadian Council on Social Development among other things called on the Mulroney government to abolish fiscal concessions to families and individuals in high-income brackets rather than turn universal income security programs into selective ones. See D. Lessard (1985).

7 The Trudeau government questioned the notion of universality as early as 1970 in its white paper on income security (Department of National Health and Welfare, 1970). For an analysis of the concept of universality see W.A. Robinson (1977: 20–33); Jonathan Cape (1956: 143–147); Richard Titmuss (1968: chap. 10). This last author maintains that a universal programme does not necessarily have to be free for everyone.

303

REFERENCES

Auld, D.A.L. and F.C. Miller (1984). *Principles of Public Finance — A Canadian Text.* (Toronto: Methuen).

Banting, Keith (1982). *The Welfare State and Canadian Federalism,* (Montreal: McGill-Queen's University Press).

Battle, Ken (1986). "Indexation and Social Policy," *Canadian Review of Social Policy,* 16-17, pp. 33-58.

Battle, Ken (1987). "Broader Base/Lower Rates: A Formula for Fair Tax Reform?," *Perception,* II, 2 (Nov.-Dec.), pp. 15-18.

Beaulieu, Carole (1984). "Les ministres provinciaux ne parviennent pas à s'entende sur un projet commun de réforme," *Le Devoir,* 5 December, p. 4.

Candian Council on Social Development (1987). "Le CCDS revèle sa stratégie fiscale pour la sécurité du revenu," *Perspective,* 5, 1 (Autumn), pp. 1–3.

Canadian Press (1984). "Mulroney affirme que son parti n'avait pas l'intention de s'attaquer a l'universlité des programmes sociaux," *La Presse,* 15 December, p. A–10.

Castles, Francis G. (1982). *The Impact of Parties,* (London: Sage).

Corina, J. et al (1982). "Do Parties Affect the Distribution of Incomes? The Case of Advanced Capitalist Democracies" in F.G. Castles, *The Impact of Parties,* (London: Sage).

Crosland, Anthony (1956). *The Future of Socialism,* (London: Jonathan Cape).

Descôteaux, Bernard (1984a). "Une nette majorité ne tient pas a l'universalité," *Le Devoir,* 19 September, pp. 1&12.

Descôteaux, Bernard (1984b). "Mulroney ne parvient pas à dissiper l'équivoque sur les programmes sociaux," *Le Devoir,* 15 December, p. 4.

Descôteaux, Bernard (1984c). "Programmes sociaux: Au tour des libéraux de faire des éclats," *Le Devoir,* 19 December, pp. 1 & 10.

Descôteaux, Bernard (1986). "Rapport Nielsen: le gouvernement canadien doit reprendre le contrôle de ses dépenses," *Le Devoir,* 12 March 1986, pp. 1&10.

Department of Health and Welfare (1970). *Income Security for Canadians,* (Ottawa: Supply and Services).

Des Rivières, Paule (1984). "Les conservateurs poursuivront les réformes fiscales lancées par les libéraux," *Le Devoir,* 6 November, p. 2.

Economic Council of Canada (1984). *Steering the Course,* (Ottawa: Supply and Services).

Epp, Jake (1985). *Child and Elderly Benefits,* (Ottawa: Department of Health and Welfare).

Epp, Jake (1988). *National Strategy on Child Care,* (Ottawa: Supply and Services).

Francoeur, Jean (1984). "Un débat en porte-à-faux." *Le Devoir,* 14 November, p. 10.

Gillespie, W.I. (1980). *The Redistribution of Income in Canada,* (Toronto: Gage).

Grosskopff, Rudolph (1986). "L'enfer en est pavé — politique familiale: plethore de bonnes intentions," *La Tribune d'Allemagne,* 14 February, p. 6.

Langlois, Richard (1984). "La 'nécessaire' universalité des programmes sociaux," *Le Devoir,* 20 December, p. 9.

Lessard, Denis (1985). "Ottawa devrait abolir les concessions fiscales au lieu de comprimer ses dépenses," *Le Devoir*, 17 January, p. 4.

Maslove, Allan (1987). "Tax Reform Process as Important as Substantive," *Perception* 11, 2 (Nov.-Dec.) pp. 24–16.

National Council of Welfare (1985a). *Opportunity for Reform*, (Ottawa: Supply and Services).

National Council of Welfare (1985b). *Giving and Taking: The May 1985 Budget*, (Ottawa: Supply and Services).

National Council of Welfare (1987a). *Progrès de la lutte contre la pauvreté* (Ottawa).

National Council of Welfare (1987b). *La réforme fiscale: facteurs à considérer*, (Ottawa).

OECD (1981). *The Welfare State in Crisis*. (Paris: OECD).

Pelletier, Michel (1982). *De la sécurité sociale à la sécurité du revenu*, (Montreal: M. Pelletier).

Preece, Rod (1977). "The Myth of The Red Tory," *Canadian Journal of Political and Social Theory*, 1, 2 (Spring–Summer), pp. 3–28.

Rice, James (1987). "Restitching the Safety Net: Altering The National Security System" in Michael J. Prince (Ed.), *How Ottawa Spends, 1987-88: Restraining the State*, (Toronto: Methuen), pp. 211–236.

Robson, William A. (1977). *Welfare State and Welfare Society — Illusion and Reality*, (London: Allen & Unwin).

Stanfield, Robert (1982). "Conservative Principles and Philosophy" in Paul Fox (Ed), *Politics: Canada*, 5th Edition, (Toronto: McGraw-Hill Ryerson).

Statistics Canada (1985). *After-Tax Income — Distribution by Size in Canada*, (Ottawa: Statistics Canada).

Task Force on Program Review (1986). *Service to the Public: Canada Assistance Plan*, (Ottawa: Supply and Services).

Titmuss, Richard (1968). *Commitment to Welfare* (London: Urwin University Books).

Vaillancourt, François (1985). *Income Distribution and Economic Security in Canada*, (Toronto: University of Toronto Press).

Wilson, Michael Hon. (1984). *A New Direction for Canada — Agenda for Economic Renewal* (Ottawa: Department of Finance).

STREAMLINING THE
ADMINISTRATIVE MACHINERY

.. the massive undertaking that is the government of Canada must be made to respond to the individual citizen, wherever and however it touches him or her. A committee of Ministers headed by the Deputy Prime Minister has begun a review of all government programs. The objective is to reform and simplify the operations of government. From the citizen's standpoint, government will be made more understandable, more accessible, and more sensitive.

— Speech from the throne, November 5, 1984.

Mulroney's Broker Politics: The Ultimate in Politicized Incompetence?

COLIN CAMPBELL, S.J.

This essay examines the performance of the Mulroney government with respect to two central objectives of a management style. The first of these is maintenance of partisan responsiveness. The second is engagement of the state apparatus. It will examine closely the plans that Mulroney and his advisers developed — during the transition — for assuring that the administrative apparatus would become responsive to their partisan program. It then analyzes the actual fate of the government from the perspective of its failure to maintain political responsiveness and — notwithstanding its reasonably effective management of the economy — to establish itself in the public mind as actually being in command.

The chapter argues that the government grossly underestimated the difficulty of the task it faced from the outset. It also notes that the purely political considerations connected with the difficulty of sustaining relative harmony in the Progressive Conservative party forced Mulroney to hobble himself by sharing his prerogatives with Erik Nielsen — the deputy prime minister. Meanwhile, the inexperience — often ineptitude — of individual cabinet members hampered their ability to gain control of the bureaucracy. The ensuing disarray resulted in politicized incompetence.

ON SEIZING CONTROL OF THE STATE APPARATUS

This section attempts to introduce some theoretical issues that rest at the centre of the polarity between political executives and career bureaucrats. It focuses on how new governments should set up their advisory systems. In Canada, this takes in a host of problems: how the new prime minister should staff and organize the Prime Minister's Office, how this should relate to the Privy Council Office, whether he should look for permanent officials sympathetic to his party to assume key posts in PCO and in the departments, whether he should shuffle deputy ministers, whether he should appoint individuals from outside the career public service to top posts in departments, and how cabinet will be organized.

At the outset, it is useful to keep one distinction in mind regarding appointees. The problems associated with the proliferation of officials who occupy various strata of bureaucratic organizations are distinct from those concerning the politicization of the public service (Aberbach, Putnam and Rockman, 1981). Virtually every system over the last two decades has encountered an intensification of top officials' — appointive or career — conscious involvement in executive-bureaucratic gamesmanship (Campbell, 1988). However, even systems observing the Westminster model have followed substantially different practices regarding the appointment of party-political advisers and operatives to positions within departments and agencies (Campbell, 1985; Weller, 1985).

Engagement of the state apparatus constitutes the other goal of any political leadership. Chief executives and/or cabinets all attempt to some degree to seize control of and direct toward their own purposes the ongoing bureaucratic establishment. And, this enterprise requires the institutionalization of control and guidance mechanisms in the cores of departments and agencies, and at the centre of the entire executive branch. In systems where partisan appointees assume key positions in coordinative units, the political leadership will increasingly seek established policy professionals for such roles (Salamon, 1981: 193, 199). In systems which continue to place a high value on the neutrality of officials, prime ministers and cabinet secretaries will nonetheless strive to fill the most sensitive positions with career public servants who possess

proven skills at the executive-bureaucratic gamesmanship necessary for the integration and implementation of their policy objectives (Campbell, 1980).

The institutionalization dimension also takes in formal machinery for processing executive-branch business. Here much depends
on the presence or absence of a constitutional norm whereby
executive authority is to be exerted collectively. The former situation usually has resulted — in response to the increasing complexity of government — in the proliferation of standing and ad hoc
cabinet committees (Mackie and Hogwood, 1985: 7–9). In non-
cabinet systems, such developments rely on proven instrumental
utility rather than constitutional conventions. In part, this explains
why the evolution in the U.S. of the shared exercise of executive
authority associated with "cabinet government" has lagged behind "Westminster" systems.

In considering the interplay between the responsiveness of political leaders and their ability to engage the state apparatus, we can
conceive of four quadrants (Campbell, 1986: 16). Political leaders
who achieve some level of policy competence occupy the area bor-
dered by relatively high responsiveness and engagement of the
institutionalized state apparatus. The rare chief executive, indeed,
would not strive in some way for policy competence. However, he
or she could drift toward another quadrant by failing to achieve
an appropriate mix between partisan responsiveness and utilization of the standing machinery of government. Those who stress
the former at the cost of the latter run the risk of winding up with
politicized incompetence. Those who defer to custodians of the
state apparatus over those concerned with partisan responsiveness
flirt with a variant of neutral competence. This state leaves observers wondering whether the stylistic and partisan nature of a
given political leadership makes any real difference. Finally, some
governments or administrations might become so mesmerized by
imponderables in the blending of responsiveness and institutionalization that they slip into a weak mixture of both and land in nonpoliticized incompetence.

The upper right-hand quadrant in Figure 1 locates schematically
four approaches which might be adopted by a political leadership.
In delineating these styles, I distinguish between governments or
administrations which foster countervailing views in the advisory
system and those which seek to limit conflict. I also differentiate
between those which rely heavily upon central agencies and those

311

which prefer as much as possible to have line departments settle quotidian affairs on their own. Under this framework, a priorities and planning style emerges when the political leadership encourages competing advice. It simultaneously entrusts central agencies with the development of overarching strategies and assuring that substantive decisions adhere to these. Broker politics results when countervailing views abound but central agencies play only restrained roles in the integration of policies. Survival

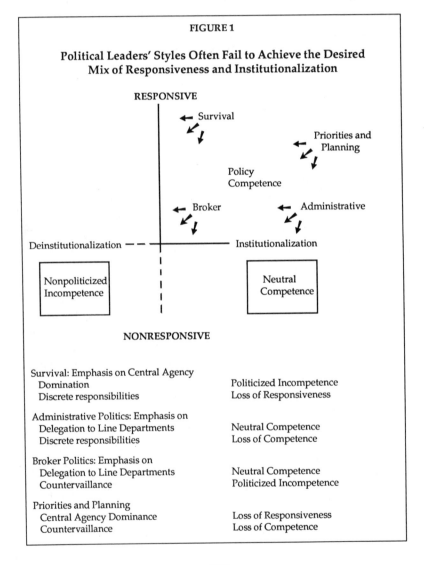

FIGURE 1

Political Leaders' Styles Often Fail to Achieve the Desired Mix of Responsiveness and Institutionalization

Survival: Emphasis on Central Agency
    Domination
    Discrete responsibilities

Politicized Incompetence
Loss of Responsiveness

Administrative Politics: Emphasis on
    Delegation to Line Departments
    Discrete responsibilities

Neutral Competence
Loss of Competence

Broker Politics: Emphasis on
    Delegation to Line Departments
    Countervaillance

Neutral Competence
Politicized Incompetence

Priorities and Planning
    Central Agency Dominance
    Countervaillance

Loss of Responsiveness
Loss of Competence

politics prevails in the opposition situation. That is, central agencies increasingly draw issues into their orbit and expressly seek to dampen competition between advisors. Finally, administrative politics develops when the political leadership tends neither to encourage a diversity of views nor rely heavily upon central agencies for guiding and controlling the rest of the executive branch.

With respect to whether governments or administrations ultimately arrive at policy competence, politicized incompetence, neutral competence or nonpoliticized incompetence, a political leadership's mix of the two elements of style can present clear dangers. Figure 1 summarizes these. A priorities and planning style which emphasizes central-agency intervention to the detriment of countervailing views will open itself to a loss of responsiveness while the opposite condition might lead to diminished competence. With broker politics, tipping the scales toward delegation to line departments lends itself to neutral competence while an overabundance of countervailing positions might bring about politicized incompetence. Under survival politics, overcentralization might result in politicized incompetence while severe reliance upon compartmentalization might hamper responsiveness. And, an administrative politics which rests too heavily upon delegation to departments might slide into neutral competence while one which tries too hard to limit open contestation might suffer a loss of competence.

Priorities and planning, thus, comes out as the safest style from the viewpoint of maintaining policy competence. Notwithstanding its desirability, priorities and planning usually encounters systemic constraints which make it somewhat elusive. We can divide these into institutional and personnel-related factors. With regard to the former, we should keep the following caveats in mind:

1) The absence of reasonably strong policy-oriented shops working directly and exclusively for the chief executive will limit the extent to which he or she will receive countervailing advice.

2) The absence of reasonably strong secretariats dedicated to brokerage of conflicts between departments will hamper a cabinet's capacity for open contestation.

3) The absence of a reasonably well structured system of standing cabinet committees will restrict the political leadership's

ability to plan rather than simply muddle through.

4) The presence of strong representational imperatives which inflate the size of a cabinet might turn it into a surrogate legislature rather than an executive council. In turn, this situation will cancel out many of the benefits to collective responsibility potentially derived from structured committees and secretariats.

5) The absence of reasonably effective analytic and coordinative units within operational departments will impair the ability of these organizations to relate to central agencies and vice versa.

Concerning personnel-related constraints, the following points arise:

1) If the legitimacy of party-political advice either in the chief executive's office or in departments is questioned to the point where it carries no weight, the political leadership will lack the support and imaginative approaches necessary for open contestation of views.

2) A weak tradition of policy-oriented professionalism among party-political appointees negates the advantages of countervailing views.

3) A very strong ethos of compromise among career civil servants can deny political leaders a view of the full range of options.

4) Career civil servants who are weak in analysis will tend to focus their attention on matters of process rather than substance.

PECULIARITIES OF THE CANADIAN SYSTEM

Regarding structures, the Canadian system boasts three advantages. First, we have enjoyed a strong tradition of secretariats supporting cabinet deliberations. The title, Clerk of the Privy Council, dates back to Confederation and the Privy Council Office became a clearly delineated institution in 1940. As well, the Treasury Board Secretariat emerged in 1965 as an autonomous department responsible for supporting the Treasury Board — a cabinet committee which also has existed since Confederation. Second, with the exception of John Diefenbaker's government, cabinet has organized itself along relatively differentiated committee lines since the late 1930s (Campbell, 1985: 63–4). Third, senior permanent officials in Canadian line departments have sustained a reasonably high level of professionalism — including an analytic aptitude commensurate with the times — at least since the 1930s. Granatstein's research (1982) on the exceptionally intelligent and well-trained men who dominated the standing bureaucracy from 1935 to 1957 drives home this point.

On the negative side, by 1968 in the Prime Minister's Office we had not seen anything remotely comparable to the small units of party-political policy advisers which have operated — albeit sporadically — in Britain's No. 10 Downing Street since David Lloyd George's "garden suburb" (Turner, 1980). Further, our cabinet has always labored under a strong representational imperative which has bloated its size and hampered its effectiveness (Mallory, 1971; Wilson, 1981).

With respect to personnel-related considerations, the Canadian experience before Trudeau was a draw. Units which brigade party-political policy advisers in offices working directly to the prime ministers or ministers have had trouble attaining legitimacy. That is, attentive observers usually let out anguished howls whenever it appeared that a government had increased the resources available to the political leadership for partisan advice on policies.

Concomitantly, in Canada we lack the "public careerist" (Heclo, 1984: 18–20). Such appointees, notwithstanding their overt partisan affiliations, have learned, through several stints in government, how to maneuver in the executive-bureaucratic labyrinth. On the positive side, our public service tradition has inculcated in senior officials a high regard for the analytic method. It also has fostered an ethos that permits senior officials to challenge their ministers on substantive issues (Heeney, 1949: 291; Robertson, 1971: 449–51).

If we compare our system to other Anglo-American democracies, the priorities and planning approach finds reasonably fertile ground in Canada, but less than in the U. K. for two reasons. First, as noted above, we lack a tradition of party-political policy advisory units attached to the prime minister and ministers. Second, our cabinet labors under immensely greater pressure for representation. Indeed, regional representation — a major factor in the inflation of cabinet size in Canada — hardly rates consideration in the U.K.

The generalist nature of Whitehall narrows the edge that the U.K. system might have over the Canadian system. Both analytic approaches to policy making and central planning units which attempt systematic coordination of policies have failed to take a very strong hold in the U.K. As well, senior officials in Whitehall lack the direct access to ministers afforded their Canadian counterparts through attendance at cabinet committees. They have not, thus, developed adroitness at direct confrontation. They tend to serve up advice as received wisdom and work behind the scenes to undermine initiatives which they find threatening. Neither inclination advances the creativity required of priorities and planning.

Allowing for time lags, the Australian higher civil service has professionalised along the lines of its Canadian counterpart. That is, it has eschewed generalism and adopted an analytic orientation toward policy making and a rigorous perspective on management as a science. Interestingly, Australia has moved more rapidly than Canada in permitting prime ministers and ministers to avail themselves of partisan policy advice (Weller, 1985: 139–41). It has not — especially when you consider its smaller and somewhat less diverse population — restrained the tendency to inflate the size of cabinet (Halligan, 1987; Wettenhall, 1989).

For all three "Westminster" systems, the U.S. looms very large as the alternate model. Still, it does not lend itself to priorities and planning. While there is no lack of party-political policy advice, the Americans have lagged desperately behind Canada, the U.K. and Australia in regularized cabinet deliberations and neutral-brokerage secretariats. This state of affairs owes to a number of factors imbedded in the constitutional system — namely, the separation of powers, the concentration of executive authority in the president — as opposed to the cabinet, and the resulting overload which often makes it impossible for administrations to resolve fundamental conflicts much less plan and prioritize.

Here the U.S. career civil service actually exacerbates the fragmentation. While expert within their chosen fields and highly managerial, the permanent bureaucracy operates almost totally devoid of a common *esprit*. Thus, those wishing to transfer officials within departments — let alone outside — frequently will find that they are not interchangeable. Usually, they are too steeped in their unit's agenda and too ignorant of the substance and procedures of other shops.

THE MULRONEY GOVERNMENT'S APPROACH

When Brian Mulroney took office in September 1984, some foreign observers expected that he would strike out in the same neo-conservative direction pursued by Margaret Thatcher and Ronald Reagan. That is, they anticipated the same type of "conviction politics" which already had brought immense changes in the U.K. and the U.S. If we stopped to consider the overwhelming majority won by the Progressive Conservatives — 211 seats in a 282 seat house, Canadians might even have concluded that Mulroney found himself in an extremely strong position to deliver his party platform.

A number of factors suggested caution in projecting bold action on the part of the new government. To begin, the Conservative campaign had not actually put forward a "conviction" agenda. That is, it did not embrace and promote the neo-conservative perspective in any coherent way. As well, polling data revealed that the surge toward the party and Mulroney was relatively soft. Voters had rejected the party of Pierre Trudeau more than they had committed themselves to a Progressive Conservative government. The public seemed to say "Forget our belief, its our unbelief that you should start worrying about."

Although they might not all have used the term, members of Mulroney's transition team recognized that he would most profitably strive for broker politics. On the one hand, a lack of a policy-oriented electoral mandate would inhibit the ability of even a relatively cohesive party to achieve a high degree of programmatic responsiveness. In fact, the immensely bloated numbers of the Progressive Conservative magnified the already intractable divisions within the party. Thus, the huge majority exacerbated rather than ameliorated the party's tendency toward fragmentation.

On the other hand, those involved in the transition acknowledged the ineptitude of the party when it previously formed a government in 1979. This time, they better understood the magnitude of the challenge they would face in getting the permanent civil service to execute its will. It would be foolhardy to engage the standing apparatus in an elaborate "dialogue" on policies and programs along the lines of priorities and planning. This constraint meant selective engagement of the state apparatus. However, it would also limit the ability of officials to obfuscate.

This author has found in other settings a disjunction between a political executive's leadership style and the approach that he and/or those advising him select for operation of an administration (Campbell, 1986: 270–1). For instance, Jimmy Carter set up a steering apparatus in the White House which barely could achieve administrative politics. However, he personally involved himself so profoundly in virtually every conceivable issue that he single-handedly attempted priorities and planning.

In his first term, Reagan convinced many of his faithful that he was preserving a devotion to ideological commitments worthy of survival politics. That is, he worked to maintain a crisis syndrome in his effort to keep the public convinced that radical measures were called for. In fact, his administration — while accomplishing many sweeping reforms — operated with an astute capacity for institutional brokerage. It knew how far it could push and it did not ignore networking either with Congress or the bureaucracy. In this case, the disjunction between rhetoric and practice proved relatively functional. The second term, on the other hand, saw — largely through the auspices of Donald Regan — the erosion of Reagan's capacity for brokerage politics. Especially in light of the Iran-Contra Affair, it became increasingly clear that — in the absence of an effective gear box — "heart" had overtaken "mind" as a factor in the administration.

Two points emerge from these observations. First, broker politics does not constitute a minimalist strategy which administrations attempt when they cannot aspire to priorities and planning. It calls upon considerable skill whether it is being established or simply maintained. Second, students of the Mulroney government should be loath to take on faith the view that the administration actually achieved broker politics.

We should probably concede that Brian Mulroney's personality would be well suited to broker politics. He does not have anywhere near the intellectual depth of Pierre Trudeau. Like Reagan, he comes across as cunning and smart but far from learned or profound. Unlike Reagan, he lacked baggage which would force him into a survival politics rhetoric. Canada had not turned its back on the welfare state; the campaign had not left the public with the belief that the Conservatives would introduce radical changes;

Mulroney temperamentally fitted well within the moderate wing of his party.

Mulroney is not a systematic person. He hates meetings and does very poorly at running them. He spends a seemingly inordinate proportion of his working day on the telephone. Even when alone in his study at home pouring over briefing books, he cannot resist the temptation to get the bottom of things by calling the people behind the paper. He would go mad trying to replicate Trudeau's almost monastic ability to insulate himself from the more "worldly" dimensions of governance and focus — often in seminar-style discussions with cabinet colleagues and charmed officials — on what was truly the "best" possible policy. In this respect, Peter Aucoin has identified what he terms brokerage politics as that most suited to the prime minister:

> ... Mulroney's leadership style (in contrast with Trudeau's) is transactional rather than collegial. His preference is to deal with individuals on a one-to-one basis rather than on a collective basis. The logic here, of course, is that this transactional style better facilitates the negotiation of compromises among differing points of views than does the collegial process, where the checks and balances more readily lead to stalemates if different points of views are strongly held (1986: 18).

The adoption of broker politics by no means implies the abandonment of the mechanisms available for coordination through central agencies and collective decision making in cabinet. Rather, the assumption of such a sharply minimalist strategy would constitute administrative politics (Campbell, 1983: 23–4). Broker politics amounts, thus, to a tactical retreat from the bolder aspirations of priorities and planning. Aucoin places due emphasis upon this point:

> ... (this) does not imply that Mulroney places little or no priority upon a consensus among his colleagues as a corporate executive. Indeed, as a strategy of management, a high priority is given to consensus as an end in itself. In this sense Mulroney's style requires that he be manager of a "team" (1986: 18).

At this stage, Aucoin offers a caveat which presents difficulties. He asserts that Mulroney's team-oriented management style did not require "collegial decision-making in the manner of the

Trudeau design." I can accept this proposition if "manner" means in the same "degree." However, I would have to reject it if Aucoin has asserted that Mulroney's style eclipsed the utility of collective decision making. In fact, Aucoin himself advises Mulroney to make greater use of the existing cabinet committee and central agency structure (1986: 25).

Aucoin and I are in agreement on this point. However, an assessment of Mulroney's management design and its implementation calls for a better understanding of the reasons why collective decision-making holds such sway in our system. The approach enjoys standing as a constitutional convention upon which the very nature of our brand of executive leadership rests. The effective operation of interdepartmental coordination in the Government of Canada relies very heavily upon collective decision-making. Further, lessons from the American case — not the least of which is the Iran-Contra episode — highlight the extent to which observance of the canons of collective decision making might yield instrumental benefits even if the approach is not expected constitutionally. Finally, any team requires group dynamics. And, no prime minister can maintain these through bilateral exchanges with ministers — largely on the telephone.

Any political leadership when initially taking power must rapidly switch gears from electioneering to governing. In passing through the transition phase, the new government must keep two things in focus. First, what needs to be done to the civil service and machinery of government to enhance its adaptiveness to the style and agenda of the new administration? Second, what are the peculiar circumstances impinging upon the incumbent government which expand or constrict the ease with which it can effect change in the bureaucracy and the state apparatus?

Regarding the adaptability issue, the Conservatives faced two main difficulties. First, they had to work toward a simplification of the cabinet decision-making process. By the end of the Trudeau era, it was manifestly clear that complexity had led to paralysis. Second, the new government had to devise a way in which it could reorient the permanent civil service. This would likely require a combination of political appointments and assertiveness with the standing bureaucracy which might gradually turn a state apparatus impregnated with the Liberal agenda and style of governance around to Conservative priorities and ways of operating.

With respect to the second matter requiring close attention —

circumstances affecting the art of the possible in the transition process, the Conservatives first — as we saw above — had to recognize that they lacked a clear mandate for change. Especially with regard to political appointments and efforts to change the folkways of the bureaucracy, new Canadian governments find themselves severely restricted under the best of circumstances. The lack of clarity in Mulroney's mandate would automatically add to doubts about the legitimacy of actions which would in any case raise fears about tampering with Canadian traditions.

TINKERING WITH CABINET AND ITS DYNAMICS

John Turner did Mulroney a huge favour by taking from the menu of things to do simplification of decision making structures. When he took power for his brief term on June 30, 1984 he expressly dissociated himself from the Trudeau approach by styling it as "too elaborate, too complex, too slow and too expensive." He further condemned the system for having "diffused and eroded and blurred" the authority of cabinet ministers. Turner backed up this stinging indictment with actions. He cut the size of cabinet from 37 to 29 ministers. He also reduced the number of its committees from 13 to 10.

Turner abolished the ministries of state for economic and regional development and social development. He did not abolish the Policy and Expenditure Management System (PEMS). However, he introduced a number of restrictions on the volume of paper flowing through the cabinet and its committees. He also sought to curtail "mirror" committees of deputy ministers which had shadowed the work of cabinet committees under Trudeau and officials' participation in cabinet-level meetings.

These various moves addressed several central elements of the overarching requirements for streamlining collective decision-making and limiting the roles of career civil servants. Their introduction by a Liberal prime minister lent bipartisan legitimacy to the view that Trudeau's system had failed abysmally. If Mulroney worried about such matters on June 30, 1984, his concerns were disposed of by Turner in a single stroke.

Mulroney followed through on Turner's reforms with one glaring exception: He inflated the size of cabinet from 29 to 40. As well, he was unable to limit official participation in cabinet committees to the degree anticipated in Turner's directive. He did eliminate a further cabinet committee — Foreign and Defense Policy. However, he subsequently reestablished the committee. Finally, he reduced the number of expenditure envelopes by merging "Energy" with "Economic and Regional Development," and "Justice and Legal Affairs" with "Social Affairs."

Mulroney found himself hobbled in reaping the benefits of the streamlined system. To understand why, we have to recall that he inherited an extremely fragmented party when he assumed the leadership of the Conservatives in 1983. Mulroney felt compelled to accommodate as many segments of thought as possible in his cabinet. In addition, he clearly attempted to begin the process of developing a cadre of Quebec ministers who could assume senior cabinet posts. He gave portfolios to 11 from that province even though precious few of these ministers had served before in Parliament let alone in cabinet. He eventually incurred immense damage from his inclusive approach to cabinet building. Yet, Mulroney might have succumbed simply to the realities of dealing with representational pressures from within his caucus. As well, his colleagues' woeful lack of experience with governance made on-the-job training essential to its performance.

Not unrelatedly, Mulroney had to deal with Erik Nielsen. Nielsen — who had earned his spurs as the Conservative's wiliest parliamentary strategist — had served as interim leader of the party before it selected Mulroney as leader. Upon Mulroney's selection, Nielsen had announced to the convention that the new leader was not his first choice but that he would back him entirely. Apparently in an act of magnanimity, Mulroney responded by saying that he would be chairman of the board for the party but that he was asking Nielsen to serve as his chief of operations. A year ensued in which the future prime minister as opposition leader devolved many of his functions to Nielsen — not the least of which was the effective chair of the shadow cabinet. Mulroney had made a habit of missing shadow cabinet meetings. When present, he far from distinguished himself. We can understand Mulroney's empowering of Nielsen as an exercise in ward healing. However, Mulroney should have gradually retreated from this arrangement even if this meant antagonizing Nielsen's wing of the party.

Mulroney came under very strong pressure during the transition phase to enshrine Nielsen's position in the new government as much as it had been in the shadow cabinet. At one stage, Nielsen's people had even pushed for an arrangement whereby Mulroney would make Nielsen chairman of all cabinet committees which decide allocations within expenditure envelopes. In the end, Nielsen became deputy prime minister and vice-chairman of cabinet.

The latter title, of course, had never been employed before. It suggested a peculiar arrangement — in constitutional terms — whereby Nielsen would be somewhat less than first among equals but somewhat more than equal! Nielsen also assumed the vice-chairmanship of two committees — Priorities and Planning which is effectively the steering body for cabinet, and the Special Committee of Council. He sat as an ex-officio member of all other committees. Previously, not even the minister of finance enjoyed as much mobility through the inner councils of government. When Robert Coates resigned as defense minister less than six months into the new government, Nielsen added this portfolio to his unprecedented collection of cabinet trophies.

Mulroney had not put forward a strong neo-conservative motif in the 1984 campaign. However, he did incant the standard oaths committing his new government to the eradication of wasteful, redundant and outdated programs. Consistent with his chief of operations role, Nielsen assumed responsibility for pressing the government's efforts to make the tough decisions necessary to achieve greater efficiency and effectiveness. He chaired the Task Force on Program Review which included the president of the Treasury Board and the ministers of finance and justice. This body launched upon an elaborate examination of each cabinet portfolio with a view to identifying ways in which departmental programs, regulations and delivery mechanisms might be consolidated.

Mulroney's arrangements for cabinet — including his granting virtual surrogate status to Nielsen — did a great deal of damage to collective decision-making in the new government. Full cabinet began to meet once every two weeks rather than weekly. Often, the prime minister would not preside. In this regard, it is important to remember that ministers will take such proceedings much less seriously if they know that the person ultimately responsible for government policies will absent himself or let someone else actually run the meeting. The fact that the Priorities and Planning Committee convened weekly meant that it essentially began to function as the executive council for the government.

On the other hand, the appointment of the Task Force on

Program Review with Nielsen as head could have comprised a stroke of genius. In 1979, Mrs. Thatcher used a similar body to impose spending cuts which her advisers had worked out even before taking over the government. Eventually referred to as the "Star Chamber," this committee has in fact become a permanent instrument for knocking ministers' heads together on resource issues. Nielsen's task force consisted of exactly the collection of ministers which would have enabled the new government to pursue a similar tack.

Unfortunately for Mulroney, the Conservatives came into power with no clear view of which programs they would cut. Further, Nielsen — who in Joe Clark's government was only minister of public works and did not even belong to Priorities and Planning — struck observers as far too muddled to effectively direct such a large undertaking. Indeed, Nielsen presided over a mind-bogglingly comprehensive examination of virtually every government program which involved over 100 private sector "volunteers" and took nearly 18 months to complete.

In the course of this lengthy process, it became clear that the government had no will to strike when the iron was hot. Thus, those who expected it to deliver upon its campaign rhetoric became increasingly disillusioned. Even worse, piecemeal leaks and official disclosures of the various studies' findings gave away numerous hostages to the opposition. The 21-volume final report simply deepened doubts. If the government could document so extensively inefficiency and ineffectiveness in the public service, why did it still lack determination to act decisively?

More fundamental, the task force represented a bifurcation of management style. The prime minister functioned with the certainty that he was the past master of broker politics. Meanwhile, Nielsen piously observed the rubrics of priorities and planning. The near schizoid state of executive leadership amounted essentially to politicized incompetence. To be sure, the deficiencies of the government did not rest on an unwillingness on the part of the prime minister to wheel and deal with his political cronies. They stemmed from the lack of a gearbox. That is, the principal executive authority eschewed involvement in the very dynamics which might lend cogency to the project of governance. His surrogate operated as if he was chairing a royal commission inquiry into public service management.

324

STAFF SUPPORT AND RELATIONS
WITH THE STANDING BUREAUCRACY

In the U.S., cabinet-level dynamics rarely fulfill satisfactorily the gearbox role in the intricate process of reconciling the countervailing partisan aspirations of an administration and effectively engaging the state apparatus. Thus, the White House and the Executive Office of the President usually strain and often overheat — even overreach constitutional and legal constraints — in trying to fill the void.

In Canada, the highly routinized and legitimized role of the PCO in interdepartmental coordination frequently has covered a multitude of shortfalls in cabinet performance. Only relatively rarely has the PMO played a substantial role in integrating issues which cabinet cannot resolve. The decision under Trudeau in 1975 to adopt a mandatory program of wage and price controls serves as one example of the PMO strongly asserting itself (Campbell and Szablowski, 1979: 65–6). As well, the PMO involved itself directly in Trudeau's dramatic public expenditure cuts in the summer of 1978 (Campbell, 1983: 194). In both instances, however, the PMO worked in close collaboration with PCO. Trudeau did not look to the PMO as his back up system for engaging the state apparatus. He already had a largely sympathetic reserve gearbox in the PCO.

When taking power in 1984, the Conservatives harbored strong suspicions of the willingness of the permanent bureaucracy to respond to their program. Two approaches presented themselves as ways in which to assert the new government's authority. First, Mulroney could tamper with career civil service appointments. This tack might centre on replacement or shuffling of deputy ministers and efforts to make the PCO more politically responsive. In either case, such moves would probably evoke concerns that Mulroney was departing from time-honored Canadian traditions. Further, the prime minister would be going back on his word — he had indicated earlier that he would not bring a purge down on the bureaucracy. Apart from a few deputy minister appointments from outside the federal government well into the first term, Mulroney pretty much adhered to conventional practices in the selection of deputy ministers.

Mulroney confined himself, thus, to moves that would not attract criticism on the grounds that he had tampered with the career civil service. He first bolstered the policy role of the PMO. And, he also allowed ministers for the fist time to appoint to their own offices senior partisan advisers. In this regard, ministers previously could rate their top staff person "executive assistant." Now they could hire a "chief of staff." This person would enjoy the same rank and salary as an assistant deputy minister in the permanent bureaucracy.

Expectations for an enhanced PMO role in policy centered largely on the Policy Development Group. This staff of some five advisers was headed by Charles McMillan who was on leave from the Administrative Studies Faculty at York University. Even if collective decision-making in cabinet operated smoothly, one wonders how effective McMillan would have been. He was not noted for his organization. And, he brought with him no previous experience in such a role.

Of course, an immense weight of unresolved issues bore down on the PMO because of the prime minister's preference for personalized brokerage. This badly overloaded McMillan's unit. Once again, the concept proved unworkable in the Canadian context — notwithstanding its relative success in the U.K. and Australia. Similarly, the ministerial chiefs of staff approach produced — at best — mixed results. Doubtlessly, the Conservatives have been able to use these positions to give some able aides just the type of experience which might increase the party's pool of policy advisers with exposure to government. However, too many of the 1984 appointments went to party operatives far more interested in political organization than policy.

Two features of Mulroney's approach to the PMO inhibited direct contact with the PCO. First, Mulroney spends most of his time in his office in the Centre Block of the Parliament Buildings. Trudeau, on the other hand, tended to work in the Langevin Block — using the other office only when the press or parliamentary business necessitated his presence there. Mulroney's practice tended to distance him from the PCO which shares quarters with the bulk of the PMO in the Langevin Block. Moreover, Mulroney departed from Trudeau's ritual of daily 9:30 AM meetings with top officials of both PMO and PCO. Instead, Mulroney's senior PMO staff meet around 8:30 every morning without the prime minister and their opposite numbers in the PCO. The only time that Mulroney regularly interacts with a member of PCO is in his weekly meeting with the clerk of the Privy Council each Tuesday morning just before he goes into the cabinet's Priorities and Planning Committee.

Even the most strenuous critics of the rise of PCO under Trudeau should not rush to celebrate its apparently weakened role under Mulroney. There is no doubt that Mulroney's view of the PCO is of a piece with his attitude toward regularized cabinet dynamics. We can only speculate whether inclusion of PCO officials in PMO meetings might have given greater cogency to the government's program. We might at least expect that the inexperienced administration might have avoided some of the extremely costly pratfalls had it learned how to utilize the resources available in the PCO — at least in a selective way.

In Britain, a locked door — the key to which is kept in the secretary of the cabinet's office — separates No. 10 Downing Street and the Cabinet Office. Yet, recent history fails to present a single British prime minister as cut off from career civil servants as Mulroney is. First, all prime ministers have working in their private offices five senior permanent officials who maintain an independent switchboard for links into Whitehall. Second, the cabinet secretary freely visits the prime minister during the day as events might require. Third, the top officials of No. 10 and the Cabinet Office come together each week to focus on pending issues which require close attention three or four weeks down the road. The fact that — since the war — the two main parties alternated with substantial intervals of power has facilitated these dynamics. Before Mrs. Thatcher's hegemony, Whitehall had not become so manifestly impregnated with the agenda of the political masters of the day that it lost credibility with the party out of government. Mulroney's failure to engage PCO more fully is regrettable but understandable.

MIDCOURSE CORRECTIONS:
DEEPENING THE BIFURCATION

On January 26, 1988, Jeffrey Simpson of *The Globe and Mail* wrote an article in his column proclaiming that the Mulroney government was off the ropes. He attributed this recovery to the "strategic prime ministership" — a phrase coined by Trudeau's former principal secretary, Tom Axworthy. Axworthy had argued that the PMO must orient itself toward giving the government a strong sense of direction. This task involves selectivity over the issues that the prime minister engages himself with, a strong instinct for the right political tactics and personnel who know how to extract what they want from the civil service. Most centrally, the approach has required that the prime minister associate himself with only major and — ostensibly — winnable issues. Simpson cites Mulroney's apparent successes with the Meech Lake accord and free trade as proof positive of the immense payoffs of the strategic prime ministership.

In some respects, Simpson's assessment could not be further from the reality. The entire issue centers on what is meant by "strategic." Terry Moe claims in an analysis of the putative "success" of Ronald Reagan's first term (1985: 239, 244–5, 258) that students of the presidency have missed the point of executive leadership. Ronald Reagan might well have failed at creatively engaging the state apparatus. Yet, he sufficiently manipulated his institutional resources to maintain his "responsive competence." That is, he did what he had to do to win another mandate. If this required circumventing established organizations and vested interests, so be it.

Notwithstanding the populist appeal of such an argument, several authors have maintained strenuously that the wise president eschews the temptation to downgrade the salience of the state apparatus. Thomas Cronin cautions that the "complexity, diversity, jurisdictional disputes, and bureaucratic recalcitrance" served up by the bureaucracy comprise very real dimensions to the task of governance (1980: 224–5). Bert Rockman urges that only by striving for policy competence and concomitant engagement of the state apparatus do political executives activate their "managerial propensity" (1984: 195). Only this trait can allow them to "move decisions along, effectively coordinate them, and have a sufficient information base to make them." We can safely say that Mulroney's managerial propensity is not better than Reagan's, nor has his activation of his aptitude along these lines put him ahead of the American president.

In fact, Mulroney shifted at mid-term from broker to a highly risky brand of survival politics — so dangerous, in fact, that the stakes involve the very character of the Canadian nation. His former approach had landed him in politicized incompetence. We have yet to see whether survival politics will gain for him some semblance of policy competence. If Mulroney wins a few shakes of the dice, he will reap a windfall. If he loses, he will ruin his political future. Some readers might add that he already has placed the country in perilous waters.

Meanwhile, we have to account for a new deputy prime minister — Donald Mazankowski. Unlike Nielsen, Mazankowski at least demonstrates some administrative ability. Mulroney has relegated to Mazankowski responsibility for the day-to-day operation of the government. From August 1987 to March 1988, he further burdened Nielsen's successor as chief of operations by making Mazankowski the president of the Treasury Board.

This move suggested the degree to which the prime minister still had not grasped the intricacy of routine governance. For instance, who had reflected on the likely institutional consequences of Mazankowski's dual role? Under it we had two central agencies — Finance and TBS — whose ministers could freely participate in virtually every cabinet committee. Since there is no way in which these two could personally cover their committee obligations, we can assume that ministers frequently faced a situation where they had to explain their proposals and programs in the presence of officials acting on behalf of the minister of finance and the president of the Treasury Board. We might further consider PCO's situation under the arrangement. It still controlled the procedural context in which meetings took place. However, PCO's whale — the prime minister — would not play with the other whales. And, it had to share his substitute with TBS.

Some observers have made much of the fact that Mazankowski created when he became deputy prime minister an Operations Committee (Ops) (Aucoin, 1988; Simpson, 1988). This comprises a more exclusive body than the Priorities and Planning Committee. Theoretically, it narrows participation to ministers who either shoulder responsibility for central agencies or chair the cabinet committees which oversee the three main policy sectors of government. The exception here is Senator Lowell Murray — the Minister of State for Federal-Provincial Relations. Mazankowski chairs Ops and the prime minister does not attend.

When it first began functioning, ministers who were not members of Ops often did not even know when the committee would be considering their submissions. More recently, ministers whose matters have come before the committee have attended on an *ad hoc* basis. Significantly, several officials participate in Ops on a regular basis. These include two people from PCO — the clerk/secretary and his deputy secretary for plans, the secretary to the cabinet for federal-provincial relations, the deputy minister of finance and the secretary of the Treasury Board. Further, the chief of staff and principal secretary at PMO both enjoy the right to join meetings at will. Further, ministers — whether members or *ad hoc* participants — do bring their chiefs of staff along to Ops when they believe that their attendance would be useful. On occasion, non-Ops ministers might appear with their department's deputy minister in tow. These multiple avenues of access point in one direction. Ops might well have cut some members of Priorities and Planning from regular involvement in the more significant decisions of the government. However, it has not advanced the original objective — namely, striking a core group that would be substantially less unwieldy than Priorities and Planning.

Initially, Ops functioned as a steering committee for the government while Priorities and Planning would continue to serve as the executive committee of cabinet. Thus, the former focussed on coordinating the government's timetable for the coming week. However, Ops has evolved into a supra-committee for Priorities and Planning. It meets each Monday and effectively decides the crucial policy issues which require cabinet assent. In many instances, this has led to a downgrading of Priorities and Planning's function. Often it merely makes the formal record of decision on behalf of cabinet. In many cases, little of substance hinges on its deliberations.

The representational imperatives which have inflated the size of Canadian cabinets have impinged over the years upon Priorities and Planning. Trudeau coped with the resulting deficit in Priority and Planning's capacity to expedite cabinet business by resorting to exclusive groups of senior officials. Operating under various guises during the Trudeau years, the members of these bodies attempted to accelerate agreement between departments on contentious issues by employing their ability — as heads of central agencies — to extract compliance from recalcitrant colleagues. Rank-and-file ministers and less strategically placed officials deeply resented such efforts to enforce harmony through exclusive committees. And serious backlashes arose frequently — especially in the latter days of the Trudeau years.

Ops tries to maneuver around the representational imperative as well. However, it shoulders the added burden of compensating for a prime minister who does not want to engage himself in face-to-face discussions of the central issues which his government must resolve on a week-to-week basis. Ops worked fairly effectively at the outset as a staging device. However, the press of business as the government tries to clear its decks during the run-up to the election has overloaded this device. Techniques do not supply political will. Most players will still look to the prime minister to weigh-in before they will resolve disputes over the priority and resources that various initiatives should receive. Mutterings in the Conservative caucus suggest that Ops has begun to loom in some MPs' minds as a non accountable board of directors. In this respect, a processing deficit for the system might become a legitimacy loss for Mulroney's style of leadership.

To leave his mark on the way in which the affairs of state are conducted, Mulroney must go beyond simply assigning a faithful and assiduous trustee. Devolution of the exercise of such a substantial proportion of his prerogatives simply quickens the gradual slippage to the administrative side of the bifurcation which has widened the further we get into the Mulroney years. The government — overloaded with the task of sorting through political wish lists — increasingly defers to the public service in disposing of the routine items on the menu of issues calling for attention from cabinet and the prime minister.

Two other mid-term changes warrant mention here. Mulroney did bring about a fairly substantial reform of the PMO in Spring 1987. In the preceding summer, he had departed from conventional practice and appointed the Conservative's most seasoned political operative — Dalton Camp — as a senior adviser to the cabinet housed in the Privy Council Office. The reorganization and restaffing of PMO have resulted in appreciably better performance in that agency. This owes in no small degree to Mulroney's appointment of a career civil servant from the Department of External Affairs — Derek Burney — as PMO chief of staff. Burney has run a much tighter ship than did Bernard Roy. The latter retains the title "principal secretary." However, he focuses his attention primarily on Quebec affairs.

It does not appear that Burney has substantially restored the collective dynamics between the PMO and the PCO which prevailed in the Trudeau years. For instance, the morning staff meeting — now chaired by Burney — still only includes members of PMO. However, Burney's admission to the PMO might provide a precedent for prime ministers' ultimately operating a "private office" of career civil servants in the PMO similar to that based in the U.K.'s

No. 10. As for Camp, he has played a largely indeterminate role. During the transition, some Mulroney people wanted to establish a policy think tank in the PCO which would essentially eclipse or replace entirely the career staffed secretariat which supports the Priorities and Planning Committee. The new unit would contain a mixture of political appointees and career civil servants similar to that of Central Policy Review Staff which functioned out of the British Cabinet from 1970 to 1983. Camp may attend cabinet meetings at will. And, he tracks several issues important to the government. If, however, he is a harbinger of a Canadian version of the Central Policy Review Staff he is an exceptionally low-key one.

CONCLUSION

This chapter has attempted to ascertain the nature of Brian Mulroney's management style and its consequences. It has focused on the all-embracing objective of political leadership — namely, policy competence. It has concluded that Mulroney has failed to achieve this goal. This owes both to his innate weaknesses as a political executive and several faulty design features in his cabinet and advisory systems. Mulroney's approach, in addition, has lead to a serious bifurcation in the government. On one hand, the prime minister has engrossed himself in a survival politics largely focused on his regaining his electoral appeal. On the other, his surrogates have busied themselves in a hopeless task — taking control of the state apparatus while lacking the engagement of the prime minister.

Under the circumstances, one does not relish the idea of another Mulroney term. Neither does one salivate over the prospect of a government headed by one of the alternatives. Nonetheless, Mulroney's survival politics locked us into the campaign long before the election was called. Just look at the menu of policy objectives: passage of the Meech Lake accord by Parliament and all ten provinces, Congressional approval of the free trade pact, the consumer tax portion of tax reform, the establishment of a fleet of nuclear submarines for Arctic patrols, the partial privatization of Air Canada. This is a high stakes poker game indeed. Fortunately for the government, it does not have to deliver on any of these objectives before the election set for November 21.

REFERENCES

Aberbach, Joel D., Robert D. Putnam, and Bert A. Rockman. (1981). *Bureaucrats and Politicians in Western Democracies*, (Cambridge, Mass.: Harvard University Press).

Aucoin, Peter (1986). "Organizational Change in the Machinery of Canadian Government: From Rational Management to Brokerage Politics," *Canadian Journal of Political Science* 19:3–27.

Aucoin, Peter (1985). "Institutional Changes: Priorities, Positional Policy and Power" in Andrew B. Gollner and Daniel Salée (eds.), *Canada Under Mulroney: An End of Term Report*, (Montreal: Véhicule).

Campbell, Colin, and George J. Szablowski (1979). *The Super-Bureaucrats: Structure and Behaviour in Central Agencies*, (Toronto: Macmillan).

Campbell, Colin (1980). "Political Leadership in Canada: Pierre Elliott Trudeau and the Ottawa Model" in Richard Rose and Ezra N. Suleiman (eds.), *Presidents and Prime Ministers*, (Washington: American Enterprise Institute).

Campbell, Colin (1983). *Governments Under Stress: Political Executives and Key Bureaucrats in Washington, London and Ottawa*, (Toronto: University of Toronto Press).

Campbell, Colin (1985). "Cabinet Committees in Canada: Pressures and Dysfunctions Stemming From the Representational Imperative" in Thomas T. Mackie and Brian W. Hogwood (eds.), *Unlocking the Cabinet: Cabinet Structures in Comparative Perspective*, (London: Sage).

Campbell, Colin (1986). *Managing the Presidency: Carter, Reagan and the Search for Executive Harmony*, (Pittsburgh: University of Pittsburgh Press).

Campbell, Colin (1988). "The Political Roles of Senior Government Officials in Advanced Democracies," *British Journal of Political Science*, vol. 18, pp. 243–72.

Cronin, Thomas E. (1980). *The State of the Presidency*, 2nd ed., (Boston: Little, Brown).

Granatstein, J.L. (1982). *The Ottawa Men: The Civil Service Mandarins, 1935–57*, (Toronto: Oxford University Press).

Halligan, John (1987). "Reorganizing Government Departments, 1987," *Canberra Bulletin of Public Administration*, No. 52: pp. 40–7.

Hartle, Douglas (1983). "An Open Letter to Richard Van Loon (With a Copy to Richard French)," *Canadian Public Administration*, vol. 26, pp. 84–94.

Heclo, Hugh (1984). "In Search of a Role: America's Higher Civil Service" in Ezra N. Suleiman (ed.), *Bureaucrats and Policy Making: A Comparative Overview*, (New York: Homes and Meier).

Heeney, A.D.P. (1946). "Cabinet Government in Canada: Some Developments in the Machinery of the Central Executive," *Canadian Journal of Economics and Political Science*, vol. 12, pp. 282–301.

Mackie, Thomas T., and Brian W. Hogwood (1985). "Cabinet Structures in Comparative Perspective," In Thomas T. Mackie and Brian W. Hogwood (eds.), *Unlocking the Cabinet: Cabinet Structure in Comparative Perspective*,

(London: Sage).

Mallory, J.R. (1971). *The Structure of Canadian Government*, (Toronto: Macmillan).

Moe, Terry M. (1985). "The Politicized Presidency" in John E. Chubb and Paul E. Peterson (eds.), *The New Direction in American Politics*, (Washington: The Brookings Institution).

Rockman, Bert A. (1984). *The Leadership Question: The Presidency and the American System*, (New York: Praeger).

Salamon, Lester M. (1981). "The Presidency and Domestic Policy Formulation" in Hugh Heclo and Lester M. Salamon (eds.), *The Illusion of Presidential Government*, (Boulder, Colorado: Westview).

Simpson, Jeffrey (1988). "Operations Unlimited," *Globe and Mail*, 19 May: A6.

Szablowski, George J. (1977). "The Optimal Policy-making System: Implications for the Canadian Political Process." In Hockin (ed.), *The Apex of Power*, (Scarborough, Ontario: Prentice-Hall).

Turner, John (1980). *Lloyd George's Secretariat*, (Cambridge: Cambridge University Press).

Weller, Patrick (1985). *First Among Equals: Prime Ministers in Westminster Systems*, (London: George Allen & Unwin).

Wettenhall, Roger (1989). "Recent Restructuring in Canberra: Same Policy Implications," *Governance: An International Journal of Policy and Administration* no. 2: in press.

The Mulroney Government, 1984–1988: Priorities, Positional Policy and Power

PETER AUCOIN

INTRODUCTION

This paper examines the structures and processes of governance introduced and deployed by the Mulroney government in the executive-bureaucratic arena in the 1984–1988 period. It examines these structures and processes as changes in "positional policy" which were designed to pursue the government's substantive policy priorities and in so doing to alter the configuration of power in the executive-bureaucratic arena (Aucoin, 1971). These changes represent in some respects an evolution in the machinery of government at the federal level that began before the Mulroney government assumed power in 1984. In other respects, however, they represent an explicit attempt to institute an organizational design that best accommodates the "brokerage politics" governing paradigm of the Prime Minister and the "neo-conservative" (or neo-liberal) strategy of his government (Aucoin, 1986). In this essay an attempt is made to sort out these different influences on organizational change and to determine the relationship between the government's strategy and the design put in place since 1984.

POLICY PRIORITIES

With the hindsight of four years, it is now clear that the Mulroney government assumed office with a strategy for governing that contained a much greater sense of direction and coherence than it was given credit for in 1984 (Prince, 1986). It must be acknowledged that it took some time for the implications of a good deal of this to emerge and one should not read a logical rationale into what only emerged after some deliberation on several options, some experimentation, and the experience of trial and error. At the same time, one can find in the Conservatives' election platform, the instructions given to the Ministerial Task Force on Program Review that was established immediately on the Conservatives gaining access to the levers of power (Canada, 1986), and especially perhaps in the early enunciation of the government's economic policy objectives and strategy much evidence to support the contention that in general terms the government had a plan of action (Canada: 1984).

A good deal of what the government wished to accomplish was not unique to the federal Conservative party. As such, it was and has been able to borrow from the experiences of other political regimes, in Canada and elsewhere. Neo-conservatism is a global phenomenon and in this respect the Conservatives have benefitted from the fact that they came to power when they did — that is after neo-conservatism had become the ruling ideological paradigm in several other jurisdictions, especially in Great Britain and the U. S.

In at least two respects the Conservatives' strategy followed mainstream neo-conservatism. This was the case in regard to its intentions to contract the role of the state on the one hand and to make productive management a political priority on the other (Aucoin, 1988). Its intention to contract the role of the state followed the pattern of restraint, downsizing, deregulation and privatization that has characterized other neo-conservative regimes. From the perspective of other neo-conservative regimes the Canadian federal experience has been moderate perhaps (Prince, 1987), given that the governing paradigm of the Prime Minister is one of "brokerage politics" and because, related to this, the government has also wished to pursue a policy of national reconciliation. This policy has served to moderate the policy of contraction. It should be noted in this regard, moreover, that "national reconciliation," as understood in the Canadian context, does not constitute an element in neo-conservative thought; indeed, in other conservative regimes, and for some neo-conservatives in Canada, it represents the antithesis of a limited role for government in the economy.

The priority given to productive management does of course fit well with neo-conservative ideals (Campbell and Peters, 1988). In one sense it represents an attempt to restrict the role of the bureaucracy in policy formulation. It does so to the degree that it posits a greater role for elected representatives, and their personal partisan advisors, in the determination of public policy. Greater ministerial direction is to replace policy initiation from within the bureaucracy in order to ensure the institution of the neo-conservative policy strategy. In another sense, it is to restrict the role of the bureaucracy to policy implementation but within a framework that allows for greater discretion and flexibility in the actual administration of programs, resources and personnel. In so doing it is to assert a more explicit "managerial" approach to public administration, that is a debureaucratization of the public sector to bring it more closely into line with managerial practices in the private sector.

The priority given to national reconciliation is, as noted, a distinctive Canadian objective. It derives in some large part from a reaction to or negative assessment of the state of federal-provincial relations inherited by the new federal government, and in particular the perception of the appropriate role of the federal government in response to the regional diversity of Canada and the way in which this level of government ought to relate to provincial governments. One dimension of this issue was and is constitutional in character, and for this reason it has been the most publicized dimension. Another dimension, of more direct interest to this chapter, concerns the priority of incorporating regional interests in the public policies of the national government. As pointed out above this priority may be at odds with the neo-conservative credo, for regional interests often are perceived as requiring an interventionist state if the spatial dimensions of public policy are given consideration in the formulation of national policies. At the same time, however, it can be argued that a more regionally sensitive national government may counter to an extent certain interventionist biases of a centralized federal government policy-making system. In so doing the result may be less government intervention, at least of a certain kind.

POSITIONAL POLICIES

The policy priorities of the Mulroney government relating to economic renewal, national reconciliation and productive management have led to changes in the executive-bureaucratic arena. The positional policies of the government have sought to alter the structures of influence and power within the executive-bureaucratic arena. In a good number of respects this has occurred. In some cases no formal organizational change has been effected because the Prime Minister has been able simply to use the existing machinery to suit his style and requirements; in other cases new organizational designs have been effected.

1. Economic Renewal

The economic renewal policy priority of the government has resulted in the least amount of formal organizational change. The Minister and Department of Finance have assumed a prominence in the policy process that was perhaps not nearly as pronounced for much of the Trudeau regime. But it must be noted that changes in this regard preceded the coming to office of the Mulroney government (Van Loon, 1984). These changes were the result of a combination of several factors including fiscal restraint, especially as undertaken within the operation of the Policy and Expenditure Management System that was put in place in the very late 1970s, and the impotence and then abolition of the Ministry of State for Economic and Regional Development portfolio and agency prior to the Conservatives coming to power (Aucoin and Bakvis, 1982). The preeminence of Finance was manifested early on in the Mulroney regime with the publication of the government's strategy for economic renewal in *A New Direction for Canada* (1984).

The position of Finance fitted well with the new configuration of power in the federal government for it meant that there was once again a clearly established focal point for economic policy generally within the complex of federal portfolios and departments (Phidd and Doern, 1978). It also enabled the reestablishment of a more simplified "interface" between the policy and political centres of power. Hence, Finance could relate to the Prime Minister and his

Office in ways that were unencumbered by what had been under the Trudeau regime a very crowded apex of executive and bureaucratic power (Campbell, 1983). In some part the centre had become less crowded by virtue of the fact that the Privy Council Office under Mulroney has assumed a more traditional or passive secretarial role, at least in comparison to the role that it performed under the Trudeau government.

Some redesign of the machinery of government has occurred to pursue the economic strategy of the government. First and foremost has been the establishment of the Trade Negotiations Office (TNO). This Office, headed by the chief trade negotiator who reports to the Minister of Trade, is separate from the Department of External Affairs although considered part of the Department for budgetary purposes. The Minister of Trade portfolio, moreover, has been upgraded from a junior minister to the Secretary of State for External Affairs to a senior portfolio in its own right, including membership on the Priorities and Planning Committee and as well the chairmanship of its subcommittee on trade negotiations. This subcommittee, it should also be noted, is supported by an interdepartmental committee of deputy ministers, chaired by a senior official from the TNO (Von Riekhoff, 1987).

A second change in the machinery of government has involved the creation of a ministerial portfolio and agency for the purposes of privatization and deregulation (Doern and Atherton, 1987; Smith, 1987). Responsibility for the former was originally assigned to those ministers under whom were to be found crown corporations singled out for possible privatization. This approach gave way to a more centralized and coordinated effort under the aegis of a single organization. Responsibility for deregulation (or regulatory "reform") had a somewhat similar evolution in that it has gone from being a strategy with a diffused responsibility system to the primary concern of a single minister and agency. The culmination of these parallel developments occurred in late 1986 when the government created the Office of Privatization and Regulatory Affairs (OPRA) headed by the Minister of State for Privatization and Regulatory Affairs. This portfolio, now held by the Deputy Prime Minister, also heads a new Cabinet committee whose responsibilities encompass the government's privatization and regulatory reform strategies (Clark, 1987). This means, among other things, that the regulatory process is now fully integrated into the central decision-making process of cabinet with the responsible minister and cabinet committee served by a central agency — OPRA.

The above developments in terms of ministerial responsibilities and organizational design took some time to unfold. So too has the Mulroney government's approach to industrial policy emerged only in steps. In part this was because the general economic strategy was to reshape what was perceived as an excessively interventionist policy regime as inherited from the Liberal government of Pierre Trudeau. The formulation of a new strategy has thus involved not only Finance with regard to fiscal policies and proposed tax reform but also the apparatus established to negotiate the free trade deal with the United States. These initiatives have an obvious impact on industrial policy. To complicate matters further, the machinery inherited by the Mulroney government included an industry portfolio and department which had the lead responsibility for regional economic development policy as well. This had come about because the short-lived Turner government had eliminated the Ministry of State for Economic and Regional Development portfolio and agency responsible for regional economic development policy and left this responsibility with a junior Minister of State for Regional Development whose relationship to the Minister of Regional Industrial Expansion, whom he was "to assist," was not made clear (Aucoin and Bakvis, 1985). The Mulroney government on assuming office gave full responsibility for regional economic development policy to the Minister of Regional Industrial Expansion. But it was clear from the outset that this could not be but an interim measure for reasons to be considered later (Savoie, 1986, 1987a).

Disentangling industrial policy from regional economic development policy was not the only dimension of industrial policy that had to be sorted out however. The Conservatives' economic strategy also placed emphasis on the promotion of science and technology, an emphasis that became even more critical as the government moved towards its position on free trade. In retrospect it is not surprising that what eventually emerged was the merger of industrial policy and science and technology policy responsibilities under a single minister and department — the Department of Industry, Science and Technology. The second set of responsibilities were taken over from what had always been a junior portfolio and ministry of state agency with little clout in federal decision-making (see Aucoin & French, 1974). The elevation of this second set of concerns is likely of course to introduce a much more industrial and commercial policy focus, for which there is already considerable evidence. This is not out of line with the overall economic renewal strategy needless to say. Just what influence or positional power this new ministerial portfolio and department will have within a government that is committed to less state intervention of the kind traditionally associated with departments of industry is not at present clear however.

2. National Reconciliation

The decision to disentangle regional economic development policy from industrial policy took some time to emerge. Although the Conservatives in opposition and on the campaign trail had been highly critical of the Liberal government's record in the field of regional economic development policy, and were supported in their criticisms by provincial governments, particularly those of the less developed regions, their criticisms centered around the bureaucratic structures of the federal government on the one hand and the perceived "failures" of Liberal policy on the other. These failures were in part related to the perpetuation of regional disparities in employment and earned income, that is the inability of regional economic development programs to generate new business activity. In this respect the criticisms dovetailed with the neo-conservative critique of Liberal interventionism generally. But they also centered on what was claimed to be a centralist bias in the federal decision-making process in both its executive and bureaucratic dimensions. In this respect there was an obvious need — obvious to the Conservatives that is — to restructure the decision-making process to make it more responsive and sensitive to the interests, needs and opportunities of the regions which were "left out," most notably the West and Atlantic Canada (Savoie, 1987a; Mulroney, 1987).

The priority of national reconciliation involved several things. First, and perhaps most importantly, it involved tackling the issue of constitutional change in regard to relations between the federal and provincial orders of government. In this development, the portfolio of Minister of State for Federal-Provincial Relations was reactivated and the Federal-Provincial Relations Office assumed a new importance given the placing of a new constitutional scheme on the policy agenda. The basic thrust of the Meech Lake accord,

341

whatever its merits, has introduced an element of federal-provincial collaboration with implications for the second feature of national reconciliation, namely the formulation and implementation of regional economic development policy.

At the outset of the Mulroney government, however, there was not a clear sense of how the government would effect national reconciliation in regard to regional development policy. For one thing the prime minister decided not to continue the practice of singling out certain ministers as "regional ministers." This largely informal but not inconsequential practice has varied in its application throughout Canadian political history but under the Trudeau regime was an important feature of cabinet decision-making (Bakvis, 1986). In fact it was strengthened over the life of this regime to the point where during the latter years, that is in the 1980–1984 period, regional ministers gained a measure of even formal recognition, particularly in relation to certain regional economic development programs (Aucoin and Bakvis, 1985). This occurred at a time, of course, when Western representation in the cabinet was weak, at least numerically. The Mulroney cabinet, on the other hand, had no deficiencies in regard to regional representation from all regions. Moreover, its enunciated economic policy left less room, at least in principle, for the kind of leverage that regional ministers under the Trudeau regime had exercised.

A combination of several factors served to reintroduce the question of regional representation in cabinet decision-making. These factors included a demand from provincial premiers, especially from Atlantic Canada, that regional economic development policy not be downgraded. Given that the Liberal government was perceived to have done so, especially after the elimination of DREE in 1982, it was not surprising that the Mulroney government agreed to keep regional economic development policy on the agenda (Canada, et al., 1985). Secondly, among other factors, the perceived "communications" problems experienced by the Mulroney government in its first two years in office led to the reestablishment of a system of identified regional ministers for all provinces. Thirdly, both Western and Atlantic Canada ministers in the cabinet were interested in devising new ways to ensure that regional considerations were more effectively brought to bear on national policy development, decision-making, and implementation. To this end some organizational change was obviously required.

The major organizational result to this point in time has been the creation of three new agencies, each headed by a regional minister (that is a minister who also possesses another portfolio). The three agencies are the Atlantic Canada Opportunities Agency (ACOA), the Western Diversification Office (WDO), and the Northern Ontario Development Corporation (FEDNOR). As region specific organizations, there are variations among these three. ACOA and FEDNOR are in some respects in the tradition of regional economic development agencies. Each has an advisory board of regional representatives appointed by the federal government, although in the case of ACOA the four provincial governments did have some input to the appointment process in the spirit of the Meech Lake accord. ACOA and WDO, moreover, are meant to enhance the capacity of the cabinet to respond to the perceived need for greater attention to regional interests in the making of national policies generally. In the case of ACOA, this has been termed the "advocacy" role of the agency (Savoie, 1987a: 69–76). Both agencies have assumed full responsibility for regional economic development programs of the Department of Regional Industrial Expansion and with them the offices of the Federal Economic Development Coordinators (the last vestige of the defunct Ministry of State for Economic and Regional Development). Each is meant to have a strong coordinating role vis-à-vis other line departments and agencies in the economic development sector. Finally, each is to have a regional fund in the order of one billion dollars over a five year period — ACOA for new "opportunities"; WDO for "diversification."

In making these new agencies region specific the government has enhanced the role of regional ministers by enabling regional policy to be "tailored" to each region. In order to do so, "bureaucrats in Ottawa" are to be replaced by decision-makers in the region (Mulroney, 1987) albeit still federal bureaucrats headquartered in Moncton for ACOA and Edmonton for WDO and supported by four provincial offices in each case. The latter are constituted by what were the Federal Economic Development Coordinators' offices. In each case a much greater degree of flexibility has been introduced for program design, as this relates both to interdepartmental cooperative ventures involving the new regional agencies and other federal government departments and to intergovernmental programs between the federal and provincial governments.

3. Productive Management

Productive management was enunciated as a "top political prior-ity" by the Conservatives in their 1984 election campaign (PC, 1984). Not a great deal of attention was given to this during the election campaign, except insofar as it related to the more general economic policy proposals of restraint, downsizing, privatization and deregulation on the one hand and the attempt by the Conser-vatives to suggest, on the other hand, that savings could be achieved through productive management in order to accom-modate those new spending initiatives which they had proposed during the campaign. Although not spelled out in great detail, the campaign proposal for productive management drew heavily on the 1983 report of the Auditor-General wherein was found an en-tire chapter devoted to "Constraints to Productive Management in the Public Service" (Canada, 1983: 53–87).

This 1983 report had detailed the extensive and accumulated bur-den of central agency, common service department and internal department policies, regulations and procedures on departmental managers, from deputy ministers on down the hierarchy and to some important extent on departmental ministers themselves. These financial, personnel, and administrative controls were viewed by the Auditor-General (ironically whose reports have caused a not inconsiderable proportion of these same controls (Sutherland and Doern, 1985) as debilitating in the cause of pro-ductive management. In taking up this cause, the Conservatives promised "to shift from reliance on regulations, controls and detailed procedures towards greater reliance on managers' com-petence and their achievement of results. Our goal is to simplify government — and (echoing the Glassco Royal Commission on Government Organization of the early 1960s) "to let managers manage." (PC, 1984: 1). The Conservatives also promised to review the legacy of programs from the Trudeau regime from the Auditor-General's much prized perspective of "value-for-money."

In coming to office the Mulroney government immediately esta-blished a ministerial task force on program review headed by the Deputy Prime Minister, Erik Nielsen. This undertaking was unprecedented in two respects. First, it constituted an across-the-board examination of almost a thousand federal government programs. Second, it involved private sector representatives in a massive way in this evaluation. This review was, in the words of the Prime Minister, "to overhaul government programs so that they would be 'simpler, more understandable and more accessible to their clientele' and that decision-making should be 'decentralized as far as possible to those in direct contact with client groups' " (Canada, 1986:46).

The consequences of the task force reviews were, as might be expected, uneven in their impact across departments and agencies but they were not inconsiderable in certain quarters. In part this was due to the fact that public servants were also used in these reviews as officials seconded to the task force. In some cases, accordingly, changes were made that had an evolutionary character, that is movement was already present in terms of attitudes and prescriptions extant in the bureaucracy. A more general development of this sort, is one extending across the bureaucracy, involved the perceived need to move away from the extensive control over departments by central agencies. Even before the Conservatives came to office, both the Treasury Board and the Public Service Commission had begun to take initiatives in these regards (Aucoin and Bakvis, 1988). The Conservatives' concern for "productive management" lent further support to these initiatives.

The result of this momentum was the February, 1986 decision of the Treasury Board to undertake an initiative entitled "Increased Authority and Accountability for Ministers and Departments" but which has been retitled for public consumption as "Increased Ministerial Authority and Accountability" or IMAA. This initiative is meant to enhance the autonomy and authority of ministers and departmental official in the use of financial and personnel resources by way of the removal or reduction of central controls over ministerial and managerial decisions within departments. This is to be achieved by way of agreements between the Treasury Board and individual ministers and departments in order that there can be a tailoring of central regulations and delegated authority and thus as well accountability regimes to fit the particular requirements of individual departments. This initiative, which has now been realized with at least a half dozen departments, is paralleled by a Public Service Commission program, entitled "Administrative Reform," that has been underway for some time and to the same end, that is tailoring its central regulations department by department.

These developments are hardly the focus of media attention and as a consequence have not been widely reported. They have had, however, the effect of moving the federal government's decision-making and administrative systems away from the excessive "fascination" with centralized control and coordination that characterized the Trudeau regime (Campbell, 1983). They constitute a recognition that excessive efforts to control and coordinate from the centre have not been very effective, let alone conducive to good management. In this sense they also represent an acknowledgement of the de facto diffusion of power in the federal administration system (Pross, 1985).

It should be recognized that the movement to greater ministerial and departmental discretion has been facilitated, even required, by the reality of expenditure restraint, a reality that set in before the conservatives assumed office but one further reinforced by the fiscal policies of the new government. The effect of expenditure restraint has been twofold. On the one hand, it has forced ministers and departments to try to find from within their own approved budgetary resources the monies to fund new or expanding programs. The IMAA initiative was in part no more than a practical response to the inability of the Treasury Board to handle the numerous requests from ministers and their departments for Board approval of such intradepartmental reallocations. On the other hand, this same development constitutes a recognition of the inherent limitations of the Policy and Expenditure Management System (PEMS) wherein sectoral cabinet committees are meant to allocate budgetary "envelopes" among the programs of the ministers who comprise these committees (Van Loon, 1983: Kernaghan and Siegel, 1987: 510–566). The inherent limitation is that ministers do not willingly give up their departmental resources in order that other ministers might use them, whatever the rhetoric of the PEMS philosophy. The natural outcome of committee deliberations, accordingly, is to seek new resources from the Priorities and Planning Committee as the executive committee of cabinet or from the Treasury Board with respect to the expansion of the existing programs. This is hardly the exercise in restraint budgeting that PEMS was designed to effect. Under this system, PEMS is, as one official put it, a "pretty expensive management system"!

The resolution to the deficiencies in PEMS has emerged in the form of an Operations Committee, headed by the Deputy Prime Minister. Formed after the arrival of Don Mazankowski as Deputy Prime Minister, this committee constitutes a "general managers' committee" with the Deputy Prime Minister as the general manager and committee chair. On this committee are the chairs of the three major sectoral policy committees — Economic and Regional Development, Social Development, and Defence and Foreign Policy, the Minister of Finance, and four officials — the Prime Minister's Chief of Staff, the deputy minister of Finance, the secretary of the Treasury Board and the secretary to cabinet/Clerk of the Privy Council. This committee manages the work plan of the government in respect to emerging issues, interdepartmental assignments, major announcements, and any crisis confronting individual ministers (in which case such ministers may join this committee to consider their approach to the same). Most importantly, however, it is at the sessions of the committee that the ministers involved tackle the matter of allocating budgetary resources. It is here that the tradeoffs are made between these key ministers, rather than in Priorities and Planning or in the sectoral cabinet committees. As such the role of this committee represents a major departure from the basic format of the PEMS approach.

Although PEMS has been heralded as an important breakthrough in rational decision-making, in a number of crucial respects it is not better, and perhaps even worse, than its predecessor — the Planning, Programming, and Budgeting System (PPBS). It has not solved the incremental character of expenditure decision-making for the basic dynamic of committed resources remains. Ministers are willing to make only very marginal changes to the existing resources — their "A base" budgets — and thus are even less inclined to engage in significant cutting exercises — the "X budget" approach. They thus are inclined to demand more to cope with new proposals. In a context where the government wishes to exercise restraint on the one hand and to introduce major new programs on the other, it is inevitable that the pressures on the system will push decision-making up the hierarchy. This is what has occurred and the Deputy Prime Minister's Operations Committee has become the decision-making arena for the critical decisions. In this sense it is an integration of functions that PEMS assigns to Priorities and Planning, sectoral cabinet committees and Treasury Board. The integration has occurred because P&P cannot be expected to give other than broad direction, the sectoral cabinet committees have not proven themselves able to make the critical tradeoffs without pressuring the system for more resources, and the Treasury Board has both too much to do in terms of its management of government administration functions and too little status in terms of its ministerial membership to function as a "high policy" expenditure decision-making body.

POWER

The organizational changes described above have been determined in a number of important respects by the priorities of the Mulroney government since 1984. They also have been determined by the "brokerage politics" paradigm of the Prime Minister that I have described elsewhere (Aucoin, 1986). In terms of the power structure in the federal executive-bureaucratic arena, this combination of determinants has led to significant changes over the past four years.

With regard to the political-bureaucratic interface, there has been a major change in that a much greater degree of ministerial direction of government has occurred. In part this is due to the fact that the Conservatives did have an agenda when they assumed office. On the basis of this agenda, and a full one at that, the capacities of ministers were enhanced in relation to the bureaucracy. Ministers who know what they want to do are obviously much less at the mercy of their public service advisors; the task of the latter becomes one primarily of advising on implementation rather than objectives.

This change was also due, however, to the insistence of the Prime Minister, and other senior ministers, that the initiative for policy be the responsibility of the government and not the public service. As David Zussman notes "Mulroney promised that 'in a Tory government the Minister will run his department. And any Deputy Minister who doesn't understand that will have a career notable for its brevity.' " According to Zussman, "this statement was a direct warning to the public service that the Trudeau regime's practice of creating strong working ties between the deputy ministers and the Privy Council office which Michael Pitfield, Clerk of the Privy Council, had developed would not be encouraged" (Zussman, 1987: 258–9). The implication in this was that the Prime Minister would also constrain his public service deputy minister, namely the Clerk of the Privy Council.

The result of this approach was an enhancement of the "political arm of government," that is the partisan political advisors of the prime minister and ministers — the Prime Minister's Office and Ministers' Offices (Osbaldeston, 1987). The PMO was not only expanded accordingly but was intended to exercise greater influence relative to the public service in the provision of advice and the management of government business. Ministers' Offices were also strengthened, particularly in regard to the status of their principal political assistants whose positions were to be elevated in status and influence. This enhancement did take place but not with the desired result. For a variety of reasons, but relating especially to a series of scandals and the political mismanagement of them, the government had to regroup, especially at the centre, Within the PMO a division of responsibilities was created so that there came to be both a Principal Secretary to the Prime Minister and a Chief of Staff, with the latter becoming in effect the official responsible for the management of the PMO, particularly insofar as this agency relates to the cabinet system and the public service. Ironically, the person chosen to perform these duties was seconded from the public service in recognition of the need for the government to rediscover trust in the public service to keep it out of political trouble. Within Ministers' Offices a similar kind of regrouping has occurred insofar as the Chiefs of Staff to ministers, as they are now called, have either reverted to the more traditional roles of executive assistants or have at least restricted their functions to what are clearly the partisan advisory roles most appropriate to such non-administrative positions.

In some large part, the political arm of government has diminished in importance, at least in regard to initial expectations, by virtue of the fact that the PCO and departmental deputy ministers especially have sought to accommodate greater ministerial direction. The fact that the government had a clear agenda obviously has helped here for it has facilitated relations between the government and the public service in terms of their respective roles. To a degree, this has made the political arm of government less necessary. This accommodation has been effected by the PCO taking the necessary steps to ensure that its own internal structures and processes are organized in ways that enable it to meet the requirements of greater ministerial direction. It has done this primarily by being more formalized as an organization; a requirement dictated by the less formalized ministerial system. At the same time, efforts have been made to enhance the capacity of PCO officials to ensure that the entire bureaucracy functions in a similar mode vis-à-vis the government. This has involved essentially two initiatives. First, the most senior positions just below the level of the Clerk of the Privy Council/Secretary to Cabinet have been upgraded so that these central agency officials relate to deputy ministers as peers in their own right and not merely as representatives of the Clerk as the most senior deputy minister in the public service. Second, the Clerk has taken steps to increase the degree of communications between deputy ministers on a regular and frequent basis. A greater effort has been made, in short, to enhance the corporate character of the most senior ranks of the public service, once a hallmark of the senior public service but a phenomenon that had diminished with both the expansion of officials at this rank given the growth in the number of departments and the greater hierarchal differentiation which accompanied the expansion of central agencies.

It is also worth noting in this regard that deputies are now once again more fully involved in the work of cabinet committees but as individual advisors and not as substitutes for their ministers. Moreover, with the exception of the deputy ministers' committee to support the Priorities and Planning Committee's subcommittee on trade negotiations, there are no committees of deputy ministers to "mirror" cabinet committees as there were during the last years of the Trudeau regime. Their involvement represents a recognition by the government of the crucial roles of the public service in ensuring the most rigorous consideration of policy. The way in which they are involved, on the other hand, constitutes the establishment of a clear(er) separation of ministerial and public service responsibilities.

Prime Minister Mulroney's relations with his ministers was originally characterized by a good deal of prime ministerial intervention on an individual basis. In this he concentrated a good deal of power to himself and his Office. In addition to the changes noted above with respect to the role of his Office, his interventions have become more selective and strategic, in part because he is being better advised by his Office, in part because he has been willing to devolve more power to his senior ministers, and in part simply because the government's agenda has been such a crowded one. In addition there has been stability in the ranks of the most senior ministers and for the greater part continuity in their posts.

The result is that there has emerged an inner circle of ministers that revolves around personal relations with the Prime Minister on the one hand and a largely informal but nevertheless regularized working group headed by the Deputy Prime Minister. The formalities of the cabinet committee system as well as the Policy and Expenditure Management System are still observed, although some rationalization of the former and some streamlining of the latter have occurred. But, in a number of important respects, the cabinet structure contains a dynamic that is more difficult to describe in purely formal organizational terms. The inner circle referred to above is not quite an inner cabinet as we have come to use the term for it is not formally structured as such. As a multi-faceted pattern of relationships between ministers, including the Prime Minister of course, this inner circle does not lack organizational coherence. At the same time, however, the essentially flexible character of this arrangement offers enough prime ministerial room to manoeuvre without complete loss of order.

It is the flexibility of this arrangement that has caused the planning system within the cabinet to be largely informal with a certain measured degree of adhocracy. This works precisely because the Deputy Prime Minister with his Operations Committee is able to function as a steering committee for both the cabinet and the public service. The power structure is no less centralized; indeed, as measured against the Trudeau regime in this respect it is clearly more effectively centralized.

In addition to the centralization that is represented by this development, two other developments have served to centralize decision-making power. The first is the trade initiative which has required an obvious measure of prime ministerial intervention and central coordination, primarily by way of P&P's subcommittee of the subject, the authority given to the minister and office for trade negotiations, and the use of a mirror committee of deputies. The second has been the centralization of the government's approach to privatization and the central coordination of regulatory affairs policy. In each of these cases, policy priorities have demanded a corporate approach and centralization has fitted with the general management approach of the government.

The fact that the cabinet system has had the above centralizing elements has not meant that collegial or collective decision-making has been a norm, as it was under the Trudeau design. Rather, the norm has been to shift responsibility more to individual ministers for all those matters that need not be dealt with by the above structures. Both the practical constraints extant within the system as

351

well as the principles underlying the Increased Ministerial Authority and Accountability scheme have served to introduce a greater
measure of individual ministerial and departmental autonomy
from cabinet committee and central agencies. There is, to be certain, an element of managerial rhetoric in play here but more is
involved. There is also an increased appreciation of the need to
selectively decentralize governmental operations, in part because
they had become too centralized and in part because the diversity
within the government's policy and political environments
demands a considerable degree of decentralization.

It is not easy to manage these twin developments of some centralization and some decentralization but they are not necessarily
contradictory. Properly designed, an organization can have a
"tight-loose" fit of the two. It is in this respect that the organizational innovations that are represented by the government's new
and region specific economic development agencies — the Atlantic Canada Opportunities Agency, the Western Diversification
Office, and the Northern Ontario Development Corporation —
constitute the ultimate challenge problematic to the system. In one
regard, they clearly represent an expression of the government's
desire to decentralize decision-making for program design and
delivery to the regions, that is to regional agencies of the federal
government.

In another regard, however, they represent the demands of
regional ministers that the regional or spatial dimensions of
national policies and programs be given a higher profile and
priority in ministerial decision-making. Hence, ACOA and WDO in
particular are meant to perform regional advocacy and interdepartmental coordinating functions within the federal decision-
making system. These functions are inherently corporate and thus
centralizing, if not with respect to the specifically internal operations of ACOA and WDO, then at least with regard to the ways in
which these two agencies and their respective ministers attempt to
intervene in decision-making concerning other federal departments. Such intervention has not succeeded to any great extent in
the past (Savoie, 1986; Aucoin and Bakvis, 1985). Whether this new
approach will prove different in this respect is still an open question. Under a tight-loose configuration of centralization-decentralization, this new approach may work if the interventions are
few in number, strategic in character and motivated by policy, as
opposed to merely partisan political, reasons. Policy reasons are

required if ministers collectively and individually are to support them; otherwise only brute prime ministerial or senior ministerial clout will win out, given that there are inevitably conflicting regional interests in cabinet. Such clout may be required even for sound policy reasons but if partisan reasons are the only basis for "program bending" then, as experience demonstrates, there will be little on-going attention given by most ministers and departments to the regional dimensions in national policies.

CONCLUSIONS

Over the past four years, the Mulroney government has had a major impact on the organizational design of the executive-bureaucratic arena. Greater ministerial direction of the policy process had been led by the Prime Minister and taken up by senior ministers. This has not resulted for the greater part in a politicization of the bureaucracy, notwithstanding some early fear and some continuing suspicion in some parts of the bureaucracy. The influence of the bureaucracy had been restricted in some important respects to be certain. This has occurred primarily as a result of greater ministerial direction, but also because the government has sought *ad hoc* and temporary outside advice, such as in the Ministerial Task Force on Program Review, on the one hand, and has sought to institute regular consultative mechanisms, such as for ACOA or FEDNOR, on the other. What has not been transformed, in any major way, is the political arm of government, that is the partisan political advisory structure of the ministry and individual ministers. The PMO especially has failed to bring this about. Its role is not an unimportant one but at best it now functions as it did under both Pearson and Trudeau. The same can be said about ministerial political aides.

Within the strategic apex of power there has been a greater concentration of authority and control both under the Prime Minister and especially under the Deputy Prime Minister with a coterie of senior ministers belonging to an inner circle. Greater informality, streamlining and flexibility characterize the planning and decision-making system as a result. The central agencies of government have had to adjust to this reality and it would not be surprising if some reorganization occurs in the near future to rationalize the central agency apparatus.

At the same time as there has been this greater concentration of power, there has also been an increased deregulation of departmental decision-making and management. Sectoral cabinet committees have become less important and central agencies have given ground to departmental ministers and their officials. Furthermore there has been an increased emphasis given to administrative decentralization within many departments, and of course new agencies with a decidedly decentralized structure have been established. In some respects this has had a "fracturing" effect on the corporate ministry system in terms of a greater emphasis on both departmentalism and regionalism. As noted, the latter emphasis introduces a problematic in relation to the former but this is so recent that the dynamics of this relationship have yet to be played out. This will clearly test the brokerage capacities of the government. It may also lead to some rationalization of portfolios, along the lines of the integration of portfolios, as in the case of industry, science and technology.

Finally, we need to note that all of these developments have taken place over a period of time during which the government had a very full policy agenda. To a significant degree, accordingly, it is difficult to say whether the power structure that has emerged over the past four years is one that will survive the urgency of this agenda, assuming, that is, the re-election of this government. Both Canadian and comparative experiences suggest that it would: fundamental changes occur only with new regimes.

REFERENCES

Aucoin, Peter (1971). "Theory and Research in the Study of Policy-Making," in G. Bruce Doern and Peter Aucoin (eds.), *The Structures of Policy-Making in Canada*, (Toronto: Macmillan), pp. 10–38.

Aucoin, Peter (1986). "Organizational Change in the Machinery of Canadian Government: From Rational Management to Brokerage Politics," *Canadian Journal of Political Science*, vol. 19, no. 1, pp. 3–27.

Aucoin, Peter (1988). "Contraction, Managerialism and Decentralization in Canadian Government," *Governance*, vol. 1, no. 2, forthcoming.

Aucoin, Peter and Herman Bakvis (1982). "Organizational Differentiation and Integration: The Case of Regional Economic Development Policy in Canada," *Canadian Public Administration*, vol. 24, no. 3, pp. 348–371.

Aucoin, Peter and Herman Bakvis (1985). "Regional Responsiveness and Government Organization: The Case of Regional Economic Development Policy in Canada," in Peter Aucoin (ed.), *Regional Responsiveness and the*

National Administrative State, (Toronto: University of Toronto Press), pp. 51–118.

Aucoin, Peter and Herman Bakvis (1988). *The Centralization–Decentralization Conundrum: Organization and Management in the Government of Canada,* (Montreal: Institute for Research on Public Policy).

Aucoin, Peter and Richard French (1974). *Knowledge, Power and Public Policy,* (Ottawa: Information Canada).

Bakvis, Herman (1986). "Regional Ministers, National Policy and the Administrative State," a paper presented to the Canadian Political Association, University of Manitoba.

Campbell, Colin (1983). *Governments Under Stress,* (Toronto: University of Toronto Press).

Campbell, Colin and B. Guy Peters (1988). "The Politics/Administration Dichotomy: Death or Merely Change?," *Governance,* vol. 1, no. 1, pp. 79–99.

Canada (1983). *Office of the Auditor General, Report to the House of Commons for the Fiscal Year ending 31 March 1983,* (Ottawa: Minister of Supply and Services, 1983), pp. 53–87.

Canada (1984). *A New Direction for Canada,* (Ottawa: Department of Finance).

Canada (1986). *Task Force on Program Review. An Introduction to the Process of Program Review,* (Ottawa: Minister of Supply and Services).

Canada, et al. (1985). *Intergovernmental Position Paper on the Principles and Framework for Regional Economic Development, by the Government of Canada, and the Governments of the Provinces of Ontario, Quebec, Nova Scotia, New Brunswick, Manitoba, British Columbia, Prince Edward Island, Alberta, Newfoundland and Labrador and the Governments of Yukon and the Northwest Territories.* (June).

Clark, Ian (1987). *Recent Changes in the Cabinet Decision–Making System,* (Ottawa: Privy Council Office).

Doern, G. Bruce and John Atherton (1987). "The Tories and the Crowns: Restraining and Privatizing in a Political Minefield" in Michael J. Prince (ed.), *How Ottawa Spends, 1987–88: Restraining the State,* (Toronto: Methuen).

Mulroney, Brian (1987). *Statement by the Right Honourable Brian Mulroney on the Announcement of the Western Diversification Initiative.* (August 4).

Osbaldeston, Gordon (1987). "The Public Servant and Politics," *Policy Options,* January, pp. 3–7.

Phidd, R.W. and G.B. Doern (1978). *The Politics and Management of Canadian Economic Policy,* (Toronto: MacMillan).

Prince, Michael J. (1986). "The Mulroney Agenda: A Right Turn for Ottawa?" in Michael J. Prince (ed.), *How Ottawa Spends, 1987–88: Tracking the Tories,* (Toronto: Methuen), pp. 1–60.

Prince, Michael J. (1987). "Restraining the State: How Ottawa Shrinks" in Michael J. Prince (ed.), *How Ottawa Spends, 1987–88: Restraining the State,* (Toronto: Methuen), pp. 1–37.

Progressive Conservative Party of Canada (1984). *Towards Productive Management — The PC Approach, Background Note no. 2.*

Pross, A. Paul (1985). "Parliamentary Influence and the Diffusion of Power," *Canadian Journal of Political Science,* vol. 18, no. 2, pp. 235–266.

Savoie, Donald J. (1986). *Regional Economic Development,* (Toronto: University of Toronto Press).

Savoie, Donald J. (1987a). "Establishing The Atlantic Canada Opportunities Agency," Office of the Prime Minister, Canada.

Savoie, Donald J. (1987b). "Atlantic Canada Opportunities Agency Announced," Office of the Prime Minister, Canada.

Smith, Janet (1987). "Privatization of Crown Corporations," a paper presented for the annual conference of the Institute of Public Administration of Canada, Saint John.

Sutherland S.L. and G.B. Doern (1985). *Bureaucracy in Canada: Control and Reform*, (Toronto: University of Toronto Press).

Van Loon, Richard (1983). "The Policy and Expenditure Management System in the Federal Government: the First Three Years," *Canadian Public Administration*, vol. 26, no. 2, pp. 255–285.

Van Loon, Richard (1984). "Conclusion" in Richard D. French, *How Ottawa Decides*, 2nd edition, (Toronto: James Lorimer).

Von Riekhoff, Harald (1987). "The Structure of Foreign Policy Decision Making and Management," in Brian Tomlin and Maureen Appel Molot (eds.) *Canada Among Nations, 1986: Talking Trade*, (Toronto: James Lorimer).

Zussman, David (1986). "Walking the Tightrope: The Mulroney Government and the Public Service," in Michael J. Prince (ed.) *How Ottawa Spends, 1986–87: Tracking the Tories*, (Toronto: Methuen).

New Trends in Public Service Management

CAROLLE SIMARD

Politicians come and go, but public servants linger on, to paraphrase an old saying. In fact, politicians never know what tomorrow will bring, whereas the public service, taken as a whole, is generally assured of its future, despite having to adjust to ongoing change in various areas.

In theory, this implies that Canada's public administration functions in relative independence. Of course, changes in the administration are never completely divorced from the social context, since they are affected by the institutions directly involved, and in turn have a bearing on the subsequent development of these same institutions. The public service, however, has its own dynamic — a system of evolution that I have attempted to study through examining the principal changes that have occurred in the management of public service personnel.

During the 1980s, the Canadian government's underlying concern vis-à-vis the public service has been to produce efficient administration, emphasizing rationalization, programming, planning, evaluation, and control of resources. Public servants have had to adapt to new ideas that have engendered a series of changes in the area of personnel management.

Under the Mulroney government, there has been a sharp reduction in the number of person-years in the public service, in line with the aims laid down in the 1985 budget, which provided for a reduction of 15,000 person-years before the end of the 1990–1991 financial year. (According to the Public Service Commission's *Annual Report* for 1987, 13,587 employees have been affected by this policy since May 1985.) The reduction was accompanied by a whole range of measures designed to help management adapt to the new policy of reducing and redeploying personnel. Various steps were also taken with regard to the employees themselves. Since 1985, the following policies have been applicable:

For management:

Public service managers are trained to view personnel cutbacks from a positive angle and to minimize their effect on work organization. They are shown how to handle staff reductions and how to inform employees of their redundancy. In other words, they are undergoing the kind of management training that deals with personnel reduction and policy changes in personnel management.

For employees:

Placement clubs have been set up for redundant employees, on the basis of a model created by Employment and Immigration Canada. These clubs are designed to help employees who are living through budget cuts to maximize the skills and experience that they have acquired, both inside and outside the public service.

Hiring and placement procedures:

The agencies in charge of managing public service personnel are responsible for setting up a simpler hiring and placement procedure. As early as 1980, the Public Service Commission began to reform hiring and placement by delegating greater powers to the ministries. The various agencies and departments then adapted these new measures to their particular circumstances. By the end of 1984, the revamped hiring and placement procedures had helped reduce public service personnel and improved overall efficiency.

In actual fact, it is a question of increasing the margin of manoeuvreability for deputy ministers and ministries. At the same time, the principle of management accountability has been brought to the fore. Policy regarding areas of competitive examination has been reviewed in order to accommodate the particular needs of each ministry and the career pattern of the employees. Deputy ministers can now work out examination policies for their ministrys, following consultation with the unions.

In its 1987 *Annual Report*, the Public Service Commission discusses this new hiring and placement procedure, giving examples in which the procedure has been speeded up by the following factors:

— elimination of application forms

— initiation of hiring and placement measures by telephone

— control of finances and person-years to be administered independently of hiring and placement

— establishment of a procedure involving managers and placement advisors from the beginning of the placement process.

The changes also led to a revision of hiring standards and procedures. Managers now have more freedom in hiring. They have greater flexibility in naming posts and determining the qualifications required. When it comes to evaluating personnel skills, they have greater discretion and can alter requirements to suit the special nature of various vacant posts.

New measures have been adopted to speed up the appointment procedure. Under this new regime, appointments made by ministries after the reclassification of posts need no longer be approved by the Public Service Commission. Furthermore, in certain circumstances, the PSC has authorized the ministries to proceed with specified term appointments without competitive examinations, as the following examples show:

— The PSC or delegated deputy ministers can redeploy managerial staff according to need, as long as their group and level remain the same.

— Employees who have been designated redundant may be given priority in appointments to new posts.

In the federal government, responsibility for personnel management lies increasingly with the ministries, since they fill more than 98% of available positions. The following trends are evident:

— Emphasis is placed on management decision-making. The way in which the PSC, personnel officers, and managers share responsibility for hiring and placement is now being redefined.

— Delays in recruiting, selecting, and appointing have been

curtailed. The PSC intends to decrease even further the time spent administering these procedures.

— Steps have been taken to ensure better planning in relation to human resources needs, in the short and middle term.

— Greater flexibility in competitive examination policies has enabled management to accommodate the employees' legitimate ambitions as well as the principle of efficiency — that is, to respond to both the organization's functional needs and its social objectives at the least possible cost.

These are new elements in federal public service management. Nevertheless, however much management may take them into account, it must still respect the principle of merit and the measures applicable for employment equity.

A LOOK AT SOME OF THE ELEMENTS

The changes noted in personnel management are accompanied by a change in administrative language. This is never an entirely neutral factor. Language adapts to new realities and reflects, however imperfectly, the interests at stake. Administrative language dealing with personnel management in the Canadian public service has been gradually modified to show the reduction in numbers. This reduction is being dealt with in line with administrative reforms designed to guarantee fair and efficient management in the area of hiring and placement. Management accountability and quality of management decisions are emphasized, rather than increased regulation which, according to some, runs counter to the aims of reform while multiplying bureaucratic inconsistency.

This new language does not disguise the changes that are taking place. In a period of cutbacks in person-years (announced, it will be remembered, in the 1985 budget) and personnel redeployment, it is possible to make certain observations based on figures given in the PSC *Annual Report* for the years 1985, 1986 and 1987.

— Placement now primarily involves finding posts for employees who have priority rating, whereas previously this branch of activity was largely concerned with recruitment.

— There has been a general decrease throughout Canada of personnel training and continuing education.

— The number of appeals lodged has dropped significantly.

— The language training program has been revised to emphasize acquiring a working knowledge on an individual basis. In addition, the length of training is now shorter. While registration for continuing education courses diminished by 14% in 1986, registration in other courses increased by 28% in the same year.

— In 1987, the PSC reduced by 16% the person-years assigned to language training.

— Since 1985, there has been a drop in hiring personnel for an indeterminate period.

A more detailed look at some of the statistics shows that some fairly interesting developments have occurred in the sectors of language training, hiring and placement, examinations, appeals and investigations, administration, and professional management training. In all these sectors, with the exception of hiring and placement, the number of person-years decreased during 1986–1987. In general, the number of full-time and part-time public service employees has dropped, as reflected in the combined figures shown below.

TABLE 1

Total Number of Employees	Year Total Number of Employees
1984	224,026
1986	217,223
1987	214,930

— All professional categories dropped in numbers of employees except for management.

— Personnel cutbacks have mainly affected the categories of development, administrative support, administration, and external services.

— The number of redundancies doubled between 1984 and 1986, and fell slightly the following year.

TABLE 2

NUMBER OF REDUNDANCIES

Year	Number of Redundancies
1983–1984	494
1986–1987	955
1987–1988	788

— The reason given for most redundancies was ministerial reorganization.

All professional categories are subject to redundancy cutbacks, although management and technical staff are significantly less affected.

TABLE 3

REDUNDANCIES AND PROFESSIONAL CATEGORIES

Professional Category	Total	— 1984–1985	Breakdown 1986–1987	— 1987–1988
Management	27	9	8	10
Scientific and professional	336	64	158	114
Administration and external services	420	110	210	100
Technical staff	191	54	64	73
Administrative support staff	510	152	190	168
Development	753	105	325	323
TOTAL:	2237	494	955	788

The proportion of professional components in the federal public service has gradually changed. Support categories have decreased in favour of officer categories. At the beginning of the 1970s and until 1980, support categories formed the largest public service group. Today officers are slightly ahead. These proportional changes within the professional sector are mainly due to the introduction of office computer systems and new technologies.

The proportion of promotions has also dropped. Seventeen out of every 100 employees were promoted in 1977, whereas in 1988 the number was reduced by half. Furthermore, since 1983, the average time during which an employee remained within the same group and level increased from 5 years in 1983 to 6.2 years in 1987.

These examples should be taken for what they are, however. They illustrate how administrative reform is being carried out on the level of human resources, and offer some insight into the general trend of changes in public administration. Reduction management is nothing new. Neither is the often asserted political determination (even under the Trudeau government) to reduce the number of employees on the public payroll (266,733 in 1979). Year after year, slowly but surely, the number of employees has dropped. Such changes have to be implemented gradually. They take time and are part of a long transformation process.

The Mulroney government has played a fairly significant role in achieving change in the public service. Although reform had been in the planning stages since the late 1970s, it had to be put into effect. The Conservative victory speeded up the process.

In the main, the Conservative role has been to turn planning into action by giving a decisive thrust to the move for reduction already initiated under the Liberals. True, such changes do not affect the basic organization of public service personnel, since the statutes governing them remain unchanged (the Public Service Employment Act, the Financial Administration Act, and the Public Service Staff Relations Act). Nevertheless, a process of reform has been launched that involves adjustments to new realities and changes in outlook. Furthermore, the approach to public service administration is now totally altered, and is concerned with keeping employees happy rather than revamping the organizational framework. It almost seems as though the symbolic power long vested in structural changes were shrinking, if not disappearing altogether.

In general, administrative changes avoid extremes as much as possible. All change is the complex and contradictory result of a long process, and the new administrative reality is necessarily determined by the old.

It is my view that under Brian Mulroney's government the field of public service personnel management has undergone real transformation, with significant breakthroughs. That being said, the overall administration is in excellent health. The relative decrease of one of its most visible components, the world of public servants, should not be interpreted as a sign of failing power.

Translated by Jane Brierley

CONTRIBUTORS

ARPAD ABONYI is the Former Director of Investment Research and Policy with Investment Canada. Mr. Abonyi is now the president of Prospectus Inc., an Ottawa-based consulting firm. He is an expert on investment and industrial policies and has written several articles on the subject. He has also lectured extensively in U.S. and Canadian universities on international political economy.

AGAR ADAMSON is the Chairman of the Department of Political Science at Acadia University in Wolfville, Nova Scotia. A student of Eastern Canadian politics, he has written on party politics and federal-provincial relations in the Maritimes.

PETER AUCOIN teaches in the Department of Political Science and in the School of Public Administration at Dalhousie University in Halifax, Nova Scotia. His recent research activity includes the forthcoming publication (with Herman Bakvis) of *The Centralization-Decentralization Conundrum* (Montreal: Institute of Research in Public Policy). He was also research coordinator with the MacDonald Commission for which he edited three background studies on Canada's parliamentary system and administrative state.

GÉRARD BOISMENU is an Associate professor in the Department of Political Science at the Université de Montréal. Professor Boismenu has written on a variety of topics ranging from legal theory to technological transfers. He is well known for his works on Quebec politics, federal-provincial relations and the Canadian state. He is the author among other things of *Le duplessisme* (PUM), *Le Québec en textes* (Boréal), and *Espace régional et nation*, (Boréal).

COLIN CAMPBELL is currently University Professor at Georgetown University in Washington D.C. where he holds the Isabelle and Henry Martin Chair of Philosophy and Politics. Professor Campbell is known internationally for his works on executive power and bureaucratic politics in the modern state. He is the author of *The Superbureaucrats: Structure and Behaviour in Central Agencies* (with George Szablowski) (1979), *Governments Under Stress: Political Executives and Key Bureaucrats in Washington, London and Ottawa* (1983), and *Managing the Presidency: Carter, Reagan and the Search for Executive Harmony* (1986).

TED CARMICHAEL is Vice President and Director of Policy Research at the C.D. Howe Institute in Toronto, and is also the editor of the Institute's annual *Policy Review and Outlook*. Although Mr. Carmichael's research interests cover a broad range of policy issues he has developed a highly respected expertise on the question of the deficit. He is the author of *Tackling the Federal Deficit* (C.D. Howe, 1984).

HAROLD CHORNEY is Associate Professor in the Department of Political Science at Concordia University. He has also worked as an economist and consultant for the Governments of Manitoba and Saskatchewan and various public sector bodies. He is a regular commentator on economic and public policy for the CBC and CTV. Professor Chorney is the author of numerous articles and reviews and has written extensively on public finance and public debt management.

LOUISE DULUDE is a lawyer who has been working in the field of women's rights for several years. In 1982, she was elected on the executive of the National Action Committee on the Status of Women (NAC), the largest women's organization in Canada, with more than 500 member groups whose individual membership includes over three million women. Louise Dulude was Vice-President of NAC for two years, and has been President since June 1986. She is the author of ten reports and studies on women. The latest one *Love, Marriage and Money*, was commissioned by the Canadian Advisory Council on the Status of Women.

GINETTE DUSSAULT is an economist and Research Associate with the Montreal-based Institut de recherce appliquée sur le travail (IRAT). She has worked on labour-related questions both as researcher and as consultant with unions, the Quebec government and the Université du Québec à Montréal. She is the author of several articles and studies on the labour market and the socioeconomic problems related to employment. In 1987, she wrote *The Financial Security of Retired Women*, a study commissioned by the Canadian Advisory Council on the status of women.

ROGER GIBBINS is Chairman of the Department of Political Science at the University of Calgary. He has published extensively on questions related to Canadian politics. He is the author of a well-known textbook *Conflict and Unity: An Introduction to Canadian Political Life* (Methuen, 1985), and of numerous articles and books on Western Canadian politics and on the questions of regionalism and Indian affairs. Among them: *Prairie Politics and Society: Regionalism in Decline* (Butterworths, 1980), and *Regionalism: Territorial Politics in Canada and the United States* (Butterworths, 1982).

ANDREW B. GOLLNER is Associate Professor of Political Science at Concordia University and Director of its Graduate Program in Public Policy and Administration. He is author of *Social Change and Corporate Strategy*, of *Corporate and Public Affairs in Canada*, and of various other works on business-government relations.

ANDREW JOHNSON teaches in the Department of Political Science at Bishop's University in Lennoxville, Quebec. His major area of research and expertise is the politics of the welfare state and social policies in Canada. He has recently contributed articles in two books: *Canadian Social Welfare Policy: Federal and Provincial Dimensions* and *The Canadian Welfare State. Evolution and Transition*, both edited by J.S. Ismael. Professor Johnson is currently conducting research on the relationship of organized labour and the development of social programs in Canada.

GUY LACHAPELLE is Assistant Professor in the Department of Political Science at Concordia University. His area of expertise is public policy analysis, quantitative methods for social science and program evaluation. For the past few years, his principal area of research has been the social policies of Canadian provincial and federal governments, and he has published and presented a number of papers in this area.

DAVID LEYTON-BROWN teaches Political Science at York University. He has widely published on questions related to international relations. More recently he has been conducting research on Canada-U.S. economic and political relations.

ANDREW MOLLOY is a doctoral candidate in the Ph.D. in Humanities at Concordia University. He has been conducting research on aspects of Canadian political economy. He currently teaches Canadian government and policies, and political communication in the Department of Political Science at Concordia University.

DANIEL SALÉE is Assistant Professor of Political Science at Concordia University. His research interest focuses on the role of the state in Canada. He has published in scholarly journals such as *Studies in Political Economy, The Canadian Journal of Social and Political Theory,* and the *Canadian Review of Studies in Nationalism,* among others.

RICHARD SCHULTZ is Associate Professor of Political Science at McGill University, and also the Director of McGill's Centre for the Study of Regulated Industries. Professor Schultz is well-known for his work on the Canadian regulatory process. Among his better known works are *Federalism and the Regulatory Process* (1979), *Federalism, Bureaucracy and Public Policy* (1980), and, with A. Alexandroff, *Economic Regulation and the Federal System* (1985).

CAROLLE SIMARD is professor of Public Administration in the Department of Political Science at the Université du Québec à Montréal. Her current research is on personnel management in the federal public service. She is the author of *Les femmes coutre l'administration* (Boréal, 1983).

RICHARD SIMEON teaches in the Department of Political Studies and is Director of the School of Public Administration at Queen's University. He is well known in the academic community and in governmental circles for his work on Canadian politics, especially on policy-making and federalism. His numerous publications include *Federal-Provincial Diplomacy, Redesigning the State: The Politics of Constitutional Change in Western Nations* (with K. Banting), and the editorship of four background studies for the MacDonald Commission.

WILLIAM STANBURY is the UPS Foundation Professor of Regulation and Competitive Policy in the Faculty of Commerce and Business Administration at the University of British Columbia. Professor Stanbury has published extensively on a broad range of issues and topics pertaining to the relationship of the business community with the state. He is the author of the standard textbook on this question, *Business-Government Relations in Canada* (Methuen, 1985).

Feb